D0801674

BLUEWATER SAILOR

BLUEWATER
SAILOR

The Memoirs of a Destroyer Officer

Don Sheppard

PRESIDIO

To Pat, for reading the first several chapters of the rough manuscript and telling me she always wanted to know how a dry dock worked. And now she does. She spurred me on.

To my wife Rose, who hung in there all the way.

Copyright © 1996 Don Sheppard

Published by Presidio Press
505 B San Marin Dr., Suite 300
Novato, CA 94945-1340

Library of Congress Cataloging-in-Publication Data

Sheppard, Don.
    Bluewater sailor : the memoirs of a destroyer officer / Don Sheppard.
      p. cm.
    ISBN 0-89141-554-8 (hardcover)
    1. Sheppard, Don. 2. United States. Navy—Officers—Biography. I. Title.
V63.S53A3 1996
359'.0092—dc20
[B]   95-34771
                                                              CIP

Photographs courtesy of Don Sheppard unless otherwise noted.
Typography by ProImage

Printed in the United States of America

Author's Note

Although the places and events are true, the people, for the most part, are composites of those I served with along the way. Names have been changed, but some of you will recognize yourselves. I trust I have rendered you satisfactorily.

Some of you will not recognize yourselves; you have never seen yourselves through the eyes of others.

The ships are real; their names have been changed. The events are real but they are not always in sequence.

For the techno buffs, you may find fault with too much or too little description. This is a story of men. The equipment is used as backdrop.

This is how I remember it, twenty to forty-five years later.

Contents

═══════════

It is by no means enough that an officer of the navy should be a capable mariner. He must be that of course, but also a great deal more. He should be as well a gentleman of liberal education, refined manners, punctilious courtesy, and the nicest sense of personal honor.

John Paul Jones
1747–1792

DESTROYER

Ten thousand days
    I've lived
        and steamed ten thousand nights . . .
I've turned the tip of Borneo
    and sailed
        through northern lights . . .

The coats of gray
    upon my side
        are lost onto my ken . . .
I've danced across
    the placid sea
        and fought the crushing wind . . .

I've sweltered hot
    in burning suns
        in distant tropic seas . . .
My rigging's moaned
    from gale whipped ice
        where even blood would freeze . . .

My guns have hurled
    their deadly steel
        against my country's foe . . .
The honors heaped
    upon my name
        mystique and legend grow . . .

But all heroic
    deeds aside
        the feeling held within . . .
My finest feat,
    what I do best:
        converting boys to men . . .

DON SHEPPARD

Prologue

===

The wind flung damp sea air across San Francisco Bay. I shivered from its biting cold as I stood shrouded in melancholy's gray cocoon. The fleet destroyer *Cambridge* backed smartly from her berth and glided past me a thousand yards away. I was no longer in command of her—no longer her captain.

Her power whispered a saddened farewell as she turned to starboard to avoid an incoming tanker. I turned to port and walked away. My dream had come and gone.

I slid into my car and lit my pipe, the smoke heady as I sat there wrapped in a pleasant capsule of memory. I drifted back to an earlier time in the navy when I had just made chief and was unknowingly on my way to becoming an officer.

At twenty-six, I was too young to be a chief. They said I was a smart-ass, butt-kissing, know-it-all wise guy. They were right, except for the ass-kissing part. Not that I was above it, I just hadn't found it necessary.

I was then the youngest chief petty officer in the navy. I had made chief because I had studied. While other men on shore duty lay around and watched TV, played with their kids and their wives, and went to the movies, I studied and worked my ass off on the job—something I had not done in high school.

Granite City Community High School Warriors fielded their athletic teams, often unsuccessfully, wearing drab red and black uniforms. The school trained males to work in the steel mills of Granite City and females to mind the homes, have babies, and serve cold beers to the ex-Warriors returning triumphantly from work. Granite City, a town of forty thousand, half of whom worked in the mills, was located barely south of Nameoki Township, Illinois, and almost across the river from St. Louis.

Every male graduating was destined for the mills. Oh, there were a few who took college prep courses and were going off to fancy colleges and who would later come back to be high-stepping managers; but in the main, we would all labor in the mills until we died. In the meantime, we'd go to union meetings and bowl and buy campers and coach Little League teams and swig a lot of beer.

I could see myself as if it were yesterday—a proud ensign struggling my bag into a liberty launch at the Fleet Landing, crossing a destroyer tender's quarterdeck, making my way across three other Gearing-class destroyers, and walking aboard the USS *Henshaw*.

USS *Henshaw*

I t was 2207 on the second Sunday in September 1958. I saluted the American flag hanging limply from a rusting staff on the stern, then I executed a left turn that any marine drill instructor would have been proud of, pulled my body as erect as a bridge stanchion, and saluted the lieutenant junior grade lounging against a portable desk clipped to the bulkhead.

I looked him directly in the eye, my heart beating against my immaculate uniform as I proudly snapped, "Ensign Donald D. Sheppard. Reporting for duty, sir. Request permission to come aboard, sir." My first destroyer. Why wasn't the captain here to greet me?

The lieutenant's tieless, wrinkled khakis and lackadaisical attitude set me back. He didn't even return my salute. This isn't how it's supposed to be.

"Jesus Christ," he snapped, "knock off that 'sir' shit. You're Sheppard, huh?" He pulled his fingers out of his nose and admired the thin hairs he'd captured.

"Yes, sir," I answered, my tone deflated.

A first-class petty officer waddled over from the other side of the ship and looked at me for a moment. "Jarvis, sir," he said, tossing up a salute. "I'm the in-port OOD, also in charge of the sonar gang." His jowls swished from side to side as he spoke. I shook his pudgy hand. "Mr. Clements is the CDO, the command duty officer," he added.

Clements said nothing as I stood awkwardly for what seemed like an hour. Even in the cool night air of San Diego in the fall, I sweated under my brand-new blues with their one brilliant gold stripe on each lower sleeve. Who do these people think they are, treating me as if I were some beggar?

"I'm reporting aboard for duty, sir," I said again to the lethargic lieutenant junior grade, who had now managed to lift himself up from the desk to lean on the bulkhead.

He waited almost a minute until answering. "Yeah, I know. You're my relief. Come on up to the wardroom. Jarvis, hold down the fort." We left my bag on the quarterdeck, made our way forward, and entered the superstructure.

I stepped over the six-inch-high coaming of the watertight doorjamb, ensuring I didn't trip or scrape my shin on it. They'd warned us of this hazard in OCS, officer candidate school. I followed Mr. Clements into the wardroom—the eating and general gathering place for the ship's officers. It was just like the movies. I'd never been on a destroyer before.

"You're a mustang, huh," he stated more than asked as he poured two cups of coffee from a foul-smelling pot that must have been heating for a week.

"Yes, sir, I came up through the ranks," I answered meekly, as if ashamed of it.

"So fucking what? You think I give a damn?" he shouted, and then sat in silence for the next few minutes while he stared at me. "I'm goddamned tired," he finally blurted. "We just got in from three weeks at sea and we're shittin' due out again tomorrow at 0800. Hell, the old man would have us under way at 0500 if it weren't against the regs," he finished, mumbling the last few words. "Haze gray and fuckin' under way."

I didn't reply.

"You think I get any liberty? No! It's the shittin' brown baggers who get to go home to their little spread-legged wifies while a bachelor takes the goddamned duty. We'd like a piece of ass too, you know." His bloodshot eyes stabbed into me as if I were the seat of his discontent.

"You married, Sheppard? You a brown bagger?"

Why am I letting this guy make me feel guilty? This guy's a basket case. He didn't appear to be much of an officer as he stared at me in silence as if I were nothing to him. Finally he said, as if doing me a favor by talking to me, "As soon as we get in next Friday night, I'm a civilian and out of this chickenshit, asshole navy."

I didn't reply. I'd heard it all before from disgruntled sailors and I didn't want to hear it again. He sipped what he called coffee after berating me for wanting cream in it. "You'll soon give up that shit," he said as if I were some retarded child. "You'll give up a lot of things."

He sauntered in front of me to a stateroom, pointed inside, and walked away. My bag lay on the upper bunk. He had destroyed my excitement at reporting aboard. He had destroyed my fantasy of the captain asking me to take the ship to sea because it was a windy, foggy day and he needed someone of my skill and daring to see us safely through the nautical quagmire. I lay in my bunk unable to sleep.

Clements, you son of a bitch.

After a few abortive tries, I managed to find the wardroom for breakfast. The XO, the executive officer already seated, introduced himself, trying to make me feel at ease among these strange, noisy surroundings. Earlier from the torpedo deck, I had watched the motor whaleboat approach with the captain and the XO from Coronado, a small navy bedroom community across the bay from San Diego. Senior officers lived there. Another new ensign rode with them.

In the wardroom the XO introduced the ensign as Mr. John Henry Graffey—from Annapolis—the son of a classmate of the old man's. He said "from Annapolis," meaning the U.S. Naval Academy there, in a grandiose tone.

Mr. Graffey and I looked at each other. He fought to keep a frown from forming as he halfheartedly extended his hand to me across the table, taking it for one shake and pulling it away, as if his skin would fall off if he touched me for too long. "You're enlisted, I understand," he said, wiping his hand on his linen napkin.

Here was my competition.

"Ex-enlisted, Mr. Graffey," I replied to the snickers of the other officers who were still smiling at the XO's "from Annapolis" emphasis. They well knew that the XO was NROTC, and prima facie a second-class naval officer aboard the USS *Henshaw*.

Just before sea detail was set, the XO deposited me on the bridge with an admonishment to stay out of the way and just watch. The captain repeated, "Stay out of the way," as he passed just in front of me by inches, a pair of well-used binoculars swinging across his chest. A lieutenant junior grade who seemed to have the watch smiled at me and winked. He was the chief engineer and had seemed pleasant when we met at breakfast. I smiled back, nodding my head in appreciation of his comforting gesture as I tried to push myself further into the bulkhead.

Smoothly easing the destroyer out of her nest away from the destroyer tender, the captain twisted the ship with opposed engines and, when heading fair, ordered all engines ahead two-thirds. We steamed for the open sea. Wow!

I stood there bewildered trying to absorb my surroundings on the noisy bridge as twenty minutes passed. The XO, standing at a chart table, received bearings to landmarks from two quartermasters stationed out on the bridge wing peloruses, the repeaters from our gyrocompass. The XO crossed these bearings on the chart and called out time and courses to steer to the next turning point. The voice of the sound-powered phone talker to CIC, the Combat Information Center, called out course recommendations sent up from CIC; they used radar. It seemed odd that the captain didn't steer the destroyer like a big motorboat. Odd? I, of course, knew it all.

"Ensign Sheppard," the captain finally spoke, barely looking my way as he kept a fine eye on the myriad sailboats attempting to ruin his career by running into him. We were almost clear of the harbor.

He kept his back to me as he said, "I know you're an ex-aviation electronics technician, an AT, and I know we're not supposed to put mustangs working in their old rates," he said, "but I'm in trouble for an electronics officer. If you don't mind, I'm assigning you the job. Okay?" *If I don't mind?*

"Only one of our five UHF transceivers works and no one seems to be able to fix the rest. If this last one goes out on the fleet exercises we're heading for, the ship will have no communications and I'll have to abort. And after that, it's all deep shit."

"Yes, s . . . sir," I stammered, stupidly saluting even though I knew from ten years of service that the navy never saluted when inside. Ensign Graffey snickered at me as he stood next to the captain. Looking at them, the acid teeth of envy chomped into my body.

The XO took me by the elbow, directing me off the bridge as a report came from a telephone talker that the last UHF transceiver had just gone down. The captain turned to me, glaring as if it were my fault, and in a parting shot said, "Welcome aboard, Mr. Sheppard."

"This is the communications shack, Mr. Sheppard, with all our bad order comm gear," the XO said, then introduced me to the ETs, the electronics technicians, working on the radios.

"What's the trouble?" I asked, in the low voice I was accustomed to using with scores of other technicians over the years. The older one's left lip curled in disdain, as if he thought I was just another young punk officer who didn't know his ass from a hole in the ground, and whose interference kept him from taking care of the problem. He didn't answer, pretending he hadn't heard me as he busied himself with one of the transceivers.

"What's the problem?" I asked again, this time louder, as I touched his arm.

He looked up at me, his eyebrow rising. "Really, sir, I've got to get these bastards up again. I don't have time to explain electronics. You understand, don't you? I'm really busy. Perhaps later, okay?"

"Of course, Petty Officer"—I looked at the stenciled name over his left dungaree shirt pocket—"Jenkins, but let me see if I can help. You can afford a few minutes, can't you?"

"No transmission, just receive. No sending," he grunted. "You know what all that means . . . sir."

I didn't answer as I stared at the combination transmitter and receiver for a moment, my mind dancing with glee. I picked up a Phillips-head screwdriver, then excused myself as I moved in over the inoperative transceiver. Six months earlier I had discovered an engineering fault with these units and devised a fix that I guess these guys didn't know about yet.

Theatrically waving my hand over the open unit, tapping here and there just for effect, I said, "Here," and undid the cover plate over the power amplifiers. I asked for a pair of needle nose pliers and with them gently bent back two wires, exposing a feed coil. With a soldering gun I removed it. It looked okay, but I knew it had a minor defect that wouldn't show up under normal troubleshooting procedures.

"Do you have any of these feed coils in stock?" I asked, trying to appear calm. Jenkins, the senior technician, answered apologetically that he had no transmitter parts. I looked at him questioningly, then took a ballpoint pen from a desk and disassembled it, taking out the metal insert that held the ink. I clipped both ends with a pair of wire cutters and drained the ink—the exact same thing I'd done six months ago. I looked around at the ETs staring at me in open disgust.

The XO's consuming stare called forth in me an extra effort to control my shaking hands.

Carefully I bent the sixteenth-inch-diameter ballpoint pen tube into a shape similar to the feed coil I'd just removed. With surgeonlike deftness I soldered it into the coil's place.

After swiftly reassembling the transceiver and pushing it back into its rack with a prayer, I turned it on. The whir of the cooling fans gave me encouragement though they had nothing to do with the problem. Offhandedly I asked for the ship's call sign and with trepidation keyed the mike, saying, "Any station this net, this is Lifeblood. Radio check. Over."

During the intolerable three-second wait, pints of sweat poured down my shirt under my brand-new set of dress blues. I could smell the odor under my arms. The XO had said nothing during the entire time as he stood three feet away staring into my eyes. I'd be branded a pompous fool if this grandstand play didn't work.

"Roger, Lifeblood, this is Hellenic Hero. Read you loud and clear. Out."

I willed my heart to slow as I turned to the technicians standing around me. "I'm the new electronics officer," I said, extending my hand to the one wearing iron-on first-class stripes and a crow.

"Ah . . . Jenkins, sir,"

"Yes, I'm pleased to meet you. Do the other radios have the same symptoms?"

With a look of reverence that probably only Jesus had ever seen, Jenkins replied, "Yes . . . yes, sir. They . . . ah, do . . . sir!"

"Do the same thing to the other four and they'll work well enough. Shouldn't take more than an hour or so. Let me know if you have any problems," I said, extending my hand to him. "Glad to meet you, Jenkins." I was back in my element.

The XO smiled broadly as he reached up, keying the 1MC to the bridge. "Captain, that new ensign just fixed the last UHF with a ballpoint pen and he'll have the others on-line in an hour."

After a short silence during which only heavy breathing could be heard, the captain replied, "Well, XO, it looks like we finally got us a live one."

Seasick

he operations officer, Lt. Norman H. Bluing, USN, USNA, a surly man whose head came only to my nose, had the stateroom next to the XO's just forward of the wardroom. I'd met Bluing on the bridge at sea detail. "I just heard you're a whiz with the electronics. That's great; we've had a lot of trouble and I'm hoping you can help us," he said after the XO's official introduction.

The XO, second in command and responsible for the administration of the ship, was called "EX OH" by everyone aboard. My being the electronics officer made Lieutenant Bluing my boss. As the senior watch officer, he would assign me to watches.

Bluing hadn't offered his hand, nor did he stand up to greet me, nor did he offer me a seat as he rubbed his nose with his first finger and thumb. I noticed a U.S. Navy divers emblem on his blouse.

The ship started rolling.

"I'm assigning you the watch with me from 1200 to 1600, noon to four in the afternoon and since we're on one in three, it means we'll have the midwatch from 0000 to 0400, midnight to four in the morning. You won't get much sleep on the mids but you'll get used to it." Mr. Bluing pumped out this little speech as if I knew nothing about the navy. His droning, patronizing tone irritated me as his fingers continually rubbed the bridge of his nose. Then he added, "The captain wants you on the mids." I wondered why.

"I'll try to teach you something, though God knows ensigns can't learn shit." He didn't even offer the courtesy of looking up at me as he lectured. I fought the urge to whip out a sarcastic answer, but I'd been an enlisted man far too long to entertain such a blasphemous thought. Maybe the praise of the captain and XO had gone to my head.

I turned to leave, wanting to sit down, wanting some fresh air, wanting to get out of here. "Wait, one more thing, and it really bugs me. Don't use 'the' before a ship's name. It's not the *Henshaw*, it's *Henshaw*. It's not the *Rollard*, it's *Rollard*."

"I understand, sir."

"You wouldn't say the Las Vegas or the Chicago, would you now?"

"No, sir, I wouldn't."

"Then why would you say the *Henshaw?*"

"I never have, sir. I never would, sir."

"See, I *have* taught an ensign something."

"Yes, sir, thank you, sir." *You've taught this ensign shit, asshole.*

"Yeah, well keep it in mind. But one more thing: if USS is in front of the ship's name, you've got to use the *the*. You got all that?"

"Yes, sir. I think I can keep it all in mind. This destroyer stuff will sure be hard to remember," I answered, trying to mask my sarcasm. *This jerk doesn't even notice.*

"Well, Mr. Sheppard, that's what we older officers have to do, you know, train the younger ones." He laughed out of the left side of his mouth, letting the sound drip down his chin to lie curdling on the deck.

Jesus, it's going to be a fun time working for this guy.

In my new starched khakis I tried fighting down the urge to vomit through my first afternoon watch. Lieutenant Bluing seemed to try to understand, but I think he was incapable of expressing sympathy. He let me take the conn, the control of the ship. I was now the one who gave orders to the helmsman on which course to steer, and I was the one who told the man on the engine order telegraph which speed the engine room should give us.

I had the conn even though Mr. Bluing told me everything to do and I dutifully passed it on like a tape recorder on playback.

I envisioned an enemy submarine being detected by our constantly sweeping sonar and the captain ordering me to prosecute the contact. I'd kill it just before it launched its deadly ballistic missiles against the United States, and the chief of naval operations would pin a medal on my chest for bravery and my picture would appear on the cover of *Newsweek*.

I threw up thirteen times: the first one my dessert; the second my lunch; the next two green glutinous masses; and the last nine dry, foul-smelling gasps of putrid air along with what I envisioned to be parts of my stomach lining.

Blessedly, the watch ended. I left the bridge with my ignoble display shaming me to exhaustion. I made my way to the electronics shop like a drunken man, tripping and hitting my shins on every watertight door coaming I went through, tolerating the solicitous grins of those I passed. I'd done duty on a carrier, but it had never been like this. And the seas were calm today.

Maybe something familiar would rekindle my will to live. "Hello, Mr. Sheppard. We got all five of them mothers up. You're one helluv an electronics man, sir."

"No, Jenkins," I said mournfully to the first-class ET. "I'm a mustang, came up through the ranks. I was an AT before being commissioned. I had the same trouble with those transceivers six months ago. I've been at this shit for years. I used some of the best shops in the country to discover that coil fault." My jaws puffed out to stifle the vomit.

"Why . . . why, thank you, sir. I was feeling sorta bad that an ensign could fix something I couldn't." He paused, looking at me. I felt self-conscious with my despair and the smell of my puke filling the tiny shop. "A mustang, hot shit. We'll get something done now," he said, shaking my hand. I wondered what he meant.

"Those spare parts, Jenkins, can we talk about that later? I'm not feeling so well."

"Don't feel bad about being seasick, sir. It happens to all of us. A mustang, hot shit," he repeated as I started to leave, heading for my stateroom. "Yes, sir, spare parts are a real problem on this ship." I barely heard him as I staggered out of the shop, noticing the blood stains forming on my trouser legs from my bleeding shins.

I shared a stateroom with Lt. (jg) Roger R. Clements, USNR, who laughed as I waddled into the tiny cubicle. "Well, well, hotshot, how's it feel to be a real sailor on his majesty's most gracious rust-fucket *Henshaw?* Puked your guts out, I hear. Tsk, tsk!"

I didn't answer as I stood over him, my six-foot trim body scrunched down to almost his five-foot-eight skinny frame. In agony, I crawled into my bunk, wishing I were home, and fell asleep instantly.

"It's 2315, sir. You've got the watch. Come on, get up, sir," came the disembodied voice of some sea monster shaking me, handing me a set of red night adaption goggles.

My shins bled again from being smashed on the treacherous watertight door coaming as I staggered, making my way up to the wardroom. I just couldn't remember to lift my legs. And even when I did, I still seemed to smash into the coamings. I stumbled into the wardroom, knowing there'd be midrats prepared by one of the stewards.

I'd missed supper, and my stomach welcomed the cold, greasy pork chop sandwiches. I gulped down two of them in the surrealistic red world of my goggles, which protected my night vision. I knew I'd be leaving the sandwiches in a bucket, second time through, as soon as I got to the bridge, but I didn't feel too bad right now.

I skimmed through the captain's night orders, relieved the watch, and had the conn. "Aye, sir, steering course 270, 265 magnetic," came the word from the helmsman as he repeated his course to ensure that I, the conning officer, and he agreed.

"All engines ahead standard, turns for fifteen knots rung up, sir," the man on the engine order telegraph—the lee helm, as he was called—finished the ceremony.

"Very well," I answered in my finest Nelsonian voice. We were in formation on picket station in a circle around a carrier along with the other three ships of our division. All I had to do was keep our position five thousand yards on the carrier's port side. Piece of cake; I'd read everything there was on handling a destroyer.

"How are you feeling, Mr. Sheppard?" came the captain's low voice from the dark. Shit, I hadn't known he was up here.

"Oh! Sorry, sir, I didn't know you were on the bridge. Fine . . . fine, thank you, sir," I managed to reply, trying to hide my surprise and consternation. The JOOD, the junior officer of the deck, was supposed to know when the captain was on the bridge—actually, where he was at all times.

"Don't worry about seasickness; it happens to all of us. You'll get over it," he said to me. Then turning to my boss, he added, "I'll be in my sea cabin, Mr. Bluing. Call me if any changes occur."

"Captain left the bridge," came the obligatory statement from the boatswain's mate of the watch, reporting whenever the captain came on or left the bridge. The calm, windless night caused me no seasickness while Mr. Bluing lectured me on station keeping and bridge procedures as if I were a functional illiterate.

The minor station-keeping maneuvers I did were simple one- or two-degree rudder shifts and dropping or adding a few turns to the engines. Even so, I knew—just knew—what to do as I rubbed my hand gently across the ship's cold steel bulwarks, her immense power and her beauty reverberating through my bones. Finally, for the first time in my life I felt I belonged.

I stared into the night between my occasional glances at the radar screen. I had never really wanted to become an officer, never thought about it until one day my division officer in the aviation antisubmarine squadron to which I was assigned suggested I give it a try. I guess he liked me for the quality of work I performed with my men in electronics maintenance. I had made him look good. Or maybe it was that incident with the Russian sub. He had looked good on that one too. He had been my pilot that night.

I never made any real decision to stay in the navy or to get out. Indecision had been a pattern in my life. I'd enlisted in November 1948 simply because I didn't relish staying at the grocery store in my hometown of Nameoki, Illinois, where I had worked every night and on Saturdays all through high school.

Even though I was told that in a few years I'd be the assistant produce manager, the job didn't hold much attraction. Nothing did. And I certainly didn't want to work at the mills. I guess my grandfather had a big influence on me; I don't recall listening to anyone else very much in my whole life.

My grandfather spent a summer with us in Nameoki. He lived in Boston and told stories of his days as a commodore in the British navy. He even had a picture of himself in a white uniform. But I never took much stock in his stories because he told so many of them. And the white commodore uniform picture was also shown when he told about starting up the Good Humor man ice-cream company.

My grandfather stayed in my room, which I didn't like because it limited my onanistic pleasures, and he rolled back and forth in his bed imitating the sea. "Come up through the hawse pipe, Donny Boy, the only way to do it in the navy. Come up the hard way like I did. No namby-pamby academy . . . come up through the hawse pipe like I did," he'd drone on in his convincing, deep baritone voice.

I'd had a half-ass shot at going to Annapolis or West Point due to some senator being friends with my father, but I had no real interest in continuing school, especially at a military academy. Besides, my grades would not support an appointment.

I heard that sailors got a lot of sex, and that was really all I cared about even though good old Janice Jean and I were getting it on almost every night I could borrow my dad's car—maybe once every two weeks.

For no particular reason, I enlisted for a two-year term—a kiddie cruise, it was called—and I was to be discharged when I turned twenty-one. Then the Korean War started and the navy extended everyone's enlistment by a year. That pissed me off. I taught them a lesson by shipping over. No one was going to extend my enlistment.

"Come left to 031. Drop two turns," I ordered when the feeling eased into me that we were about to drift off station.

In about three minutes, CIC, where the men plotted everything their radars could detect, reported still dead on station.

"How'd you know that, Sheppard?" Mr. Bluing asked.

"Just felt it, sir," I replied, somewhat astonished by his question. This was no different from riding a bike or driving a car or a speedboat.

I wasn't sick the whole watch and was proud of myself for it. I crawled into my rack. For no apparent reason, my first year after boot camp drifted through my mind. It had been a traumatic period. I was Monk Evans's best friend . . . I was asleep smiling before more of the memory came back.

"Get up, sailor boy," Clements's shrill voice penetrated my sleep. "We gotta go stand in front of Jenkins and his girly technicians at quarters, then read the plan of the day—POD to them. Good thing. Those pussies can't read too well."

I managed only a scowl. I hurriedly ate breakfast in the wardroom and followed Mr. Clements out to the electronics division's muster area. It was 0715. Electronics Technician First Class Jenkins, in freshly pressed dungarees covering his slim, six-foot body topped by a blond crew cut, dutifully read out the name of each of his six men, and each answered present. Then turning to Mr. Clements, he said with a snappy salute, "All present or accounted for, *SIR.*"

Clements brushed his forehead with a gesture that might have passed for a salute, answering, "Yeah, good for you." And walked away.

Clements returned, mumbling that we'd be going to GQ, general quarters, at 0800 to fire the torpedoes and the five-inch guns at an old LST, a World War Two landing ship. "You guys can read it in the POD because

I've only got four days left in this shit-ass navy. Dis—fucking—missed."
And he turned away.

"We'll miss you, sir," came a sotto voce reply.

"Who said that?" he barked, spinning around.

"Said what, Mr. Clements? I didn't hear anything," I answered. He
glared at me for a second, then stomped off looking as though he was
long overdue to go to the toilet. The ETs smiled. "I'm sorry, Jenkins; it
won't be long," I said, noting a destroyer about two thousand yards off
our port beam. I turned; there was another off our starboard beam, and a
third steamed a thousand yards behind us.

The officer of the deck, Lt. (jg) Richard M. Bernard, USN, USNA,
who was the chief engineer, looked at the captain as he came onto the
bridge.

"If you please, Mr. Bernard, general quarters," the captain said. Mr.
Bernard nodded to the boatswain's mate of the watch, who raised his
bosun's pipe to his lips and, keying the 1MC, piped "all hands."

The shrill call sounded in every compartment and in every small hide-
away. It blasted unrelentingly and was followed by the deep voice of the
boatswain's mate saying calmly, "Now hear this, now hear this, general
quarters! General quarters! All hands man your battle stations. Now general quarters." He followed this by throwing the general quarters alarm
switch. As the BONG! BONG! BONG! of the alarm beat throughout the
ship, my heart danced in excitement. *This is what it's all about. Wow!*
General quarters.

I tried to stay out of the way as the watch swiftly changed places with
the general quarters bridge team. The XO had told me to come to the
bridge and just observe. Mr. Clements's station was in the electronics
shop, where mine would be when I relieved him in a few days.

Mr. Bernard smiled at me as he left the bridge, pointing to a helmet
and bulky life preserver lying under the chart table. "Put 'em on, Don,
it's all part of the drill," he said, scooting out the door to his GQ station
in main control. I saw the bridge team pulling their socks over the bot-
toms of their dungarees, as the movies in OCS had showed us to do. I
never understood why, but I did likewise.

Mr. Bluing ordered full speed and came about with full rudder. "We'll
join up with the other ships in the division in fifteen minutes, Captain,"
he reported.

With consternation, I saw that Ensign Graffey was the JOOD. *Why not*
me? I guessed having your father the buddy of the captain helped a little.

I hoped my disappointment of not having a real job didn't show. The captain nodded for me to come over.

"You've met John Graffey, I assume," he said. We both answered yes. "You two are fortunate today; you'll probably never see anything like this again. We're going to make a torpedo run against a real target and sink her.

"You've probably both done this in school on a maneuvering board. I'm sure John has at the academy. We've got an old LST out there. The carrier's planes will strafe it first, then our division will commence torpedo runs. I did it just once in the war, but missed as the Jap destroyer turned at the last minute."

Visions of adventure danced through my mind—*Japs, destroyers.* "I want you two on the maneuvering boards to recommend courses to the OOD. He'll be getting the same info—hopefully—from combat."

Henshaw formed up with our other three division mates in a line astern. We were second in the column. We could see the tug cast off the old LST, which the division had cannibalized of anything of value two weeks ago. At five miles out, the first flight of jets fired their machine guns at the floating target. Through the binoculars the splashes showed they were missing by quite a lot. On their third run they fired rockets, but only smoke showed for their efforts.

The commodore ordered the runs at twenty-three knots. All Ensign Graffey and I had to do was work out the course to the launch point and indicate a time to fire. Simple against a drifting target. We commenced the run. Graffey recommended course 047; I shouted 053. Combat came up with 046. S*hit!* The commodore ordered 047 for the four racing destroyers. As we rapidly closed I worked and reworked my solution to the firing point time. "Eight minutes to launch," I hazarded. "Seven and a quarter," Graffey smugly called out.

"Seven and a quarter minutes to launch. Will commence countdown at five," came the XO's voice from combat.

"Follow combat, Mr. Bluing," the captain ordered. I flushed in shame that I wasn't as good at this as Mr. Graffey. Three minutes passed. The first ship in line launched. What a beautiful sight. "Hydrophone effects from outbound torpedo in the water off starboard bow," came the voice from the sonar room in the bowels of the ship. "Running hot." The first ship's torpedo passed at least one hundred yards forward of the bow of the rusting LST.

"One minute," came the XO's voice. Then, "Five seconds, four, three, two, one, FIRE!" Nothing happened.

"No launch," reported the torpedo deck.

"XO!" the captain screamed. "Get your ass back there and find out what happened." The third destroyer missed, as did the fourth.

The commodore's voice came over the division's tactical radio net. "Tsk, tsk," was all he said. In a few minutes a new approach commenced. The captain took the conn, shouting speed and course changes as his ashen face stared at the hapless LST.

We sped in again. This time the first ship failed to fire. We got one off, but it quit running, sinking twenty yards from the hulk. The third ship's torpedo hit the LST midships but failed to explode. The fourth ship missed. "Again," came the angry voice from the flagship.

Again no score. Again we were ordered in. Again no score. "Upon return to port, all commanding officers will immediately report to the flagship," came a scathing message by blinking light. I guess being the captain wasn't always so much fun.

We formed up again in a line astern, and all four ships commenced firing broadside with our 5"/38 naval guns. It changed my world. The overpowering sensual pleasure of the deafening noise, the comforting heat of explosion, the acrid, pleasant, jamming smell of the cordite converted me into a destroyer man for life.

We hammered away for an hour. Of the 172 five-inch rounds that tore at the defiant ship, more than 50 scored direct hits, but she would not sink, even though all of her watertight hatches had been purposely left open. My heart went out to the gallant vessel as she finally started to settle by the stern. The captain requested permission to make one more torpedo run. I guess he wanted to assuage his warrior's pride.

The captain took the conn again and made the run by eyeball. Fast. A beautiful approach complemented by a perfect launch blessed his tenacity. The twenty-one-inch, ten-thousand-dollar, two-thousand-pound torpedo flashed over our port side, slicing down into the water and running hot and true, propelling its eleven hundred pounds of torpex explosives at more than forty knots, ready to sink anything in its path. The LST settled faster now. The torpedo, set to run at ten feet, whizzed right over where the ship had been ten seconds earlier.

The captain's pitiful look of utter frustration made me fight down tears in empathy with those he struggled to restrain.

Tactical Maneuvers

========================

I threw up only after we'd secured from general quarters. I retched for about an hour, watching in disgust as all my strength spewed out my mouth in a pitiful exhibit of physical weakness. Exhausted, I went to my bunk to lie down before my 1200 to 1600 afternoon watch.

"Well, I see ole Hemorrhoid Henshaw did her normal incompetent bit today. Heard three out of the five torpedoes were rusted into their tubes," Clements started on me the second I entered the stateroom we shared. I didn't answer.

"I feel sorta bad again, Mr. Clements. Do you mind if I just get in my bunk for a little rest?"

"Sure, go ahead. I always heard you mustangs couldn't take it when it got rough. Too bad you're not one of the captain's little academy boys, then you wouldn't have to stand watch when you were sick."

I didn't reply for a few minutes; I wasn't going to let him bait me. I looked down from my upper bunk, asking, "What's the problem with the spare parts for the transceivers?"

"Don't start that shit with me, you goddamned illiterate mustang. It's that fucking Rub Nose Bluing and his big campaign to look good at budget time. I'm not taking the rap for that one. What's that sonovabitch trying to do, blame me?" he screamed, jumping up and knocking over his chair as he leaped the distance to my upper bunk. His wild, distorted appearance and piercing wide eyes shot a bolt of fear through me as his shaking, unstable face leveled itself inches from my head.

"I was just asking; no one said anything. Please, sir, could I just get some rest?" I said, hoping to calm him. Mr. Bernard put his head through the doorway curtain, asking if everything was okay. With a snarling glance, Clements righted his chair, mumbling unintelligible threats.

After an early lunch, I assumed the JOOD watch. Mr. Graffey had the conn while the captain showed him various ship maneuvers. I watched and listened, controlling my jealousy under the guise of running an efficient watch. It was happening again just as it did with my father and sister.

I was a great disappointment to my father. He wanted an athlete for a son, and all he got was a fat, pimply faced wimp who did not care one iota for sports. This was reinforced by my ineptitude in doing the simplest thing with balls, such as throwing them or catching them or hitting them with bats, which I swung awkwardly without effect. I could do nothing in sports that pleased him, nor could my poor academic record lend mitigation.

My sister could do everything better. She ran faster, jumped higher, and never seemed out of breath. Her baseballs zoomed hot over home plate, scoring easy strikes on batters, and her footballs sailed spiraling true about their axis, landing exactly where she aimed. She could run rings, actual rings, around me.

She never wanted to hurt me or ever lorded it over me that she had a lithe body, outstanding athletic ability, and just naturally achieved grades of As or Bs on every report card. And my father, rightly so, showered her with the praise she deserved. None for Fat Donny.

She went to college; I didn't. I could have, I guess, if I had had better grades, but I didn't want to. I'd screw that up just like high school, and I knew that college girls wouldn't have given me any ass either.

The vile smell of my vomit brought me back from those depressing thoughts, and the disgraceful condition of my puke-spotted uniform didn't help my deflated spirits. The watch crept boringly by. I wanted it to end so I could stop by the electronics shop to talk to the ETs. But I was ashamed to face them in my debilitated condition. It spoke poorly of my manhood. Besides, one shop is just the same as all the others, and I had the experience to run any shop if I could only stop throwing up. And I was so very tired.

I took off my khakis and threw them over the side. I didn't talk to anyone, nor did I eat supper. I couldn't sleep either. *I've got the midwatch*

and, Christ, I can't sleep. My banged-up, bleeding shins were testimony
to my inability to adjust to destroyer life. I was a failure again, just as in
those early days in the navy with Seaman Monk Evans.

Monk Evans—I wondered where he was. Probably dead. We were
assigned together out of boot camp to the dry dock at the San Diego
Naval Station. We were eighteen. We hated work, and neither of us gave
a shit about anything but getting laid.

It was easier for Monk Evans. His sharp-featured face was framed by
crisply styled black hair, and his muscles rippled as he walked self-con-
fidently among the girls. I weighed a chunky 221 pounds. Monk Evans
spoke softly with a hint of mystery and adventure in his voice. I blurted
out the first words I thought of.

The scraggly old chief in charge of the dry dock assumed the holy
mission of teaching Monk and me how to be good boatswain's mates so
we could follow him along the glorious path of boatswainhood. Our specific job was building supporting stays in the bottom of the empty dry
dock so ships could be safely pulled in and settled.

Each class of ship had a standard hull pattern, so all we had to do was
build up huge wooden blocks according to the plans and place them every thirty feet or so. When we were done, someone—we never knew
who—flooded the dock, and tugs towed the ships in.

Once the ships were in position and held there by lines to capstans
around the rim of the dock, the dock would be pumped dry and the
ships lowered onto their stays. An easy procedure. We'd dock six small
ships from the mothball fleet at a time. The hulls would be inspected,
and once they had been deemed okay, the dock would be flooded and
the ships hauled out. Then we'd tear down the stays and build others
for different ships.

One problem was that it was bloody hard work, and Monk and I didn't
like it. Monk was much smarter than I, and he devised a method of strik-
ing a hammer so that the handle would break and we'd have to come out
of the dock to get a new one. The chief, never too bright during those
hours he had to spend away from the chief's club, solved this by making
us take ten hammers each down into the dock, so it wouldn't be necessary for him or the other two chiefs to go down the 132 stairs to the bottom. He trusted us with all those hammers, he said. In combination the
three chiefs weighed just under 750 pounds.

Unfortunately, those ten hammers had handles that must have been defective, because they too broke with alarming rapidity. We missed a docking. The chiefs weren't happy. We were their only two workers. The other three men assigned to the dock were third-class petty officers, each with more than ten years as rated boatswain's mates. Surely no one expected them to go down into the dock.

The chief decided that Monk and I needed more basic training, so he taught us, via his minions, to splice wire rope without heavy leather gloves. The wire ends shredded our hands.

Our bandaged, still periodically bleeding hands could not build stays, so the three petty officers had to do the work. The chief apologized to us for the incompetence of the petty officers who had not instructed us to use gloves. We got the message.

In those days the navy insisted that everyone stand watch when they had the duty every three days. Monk and I stood watches over the dry dock. Late at night I'd climb aboard one of the dead ships and make my way to the bridge. Once there, I'd stand proudly, acting like the captain giving orders to man the guns and torpedoes to fight off another sneak attack by the nefarious Japanese. In every case I saved the fleet and received the Medal of Honor from a grateful president and country.

Still tossing sleeplessly in my bunk, I forgot about Seaman Monk Evans as I heard the messenger approaching. I managed to put on a new set of khakis and stumble to the wardroom. Red goggles and slimy bologna sandwiches didn't prepare me well for the watch. The fresh air helped a little as I spent most of the time on the bridge wing.

The choppy seas and an increasing wind from the north spelled more bad weather. I felt myself drifting into sleep. I bit my lower lip until it bled. Finally, Mr. Bluing gave me the conn. Station keeping was more difficult than the night before, and the attention I had to pay to it took away some of my tiredness, but not much.

Mr. Bluing said very little during the watch. He asked me how I felt and told me again, uselessly, that I'd get used to it. I knew I never would and was doomed to a life of puke-splattered clothes and lack of sleep. He spoke of nothing personal and only once in a while mentioned something or other about the ship. He continually rubbed the bridge of his nose.

I spoke with the bridge watch finding out their names and duties until Mr. Bluing told me to stop. Just before the grand moment when the insufferable watch would be over, I asked him, "Do you detect any problems with the electronics gang?" He stiffened as if I'd asked him if his sister was a whore.

"No . . . no—what do you mean?" he demanded in a voice louder than he probably wanted it to be.

"Oh, nothing, just asking your opinion." Another ten minutes passed. "How about spare parts? Any problems there?" I hazarded.

"NO!" He paused, then added, "Not that I know of. Knock off this talk on the bridge, Sheppard; pay attention to the watch."

I had no problem falling asleep after I went below, pleased with myself for not throwing up even once on the midwatch. After breakfast and quarters on station, which meant that the men mustered in their working area rather than lining up outside on the decks, I dropped by Mr. Bernard's small engineering office. I really wanted to sleep but knew I couldn't, so I stopped in just to say hello.

"You interested in engineering?" he asked.

"Never thought much about it."

"I'll be leaving in a year or so and the job will be open. If you're at all interested, you should speak to the XO as soon as possible. I'm sure they'd want someone they know instead of the luck of the draw from BUPERS, the Bureau of Personnel. We have some problems down there," he said, indicating the boiler and engine rooms with a sweep of his hand.

I wasn't interested. "You're academy, aren't you?" I asked, trying to make conversation from my groggy state and acting as though I didn't see his ring.

He frowned. "Yes, is it obvious?"

"No, but it appears from the climate and innuendos around here that not being academy could be injurious to your health. That true?"

Mr. Bernard's mouth fashioned into a sly grin, and he laughed. "The old Protective Association of Annapolis syndrome, eh? It's more perceived than real on this ship, Don, I assure you. The captain wants good naval officers, and some of the ROTC boys don't quite cut it.

"When the captain comes down on them, they attribute it to not being academy. If they only knew what shit we ring knockers get, they wouldn't be so fast to criticize," he answered, getting up to leave. "Gotta go down and see my boys. Let me know if you're interested."

"My performance hasn't been too sterling in the time I've been aboard," I replied. "I'm not sure they'd want me to be the chief engineer."

"Don, right now, after that radio thing, you're the old man's golden-haired boy. You've got it made on good old *Henny*. We had to abort the last two exercises because of poor electronics. If it's not the radios, it's the radars; if not that, it's the sonar; if not that, et cetera, et cetera, et cetera. Think about it."

He paused for a second with his hand on the door to steady himself, his body swaying in perfect counterbalance to the rolling and pitching of the ship. "Believe me, young man," he mocked in a stern schoolmaster's voice. "The Protective Association is alive and well, and I'll be an admiral someday. Thank you very much."

He didn't hear my thanks for his offer as he disappeared down the access hatch to main control.

I walked to the electronics shack, where Jenkins and Moore, his second in charge, were busy over a black box out of the IFF—identification, friend or foe—set. Stupidly I asked, "Problems?"

Jenkins looked up at me, his face mellowing with a grin. "Oh, hi, sir. Yeah, for one thing these stupid IFF sets are built with no color coding on the wires or the resistors. Even the capacitors aren't marked. How the hell are we supposed to fix them? Stupid fucking navy—oh, sorry, sir, but it's a bitch."

"Know what you mean, Jenkins. We had the same problem on airplanes. But it's not really stupid; they were made in World War Two, and the navy was afraid they might be captured, so they were built with no markings in order to confuse the enemy, and it bloody well worked. But it confused our technicians, even though we had the manuals. And it's still confusing. In aviation, we'd just turn them in for new ones. Tough to do that out here, though. If we have the chance, we should comshaw another set for a spare."

"Yes, sir, but that isn't the problem here. Ya got any more ballpoint pens, Mr. Sheppard?"

"Why?"

"We know what's wrong with it, but we just don't have the parts to fix it." We talked for about an hour. Jenkins, a wholesome, recruiting-poster type with a crew cut, looked me straight in the face when he spoke. I liked him and trusted him.

Finally weariness and a sense of impending sickness forced me to head for my bunk. I crawled in, hoping for an hour's sleep before my next watch. Mr. Clements, reading in his rack, said nothing.

During my 1200 to 1600 watch, the commodore decided to do tactical maneuvers. We started off in a line astern formation with each ship a thousand yards behind the one ahead. The flagship in the lead gave us signals to carry out by using flag hoist codes hauled up only halfway on their signal halyards. When we understood the message, we hauled up the same set of flags.

When all ships had their flags up, the lead ship executed the signal by hoisting her flags all the way up, then rapidly pulling them down. The JOODs decoded these signal flags and passed the meaning to the conning officer. When necessary, they worked out solutions to a new station on the maneuvering board in competition with CIC. Each tried to see which one could be the fastest to give the course recommendations to the conning officer. Speed was the hallmark of a sharp ship.

We wheeled, turned, ran a line abreast, and did about everything four ships could do. Mr. Bluing did well. After about an hour the commodore split the formation, with each ship to steam away on a different course and, upon signal, return to a line astern.

But this time the distance between ships was to be only five hundred yards. It would be a bit more taxing at this distance, with a much higher pucker factor for the captain and the conning officer.

Once out on our scatter station, the captain told Mr. Bluing to give me the conn. My mouth dropped open. My eyes widened. A gush of sweat soaked my T-shirt. I'd been aboard only three days, and conning the ship during tactical maneuvers was considered a plum given only to the more experienced officers.

I looked at the captain sitting in his chair. Smugness twinkled in his eyes as if this were some monstrous joke. "Take the conn, Mr. Sheppard. That's the first step," he said, looking away.

I looked at Mr. Bluing. He nodded toward the helmsman.

Is this for real? A scene in my high school gym erupted in my memory: Fat Donny Sheppard, would-be heavyweight wrestler, being used as a training dummy for the middleweights to practice "moving flesh" around on the mats. Give a taste of mass, the coach had said to his middleweights. He'd been obliged to use me because of his friendship with my support-the-team father. "Don't hurt him," I recalled the coach saying to his bloodthirsty middleweights as they laughed at me.

"Ah . . . ah . . . Ensign Sheppard, here, I've . . . ah, got the conn." I stammered out the obligatory statement to the bridge, wishing I was in my stateroom throwing up. The helmsman and lee helmsman, as required, shouted back the course and the speed.

"You're the king of the mountain, Mr. Sheppard. Grease us in there when we go," the captain said, rising from his chair as he filled his pipe.

A slight tingle whisked through me, my fatigue evaporated, my head cleared, my stomach made peace with the rest of my body. I *was* the king of the mountain.

The flag hoist fluttered up from the flagship: "All ships join by sequence number, five-hundred-yard separation, course 000, speed fifteen knots."

"Understood!" I shouted before the signalmen could get their flags up, or before Mr. Graffey, now on the bridge as the codebook interpreter, could decode the hoist. I had memorized most of the two-letter signal codes. We weren't supposed to do that, because the meaning of the codes could change and our conditioned minds might not accept the new ones. But the codes hadn't changed in twenty years, and I couldn't help memorizing them. The captain frowned, then turned away.

Our flags zoomed up. It was the mark of a good ship if she could answer the hoists swiftly, if she could be the first in the division to respond. The signal flags on the commodore's ship flashed to full up, then were immediately hauled down. "Execute. Left full rudder; all engines ahead full; make turns for twenty-four knots," I shouted over the wind on the open bridge, feeling ten feet tall. No failure here.

Die, Fat Donny.

Twenty-four knots was the fastest we could go without the superheaters lit off.

The ship jumped ahead as she heeled over, swinging around in a beautiful arc toward the flagship. I waited for our bow to be several degrees ahead of the flagship and ordered, "Rudder midships." The helmsman repeated the order, swinging the two-foot brass wheel to the right until the rudder angle indicator showed zero degrees. I waited thirty seconds until the helmsman gave me the course we'd settled on.

"Passing 036, sir."

"Steady as she goes," I ordered, trying to remember all the fancy words my *Conning a Destroyer* book said to use.

"Passing 037, sir."

"Very well, steer course 037."

"Aye, sir, steer course 037." Ten seconds passed. "On course 037, sir."

"Very well." I could feel the sweat on my back as I tried to keep my hands from shaking.

I judged the relative closing angle. "Steer course 038 . . . no, belay that, steer course 041."

"Would you like a maneuvering board solution, Mr. Sheppard?" the captain asked, trying to mask his sarcasm. I'd forgotten about maneuvering boards and the officers and CIC behind me ready to help.

"Ahh, yes . . . yes, sir," I answered.

"Recommend course 040," Mr. Bluing replied. Mr. Graffey's was 039. Combat recommended 040.

"Very well, steer course 040," I said, conceding to protocol. It really wasn't necessary to quibble over a degree's steering at this long distance. I'd have to adjust as we got in closer anyway. I waited as we three ships raced toward the flagship. I made an adjustment to 039 and we headed for a spot one thousand yards astern of the flagship moving at fifteen knots.

The captain walked over to me and said in a very low voice, "Don't forget the length of the ship between you and the flagship." Then he returned to his chair.

Christ, I've forgotten. "Steer 040," I ordered, stealing a glance at the captain. His head nodded ever so slightly and the sides of his mouth raised maybe three millimeters, which was the closest to a smile I'd ever seen him make.

"Will she slow fast in these seas, Captain?" I asked and saw Mr. Bluing flush in surprise. A fresh-caught ensign asking the captain a question about ship handling? Never done, never done. Ensigns were supposed to learn and absorb by long hours of standing watch and paying attention.

"No, she won't," he answered. "At this speed differential of nine knots, it'll take at least four ship lengths to drop to fifteen knots," he lectured.

My mind rushed through the calculations. I didn't have the experience yet to feel it. Four ship lengths? We're 394 feet long, say 400 feet, times four equals 1,600 feet, divided by three to convert to yards equals 530, say 550 yards for safety. I'd pull power at 550 yards from station.

The palms of my hands dripped sweat over the forward bulkhead of the bridge. My hands felt the vibration of the ship; I felt as one with her. She sang merrily as we rushed to station. My hands dried.

"Range, Mr. Bluing, if you would, sir," I ordered, hoping it came out as a request. I keyed the 21MC, one of the ship's electronic intercommuni-cations systems to combat. "Combat. Bridge. Continuous range to station."

Mr. Bluing called out from behind the stadimeter, "Eight hundred yards to the bridge."

"Very well . . . excuse me, sir, thank you." *One never said* very well *to a senior.* Combat's range roughly concurred when converted from our station's location to the flagship's bridge. The numbers of the steady stream of ranges passed up to me grew smaller and smaller. Nervously I looked at the captain. His expressionless face gave no help or encourage-ment, but the tingling of my fingers against the steel told me I was doing okay.

"Six hundred yards to station," combat sang out.

"Belay continuous, call five hundred sixty," I ordered.

In a minute an uptight voice from combat came over the 21MC: "Five hundred sixty yards to station."

"All engines ahead standard; make turns for fifteen knots." We slowed fast, too fast; I should have waited another minute. *Grander,* our sister ship, was assigned the second vessel astern of *Rollard,* the flagship. *Grander* reached her position before we reached ours. But she was too far astern, encroaching dangerously on our station in the number three position. I turned to the lee helmsman, who was also the sound-powered phone talker to main control, and shouted too loudly, "Tell main control to stand by for a backing bell."

Fifteen seconds passed. We weren't going to make it. *Grander* was half in our station cocked to the line of steaming. *Sanders,* the fourth ship in line, was too far forward and still moving up. We'd never squeeze into station. I ran into the pilothouse, shouting, "All engines back full! Right standard rudder!" The right standard rudder would pull my stern away.

Seconds later the captain's voice came from behind me, saying matter-of-factly, "This is the captain. I've got the conn."

My body recoiled from shame as my humiliation spread throughout the ship and to the fleet. My first maneuvers, and the captain had taken the conn away from me. My face burned in degradation. I would resign my commission as soon as my watch was over. A flash of the dusky skies over the Granite City steel mills penetrated my woeful thoughts.

The captain changed no order as the ship gained sternway, swinging out of danger. Then in less than two minutes he said, "This is the captain, Mr. Sheppard has the conn."

The swiftness of the statement dumbfounded me, but I managed to stammer, "Ahh, Sheppard here, I've . . . I've got the conn." I waited three seconds to catch my wits, then ordered, "Rudder midships; all engines ahead standard; make turns for eighteen knots." Once moving ahead, I slowed to fifteen knots, paralleling our station out to the side at five hundred yards while *Grander* and *Sanders* sorted themselves out.

When they did I added ten turns to the engines and came left into station, overshooting it by twenty yards. I recovered by coming slightly right. When on station I came to 000, fifteen knots, sweat gushing from every pore in my body and said, "Alpha station, on station, Captain." He grunted, tamping the tobacco in his pipe.

A hoist came up from *Rollard:* "Commodore to *Henshaw,* BZ." It was a Bravo Zulu, that most sought after code for well done. A slight, ever so slight, smile crept across the captain's stoic face. Softly, in a monotone but with a grin he could barely contain, he said, "Understood. Acknowledge."

The Mids

W e played at the tactical maneuvers for another hour. I feared that my pounding pulse would betray my lack of confidence. I held onto any surface I could so no one would see my hands shake. Five hundred yards between ships left little room for error. I handled the maneuvers reasonably well, except for turning in a column.

I kept turning too late and ending up out of line. It seemed a simple matter to turn in the wake of the ship ahead, but I just couldn't manage it. Finally, the captain walked over to me, pointing to the ship ahead, and said, "Watch the knuckle of her rudder. When it's just under mount 51, throw your rudder over."

I tried, but my in-column turns remained sloppy. But so were the other ships'. I considered Mr. Bluing's statement that we were no worse than anyone else to be rather poor encouragement. I'd hate that to be my epithet. The drills ended, but my ego remained crushed from being relieved of the conn. When I reported my relief to the oncoming OOD, Mr. Bernard, the captain called me over. The XO stood behind him. My hands trembled. *This is it. I'm in for it. At least I'm not seasick.*

"Don." *Don . . . wow! Wow!* "I want you to know that that was a fine piece of ship handling for an ensign. Have you handled ships before?" the captain asked.

"No, sir, but as an aircrewman in antisubmarine aircraft, I had to work out turns and things in my head."

"Do you know why I took the conn from you?"

"No, sir, except maybe I was screwing up," I painfully answered.

"No, Don, you did all the right things, but we were in extremis, and if we'd had a collision I'd have been hung no matter what. I took the conn so you wouldn't go under with me. Remember that when you're sitting in this chair."

Sitting in this chair? Tears welled up in my eyes. I couldn't answer for the lump forming in my throat. "I, ah . . . I . . . thank you, Captain. I—"

"Go below, Mr. Sheppard," he said, waving me away, saving me from making a further fool of myself. I impulsively reached for his hand, shaking it until he pulled it away. I loved the man. Mr. Bernard nodded to me as I left the bridge floating six inches above the deck.

Over a cup of coffee in the wardroom with the comm and gunnery officers, both offered praise for my ship handling. Mr. Graffey, sitting at the other end of the table, said nothing.

At the electronics shop Jenkins and Moore lauded the hotshit division officer they were going to get on Friday. "There is a God," Moore joked. I waltzed back to my stateroom.

Clements sat with his chair leaned back on its two rear legs, his feet swinging back and forth. "Well, well," he started, "if it ain't the little uneducated high school graduate, enlisted puke, super-fucking-star kissing that fag captain's ass with a few simple rudder moves. I'll bet yo—"

He never finished the word. I grabbed him, yanking him up by his collar. His wire-framed glasses flew against the desk as I pulled him close to my face, then threw him backward. He crumpled to the deck. I stood over him with my outstretched finger an inch from his fear-crazed eyes.

"You listen to me, you miserable excuse for a naval officer. I'm going to tell you only once: you leave me alone, you don't say shit to me, and you stay out of the electronics shop. I relieve you as the electronics officer this minute. As of this fuckin' minute you ain't shit . . . you ain't shit. Do you understand me? You ain't shit."

His wailing retort that I couldn't do this to him halted when I raised my hand as if to hit him. His whining voice followed me out the door. "Don, Don, I . . . I . . . it's not my fault . . . not my fault . . . please . . ."

Holy shit, I've roughed up a naval officer. I'm going to be court-martialed. Well, in for a penny, in for a pound. I marched straight to Mr. Bluing's stateroom, where he sat rubbing the bridge of his nose.

I announced loudly enough for the XO to hear across the passageway: "I've had some trouble with Mr. Clements. I've relieved him of his duties as the electronics material officer and assume all responsibility for the division as of this minute."

Barely looking up, he simply said, "Very well, write me a letter."

For the next six months I stood the midwatches and the twelve to fours—the killer watches. I could not get to bed before quarter to eight in the evening because of my normal shipboard routine that required me to look after my division and all the shitty little jobs, SLJs. I was called for watch at quarter after eleven. At best, this was a poor three and a half hours of sleep, assuming I could get to sleep right away.

I meandered about constantly fatigued. I didn't know why I had the mids for so long. The comforting statement from others, "You'll get used to them," didn't help and wasn't coming true. My seasickness had subsided to where I got sick only in rough seas. My body defined as rough seas what others described as moderate.

The other watches weren't as bad. On the eight to twelves you at least got all your sleep at one time and could take a nap after lunch for maybe thirty-five minutes. But even on the eight to twelves, you didn't get to bed before say 0015 and had to be up by 0600 to relieve the four-to-eight early for breakfast. So you got maybe a little less than six hours of sleep; but at least it was all at one time. It looked good to me. On the four to eights you got the most sleep—about seven hours—since you could be in bed by 2015 and not get up until 0315.

That's if you had no problems with your division or you didn't have night GQ or the seas weren't that rough.

We were out at sea every other two weeks for two weeks at a time. All we did for the most part was steer in a column formation day after day. When we arrived back in port we were still on one and three, which meant one-third of the crew always had to be aboard. And of course quarterdeck watches had to be stood around the clock. In my section we had only three qualified in-port OODs, and I stood the boring, nothing-to-do quarterdeck watches in port.

This destroyer officer bullshit didn't seem right or have the romance I had envisioned. Could ex-naval officer Clements have been right? When I did get off the ship periodically and returned home to my family, I just wanted to sleep.

The underway OODs stood one in four and sometimes one in five, which meant their watch hours rotated, so we JOODs didn't work with the same OODs every watch. The three JOODs—Ensign Graffey, Lieutenant Junior Grade Chadwick, who was a lesser light, and I stayed on one in three. Whenever the little hand was on twelve, and until it reached four, night or day, I was on watch. Ensign Graffey had the eight to twelves; Lieutenant Chadwick had the four to eights. He had the four to eights because, it was said, the captain couldn't stand seeing him, and the four to eights had the least visual exposure to the omnipotent one.

Chadwick had apparently fallen out of favor and was only marking time until his release from active duty. Ensign Graffey had the eight to twelves so he and the captain could talk about the good old days when Graffey was young and he and his father and the captain went hunting and fishing together.

The worst thing about the midwatch was that it was rarely busy and it gave you a lot of time to think. If you were on watch with Mr. Bluing, he'd demand silence, then he'd stand there all watch rubbing his nose and looking out to sea or at the accompanying vessels.

The other types of OODs felt it was their God-given duty to tell you all about their lives and college days filled with abundant, never-ending, fine sex and copious drinking, or the academy, which was tough beyond endurance and could not be described to those miserable castaways in life not blessed with attendance. Worse yet were the ones who endeavored to teach you the ways of the navy and the destroyer. All of these types were bearable for a while, but then the stories got old and the lessons repetitious. I learned to enjoy the silent types.

We steamed mostly independently now and it was boring. We never did anything that was fun, such as tactical maneuvering or chasing submarines or shooting the guns or torpedoes or any of the other things I'd always thought destroyers did.

My first week aboard had been the most active, and I'd been too seasick to even understand. Almost every day we went to general quarters but nothing happened—no drills, nothing. Rumor said engineering or damage control drills might harm the ship, and by extension the reputation of the captain; therefore, they were something to be avoided.

Once in a while we'd have a lecture in the wardroom about something we all knew anyway. Neither the captain nor the XO nor even the senior junior officer, Mr. Bluing, ever talked to us about the heady matters they dealt with. That would have been interesting.

Most of the time the training lectures became bull sessions—circle jerks, the more senior junior officers called them. Mr. Bernard tried to talk about engineering once or twice but nobody really gave a damn. We ensigns dared not comment.

Two nice things about general quarters were first, they usually occurred in the afternoons after everyone awoke from their postlunch naps, and since my GQ station was in the electronics shop, I could get off that boring 1200 to 1600 bridge watch. And second, it gave me free, locked-in time to train my men.

While men at the other stations sat on their asses reading paperback books, I set out to make GQ fun for the ETs. Most of the ETs were not staying in the navy; there were too many opportunities in civilian life. Consequently, they were driven to increase their knowledge. I let the junior ETs set up the academic curriculum and the equipment they wanted more training on.

Having spent three of my enlisted years as an electronics instructor at the naval station in Memphis, Tennessee, I held most of the theory lectures. But I farmed out some of them to anyone who might want to do them, such as young Moore, a third class, who was a whiz at math and enjoyed talking about it.

We ran our own damage control drills on the equipment without the captain or XO, or even Mr. Bluing, knowing about it. We'd gather bad components from past repairs; before GQ, Jenkins and Moore would take out the good parts and put in the bad. We'd assign the problem to one of the ET teams and grade them on technique and time required to repair.

It was a great game as we rotated, letting the more junior ETs develop problems for Jenkins and Moore and often me. No one questioned why some equipment went down just before general quarters sounded and was always up before GQ was over. GQ times always appeared in the plan of the day, put out by the XO scheduling the day's activity.

One night we were steaming in our assigned geographic boxes, thirty miles square, fifty miles out from San Diego. Night steaming on station was really boring. Each ship stayed close to the center of its box in order to avoid even the remote possibility of a collision that might occur if ships wandered to their borders. Rarely did we steam in company with other ships, and then it was usually with a carrier, and our stations were five thousand yards, two and a half miles, apart.

Tonight a full moon and a slight ripple on the still water graced our view. Mr. Bluing, who always looked tired, slept silently in the XO's chair on the port side of the bridge, taking a hell of a chance of being caught if the XO or captain happened to come to the bridge. Sleeping on watch was bad enough, but doing it in the XO's sacrosanct chair was adding insult to injury. Even in his sleep Mr. Bluing rubbed his nose occasionally, and periodically he groaned a soft lament of pain. *What's the matter with this guy?*

"Bogie, an unidentified air contact, bearing 095 . . . inbound, negative squawk," came the report from CIC. Negative squawk meant no IFF indications.

What if it were an attacking Japanese bomber with an atom bomb, and my alertness in reporting it saved the country and my swift attack with machine guns destroyed it? I again pictured myself receiving the Medal of Honor from a grateful president and nation. The ticker tape parade in New York would be marvelous to behold.

"Very well," I answered, trying to work up enthusiasm. "Probably a commercial airliner from Lindbergh Field in San Diego. Keep me informed."

"IFF squawking friendly," CIC reported back in three minutes.

In ten more minutes I heard the familiar sound of a two-engine prop aircraft, a navy P2V antisubmarine patrol aircraft. I knew the type well. I could see the outline of this one as it came within two miles. An aldis lamp blinked at us from the silhouette. The signalman quickly called out, "Sending 'Who are you?' sir."

"Send back, 'What squadron?'" I whispered to the signalman so as not to awake my sleeping boss. "And keep it quiet." I saw him wink in the dim light.

The P2V came to the north, circling us. Probably no one had ever challenged them before. "He sends back, 'What ship?' again, Mr. Sheppard."

"Send back, 'Lollipop, Good Ship.'" The signal lamp flashed skyward again.

The P2V came in lower now at about two thousand feet. I was afraid the noise would stir Mr. Bluing.

The flashing light started again. "Does that mean you suck?"

I sent back, "It's the other way around; figured you brown shoes could keep that straight. What squadron?"

"PATRON 2."

"You're a long way from Whidbey Island. What are you doing?"

"Night cross-country. Interrogative your mission?"

"Digging holes in the ocean."

The two-engine patrol bomber circled us as we exchanged our cumbersome light signals. "Keep up the good work," they flashed, then pulled up heading north.

I flashed one more time, "And you and Operation Ivy."

There was a pause as the aircraft turned again, heading back. "Roger that," came from the cockpit as they waggled their wings in the moonlit sky and turned north again. Operation Ivy was the first dropping of the hydrogen bomb. I knew it well. Patrol Squadron 2, with me attached, was there.

The now quiet watch bored me again as I followed the droning engines until they disappeared. Patrol Squadron 2, my first sea duty assignment in the navy. It was all Monk Evans's doing. I smiled as my thoughts meandered back.

On the dry docks, Monk got tired of the harassment the chief boatswain's mate passed out, even though we deserved it. One day after we'd been on the dry docks for about two months, Monk read a bulletin asking for volunteers for naval aviation. You could transfer from seaman first class to airman first class if your scores on the classification battery test, which equated roughly to an IQ test, were high enough. It required a score of at least 110; 100 was average. We both well exceeded 110. The personnel man in the admin office asked why we didn't go to school right out of boot camp. We didn't know, we answered, but bloody well knew it was because we were such foul-ups.

The chief in charge of the dry docks begged us to stay. He said that things would be better and he would even put the third-class petty officers to work. But no, we were heading for adventures high in the sky in new places. We'd seen the World War Two movies, and we knew that fighter pilots got a lot of ass.

But we weren't quite fighter pilots; in fact we were sweat labor closing down old naval air stations. It was ignoble work for the grandson of a British commodore cum Good Humor man. Monk managed it so that we could screw off as much as possible. I followed along like a sheep with no mind of my own. Hell, it was fun not having to think, just doing what "The Monk" said.

We kept getting transferred from one place to another, becoming other people's problems as we moved. We ended up at U.S. Naval Air Station, El Centro, California, working menial labor on tropical hours from 0600 to 1300. We stood no duties, and every weekend we'd put on our cleanest uniforms and hitchhike to adventure.

Monk's greatest and easiest scam was for us to borrow a car, run down to Mexicali, Mexico, and promise the ladies of the night that if they'd shack up with us all night we'd run them across the border next morning in the trunk of our car. We never got caught. We were nineteen. Border crossings were different then.

One day while I was in a bowling alley in El Centro, a third-class petty officer stood next to me trying on bowling shoes. I noticed his rank device—his crow, as it was called. Of course I had seen many of them, but this one seemed magical. How beautiful it was; it spoke to me, that white-winged spread eagle hovering over the one red stripe with its specialty symbol in the center. The great breath of ambition surged through my body. I had a goal. I quit screwing off.

I worked my ass off to impress my chief, and I did. I became a control tower operator directing fighter planes for landings and takeoffs; the planes used our field for staging as they shot up the nearby desert gunnery ranges.

Three months after my transformation, my division officer called me in to comment on my work. He was proud of my turnaround, he said, and asked if I would like to go to air controlman school. I saw my crow getting closer, but then I saw it dashed when he told me a few days later that all quotas for the school were filled for three months. He couldn't have missed the dour look on my face. But he continued, "With your IQ and my recommendation, you qualify for every school the navy has. What's your choice?"

"Got anything close to St. Louis?" I asked, because I was sort of homesick.

"In Memphis, Tennessee, there are dozens," he answered. "But that's as close as we can get."

"Which one starts the soonest?"

He glanced at the paper he held. "Aviation electronics technician, AT, school starts every Monday."

In a week, without having made a true conscious decision to go, I was sitting in a front-row seat in a classroom in Millington, Tennessee, just north of Memphis, at the Naval Schools Command, determined to graduate with honors even though I had barely made it through high school. The top 10 percent of the graduates were automatically promoted to second-class petty officer, the next 10 percent to third class.

In nine months I returned to the El Centro naval air station a second-class petty officer, met a young lady, got married, reenlisted, and transferred to Patrol Squadron 2 at Whidbey Island, Washington. P2Vs. Monk Evans gone forever.

Someone closing the bridge door brought me back. It was 0330. Our reliefs would be up soon. I walked over by the XO's chair and affected a cough loud enough to startle Mr. Bluing. He harumphed a couple of times, rubbing his nose. He looked so horribly pale in the dim light of the moon.

"Yes . . . yes, of course it hurts," he mumbled unintelligibly.

I didn't understand.

OPTAR

D etermining the spares we needed was my highest priority during the first few months after taking over as the electronics material officer, the EMO. The ETs took the bite for the constant failure of the equipment when in fact the shortage of parts was the real culprit. And, of course, Mr. Clements's hostile attitude and mental degradation and his wretched leadership had driven the morale of the group to an abysmal low.

This probably accounted for the cool, almost hostile reception on my first day in the radio shack working on the transceivers. Officers, to them, were at best tolerated, at worst no better than the plague.

Spare parts were essential to our program of getting all the electronics equipment in good shape. The ETs did more than I. My bouts with seasickness kept me from participating except for the most difficult repair situations, when they asked for my help. Repairs were becoming more frequent as the gear deteriorated further. It took all my experience and skills to figure out the proper jury rigs. We were going critical.

I needed to talk to someone. The chief engineer had been friendly to me. I went to see him. "Mr. Bernard, I need your advice, sir," I said, knocking hesitantly on the open door of the chief engineer's office. I told him my problem with the lack of spares. "What should I do?" I asked. I explained what Mr. Clements had said about Mr. Bluing wanting to look good by saving money on his budget through not buying spare parts. "I'm confused. I thought the navy paid for the spare parts. I didn't think we had to buy them."

"Well, yes and no, Don," Mr. Bernard replied. "The navy does pay, but they make each ship responsible for what it spends. The type commander—that's COMCRUDESPAC, or Commander, Cruisers and Destroyers, Pacific—assigns each ship an operating target, OPTAR for short, of so many dollars per quarter. The captain in turn allots so much of the OPTAR to each department. This is our budget, or spending target, if you will.

"From this we must buy all consumables, such as paint, foul-weather clothing, mooring lines, fire hoses, and such. We don't have to pay for medical supplies, food, fuel, or new equipment, but we do pay for repair parts. Not the huge ones like new motors, but we do have to pay for most other parts . . . hence the problem."

"Let me guess," I offered. "We're evaluated on money management, right?"

"You're getting there."

"If we're given this money to spend, and we don't spend it all, it appears that we're good financial managers. If we can scrimp here and there while holding things together, our fitness reports will reflect how good we are."

"You got it, Don."

"You think that Mr. Bluing is doing that? It's an awful shortsighted policy. Wouldn't the captain or XO know about it?"

"I never discuss the conduct of my senior officers. They taught us that at the school I went to—you know, the Big A. But if a department head looks good, the old man looks better. All I can tell you is to cover your ass."

I carefully signed the requisitions and stood outside Mr. Bluing's stateroom holding them in my sweaty hands with a heartbeat half again as fast as normal. I feared hyperventilation. I knocked on his open door. He looked up at me from his desk. "What?" he barked.

I offhandedly gave him the two-inch-thick stack of flimsies as if I were just a messenger dropping off routine paperwork. "I was coming this way. Thought I'd . . . I'd just drop these off."

He looked at them, fanning through the pile, his face shading white. He rubbed his nose as if to claw it off his face, or to ensure it wouldn't come off. The movements were the same. "Jesus Christ, Sheppard, where'd these goddamn things come from?"

I tried to stand taller, wishing I hadn't done this, wishing I had some moisture in my mouth, wishing I could speak. "I, ah . . . it's, sir—it's several months' worth of spares that Mr. Clements failed to submit, sir," I lied, feigning innocence. It hadn't been Clements but Bluing himself who had turned down the original purchase requests.

He threw the requisitions on his desk, staring at me as if I had just slapped him. One of the requisitions fell to the passageway deck. I bent over, picked it up, and threw it toward the stack. It missed, drifting to the deck behind him like a leaf fluttering to the ground. When I started to step into his room to retrieve it, his hand went out in front of me as if it held a dagger ready to drive into my heart. "I'LL GET THE FUCKIN' THING! How much these come to?" he barked, snarling, his teeth bared.

"Twelve thousand two hundred thirteen dollars and fifty-three cents, sir," I glibly answered, much to my regret as his face tightened and his jaw set even more. He looked at me, fire flaring from the slits that passed for eyes.

The ship tilted in a slight roll and I braced myself as I stood there in silence. He glared at me. I tried to look like a stupid new ensign caught in a drama over his head. I could almost hear my sweat beads as they fell from my hands, plopping on the deck like raindrops.

The roll increased.

My stomach grumbled, my head lightened. *Oh, please, please don't let me get seasick now—not now.* The rolling continued. Silence filled the narrow passageway.

Color crept back into Mr. Bluing's face as he sucked in a deep breath, bringing in more air; his violent right hand softened to a caress on his nose. He motioned me in, surreptitiously sneaking away a huge jar of aspirin from his desk as he did. He motioned me to sit on the bunk.

"Now, Sheppard, why the hell do we suddenly need all these repair parts when we were getting along just fine before you came here?"

I guess he'd forgotten his first statement to me about having a lot of trouble and hoping I could help. "Sir," I hazarded, "with all due respect, we haven't been getting along. The electronics gear on this ship isn't worth shit. It's held together by jury rigs and baling wire.

"Those transceivers we fixed with ballpoint pens are still using the ballpoint pens. Their power output is down by more than fifty percent and dropping every time we use them. We've replaced the pens twice but they won't last long and the subsequent repairs will be even more expensive."

"'We've,' Mr. Sheppard? Have you been working with the ETs fixing equipment?" he asked as if I'd raped the queen of the May.

"Yes, sir, of course I have. They're good boys and they work their asses off, but they needed help and I helped them, of course I did," I answered, taken aback by his raw display of elitism. His Annapolis ring caught the light from his desk lamp, reflecting into my eyes like a death ray burning into my unworthy soul.

His eyes narrowed questioningly as he kept pulling his hand down away from his nose. "You're on the mids. When do you have time to do this? Aren't you sick most of the time anyway?" His words lashed across me like a cat-o'-nine-tails. *Pompous ass, does he think he can intimidate me?* And what a pitiful attempt to divert the subject to something personal and embarrassing to me.

I stiffened, trying to come to attention sitting on the bunk in his small stateroom. The hint of disrespect in my tone came out all too clearly as I carefully replied, "I get enough sleep, sir, and it is my duty to my ship and to my men to assist them whenever they need help." I paused, trying to reset the tone of my answer. Not a muscle moved in Mr. Bluing's face.

"As to my seasickness, sir, I deeply regret my inability to overcome the problem, and I am ashamed that I have not conquered it. But I assure you, sir, as you have well observed on our watches together, it has not affected my military job performance or my professional duties with my division, sir."

Twenty degrees dropped off the temperature as his silence followed my answer. I offered no more. He looked at the requisitions spread over his desk where he had thrown them. "You dare to lecture me, Ensign Sheppard, you dare?"

I did not reply. We sat in silence, the roll of the ship and the smell of cooking meat in the wardroom pantry punching at my stomach. The low murmur of a ventilation blower soothed me with its soft whir. "Does it have to be this much? I don't have near that amount left in my OPTAR," he finally answered, dragging the muted sounds from deep inside his churning gut.

I didn't answer. Here was a man who, for his own self-aggrandizement, let the ETs suffer, let the ship suffer, and perhaps could have put our nation in danger, for want of a nail.

"I'm going to look bad," he muttered. I heard a cough from the XO's stateroom. I still did not reply. I felt sorry for him even though I was convinced he'd destroyed Mr. Clements. "I'm going to look awfully bad," he whispered, his hands shaking as he took four pills from his desk drawer and popped them into his mouth. "Have you told the captain?" he asked almost rhetorically.

I shook my head no in disgust to the insulting question. Of course I hadn't; Mr. Bluing was my direct superior. I had to report to him first.

The head steward knocked on the door announcing lunch in five minutes. "Can we talk about this on watch, Mr. Sheppard? You've got to be mistaken."

As tradition required, I, an ensign, sat at the far end of the ten-man table away from the captain. The discussion amongst the officers dealt with the poor quality of movies received before leaving San Diego and what movie we'd show tonight. We should have been talking about what training the ship needed or what repair parts were in short supply, not something as frivolous as movies. There was much work to be done. I felt uneasy, but not from the discussion with Mr. Bluing. I was uneasy about what was going to happen next, uneasy about the upcoming charade.

The stewards had just served the main course when a knock on the wardroom door caused all heads to turn. This didn't happen often at mealtime. We officers were not to be disturbed by enlisted men during our high-level discussions while we ate. Electronics Technician First Class Jenkins came in looking around the table. He spotted me and, saying "Excuse me" to the captain, came over and whispered in my ear, then left.

"Excuse me, Captain." I rose from the table. "The surface search radar has gone down again," I said, hoping I hadn't inadvertently stressed "again."

The captain scowled, answering, "Shit, Mr. Sheppard, the weather's closing in. I thought you were going to be the big solution to our problem. XO, we gotta get rid of those ETs and get some who aren't so incompetent and lazy."

"Sir, with all due respect, they are neither incompetent nor lazy," I spoke without thinking, glancing at Mr. Bluing as I walked toward the door that Jenkins had just exited. The captain's face lost a shade of color. The XO's eyes widened and he coughed. Mr. Bluing turned nearly white.

"Excuse me," I said, passing behind the captain as the phone to the bridge by his chair buzzed.

"Yes, thank you, I know. Mr. Sheppard is on his way up to fix it now. Visibility is how far? A thousand yards! Slow to five knots until they get it fixed," I heard him say as I passed through the door.

*   *   *

I was ten minutes late for the watch. Mr. Graffey made a snide comment about good officers being on time. I apologized, reporting my assumption of the JOOD watch to Mr. Bluing. I announced that the SPS-10, surface search radar, would be up in perhaps ten to fifteen minutes. "We've used the last of the transmitter spares, and we're jury-rigging some other components. I had to cannibalize the air search radar for a few parts. It'll be down too. I think the fix will work. But if it goes down again, there will be nothing we can do."

"Captain on the bridge," came the report from the boatswain's mate of the watch. The captain looked into the cone-shaped black daylight viewing hood over the radar repeater, harumphed, and sat down heavily in his chair. Mr. Bluing reported the cannibalization of the air search as if he had ordered it.

We waited in silence for the next ten minutes, alert to the poor visibility. The slow speed accented the rolling, and my head expanded in pain as I fought the grumbling in my disloyal stomach. There had been no ships around when the surface search radar went down, and at our five-knot speed we anticipated no problems. Ten minutes stretched to fifteen, then twenty.

The fog thickened and the captain kept glancing at the dead radar screen repeater sitting there blank, mocking us for our dependence upon it. "Mr. Bluing, send Mr. Sheppard below and find out what the hell's going on. This crap'll be soup in another five minutes."

In ten minutes I was back on the bridge, just as the turning of the radar antenna high on our mainmast signaled the radar was up. The yellow line sweeping 360 degrees around the radar repeater added unerring electronic visibility through the now dense fog. "What was the trouble, Mr. Sheppard?" the captain asked, stroking his battered 7x50 binoculars as if trying to soothe them for their inability to see through the fog.

"We had a little trouble with spare parts, Captain. We—" I started to answer as Mr. Bluing cut me off.

"I've taken care of that, Captain. Mr. Sheppard and I had a talk just before lunch. I think we got it licked."

"We?" you sonovabitch!

Jenkins came to the bridge, looked into the rubber hood over the radar repeater, made a slight adjustment, and looked at me and winked.

OOD

U sually I was too exhausted to go to sleep after climbing into my bunk from the treadmill of the midwatches. I rarely got more than three hours' sleep at a time. My eyelids constantly drooped, and huge, dark bags found a home underneath them. Even though I had little to do with the electronics gear now that we'd gotten all the spare parts we needed, I had to spend countless hours on the other crummy little jobs thrown my way.

I was on Mr. Bluing's shit list even though we now enjoyed almost 100 percent availability of the equipment. He had to *borrow* money from the captain's reserve fund to buy all the parts. I reckon the captain had a few words with him. I never knew.

To add to my misery, Mr. Bluing made me the registered publications custodian with the responsibility of making the thousands of changes to our confidential and secret publications. These changes rained down continuously from some staffie Nirvana in Washington. It was a thankless, time-consuming, boring task usually given to some smart-ass ensign who had angered the ops officer. I qualified.

I often wished, lying in my bunk, that I'd become a limited-duty officer (LDO) instead of an unrestricted line officer. I was miserable from the tiredness and the menial work and the constant fear of my seasickness returning, but boredom was my greatest enemy. If all I was going to be able to do was worry about electronics, I should have been an LDO, even with its lack of promotional opportunities and limited assignments.

At least LDOs didn't have to go to sea very much. Then I wouldn't be on this horrible destroyer, battered by the sea and lying here contemplating resignation. And I wouldn't have to be the SLJO, the shitty little jobs officer, which entailed being the voting officer, welfare and recreation officer, VD control officer, charities officer, wardroom mess caterer, public affairs officer, and every other goddamn thing that no one else wanted to do. How come Graffey didn't have to do all this shit? Suck-ass academy bastard.

I didn't even have to be in the navy. I could have received a medical discharge in boot camp. I was allergic to wool. Our uniforms were wool. I broke out in a violent rash whenever I wore one. The medical board said, "Out." My company chief said no and had his wife line my wool uniforms with cotton for five dollars. I stayed in the navy and cursed him now for his seamstress wife as the pollutant stench of the steel mills wafted more gently through my truant mind. If it hadn't been for her, I could be swigging beer, bowling, watching TV, and letting my gut fall over my belt line.

Six months to the day after I arrived aboard, the captain called me into his sea cabin just off the bridge. I'd never been in it before. He had an in-port cabin two decks below, but he used it only when we were in port. His sea cabin gave him instant access to the bridge or CIC.

I sat when he motioned me to. He didn't say anything, just looked at me with his deep blue eyes under eyebrows the color of polished old silverware. His short gray hair and weatherbeaten face made him look older than his thirty-six years. His six-foot-one body sat comfortably in his chair as he meticulously filled his pipe.

"Smoke if you'd like," he said with a loose wave of his hand. I hadn't brought anything to smoke but said thank you. The sweet smell of his tobacco filled the room as I watched the vent fan draw the gray smoke into itself, consuming it with a contented purr like a giant cat lapping milk.

He leaned his chair back, adjusting it to the gentle rolling, and said, "Don, what do you think of being a destroyer officer and about life in general aboard *Henshaw?*"

The question startled me. I had thought this meeting would be an ass-chewing session for something I did or didn't do. I hesitated. *Does he know I lost that page of the confidential document . . . the XO said he'd take care of it.* He asked his question again.

"Frankly, Captain, I'm bored." His face didn't change expression. "Being the electronics officer is the same thing I've done for the past five years. The equipment is all working to specs, and the ETs are trained and organized. There is little for me to do. Being a JOOD gives me no challenge. The OODs take over when anything interesting is going to happen, and I feel little opportunity to grow."

"You're rather frank, aren't you?"

"A failing, sir. I apologize."

"Please don't, I find it a refreshing change from all the yes men who gather around me. Tell me, do you perceive that academy officers are treated more favorably than the other officers?"

Talk about a loaded question! After the second it took for my mind to absorb it, I answered, "I can only speak for myself, sir, and I have not detected it." I hesitated as his eyes bore into mine. I would not glance away first. "It does, er . . . appear, however, that you'll chew out an academy officer's ass faster when he screws up . . . and more harshly, than a nonacademy officer. This may be somewhat of a reverse favoritism. If I may hazard, though, it is a . . . a common feeling in the wardroom that academy officers receive more favorable treatment." I had said enough, probably too much. I didn't understand. Why'd he ask me such a question?

We sat in silence for a god-awfully long minute or so. My hands sweated. I wanted to look around his sea cabin but kept my eyes right on his. I'd read that was important, but he was too sharp for me. "Look around, Don. Do you like it?"

"I like it and what it represents," I said after a moment.

"Why haven't you complained about being on the mids for six months? Most officers would."

"It never entered my mind," I lied, "and excuse me, sir, but how do you know I've never complained?"

"You'll find out when you're a captain that captains know almost everything that happens on their ships."

When you're a captain. Wow! Is this some leadership ploy: dangle a carrot . . . give 'em a goal?

"I've liked what I've seen in you, Don. I know, unofficially of course, about the Clements thing and wished I could have done it myself. I know all about the spare parts and I know what you've done for the Electronics Division and the availability of our equipment.

"I know you've even done well on the SLJs. I know your conduct on the bridge is impeccable. You seem to know what to do and when to do it."

He paused, compacting his pipe tobacco with a sterling silver tamper. I flushed at his comments, not understanding what was going on. I wanted to be out of here before I confessed how truly miserable I was and that I'd already typed up my request for transfer to LDO status. *I'm not giving up any more sleep.* I didn't want his praise or his bullshit pep talks; it jumbled my mind. I wanted off this tub.

"You were on the mids for so long because you were being tested. I was testing you. I knew an ex-chief mustang would complain if he felt it justifiable. My first captain did it to me and I detested it—and him—but never had the guts to complain. Don, what do you think of becoming the chief engineer?"

I said nothing. I had for so long resigned myself to being the electronics officer that the possibility of being anything else had never occurred to me, except for a fleeting moment when Mr. Bernard mentioned it to me many months ago. "I, ah, I think I would like that . . . yes, I would like that, Captain."

"So would Mr. Bernard. He thinks you're a fine officer. He's very protective of *his* plant. See the XO; he'll take care of getting you to the Engineering Officer School."

His words stunned me. I couldn't move; I couldn't think for a second. Few but the ETs had said anything good about me since I came aboard. I always needed praise but never received enough of it. I knew this was my own hang-up; I was insecure in everything I did. I never felt I was good enough. "I . . . I thank you, Captain. I'll do a good job," I stammered, getting up to leave with visions of sugarplums dancing in my head.

"You know what impressed Mr. Bernard and me so much about your engineering savvy?" he said as I stood. He motioned me down.

"No, sir, he and I have talked about engineering only one time and then for only a minute."

"It was when we were joining up in the tactical maneuvering your first week aboard and you alerted main control to stand by for a backing bell. That took real foresight for a junior officer, first time out."

"Oh?" I answered. The captain broke into a laugh at my profound remark. "Thank you, sir," I added, starting to stand again.

"And one more thing, Don. Please sit down, for Christ's sake!"

"Yes, sir. Sorry, sir."

"Who is responsible for this ship?" he asked.

I hesitated, thinking there would be more to the question. "Why, we all are, sir," I answered, not understanding his meaning.

"No, Don, I mean ultimately responsible for this ship."

"You are, Captain."

"What about when I'm asleep? Am I still responsible?"

"Yes, sir."

"What should an OOD do when he becomes confused or the situation changes?" he asked in a schoolmarmish tone.

"Inform the captain, sir."

"And what should the OOD do if he thinks he can handle the situation and he knows the captain's dead tired from too many hours on the bridge?"

"Inform the captain, sir."

"Do you truly believe that, Mr. Sheppard? Really believe that?"

I hesitated for a split second, wondering why he now called me Mr. Sheppard instead of Don. What was all this about? Is this some kind of trap? Why was he so serious all of a sudden? We had had these answers jammed into our heads every night in the night order book.

"Yes, sir, I truly do. That's why captains get all that 'extra-responsibility' pay." I managed an insincere laugh, unsuccessfully trying to put some levity into the conversation. He didn't even smile. Extra-responsibility pay for captains was a joke around the fleet. Every once in a while someone tried to get it through Congress but it always died. Captains received no extra pay even though most people thought they did.

The captain stood, solemnly extending his hand. The ship started to roll, and my stomach started to churn. *Shit!* I automatically stood with him, reaching out and shaking his hand—I didn't know for what—as he said, "Congratulations, Mr. Sheppard, you are now a fully qualified OOD. You'll take Mr. Bluing's place in the rotation. Unfortunately, he has the mid tonight. Ensign Rice, who came aboard just last week, will be your first JOOD. He knows nothing and will, by the way, relieve you as the electronics officer."

I stared at him. My stomach settled. I kept foolishly pumping his hand until he took his left hand, grasped my wrist, and extracted himself, pulling his hand away with a sincere look of pleasure.

"But, sir, I . . . I've only done one man overboard drill and I fuc . . . messed that up horribly. And I've never had any ASW. I—"

"I think you'll do just fine, Don, just fine." And with a smile he added, "Are you questioning the captain's judgment again, Mr. Sheppard?"

Lieutenant Junior Grade—soon to be lieutenant—Bernard had the watch as I floated out of the sea cabin. He nodded his head at me, grinning. The seas were growing but I didn't care. I laughed as I dared my stomach to react. I was through with that bullshit: OODs don't get seasick.

As Mr. Bernard suggested, I reported to Mr. Bluing, who, as the senior watch officer, had the responsibility of assigning officers to their watches. "Congratulations, Don, welcome to the club," he said, standing outside his stateroom offering me his hand.

We shook hands as the XO stepped out of his stateroom. "You're the most junior officer I know who has become an OOD so fast," the XO said. "Well done, Don, you deserve it. Glad to be on the same ship with you. See me tomorrow and we'll set up the school. It's sixteen weeks at San Diego, and you should go as soon as possible. We deploy to WESTPAC in five months. Just got the word. Gotta go."

WESTPAC, the Western Pacific, the Orient, exotically beautiful women, marvelously strange sights, combat with the Communists, glory, adventure . . . Don Sheppard, boy defender of freedom, keeper of the faith, fighter for the greater good of mankind. Destroyer Man. The Nameoki Kid. Wow! WESTPAC!

"Don, you okay?" Mr. Bluing asked. "You okay?" His voice and hand on my shoulder broke my fantasy. "Here, come into my room." We sat as he offered me a cigarette. I knew he didn't smoke and offered me one just to establish rapport. *Where were you, you sonovabitch, when I really needed someone? You're my department head; I needed you and you ignored me. Fuck you, Rubadubnose.*

He leaned out of his chair, pushing his door closed. He glanced around the room as some movie super spy might do checking for a bug.

He ensured again that his door was closed and lowered his voice to a whisper. "Don, thank you for not blowing the whistle on me on that repair parts thing. I got in big trouble, but I only took the bite for bad management, not for intentionally shaving my OPTAR. Nobody but you knows about that. I've learned my lesson."

Yeah, and destroyed poor Clements along the way. The ETs know and the captain knows and certainly the XO knows and probably everyone else on this bloody ship knows, asshole. Whadaya want me to say, "Oh, that's okay"? Fat chance.

"So I just want to say again, thank you." He finished his agonizing little speech by extending his hand.

I shook it, saying, "Oh, that's okay," while he rubbed his goddamned nose.

Off San Diego

I n my exhilaration, I was on the bridge early, carefully reading the night orders before relieving the watch. Before tonight, I'd never taken them seriously. They simply belabored the obvious—except for the occasional announcement of an impending turn, which never seemed to happen on the mids—or gave the stations when we were steaming with our squadron mates or a carrier. Hell, it was the OOD's responsibility to know what was in the night orders. But tonight, tonight, I was the "OH OH-bloody wonderful-D."

Mr. Graffey, the JOOD on the 2000 to 2400, with his overelaborate courtesy barely disguising the contempt in his voice, acknowledged my assumption of the "deck." It didn't bother me, and I noticed the captain's grin when the radar repeater's sweep dimly lit his face. Mr. Rice appeared on time and reported his assumption of the watch. Mr. Graffey mumbled his relief status and stomped off the bridge like a petulant child.

"Captain, with your permission, sir," I said, "I'd like to work with Mr. Rice on some simple ship maneuvering. I'll stay within five miles of the center of our box."

He didn't reply at first. He raised himself slowly in his chair, then said deliberately, "You do know, Mr. Sheppard, that the training of watch officers is the responsibility of Mr. Bluing, the senior watch officer."

"Yes, sir."

He looked at the radar repeater sweeping its magic electronic eye over the ocean. We were well clear of the shipping lanes. He switched the range selector to fifty miles—a useless thing to do because the radar range was only line of sight, and for the height of our radar antenna this was only ten to twelve miles. Then he switched it to five. Only the sea return of the radar beam bouncing off the ocean's surface appeared on the screen.

"Very well, but stay within five miles of the center of our box, and only for an hour," he finally answered, none too happily. Was this too presumptuous on my first watch?

"And the engines, sir, can we play with the engines too?"

"We do not *play* with the engines, Mr. Sheppard," the captain replied, ice forming on his words. "We maneuver with the engines, we exercise with the engines. But we do not *play* with the engines."

"I understand, sir. Request permission to exercise with the engines, sir."

From the twisting of his face in the light of a full moon, I could see he hadn't believed I'd ask again. He looked at me, then walked toward his sea cabin. He paused as he opened the door, turned to me, shook his head, and grunted, "Permission granted." Then he slammed his door, shouting, "And keep me informed."

For an hour Mr. Rice did what I never had the opportunity to do: he got the feel of the ship in a practice situation. Someone in main control called up asking if they could train new firemen—the junior men in the engineering department—at the throttle and burners during our maneuvering. I didn't know who asked; on the bridge we didn't much care who had the watch in main control. We just assumed someone had it down there and that was good enough for us. It didn't dawn on me until we completed the maneuvering drills that I had no authority to allow the engineers to train new men. *Should I tell the captain?* I didn't.

The moon glimmered off the glassy smooth sea as we turned and changed speeds in simple maneuvers. Mr. Rice reveled in the chance to control this beautiful machine. And even though I didn't have the conn, I felt the ship, I felt her whispered response.

"Sir," Mr. Rice said as we ended the drill, "I appreciate the opportunity you gave me."

"Knock off the 'sir'; call me Don."

"But, sir, you're senior to me."

"Bob, seniority among ensigns is like chastity among whores: there is none. What did the night orders say?"

"I . . . I don't remember, sir."

"Refresh yourself, Bob."

He started to walk over to the quartermaster's stand-up desk, the nav table, where the night orders lay. "Mr. Rice," I said softly, and as he turned to me I whispered, "You have the conn, Mr. Rice, and the conn does not read night orders." He looked blankly at me, his mind in a quandary over conflicting orders. "I'll take the conn, Mr. Rice," I said, solving his dilemma.

One hour and fifteen minutes as an OOD and already I'd turned into a standard-stock pompous ass.

Two days later the XO announced over the 1MC that *Rollard* and *Henshaw* had a submarine to exercise with that afternoon. It wasn't such a big deal to me since I never got to participate in these drills. It was the Gunnery Department and the XO's bailiwick. Besides, I'd done a lot of ASW, or antisubmarine warfare, work when attached to an S2F aircraft antisubmarine squadron prior to receiving my commission as an ensign. I knew the problems and had little faith in the ability of a destroyer, or any other surface ship, to kill a sub. In my mind only another submarine could do the job efficiently.

On the fantail I watched the gulls swooping in, snatching at the garbage we threw over the stern. Off to the west two S2Fs worked over the area assigned to the ASW exercise. It'd be our chance this afternoon. The bright sun warmed the gentle breeze that was stroking the ship's sunbathers into lethargy. I wondered if the S2Fs were having any luck. The sub was probably laughing at their puny efforts, and with a cold shiver my mind jerked itself back to more than a year ago.

I was in the backseat of a two-engine S2F roaring in again for the fifth "final" approach to our ASW aircraft carrier, Lt. Comdr. Bob "Shaky" Lyons flying as command pilot.

The November wind and ice-drenched night over the North Atlantic, just off the Faeroe Islands three hundred miles south of the Arctic Circle and two hundred miles north of Scotland, reduced visibility to less than five hundred feet over the carrier. It was all instruments. Shaky bolted on the sixth approach.

We'd been searching for a Soviet submarine trying to break through the U.K.–Iceland gap. A good half of the Soviet subs were homeported on the Barents Sea's Kola Peninsula, and to get to the Atlantic, where they could do some good against the Allies, they had to run the six-hundred-mile gap between Iceland and Great Britain, or the three hundred miles between Greenland and Iceland—the Greenland–Iceland–U.K. gap. And that was where we could find them.

SOSUS, the underwater, fixed hydrophonic systems placed on the bottom of the Atlantic had called the original contact, and for five days we searched in this horrible weather. Intelligence insisted the sub was breaking out, but we never got a clue.

The aircraft cabin heat on max hot didn't keep our teeth from chattering as we came around for the seventh approach. Our five-hour mission time and long search for the carrier had sucked up our fuel. Shaky Lyons's voice belied the confidence he affected as we turned in for another approach. The icy, pitching deck battered by the Arctic storm defied the efforts of the carrier's crew to free it enough for a safe landing. The arresting wires froze in uncontrollable positions.

The destroyer in the plane guard station off the carrier's stern fell back as the Herculean seas smashed into its hull, throwing it from giant wave to giant wave. How could men live in such puny ships in such tremendous seas? I pitied them. The rescue helicopter gave up in exasperation as the storm thwarted its valiant efforts to lift off the deck. Shaky's boys were on their own tonight, with no rescue ship or helo.

I was afraid. I was not the pilot. I had no control, and Shaky Lyons hadn't earned his nickname throwing dice. As for the copilot, Lt. (jg) William A. "Rammin'" Randall, this was his first night flight in an S2F operational squadron. That was not much to engender confidence.

The S2F pulled up hard, its engines screaming at full power on the abort.

"Roger, Bobby Boy, that was almost a good one . . . now take it nice and easy for the next. We got it licked," came the voice of the LSO, the landing signal officer, in his special perch on the fantail. "Nice and easy, Bobby."

"Roger."

"You can do it, Bobby. Say state." And the copilot gave them our depressingly low fuel status.

The soothing voice of the LSO dripped with confidence. "Ya got enough gas, Bobby. You can do it, you're a little high . . . drop . . . drop . . . steady . . . power—*POWER! UP! UP! UP!*" he screamed, and we roared over the fantail, again missing it by inches.

Another voice came through the headphones in my helmet. "Bobby, this is CAG, the carrier air group commander. We know it's the shits up there. Here's the situation. This is the best course we can get. Ice has fouled the deck and we can't clear it. Arresting wires are frozen down except for number two. You're going to have to catch that one. Can't rig a net because we can't get men out on the deck.

"When you land, we'll be out there to tie you down. But if we can't— and I'll let you know—ya gotta get out and let the sea take that mother over the side. You copy?" Shaky Lyons didn't answer. His quivering hands gripping the yoke wobbled the aircraft all over the sky.

Ten seconds passed, then "Copy all," came the jaunty voice of Rammin' Randall. "And CAG," he continued, "Commander Lyons requests you hold the movie until we're aboard." *What a cool sonovabitch!* Lieutenant Junior Grade Roger "Rammin'" Randall was the typical young, handsome fighter pilot portrayed by Hollywood.

His defiant walk, devil-may-care attitude, and lack of flying discipline had bounced him out of an F-4 Phantom jet fighter squadron with the explanation that he was just too hot for the airplane. Being a superb pilot, he continually tried to prove it, much to the chagrin of his safety officer and squadron commander.

He had pushed the envelope one too many times and had been exiled to S2Fs—slow, lumbering birds compared to F-4s. This was to tone him down so he could return to the big jets with somewhat more concern for his own well-being, his wingman's life, and the government's property.

The LSO's cool, deliberately affected voice came in over the radio again. "Okay, Bobby Boy, lookin' good. Up a little. Can you see the ball? Roger, understand negative ball. I'll bring you in. Left wing up, Bobby. Little more . . . down. Up . . . up . . . catch it when the fantail's down. You're doing okay . . . great stick, Bobby, you're a great stick. Watch the deck, watch the deck . . . up. Up! Abort! Abort! Go around, go around."

I could swear I saw the deck rivets in the fantail as we flew by and lifted again.

"Hey, Chief, how you guys doing back there?" Rammin' Randall came in over the intercom. "Ya know we pilots get paid by the number of approaches we make. We'll share the extra money we get on this hop with you guys."

"Roger that," I answered knowing it was bullshit and wishing to hell people would stop trying to cheer us up.

Then Randall addressed Shaky Lyons in the same conversational intercom tone he'd used with us—but this time I noticed that the UHF radio transmitting light came on, not just the intercom. His voice would go to the carrier. It could have been a mistake and only I could see the transmit light come on in front of the UHF radio set. He had cross connected the systems. "Hey, Commander," he said, "how 'bout giving me a shot at it? Shit, Commander, I've been sitting here all night doing nothing. Come on, sir, lemme try. I need the landing for my logbook requirements."

"NO! NO! I can get this sonovabitch down. Just leave me alone, goddamn you, Randall, and all you punk fuckin' kids. Just leave me the fuck alone! I can fly just as good as the rest of you. Better in fact. I'm not messing up this one."

You clever bastard, Randall, you got that to CAG, didn't you?

The answer came in ten seconds. "This is CAG, Bobby; how's it going up there? I know it's tough," came the voice after the eleventh wave-off pulled us close over the deck and up into the black night again. My sweat froze in my survival suit. My body had no control of itself. I urinated into my suit and felt the stabs of pain as it hardened into ice. The survival suits would give us only two minutes of life in these cold waters. Without them we'd be dead in thirty seconds. But it was all academic—there were no rescue vehicles.

CAG's soothing voice came in again. "Now listen, Bobby, here's what we're going to do. I want Randall to try the next approach. I know he's new, but what the hell, let's give the kid a chance. Help him along, Bobby, he needs your experience. Gotta help him, Bobby." A weak "Roger" answered this patently face-saving message. Shaky was being relieved, but in his hyperexcited condition he probably didn't even understand what was happening.

My mind could no longer handle the impending thought of death. I'd passed the plateau of fear into indifference. Mercifully, my internal survival systems had shut down and I no longer cared.

The Twenty-third Psalm, the only prayer I knew, crossed my mind and drifted off to help someone else. "Yea though I walk through the valley of the shadow of death, I shall fear no evil for thou art with me; thy rod and thy staff they comfort me." Maybe so. I'm shut down—that comforted me.

"Paddles," Randall addressed the LSO, "I'm bringing this hummer in. I'm going to try once the normal way; if I blow it, I'm coming in hot the second time. We won't have the fuel to go around again."

"Roger, Rammin', smoke that mother in here. I'm freezing my ass off out in this weather. Watch the ball."

We aborted Randall's first pass as the stern of the carrier dropped away from us at the last moment. "Button up, babies," Rammin' Randall laughed. "We're going in shit hot this time. We're going to crab the boat; we're going home." I noticed him leaning over, tightening the straps on the now silent ex-command pilot.

"Left wing up . . . up . . . easy, you're doing great, boy, only a little way to go. Ya got it made. Keep the left wing up. Goddamnit, Randall, keep the fucking left wing up . . . good, good." We appeared to be bouncing up and down, but I knew it was the carrier's deck pitching. Randall had to catch number two wire. There was no choice—all the others were frozen.

The LSO droned on about the wings, the altitude, the predicted deck movements, and the angle of the nose as he continued his stupid, sugary praise and encouragement. My world crept by in slow motion. I just didn't care anymore.

I looked over at Snyder, the other aircrewman. Fear contorted his face as he sat scrunched over in the seat across the aisle from me. This was only his fifth flight and I had talked him into becoming an aircrewman. I reached over and squeezed his arm. His pathetic face glanced back at me, his fear intensifying my own, but it passed rapidly through me into the violently twisting black night.

In my mind we drifted over the fantail. I saw the stern of the carrier rise ever so slightly as we slowly sank down to the ice-encompassed dark gray deck. The jab of the arresting wire was but a slight pull to my ephemeral body. We were down. The noise deafened me as I unstrapped

Snyder, slapping him in the face, yelling for him to get out. He ignored me. I kicked open the side door as Mr. Randall kept the power on against the stretching wire holding us in place. He dared not let up or the wind over the ice would hurtle us from the deck.

I reached forward, pulling, guiding Mr. Lyons out the door, handing him off to sailors with safety lines. Other harnessed men tried to make their way toward us. Most of them fell on their hands and knees and crawled for us the best they could. They used the point of small crash axes to dig into the ice, pulling themselves forward twelve inches at a time.

Their courage was amazing. Any vagary of the wind could have picked them up and tossed them into the spinning props. Some of the sailors blew away from us, trundling across the flight deck to be pounded against the island or the catwalks. When they slid out of control, others in the island mule-hauled them back, the rough ice and deck scraping and cutting into them.

Snyder's hands still grasped his armrests with a deathlike strength. I smashed down on his hand over and over, forcing him by pure pain to move. "Get out! Get out!" I yelled and yelled. Then with a slight recognition of me, he allowed himself to be handed off to the waiting, shouting, safety-belted deck crew.

I made my way up the few feet to Mr. Randall, in the cockpit, where he juggled the plane's engines so as not to either part the wire or loose the tail hook's grip on it. Motioning that I was the only one left, I waved good-bye. Being dragged to safety by the waiting sailors, I heard the engines slow and die. I saw the S2F slew to port, and Rammin' Randall fling himself through the door, whipping his hands demonically in the air. I tried to break loose in a stupid effort to help him, but the safety belt and grabbing hands of the sailors stopped me.

The airplane flipped onto its side away from Randall, cocked itself into the air, lifted, banged across the deck screeching, bounced once, then again, and tumbled off the fantail into the churning sea.

The thick ice and screaming wind allowed no traction on the deck as the men inside the ship dragged me by safety lines to the security of the island.

Ten men tethered to various points raced—slipping and falling, with no time to use their crash axes—to catch Mr. Randall as he rolled and twisted away from them toward the fantail. His grasping hands miraculously found number one wire and held it in a death grip. Finally two of the tethered men—slithering, crawling, shoved and buffeted by the wind and the twisting deck—reached him, tied a line around him, and dragged him back to the island.

The Pacific sun, now burning into my thought-frozen skin, brought me back from the North Atlantic to the gently rolling destroyer and the eighty-degree temperature. I shivered from the memory and started to cry.

ASW

I wandered into the Combat Information Center, or combat, as it was called. I wanted to watch the ASW team trying to catch the sub. Torpedomen stationed on the fantail had hand grenades ready to throw over the side to simulate depth charges. Torpedomen took care of the depth charges as well as the torpedoes, and we didn't have any torpedoes left.

Earlier I'd talked with TM1c. Michael H. Roll, USN, the leading torpedoman, about this, and he told me we'd load out before deploying to WESTPAC. He joked about his being named Roll, saying it was the same word as the command to drop depth charges. "When we practice," he said, "and the torpedo officer yells 'Roll,' I say, 'What?' Always good for a few laughs, sir." *I bet it was!*

It was always dark in CIC. The illuminated Lucite vertical status boards, with grease pencil markings showing other ships and aircraft, provided most of the dim light. A small light fixture attached to a desk allowed the radarmen to do occasional detailed work. Five radio loudspeakers crackled static and unintelligible babble. The radarmen who worked here rarely saw daylight and were content to live in this fantasy arcade world of electronic vision and sensing.

Several men, headed by the XO, herded themselves around the DRT, or dead reckoning tracker. The DRT, a glass-topped table, had a "bug" underneath hooked up to sensors that recorded the ship's course and speed by shining a small dot of light up through the table onto a large piece of tracing paper. A radarman marked the moving light at specific intervals and connected the dots, thereby showing the ship's movements around the paper. Other ships were also traced, including a submarine when sonar contact provided the information.

I felt a tingle in my body as the XO set up for the hunt. A voice from a loudspeaker announced, "Sonar contact bearing 053, range two thousand yards. Echo quality poor. Possible submarine on the surface."

"Roger, Sonar. The sub's checking in for COMEX and area correlation. We'll be working with *Rollard* on this. Let's look good," the XO acknowledged.

"Sonar contact bearing 187; looks like a destroyer," came the monotone again.

The XO nodded and spoke over his mike, which was hooked up to a loudspeaker so everyone knew what was happening in combat. "That's *Rollard,* Sonar; we'll track her on radar. The sub's going to dive in five minutes. Let's get the mother this time. Exercise parameters will keep her above thirty fathoms, one hundred eighty feet, and she reports there's a thermal layer at two hundred."

I knew well of thermal layers, those bands of different-temperature water that bounced the sonar sound beams in different directions, making detection almost impossible. Submarines had the advantage here; they could hide under the layer. My bellicose theory called for launching a homing torpedo on the first hint of detection and continue doing it until you've killed the sub. It was not a universally accepted doctrine, and besides, *Henshaw* did not have homing torpedoes as the S2Fs did; she had only old-fashioned dropping or firing-over-the-side depth charges. Also we were at peace and these were our own subs. Anyway, I was just an ensign.

Sonar reported the sub diving. The rules demanded a ten-minute wait before attacking. In nine minutes *Rollard* lost contact and so did we as the sub probably penetrated the thermal layer. Like hungry, disappointed wolves, we circled the "lost contact" spot, pinging hopelessly into the vast ocean. The trailing-off "pingngngngng" evoked no answer. We increased our diameter around the hypnotic lost contact spot as if, by our worshipping it, the submarine would be delivered miraculously into our hands.

In sixty minutes the sub launched two black underwater flares, which shot up to fifty feet above the surface, indicating she was coming up. She was three miles away from us and we hadn't had a clue. The captain demanded an explanation from the distraught XO, but none was available.

I made my way into the bowels of the ship, down to the sonar room, for the next attack. I watched the ping on the cathode-ray tube go out in ever-widening circles and the return circle bounce back from the diving sub. We waited for the second COMEX while the "PINGNGNGNGNG" raced out to be answered by a lesser and weaker "pingngng."

Weak contact still blessed us at COMEX. The sonarmen bent over their machine, tending it like a god but knowing it would fail them all too soon. My eyes never left the screen as the sound pulsed out into the sea. I tried to ride each ping in my mind. I tried to merge with the ocean. I tried to see the submarine. I'd done it before with that forty-knot Russian bastard; I could do it again. But I could not interfere here. *Maybe a hint . . . if I feel something.*

For ten minutes we bore impotent holes in the ocean. The lead sonarman, PO1c. William Edward Jarvis, USN, a short, 240-pound, twenty-four-year-old friend of Jenkins, looked at me in despair. His flabby sides folded over the chair arms as it creaked with the ship's movement. "Got a ballpoint pen, Mr. Sheppard?"

I returned his facetious query with a slight grin as a hint of a twinge tickled the back of my neck. Leaning over his bulk at the big screen, which filled most of the space, I lightly touched a point in the upper right quadrant with my finger. He looked at me, smiled, and narrowed his search beam from a 360-degree, allover scan to a narrow searchlight stab.

The "pingngngng" shot out and we waited. In what seemed like hours but was really only seconds, a weaker, almost pathetic "pingngng" returned. Jarvis's body stiffened as his shaking hands keyed his mike, but his voice betrayed no excitement as he reported to CIC, "Sonar contact, weak, bearing 028 degrees, range three thousand yards, echo quality poor, no Doppler. Evaluate possible submarine."

"Bearing clear," the bridge reported, indicating no surface vessels on that bearing.

I held on as the ship leaned over in a tight turn to prosecute the contact. I felt the surge as pumps wound up and extra burners were jammed into hungry boilers, feeding the turbines' greedy need for steam. The engines leaped ahead full. We were on our way.

The sonar blanked out from the speed, with only a mush of electronic snow returning from our useless pings. In three miles we jammed to a stop, safety valves lifting in an explosive roar as the boilers rebelled from their mistreatment and the too-fast closing of the throttles. They seated in ten seconds, and all was silent save for the searching ping of the sonar.

Nothing.

Jarvis looked at me, pleading. I shrugged; no feeling came to me. We waited. I was about to walk out when the tickle returned. I searched the screen for a hint. Nothing.

Then my finger twitched, my pulse increased, and I pointed to the lower right quadrant. Out went the stabbing pulse of audio-concentrated energy, and a dot of light blessed us with the sub's location under the thermocline a thousand yards from us. We headed toward it. It was too close to get away, and four hand grenades dropped over our fantail, signaling our successful attack on her.

Over "gertrude," the underwater telephone, the sub acknowledged a hit, adding dryly that he'd gotten three solutions on us during the chase and attack. A solution meant that all kill parameters of a torpedo firing had been met. In other words, if for real we'd be at the bottom of the ocean now. I hated submarines. Submariners. *Pompous assholes.*

Jarvis turned his head up at me with what might have been a look reserved for seeing the Pope. The other sonarmen stared. I threw up my hands in front of me, laughing. "Hey! Luck, you guys, pure dumb-ass luck . . . okay?" They said nothing as I backed out through the door. I continued to laugh at my "beginner's luck" as I said, "Hey, you guys, don't say anything about this bullshit, okay? Okay?"

Their silence lasted long enough for me to get to the main deck from the sonar shack four decks below as the overbearing 1MC ordered, "Now hear this, now hear this. Mr. Sheppard please report to the bridge. Mr. Sheppard, please report to the bridge."

The XO stood next to the captain. I reported to the OOD, asking what he wanted. The captain interfered, calling me over. "What were you doing in CIC, Mr. Sheppard?"

Uncomfortably, I answered, "Just looking around, Captain, trying to learn as much as I can." I tried to factor in a little boy's plea for understanding in a big, mysterious world.

"I'm sure you were. What about Sonar? What where you doing there—same thing?"

"Yes, sir."

"Anything strange happen down there?" he asked, his eyes glued to mine. The XO fidgeted, looking as though he was ready to go for my throat.

"I don't mean to sound impertinent, Captain, but I'd never been down there when the gear was operating. I hope I didn't screw up anything." I held my hands close to my side to conceal their wayward shake.

"They say you made some rather accurate estimates on the sub's position. Can you explain that?" the XO asked with an impatient bite in his voice.

"Wild guesses, XO, wild guesses. I've had a little experience flying in ASW aircraft and helos, but never aboard a surface vessel. It just felt right."

"Surface vessel? You sound like a goddamned airedale," the XO snapped and stomped off. I'd never seen him lose his temper before.

I didn't know if the captain censured me or not for being in the sonar shack. The feel of impotency is a vicious cancer.

The word *airedale,* a slightly derogatory name for flyers, pulled my mind back. It was just about a year ago, I recalled, as I returned to my stateroom, the bite of the XO's voice still scorching my ears. It had also "just felt right" then.

There had been reports of a Russian sub running up and down the East Coast. My S2F squadron deployed aboard our carrier to hunt her down. We were a full ASW hunter-killer HUK group, with four destroyers and a squadron of dipping sonar helos. SOSUS, the underwater, fixed hydrophone system placed on the bottom of the Atlantic, provided the only contact. P2Vs added muscle but no results.

For a week we tracked the elusive contact, who would appear one place once, then show itself a day later far away. By now three HUK groups searched from Florida to Maine. Well into the third week without contact, the admiral called an end to the search. My flight was still two hundred miles from the carrier when the word came to wrap it up. It didn't feel right; I had that tingle on the back of my neck as I ran the range controls of the radar in and out, trying to see anything against the abominable sea return.

I wanted to tell my pilot, Lieutenant Martin, who was my division officer, that we should extend the search, that it was too early to quit. But we'd been at it for a long time and our aircraft and its equipment grew wearier than the men. I was bone tired, the kind of tired you get when you just don't give a damn anymore, when all you want to do is shut down and check out.

We turned inbound to the carrier. The MAD, magnetic anomaly detector, equipment showed signs of deterioration. It took a lot of maintenance, and it was too long since its periodic check. I was the chief petty officer in charge of the electronics shop.

I told Mr. Martin I was commencing the 120-hour check as we returned to the carrier. He concurred; he was the electronics officer and well knew the workload we had on the carrier awaiting us.

The MAD gear was a fine piece of detection equipment—when it was babied. The Japanese invented MAD gear during World War Two, but it wasn't very effective then.

I ran the boom containing the magnetic sensor out the rear end. The farther away from the airplane, the more sensitive it became. I didn't have the test equipment onboard to run a full check, but I could get some of it done, leaving less work for my maintenance boys. Mostly, however, I wanted something out there that could seek the underwater sub. It felt right.

A large piece of metal, such as a submarine or ship passing through the earth's magnetic field, distorts it. The MAD gear detects this distortion. The MAD boom ran out smoothly, the equipment showing only a slight degradation of efficiency. "Can you go lower?" I asked the pilot, saying I wanted to run some special test. At two hundred feet heading south, my fingers drummed in nervousness against the control panel.

"Come right thirty degrees," I said, not knowing why and quite surprised that the words came out. We banked over gently, and as we steadied on course the recording pen on the indicator panel smashed over into the stops once, then whipped to the other side of the graph, indicating a strong magnetic contact. There were no surface ships around.

"MAD MAN, MAD MAN . . . SMOKE AWAY . . . MAD MAN, smoke away!" I screamed into the boom mike attached to my helmet. Martin pulled the S2F into a tight, climbing turn to fly over the spot marked by the smoke flare I released on contact. "Mad man," I reported again, this time with more control, more composure.

"Roger," the copilot answered, reporting to the carrier as Mr. Martin went into a trapping circle. The wings dipped barely above the water as the tight cloverleaf pattern over the smoke kept contact on the sub no matter which way he turned. The sub picked up speed. I changed seats with Hanks, a new crewman, so I could work the sonobuoys. It was a crummy thing to do to him when he had the chance to do some good work, but this sub was just too important to leave to a neophyte.

We dropped a pattern of passive sonobuoys around the sub. Upon impact, these sonobuoys released a hydrophone on a long wire deep into the water, picking up any noises that a submarine might make. With the signal radioed back to us, I could judge the location, course, and speed of a sub by detecting different signal strengths from different sonobuoys. Crude, but it was all we had. There were active sonobuoys that sent out a ping, but we didn't have any. I prayed no thermoclines existed. I heard the copilot report on-station time as two hours. The carrier launched four more S2Fs and steamed toward us at flank speed. The P2Vs diverted to our location but couldn't arrive for another hour. The S2Fs would take an hour and a half.

"Mad man."

"It's just us, Chief. Can we hack it?"

"Just keep those wings out of the water, sir, and we'll do the rest back here." We were shit hot today.

"I'm tracking this hummer at forty-one knots, Mr. Martin. Can that be?"

"Roger, concur speed. I've computed his course as 040. Looks like he's headed home."

"Mad man."

"Interrogative relief time, I've got only a few sonobuoys left and we're down to five smokes," I said.

"Our buddies'll be here in thirty and the P2Vs in twenty. Helos, maybe forty-five. We got about forty minutes' loiter."

"Mad man."

"Tracking forty-three knots at 043," I reported indifferently, tired of the game. We weren't going to destroy this sub, we were only going to track him. *Big deal.* I wanted to go back to the carrier and get to work.

Recess was over.

Mad man.

Fueling Pier

I threw myself into Engineering Officer School with a fervor I'd not felt since coveting that third-class "crow" I saw on some guy's arm in a bowling alley in El Centro many years ago. School didn't come easily, but I drove myself to where I felt there was nothing I didn't know about a destroyer's main propulsion plant. Since becoming a third-class petty officer, humility had not been my strong suit.

What I truly knew was just enough to fake it if I had to. I proudly reported aboard again, this time armed with an officer's skill, not just that of a glorified electronics technician. I met with the captain, the XO, and Mr. Bernard. "From the reports, you've done well in school," said the XO. "It is our intention, Mr. Sheppard, to have you relieve Mr. Bernard in two to three weeks and in any case before we sail for WESTPAC in a month. Is that okay with you?" *Okay with me? Of course!*

Mr. Bernard took me in hand to complete my education. I wondered about the statement he'd made when I first came aboard that "we have some problems down there," but I didn't ask him, figuring he'd tell me when the time was right. My enthusiasm for the job must have been obvious, because he started out with, "They probably didn't tell you at EO school, Don, but being a chief engineer is not the greatest of assignments. You're pretty junior as an officer, and there are some commissioned secrets you might not know about.

"First, the job is not as career enhancing as operations or gunnery. Oh, you'll get good fitness reports and gain great experience that may or may not help you later, but in the main it's considered as something to be avoided or made as short as possible. It's not a ticket-punching job."

My mouth dropped; a dark cloud passed over me.

"Hey! It's not that bad," he said. "And for Christ's sake, knock off that Mr. Bernard crap. I'm only a JG." He gently patted my shoulder.

"The naval mentality still holds that a line officer has only one job, and that is to put himself next to his enemy and board with pistol and cutlass. Worrying about vacuums in the main condensers is someone else's job." The phone rang, he picked it up, said yes into it, and turned back to me.

"That's what line officer means. One who fights in the line of battle firing broadside into the sailing ship off his beam. We really haven't changed much from those days except maybe substituting a torpedo bomber for a cutlass. So what it means—if you don't have your finger on the trigger or the authority over the man's finger on the trigger—is you ain't shit."

It was quiet in the tiny engineering office. The soft, steady hum of the ventilator gave little comfort as Mr. Bernard's words pricked the tenuous fabric of the self-confidence I'd wrapped around myself.

To my chagrin, he continued: "The U.S. surface navy . . . to my knowledge . . . is the only navy in the world that doesn't have a separate engineering branch with its own path of advancement. Except for the big ships like carriers and battleships, which are chief engineered by EDOs, or engineering duty only officers, line officers are reluctantly assigned to be in charge of a very complex high-pressure, superheated steam turbine main propulsion plant. It staggers the mind that we let this happen. The nuclear submarine boys don't; all their officers are engineer qualified.

"The merchant fleet doesn't allow it. They have their own engineering branch. The chief engineer on a merchy ranks with but below the master and can, if he deems it prudent, refuse a command from the captain. He damn well better be right, though."

I lit my pipe as Mr. Bernard, standing on the mount, continued his sermon, my body sagging as his words loosened the mental nuts and bolts that held me together.

"That's the first problem—not being career enhancing. The second is, the black gangs know it and use it. Their name, you know, stems back to the old coal-fired boiler days when all engineers were covered with coal dust." I nodded understanding as he continued.

"To complicate the situation, you're also in charge of the damage control functions of the ship. Sure, you have a damage control assistant, or DCA, but he doesn't know shit about what he should.

"Usually, he's a very junior officer and hasn't had the chance to learn about steel strengths, and water pressure and fighting fires, and maintaining watertight integrity on a damaged vessel, and so on and so on. In our case, the DCA is not a fresh-caught ensign, but that's something else I gotta talk to you about.

"You should have a main propulsion assistant assigned just to help you with the paperwork, but he wouldn't know anything anyway, and the billets are usually left vacant by the anointed ones in BUPERS.

"To top this off, you have to stand all your watches and learn all about the other sleazy departments and take those goddamned correspondence courses for promotion. When do we have the time? When do we sleep? The old-timers think if you're dicking around with engineering, you're not spending your time wisely learning about the real navy of operations. I'm tired, Don. Bone-ass tired."

I hadn't said a word during this welcome-aboard speech. "In other words, you and the captain have screwed over this here poor old country boy good and proper like?" I finally asked in preference to screaming.

He paused before answering, "No, Don, we haven't. The captain thinks you're a good officer. His daddy's an admiral, and his daddy's daddy was an admiral and good ole Commander David P. Baker will be an admiral. I'm off to be the ops officer on a guided missile destroyer, brand new, the latest in the fleet. Now that's career enhancing.

"He took care of me as he'll take care of you. He asked me to tell you all this. He'll never mention it . . ." His voice trailed off to a whisper. "Nor," he pointed a finger at me, "should you."

"I guess that makes up for it somehow," I all but whined. "I wish he'd said something before I accepted the job."

"Accepted the job? Are you goddamn stupid or naive? Wake up—he could have assigned you to the job without so much as a 'kiss my ass.' And don't go feeling sorry for yourself. What I said is all true, but look at it this way. You'll be the only ensign in the Pacific Fleet who's a chief engineer and a department head of a destroyer. That'll look damn good on your service record."

"Yes, sir."

"And another thing you should know is that ole Captain Baker put his

ass on the line for you. COMCRUDESPAC's engineering four-striper
damn near shit a brick when he heard the captain was making an ensign
the chief engineer. They worry about things like that. He asked him to
change his mind—if he would—but the old man said no . . . with all due
respect, of course, and the staffies had to acquiesce to a commanding
officer's decision. It's history now, but they'll be watching, and waiting
for you to blow it, figuratively speaking, of course. Watch your six."

His arm went around my shoulder, and he laughed as he patted my
upper arm. "It's okay, Don, you had no way of knowing. Keep it quiet.
The ole man doesn't want the staff's opposition known, but he wanted
me to mention it to you so you'd know the lay of the land . . . or ocean,
in this case."

A mumbled, inadequate thank you was all I could muster as we began
a tour of the engineering spaces. I'd been down here once before, and
then the jammed-in complexity had left me baffled and uninterested.
From EO school, I knew the layout, but this one was going to be mine.
We started at the forward boiler room, and Mr. Bernard . . . no, Richard,
explained things as we went.

"As you know, Don, we have two separate plants. They are identical
except for the placement of the engines. One's on the starboard, the other
on the port—a clever solution for a twin-screw ship. The propulsion
plant takes up one-third of the ship and the fuel tanks take up another
third. We have complete redundancy, and any boiler can feed any engine;
any system can substitute for any other. It'd be rare that we could ever be
dead in the water."

Our division was getting under way for WESTPAC via Seattle, Washington, in three days, and the engineers were finishing up the repairs they
had begun during the last two weeks in port tied up to a tender. Richard
reintroduced me to Chief Maclin, the senior enlisted engineer of the department. We, of course, knew each other, but Richard wanted to offi-
cially introduce me to the mainstay of the plant.

Chief Maclin was a five-foot-eight-inch barrel of a man with thinning
hair and the arms of a gorilla. He wielded great power and was the first
to be called when things went wrong. He determined what to do and
whom to tell. Chief Maclin knew me by reputation with the ETs, who in
his mind were pansies; by extension, anyone who had anything to do
with them were pansies. His greeting bordered on rudeness. There was
going to be a problem here.

"You just met the symbol of another type of difficulty that chief engineers of destroyers face—the chief machinist mate," Richard continued after Maclin left. "Since captains rarely know much about main propulsion engineering, when things go wrong they want to talk to someone who isn't getting his information secondhand, like me, the chief engineer. The chief machinist mate is the man he goes to. This sort of thing undermines authority.

"All casualty control drills are run by the chief machinist mate because he knows what's going on. I tried it once and got so screwed up that Chief Maclin had to take over—embarrassing, lesson learned. I never tried it again. Even at sea detail the chief's in charge. It's too dangerous to allow the impotent chief engineer to participate in critical situations. Besides, we have to be on the bridge when it's our turn to conn her into port.

"Maclin's a good engineer, but he damn well knows he's the big cheese down here, and he can become quite insufferable at times. I reluctantly give him his head, and everything seems to work out. He's a good man and knows just how far he can bullshit or push me."

We had just finished touring the after engine room, and as I wearily made it to the main deck I noticed Richard perspiring and a little out of breath. It pleased me that I wasn't.

In the last three hours we'd covered all four main spaces of the plant: two boiler rooms and two engine rooms.

In the forward engine room, Richard rubbed his hands lovingly over the starboard engine. It was the size of a two-car garage. A glaze softened his face. "Sixty thousand shaft horsepower we've got between the both engines. That's the same as about four hundred cars. We've got lots of power."

We'd climbed up and down a hundred ladders. We'd gone around the boilers and on top of them. We'd crawled under the turbines. We'd touched every bearing, every pump, and looked into every bilge and cranny.

"Because the captain knows very little about engineering—and I'm being generous here—we rarely hold casualty control drills in fear that we'll mess up the plant. It needs to maintain a delicate balance, and messing with the machinery can wrack it up quite badly. It's like taking the parts out of a car as fast as you can, throwing them back together even faster, and then expecting the car to run properly. Multiply that by a thousand, and you might understand the problem."

I didn't comment as we walked to the engineering office. I sat back, pulling out my pipe. I lit it, not knowing what questions to ask.

Bernard spoke first. "I know, Don, from what I've heard about you and the ETs, you're a great believer in drills. Good luck!"

Trying hard not to make it sound like bragging, I said, "I found conducting engineering drills quite exciting on the school ship we had for a couple of days. They didn't seem hard."

"I'm sure they didn't, but the chief machinist mate on that ship probably had you covered with half a dozen extra men, and he would have kicked out your ass in a moment if you started to screw up his plant."

"Richard," I asked in deadly earnest, "is there a spare parts problem?"

He looked at me, his face equally earnest. "No, Don, there isn't."

Under way at 0800 for Seattle, the winds were light, the skies slightly overcast. I was on the bridge with Mr. Bluing, requalifying after my four months on the beach. I hadn't forgotten anything, but the captain insisted I requalify anyway. "Mr. Bluing, give the conn to Mr. Sheppard," the captain said as we headed far away from the tender where we had been moored.

Our first stop was the fuel annex just south of Shelter Island to top off our fuel for the trip. The squadron was getting under way in an hour; we'd rendezvous at the sea buoy. We had plenty of time to fuel and beat them there.

"This is Mr. Sheppard, I have the conn." And the helmsman and lee helm gave their reports. I answered, "Very well," in what I considered a most nautical tone.

"Recommend course 310," the XO said matter-of-factly from his bent-over position working on a chart of San Diego Bay. He used cross bearings from the quartermasters, taking sight angles on various landmarks from the peloruses on each bridge wing.

"Aye, sir, come left to course 310," I ordered, and stayed on 310 for three minutes until recognizing that it wasn't the best course. I ordered the rudder over to steer 314. The captain gave me a puzzled look, and the XO straightened up from the chart table as if I'd kicked him in the groin.

"I recommended 310, Mr. Sheppard," he said patiently in reprimand.

"Aye, aye, sir. Steer course 310," and the helmsman swung back four degrees.

"Combat recommends course 312," came the sound-powered phone talker hooked to CIC. I acknowledged. The radarmen in combat got all their fixes from radar, which wasn't as accurate as the pelorus bearings worked by the XO.

We steamed in silence for eight minutes. "Tell main control there are a lot of small boats out here this morning, so be prepared for a back down," I said to the main control telephone talker, who was also the lee helm. I was in fact alerting him too. "Steer course 315," I ordered. The XO looked up at me as though not believing what he was hearing from some smart-ass ensign. Not taking course recommendations from the XO, who was the navigator and acting in that role now, was unheard of.

I didn't need all those recommendations. It was a beautiful day with unlimited visibility. Shit, I knew where I was and I knew where I wanted to go—all I had to do was steer the ship that way. I wasn't a talking robot.

"Mr. Sheppard," he said with a scowl, "are you familiar with San Diego Bay?"

"Yes, sir, of course, sir, we've been in and out of here many times since I've been aboard." But before the XO could address my impatient answer, the captain walked over and whispered something into his ear.

"We'll try it your way, Mr. Sheppard," he said, returning to his chair and looking at me as if I'd walked over the Pope's grave.

"XO, if you please, sir, let me know if our heading is more than five degrees off your plotted course," I requested.

"Aye, aye, sir," he answered, splattering his sarcasm around the bridge. I gave the same request, now phrased as an order, to combat.

"Right ten degrees rudder," I said as we passed the downtown Broadway Pier on our starboard hand. The helmsman called out the heading every five degrees as the compass swung through them. San Diego Bay has only a narrow channel, but it is well marked with buoys. "Rudder midships." I waited while the ship settled from her turn. When the bow headed generally to where I wanted to go, I said, "Steady as she goes."

"Steady as she goes, sir, steering 350."

"Very well." I was off a degree or two. "Steer course 352."

The captain sat in his chair apparently relaxed, but periodically he got up to walk to the bridge wing to look aft. He didn't want a huge ship bearing down on us from astern. Neither did I. I was constantly checking and a little put out that he might think I wasn't. But captains have their little hang-ups about their careers. I can't believe I was being so arrogant about this. Here the captain had overridden the XO and given me my head and I was complaining when he took the liberty of checking his stern.

Only the mild flapping of our flag hoist indicating our international call sign disturbed the quiet. The gentle breeze from our forward motion felt good in the silence. So many things external to the ship could be heard without the constant recommendations and directions being given from the XO and combat. Quiet begot quiet and few words were spoken by the bridge team, and those only in whispers. It was nice. Two seagulls swooped over the bridge, cawing their welcome.

"Left ten degrees rudder . . . steady on course 270." We passed Lindbergh Field and Harbor Island on our starboard hand. I noticed a large navy transport, an APA, steaming inbound as we came left to a more southerly course of 220. The bridge seemed lulled into apathy by the change of routine and the silence. Not the captain nor the XO, of course, they evaluated every move I made as Shelter Island moved steadily down our starboard side.

From the port side, a sudden roar of jet fighters, kicking in their afterburners on takeoff from the U.S. Naval Air Station, North Island, assaulted our tranquillity. It offended me.

The APA was fully recognizable now; we'd have to render honors, as was naval custom, as she passed. Most APAs had a full captain, a four-striper, for a CO; thus we would be junior and have to salute first. I looked at the captain; he knew what I was thinking. I had no official status here on the bridge since Mr. Bluing was the OOD and Mr. Graffey the JOOD. I was just the conning officer. It was not the conning officer's job to see to it that proper honors were rendered. The captain winked one of his sly near smiles at me. I got the message.

"Mr. Graffey, stand by for honors to port, if you please," I said, and he damned near smashed into the XO as he bolted to the port side. I caught a glimpse of Mr. Bluing glaring at me for calling out his inattention to duty. I'd made no friends here.

Under orders from Mr. Graffey, the boatswain's pipe called the ship, actually just the deck force and the signalmen, to attention over the 1MC. Mr. Graffey waited for the other ship to call attention. Then he called hand salute and waited until the other ship saluted, then called "two," which ended the salute; then he said, "Carry on."

He marched back into the pilothouse, reporting, unnecessarily, "Honor's rendered, SIR!" The heat of his scorn blistered the air between us.

"Mr. Sheppard," the captain said conversationally as he came over and stood next to me. "The winds can become vicious at the fuel pier as they roll down over Point Loma. It may look calm now, but without warning, thirty to forty knots of wind can whip in broadside to us. It can be tricky, and you've never made a landing before." The one thing I faulted him for was his reluctance to let anyone make a landing but himself. I'd seen Mr. Bluing make one and the XO two—but no one else. I was pleased he was letting me make this one. I prayed I wouldn't screw it up.

"Yes, sir, I understand," I said, wondering why he bothered telling an ace ship handler like me such a trivial thing like what the winds *could* do. Mild winds prevailed and no hint of anything greater was in sight. Yet the fact that he mentioned it unnerved me.

"Would you like to have someone else take her in so you can watch?" he asked without censure in his eyes.

I furrowed my brow, looking at him like a ten-year-old child might if you questioned his ability to ride a bicycle.

"Why, no, sir!"

An LCM-6, a MIKE boat, with huge mat fenders draped over its bow got under way from the fuel piers. A MIKE boat was a large, powerful, two-engine landing craft designed to run up on a beach, lower its ramp, which formed its bow, and let two large tanks roar out. Since the United States had no beaches to storm, the boats were used for utility purposes.

As I pointed our bow toward the fuel docks, the XO came over with a chart, telling me to put the bridge right next to the yellow markings on the pier so the fuel connections would line up. "Watch the winds," he whispered. "If you need help, that MIKE boat there," he pointed, "will give you a push. You may need him."

I'd never made a landing; I was apprehensive even though I'd watched dozens. As we got closer, my thin veneer of confidence started to crack. This landing seemed ridiculously simple. *Wind?* We came up on the fuel dock slowly. The captain cautioned me on this: if we banged into the pier we'd break fuel lines and contaminate the bay. "We could both end up in Portsmouth, the navy prison," he chuckled in dead seriousness.

Our bow was fifty feet from the pier where I wanted it to be as I ordered number one line put over. Number one line was the farthest line forward and usually led out through the bull nose. The sternmost line was number six. Lines two and three came from forward of midships and four and five lay aft of midships. When the ship was properly moored, lines two and three crisscrossed each other as did four and five in order to control the forward and backward movement of the ship.

Number one line snaked out of the bull nose and to our starboard side as the line handlers heaved it in. "Moored," the boatswain's mate announced as soon as the eye at the end of the line was slipped over the pier bollard. The shallow angle that I came in at would allow number six to be made fast in a minute or two. *Piece of cake.*

As I stood on the starboard wing, proud of myself, the trees up the shallow cliffs of Point Loma rustled more noisily. Some of the smaller branches bent down toward me. The breeze against my face freshened. Dust meandered on the pier and the approach roads. Scraps of paper raised from their discarded positions and twisted into the sky. The stern blew away from the pier before number six could be secured, and the thin hauling line was let go by the line handlers before it dragged them into the water.

Number one line took a strain and was let out before it could part. We were damn near vertical to the pier in minutes. I looked at the captain in questioning dismay. "It happens sometimes," he said, looking aft and up and down the channel. "Twist her in."

Shaken, I ordered right standard rudder, the port engine ahead two-thirds, and the starboard engine back two-thirds. Our stern confusingly refused to twist. It should have been going to the right. I stood in consternation as I saw my career disappearing.

"Wrong combination, Don," the captain said, his strained patience ebbing. "Do it right, Mister."

My mind cleared and the pages of my *Conning a Destroyer* book flashed in brilliant clarity. "Port engine back two-thirds, starboard engine ahead two-thirds, left standard rudder," I quickly ordered, and as they took effect with number one line still fast to the pier, the stern, ever so slightly, started coming around to the right—the correct direction. This combination of engines and rudder put a twist on the ship around its turning point just forward of the bridge. At best, though, it could only get me parallel to the pier still one hundred feet out.

I didn't know what to do. My guts churned in confusion. The captain whispered, "Take number one line to the windlass and haul in the bow while you're twisting the stern . . . easy on the strain on number one."

Ten minutes passed as we fought the wind with engines and number one line groaning against the windlass, moving us in inches at a time. The wind did not let up. The starboard engine going ahead was more efficient than the port going astern, and this gave us headway, which I had to kill by dropping the starboard engine to ahead one-third for a minute in every five. In my mind, minutes warped into hours as nothing seemed to be happening. "What more can you do, Mr. Sheppard?" the captain asked with a sharpness he'd never used with me before.

I looked at him, my eyes begging for an answer. The captain was always there to help, always had the right answer. Was he failing me now? Where was Mr. Bluing? He should help me, but he and Mr. Graffey stood on the port wing with shit-eating grins on their faces. The captain's eyes penetrated my soul, looking deep into the quagmire of insecurity that I hauled around.

"The MIKE boat, Mr. Sheppard. It's there to push you in when you need it," the XO whispered softly as he deliberately brushed by me. I turned quickly from the starboard wing to call it in, but the XO stopped me by touching my shoulder and nodding toward the grinning Mr. Graffey. *What a gentleman, the XO.*

"If you please, Mr. Graffey, call in the MIKE boat for a push midships," I asked—ordered.

Glowering at me, he motioned in the boat, which was only a few yards off our stern awaiting instructions, probably wondering what stupid lout of an officer they had up there conning. The two powerful engines of the MIKE boat pushing us broadside added greatly to our sideways speed. Another smaller landing craft, and LCVP, pulled away from the small shack on the fueling pier and came alongside our starboard quarter.

The chief boatswain's mate on the fantail requested permission to put number six line into the LCVP so they could take it ashore for us. The fantail crew had earlier scurried about busting their ass pulling in number six line before my inept ship handling tangled it in the screws. I hadn't thought of using a boat to take in the line. I looked at the captain for permission, and with icy sarcasm he said, "Why, I think that would be a great idea, Mr. Sheppard."

With number six line made fast to the pier and fair-led to the midships winch; with number one line to the windlass hauling the bow steadily in; with the MIKE boat chugging, pushing, shoving against us; and with the engines twisting, surging, stopping, slowing all in a massive unrehearsed choreography, we finally made fast to the fuel pier forty-two minutes after I had first ordered number one line over.

Fueling took an hour and ten minutes as the wind pushed relentlessly against our six strained lines. The captain kept me on the bridge. Twenty minutes after we had moored, the other seven ships of our squadron steamed by in a close column. The two words I could read from the flagship's signal light was "is unacceptable." I wanted to run away and hide. Just before we finished, the captain set the sea detail, and as soon as we completed fueling, he ordered me under way.

I had been berating myself for forgetting everything my destroyer book had told me. I'd read about landing situations such as this. I knew what to do. My supreme ego had led me into another trap. I'd figured he'd never let me conn the ship again.

I let go all lines but number one and six. Easing the tension on number six, I let the wind ease my stern out. Then I eased number one, letting the bow fall off more than the stern, cocking me heading fair down the channel. I had both lines let go simultaneously and waited for the fantail crew to haul in number six. I was not about to tangle this after line in the screws. When the line was safely aboard, I simply ordered both engines ahead two-thirds. It was easy but cost me a gallon of sweat. I'd never be a smart-ass, know-it-all asshole again. *Yeah, sure.*

Drained of bravado, I looked at the XO. He looked at me as if I were a child as I asked in a voice a little too high pitched for an "ace" conning officer, "If you would, sir, request course recommendations."

Mr. Chadwick

E xecute!"

Eight sleek destroyers in a column turned westerly making the bend out of the Pacific Ocean into the Strait of Juan de Fuca. The whitewashed wakes from our close formation extended seemingly to the horizon. Occasionally a small wind rippled the glassy surface of the outwardly rolling water. The clear skies and smooth seas on the journey up from San Diego were a godsend; I was sick only once.

We were a destroyer squadron proudly heading for the Orient, via Seattle, to protect the free world from the godless aggression of the Communist hordes. Some of the younger sailors had their mind only on getting a lot of cheap ass.

A destroyer squadron consists of two divisions of four ships each. Each division has a full captain, a four-striper, as a division commander, and a commodore. A commodore is one who commands two or more seagoing vessels and is required to fly a small, dovetailed flag called a burgee pennant to indicate which ship he is aboard.

This stems from the old days of sailing ships when in the heat of battle one had to know which ship carried the commodore, the flagship. Admirals, when embarked on a vessel, flew a flag indicating their rank. A rear admiral rated two stars, a vice admiral three, and a full admiral four, hence the term *flag officers*. Commodore is not a rank but a position even though it used to be a one-star rank.

All this business about stars and flags and ranks did not bother me at this time. Hopefully, someday it would. But for now, I had more important things to think about, such as not getting seasick and ensuring the plant worked well and not banging my scarred shins on the watertight door coamings.

In the destroyer hierarchy the senior of the two division commanders is also the squadron commander—hence, commodore of the squadron. It is rare that a full squadron ever sails together. However, we were doing it now, steaming into the Strait of Juan de Fuca heading inbound to Seattle to give a naval dog and pony show on our way to WESTPAC.

This was familiar territory. I'd been attached to a P2V squadron out of Whidbey Island, just north of Seattle, a few years back and had flown these waters many times. I listened as the sound of powerful engines betrayed the approach of two P2Vs coming in low from the north. They skimmed the water like fighter planes, lifting no more than two hundred feet as they buzzed over us heading outbound—our fellow dog and ponyers practicing.

The relief of Mr. Bernard had gone well, with just minor discrepancies reported in the turnover letter. When a department head is being relieved, the relieving department head has to make an exhaustive inspection of the department and list all discrepancies found. A letter is then prepared, and signed by both men. Then the new department head takes responsibility for the department.

A poor letter could kick a man's career in the butt. In the relief of Mr. Bernard, the turnover letter revealed several problems such as leaks and a shortage of repair parts and poor training, especially in the damage control parties. The worst thing was the sad condition of the damage control lockers. These lockers held all the equipment necessary to fight fires and keep the ship afloat.

All but the damage control lockers were really minor faults that all destroyers had. I could take care of them. I didn't list them in the letter, nor did I list the lockers.

Mr. Bernard befriended me when the other officers were merely coldly courteous to a mustang. *Not quite our kind . . . he's never been to college, has he?* I had no reason to make Bernard look bad. He had already confessed he'd paid scant attention to the department, letting MMC Ernest B. Maclin, USN, with twenty-two years in this man's navy, take care of everything. Chief Machinist Mate Maclin, I suspected, wasn't quite as good as people thought he was. He kept too much information to himself and probably covered up any deficiency that might make him look bad. I wasn't quite sure of this, but I suspected. I'd seen the type.

In the turnover meeting with the captain and XO, Mr. Bernard laid out all the discrepancies, mentioning several I had not put in the relieving letter. We'd made the official inspection together and Bernard had kept his own list.

The captain passed a questioning look to the XO and then to me. I answered, "It's okay, Captain, nothing we can't take care of. Mr. Bernard has taught me a lot. I wish the letter to stand."

The captain looked again at the XO, who shrugged. Then, turning to me, he said, "Good enough, let's keep our dirty laundry on our own line." Relieving letters went to the division commander and to the type commander. "The less they know, the better, but . . ." He paused, looking directly at me, then added, "That does not apply between you, the XO, and me, Don. You tell us everything . . . understand?" *Sure, Captain, sure!*

Bernard and I shook hands as he departed the ship with, I'm sure, a glowing fitness report. "If I can ever be of any help to you, Don, let me know." He saluted and left, and I was the chief engineer of a sleek, sixty-thousand-horsepower man-of-war. At meals, I used the sterling silver napkin ring engraved: CHIEF ENGINEER.

We steamed in tight formation all the way to Seattle. There was no time to conduct engineering casualty control drills. Steaming like this seemed a little foolish, since in any future war the threat of nuclear attacks demanded that the ships be separated—dispersed, the book called it. But old habits die slowly, I reckon.

At Pearl Harbor on 7 December 1941, and the next day in the Philippines, the Japanese destroyed most of our aircraft on the ground because we had them so neatly arranged, lined up in rows. Don't we ever learn?

The P2Vs continued down the strait until out of sight. I watched from the main deck, getting a breath of fresh air after the stuffiness of main control. I stared at the watertight door leading into the superstructure by the engineering office, and fumed.

The rubber gasket around the door that was supposed to wedge tightly against the blunt knife-edge coaming of the jambs had deteriorated and split in several places. Water could easily leak through, destroying the watertight integrity of the ship.

The damage control assistant, the DCA, worked for the chief engineer with the responsibility of checking things like this. He was in charge of the Repair Division. It pissed me off that he wasn't doing his job, and I waited for the proper time to chat with him about his duties. The more I looked at the door and the rusty knife edges and the deteriorated fire hose coiled on the bulkhead next to it, the angrier I became.

The DCA, Lt. (jg) Chester H. Chadwick, USNR, NROTC, Harvard—with extraordinarily poor timing—put his head out the door, and seeing me, pulled back instantly. "Mr. Chadwick, come over here, if you would please," I called out after him. He ignored me, pretending he hadn't heard until I called again much more sternly.

He turned reluctantly and walked toward me. His face barely contained his disgust as he stood there in his freshly pressed khaki uniform looking to all the world like the recruiting poster's image of the navy's handsome, ideal destroyer officer. He made me feel old, fat, and ugly.

"YES, SIR?" he snapped out as if replying to a Marine Corps drill instructor.

"I guess we'd best get this out of the way now. You're obviously unhappy because they made me the chief engineer while I'm only an ensign and you outrank me as a JG."

He smiled. "How perceptive of you, sir. Perceptive, as you *might* know, means recognizing things or events with a minimum of intelligence or education." His eyes burned hate.

"Why, thank you, Mr. Chadwick," I answered with a calm I did not feel. "I always wondered what that there word meant. Shit fire man, us poor country boys don't even know how to pronounce it much less spell it. It ain't in none of the comic books I try to read." His eyes turned from hate to puzzlement. I could feel mine growing cold, I could feel the chill in my veins and the blood drain from my face.

"However, Mr. Chadwick, what I do know how to spell is *insubordination*. And I can find someone else to help me with the really big words such as *incompetence* and *dereliction* of duty in a letter relieving you for cause," I said in a scathing voice barely above a whisper.

The tightness around his jaws loosened, his face sagged, his shoulders slumped. He opened his mouth to speak, then stopped, apparently thinking better of it as I continued. "Though you may not now have a letter of reprimand in your service jacket using those words, Mr. Chadwick, you certainly deserve it. The condition of your damage control lockers is at best atrocious, and the state of training of the damage control parties borders on criminal negligence—criminal negligence, Mr. Chadwick."

"But . . . I . . . I—you can't talk to me that way—I . . . tried to do a goo—"

"Bullshit, Chadwick. You don't give a shit, and Bernard was too nice a guy to call you on it. But, Mr. Chadwick, I'm calling you on it right now. Please consider this an official verbal reprimand. Further, when you get off watch this afternoon, report to me immediately, because you and Chief Burton are going to inventory *your* damage control lockers."

"But I've got the mids . . . I'll need to sleep. Why, it'll take hours to inventory those lockers."

"When did you inventory them last, Mr. Chadwick?"

"Why . . . I . . . don't know. Maybe a year ago, maybe six months ago . . . Hell, I don't know. The chief takes care of that petty shit."

"How often should they be inventoried, Mr. Chadwick?"

"I . . . I don't know."

"Every quarter, Mr. Chadwick, every quarter."

"Yes . . . yes, I remember now," he answered, his cool Harvard panache crumbling around him.

"You have signed every three months, Mr. Chadwick, that you have personally supervised the inventory of these lockers. In fact, you have not, thus adding to your incompetence the court-martial offense of making false official statements." I paused for effect; this man made me sick. If we needed the repair material in those lockers and it was missing, lives could be lost or the ship could sink. *For the want of a nail.*

"But the chief assured me everything was okay. He—" My blood boiled over from this reprehensible reply as I moved in, inches from his face. He dared not budge.

"Do not, Mr. Chadwick, compound your own shortcomings by blaming your men. It is the lowest and most disgusting form of defense."

I paused, hoping this registered. "I shall deal with your chief damage controlman, Sachel H. Burton, very shortly. He is an accessory to your misconduct, and he will be very lucky to still be a chief. And then you, Mr. Chadwick, fun boy, part-time DCA, ace cribbage player in the wardroom while you should be inspecting the ship, you can wallow in your own disgrace while sharing in his humiliation and his family's lower standard of living.

"Surely his court-martial will bust him back to first class, at the very least, if this gets out." I paused again, letting the statement ricochet around his lazy, fear-crazed mind. The wind rose and the strait obeyed with a chop. My stomach waltzed around itself as the ship commenced her relentless rolling.

"If it gets out? You mean you haven't reported this to the XO yet?"

"No, I haven't."

"You mean . . . you mean I can . . . I—"

"Perceptive of you, Mr. Chadwick, very perceptive. Now get the fuck away from me."

The P2Vs buzzed over us again as they turned to the north to recover at Whidbey Island. I watched until they disappeared, then I returned to the engineering office. Throwing my feet up on the desk, I lit my pipe. The encounter with Mr. Chadwick left me unnerved. I shouldn't have come down on him so hard. I felt bad about it; it wasn't my style of leadership. Bernard should have caught this. Chadwick was immature; he needed help from his chief but was too tied up in his Harvard, fun-loving bullshit to recognize it.

The chief damage controlman should have taken it on his own to educate him. Senior petty officers in the navies and noncoms in the armies of the world have shouldered the burden of junior officers since time immemorial. The chief was a pretty good man, and the lockers weren't in such bad shape that we couldn't fix them. But goddamn it, Chadwick should have known this.

I'd already chatted with the chief on the locker conditions, and no doubt he'd related it to Chief Maclin—who, I'm sure, lurked waiting to take that wise-ass mustang ensign down a peg.

The gentle rolling of the ship and the smoke from my pipe curling in gray clouds toward the overhead lulled me into recollection as I thought of the P2Vs. Just about now they'd be turning on their final approach for landing. I remembered as a young second-class petty officer how excited I'd been reporting to the squadron, thrilled with my first operational assignment. Everyone looked so cool in their flight suits and macho decorated helmets.

I wanted to be one of them. I recalled when I first checked in watching a P2V as it taxied. A man stood in an open hatch just aft of the cockpit windshield. He was like an awesome medieval knight riding his steed home after a great battle to save the kingdom. I reckoned he was guiding the pilot to his parking area.

From that moment I wanted to fly. I asked the squadron XO but it did no good. He had other ideas, such as the electronics repair shop. Officers were like that: they had the prettiest girls, the fastest cars, and the finest education, but they didn't care shit about their men. I wanted to be an aircrewman and they wouldn't let me. They treated me as if I were a child; hell, I was twenty-one and knew most everything important already, but they wouldn't let me fly.

It proved they didn't give a shit for their men. It wasn't like that in the books I'd read or the movies I'd seen. The benevolent officers always gave their men what they wanted—or mostly so—well, in some of the movies at least. Well sometimes they did. I saw it once.

Despite this setback to my ambitions, I worked hard. The squadron's equipment was in pretty good shape and we had a lot of ATs. Repair parts were plentiful so the work proved easy; we didn't have to cannibalize. I had a lot of time on my hands to bug my division chief and division officer to let me fly. After three months they assigned me to a crew. I had no training; they just assigned me to a crew as the radar operator. And I got flight pay. I was rich.

The APS-20, the long-range radar hanging in the aircraft's huge, bulky radome under the fuselage, was my baby. I'd studied hard in the squadron to know all about it, and I was ready. No treacherous lurking submarine periscope would escape my search, nor any attack on it suffer for my lack of attentiveness. God, I looked good in my khaki flight suit and flight helmet, although the helmet remained unpainted in its issue, nonmacho white.

I walked around the aircraft with the crew chief as he showed me what to look for in a preflight. Everyone in the crew gave the plane a preflight in their particular area. I had the responsibility of the radomes and radio antennas, but I dutifully checked the engines and tires and skin and everything the crew chief checked.

We did this while the officers sat in mission briefing. I wanted to sit in on the briefing, but no low-life second class ever got to. The officers came out fifteen minutes before start time, made a quick round of the plane, and ordered us aboard.

With electricity from an APU, auxiliary power unit, the starters kicked the engines over nicely. The smooth roar and slight vibration of the engines proving themselves to the crew chief made me proud to be an

American. My shoulder straps were too tight and the vibration of the engines slowly rubbed them across my groin. It gave me an erection, sending tingles up and down my body. It was going to be a great flight.

We taxied out. I was too intent on making final adjustments to my APS-20 to pay much attention to what was going on around me. Later when I had proved myself I'd pay attention, but for now my "20" would be the best in the air, in the fleet. I knew we were at the runway's threshold from the noise of the engines turning up to takeoff power. I was just about ready to energize my transmitter when I noticed out of the corner of my eye figures in a haze passing my radar console. No time to wonder—too many adjustments to be made before takeoff.

I smelled raw gasoline and the faint odor of smoke, but I'd never been on a flight before and paid scant attention to it. The noise slackened as if the engines throttled back. I called on my intercom to say I was losing power on my radar. It was getting hot. My radar flickered once, tried to recover, and went dead. As I turned to look, I saw I had forgotten to plug in my headset. No wonder it had been so quiet. I thought it was good crew discipline.

The lights went out; smoke irritated my lungs. I looked around. The airplane was on fire. I beat against my chest where I knew the shoulder harness quick-release tab had to be, but my smashing, panicked fist couldn't find it.

I remembered tears coming to my eyes—I knew I was going to die. A harsh fist jammed me back into my seat as a stunning blow to my chest snapped the harness loose. A gorilla-like hand grabbed my shoulder, yanked me out of my seat, and bounced me down past my precious APS-20 compartment on the plane's lower level.

The steel hand lugged me, colliding me into every obstacle and protrusion, out to freedom's fresh air through the nosewheel access ladder and fifty feet beyond, my heels dragging every inch.

The copilot had braved the flames and possible explosion to come in and get me out. *That stupid new kid who didn't even have sense enough to evacuate a burning aircraft.* I guessed officers cared about their men after all.

The searing heat, even from one hundred feet away, frightened me as the fire trucks spewed fog and foam against the deteriorating metal. The high vertical stabilizer lay crumpled on the ground, and the two huge engines hung down from the thick, distorted wings. The searchlight and high-definition APS-38 radar in their pods on each end of the wings drooped sadly. The long, thick fuselage screamed once and crumbled in half. A van came out to pick us up. I wondered how good that preflight inspection had been.

Not much of a first flight, I remembered thinking as I stood there on the runway in white-faced fear asking myself, Do I really want to be an aircrewman? How much was that flight pay?

"Thank you," I whispered to the steel walls of my small engineering office. "Thank you again, Lieutenant Junior Grade Whateveryour-namewas, thank you . . ."

Petty Officer Roll

Lieutenant Junior Grade Chadwick was unable to attend the party the civilians gave us that night in Seattle. Unfortunately, it had taken him and Chief Burton too long to conduct the inventory of the damage control lockers. We spent a restful night moored to the downtown piers and were under way at 0600 to be in position for the show by 0900.

A slight breeze blew in from the sea as the sun rapidly burned off the morning's haze. We did the standard destroyer tactical maneuvers to impress the locals on how well we spent their tax dollars.

The dignitaries sat on a large observation barge in the middle of the harbor so they could have a good view while we steamed around them. A rash of sail- and powerboats clustered around the reviewing barge. The final event, the honor of dropping depth charges, fell to three ships of our division. We steamed in a line abreast at fifteen knots, and as we came parallel to the barge all three of us were to drop our depth charges simultaneously.

Outside of the movies, I'd never seen a depth charge drop. The command to drop a depth charge was "ROLL," followed by the number of cans to be released. The depth charges were launched by pulling a braking lever loose on the holding ramps letting the depth charge—more than two feet long and a foot and a half in diameter—roll down the inclined ramps on the stern of the ship.

I was on the fantail as an observer. I should have been in main control where my sea detail station was, but I was nosy. Anyway, Maclin was down there and I didn't feel comfortable enough yet being around him. So I rationalized.

"Set depth for one hundred feet," the talker to the bridge repeated. The torpedo officer passed it on. Petty Officer Roll, with a Y-shaped fuse wrench, bent over the depth charge, inserting the yoked end. In a second he called out, "One hundred foot depth set." The torpedo officer passed it to the bridge.

"Stand by for depth charge drop," came over the 1MC, followed by, "All hands assume the position. Stand by. Stand by! Assume the position." The men on the fantail took the position: a flexed, deep knee bend to absorb the shock, which could shake the hell out of the ship if the depth charge went off too close.

I glanced forward just as we approached our drop point and saw a sailboat suddenly appear from nowhere, crossing our bow. The harsh whine of emergency backing steam assaulted my ears as the captain backed full to avoid a collision.

"Cancel the drop!" the phone talker shouted to the torpedo officer as we rapidly slowed. The torpedo officer instantly yelled to his petty officer in charge, TM1c. Michael H. Roll, USN.

"Hey, Roll!"

"Roll one," Torpedoman Roll immediately answered, yanking the braking lever forward, letting the lethal charge roll into the large and deep Seattle Bay.

"My God!" the torpedo officer screamed. The sound-powered phone talker connected to the bridge blurted out that we dropped a depth charge when we were near dead in the water.

I could swear I heard the captain's, "All ahead emergency flank," and could see in my mind's eye the lee helmsman slam the engine order telegraph levers forward against the stops, pull them back to stop, then jam them to flank ahead. The ship leaped forward as the huge screws dug deep into the water.

But too late.

A huge explosive bubble formed, like a giant rising, thirty yards behind us, throwing our stern five feet out of the water. The unrestrained propellors screamed at their freedom, running wild in free air.

In seconds we crashed down, a twenty-foot splash throwing us to the deck. My legs screamed from the pain.

The boiler safeties lifted with their horrible shriek of high-pressure steam. The throttle men had spun their throttles closed too rapidly against the runaway screws, dramatically reducing the steam needed, and the boilermen were unable to pull their burner barrels out of the fireboxes fast enough on their hot boilers.

We sat there dead in the water, waiting until the banshee wail of the safety valves stopped. The lights went out, and the gyrocompass power-failure alarm squealed its pitiful shriek. We'd lost all power as the generators kicked themselves off the line from the shock. It took me what seemed an hour to get my wobbly legs down to main control, not that I could do anything, but I was in charge and I should've been there from the beginning.

I swore it'd never happen again as I reached the control board and saw Chief Maclin nonchalantly bringing the plant under control while several men lay on the floor plates rubbing their legs, moaning. They'd not assumed the position soon enough. Steam leaks hissed through the engine room, each breath a soggy condensation.

I felt cheated by my own ineptness and my inexcusable absence from main control during a live depth charge drop.

The boiler safeties set after the steam pressure dropped. The diesel emergency generators had failed to start automatically as they should have when the main power dropped. The men did their work under the barely sufficient light from the few battle lanterns they could get working. There was hardly enough pressure left in the boilers to get the main generators rolling again and back on the line.

Chief Maclin turned to report to me, "Several small steam leaks in all the spaces, but nothing we can't handle in a few hours. We're ready to answer all bells . . . sir." I passed the message up to the captain, thankful to the chief for giving me the consideration of letting me report our status to the bridge.

"What do you think, Chief—what major damage do you think the plant could have suffered from the explosion?" I asked.

He furrowed his brow, glaring at me. "Damage, sir? We'd know about any major damage by now if the plant suffered. I don't think we got any problems, *sir*," he answered—patronizingly—in a civil enough tone, but barely so. *Who was I, an interloper, to dare question the Prince of the Plant.*

Undaunted by his haughty answer, I said, "I saw a movie in Engineering Officer School showing that after a smashing like we had, there's a good chance of damage to the stern tube packing and to the spring bearings, and maybe all the way up to the reduction gears." I added no more as I looked at his face, hesitantly hoping for a concurrence. None came. The hiss of escaping steam made talking difficult. The men scurried around tightening bolts and cursing burns.

Spring bearings supported the long length of the main shaft from the engine reduction gears out through the stern to the screws. They supported the shaft's heavy weight by providing a continuous oil film over a soft metal bearing surface. If a bearing failed—wiped, as we called it, because the failure "wiped" away the soft "bearing" metal—the shaft would sag, throwing itself out of alignment and grinding the delicate main reduction gears to the status of discarded tin cans.

The shafts, being whipped around as they had been, could have crushed the bearing material enough so that an insidious wiping failure could be lurking in the quiet support pedestals.

"Maybe in some of them fancy movies it happened that way, *sir,* but nothin's wrong here," he answered too loudly and with too many people around, and with too much emphasis on the "sir." He was circling his wagons; here's where he'd make his stand. His very tall, very black assistant, MM1 Albert J. Langston, USN, who was in charge of this forward engine room—called main control—moved symbolically to his right side as if preparing to protect his knight.

Shit, too early, the issue too important for me to cross swords on this.

"Main control, shaft alleys flooding—both of them—and it's bad," the man on watch in after steering reported over his sound-powered phones.

I smashed down the bridge button on main control's 21MC and in a voice betraying my excitement blurted out: "Captain, we lost the packing out of both stern tubes. Taking water bad. Request you stop engines immediately before we lose the securing rings. I don't know how bad it is yet. Chief Maclin's on his way back there now." There was a slight pause and the ship heeled to starboard as we pulled out of formation. The engine order telegraph from the bridge rang its bell as the handles chimed to STOP in electrical obedience to the bridge's command.

I went back to the shaft alley, but by the time I got there the machinist mates under Chief Maclin's guidance had almost completed replacing the packing on the starboard shaft.

Where the nearly three-foot-diameter shaft passed through the stern tube, through the ship's hull, leading out to the screws, a water-lubricated packing had to be fitted tightly around the shaft and held in place by a huge ring bolted down around it, with some leakage allowed to lubricate the shaft.

The close-in explosion had weakened the packing material and blown it past the rings, allowing the shaft to chew up what remained. Just like in the movie. Replacing the packing wasn't a difficult job except so much water continued to flood the shaft alley that the machinist mates had to work underwater and repair them by feel. If the shafts had continued to turn, they'd have rubbed against the bare metal of the stern tube, enlarging it so that the packing wouldn't seat. The stern tube itself would have had to be replaced. A job for a dry dock.

Machinist mates from number two engine room repaired the port packing, and in forty-five minutes we were under way. While I waited in main control to congratulate the chief, I tried talking to Petty Officer Langston but failed. He went to great pains to defeat the conversation, answering only yes or no or with the minimum words required, the chill of his voice ominous on the words he did use. I obviously was not one of his favorite people.

He was the second senior machinist mate. His counterpart, MM1c. C. J. Summers, USN, in number two engine room—the after engine room— was third in charge. Between the three of them, one was always on watch as the "engineering officer of the watch" when we were under way. Destroyers were too small to rate an actual officer on watch. Even if we had extra officers, they'd just have been in the way and wouldn't have known what to do anyway.

The bigger ships, cruisers and carriers, used their EDO officers to stand watches in main control. They were *restricted* line officers, restricted to serving only under their specialty, and therefore rated much lower on the food chain than the *real* naval officers, the unrestricted line officers. Limited-duty officers such as EDOs, LDOs, and staff corp officers such as doctors, supply officers and lawyers, and the like could not aspire to or take command of a vessel or an aircraft.

Chief Maclin returned to main control and barely acknowledged me standing there as he gave Langston a dirty, questioning look. I guessed he smarted a bit from my statement that the movie said there was a chance of stern tube failure. He said nothing to me as he scanned the myriad gauges on the throttle board that told him the condition of the entire plant.

"Okay?" he asked Langston, who answered with a nod, then picked up a phone to inform the bridge he was ready to answer all bells.

The throttle man, whose job it was to control the opening and closing of the huge valves that metered the flow of steam to the turbines, and who did double duty as the sound-powered phone talker to the bridge, turned to me. "The captain wants to see you, sir."

I was glad to have an excuse to leave the dense, nerve-strained denseness of main control. As I reported to the captain, he asked, "Don, what's the condition of the plant?"

"The stern tubes appear okay, sir, but I'm concerned about the spring bearings. I think they might wipe if we continue on."

"What does Maclin say?"

"He doesn't agree, sir."

"What makes you think the spring bearings will fail, Mr. Sheppard?" the XO asked with a bite in his voice as he stood next to the captain's chair.

Butterflies fought for space in my stomach. The XO was usually pretty calm about this sort of thing. I didn't answer for a moment, afraid of betraying a lack of knowledge. Finally, as both the captain and XO stared silently at me, I replied, "I saw an old World War Two movie in Engineering Officer School that said after a close-in explosion, the spring bearings and stern tube packings were vulnerable to failure." Neither of them spoke or changed their expressions. "And I suspect that the runaway screws, when they came out of the water, didn't help much either," I added.

Silence. My confidence crumpled as the pilothouse closed in around me. *What were they thinking?*

"Commodore won't like that, Skipper," the XO said.

"How much time will it take to check them out, Don?"

I hesitated. "I don't know, sir." In answer, the captain called for Chief Maclin to come to the bridge.

We went into the sea cabin. *Shit, this isn't going to be fun.*

"Chief," the captain began as he seated himself at the small desk and the rest of us sat on the couch that opened up into a bed at night. "Mr. Sheppard, here, thinks there might be some damage to the spring bearings based on a movie he saw in EO school."

"Yes, sir, he told me," the chief answered without reflection and in the dry voice of someone talking to himself, his arrogance gone. He still wore his wet khakis that dripped over the standard brown Naugahyde covering on the couch. Sweat pushed its way out of his pores. He was in high officer country and didn't appear to like it one bit.

"What do you think, Chief Maclin?"

We waited for his answer. I could just imagine the torture in his mind. His tight face showed he was thinking hard on the proper response. On one hand after the stern tubes failed, I might be right. On the other, he had his ego and kingdom to protect. If he went against me, and the captain agreed, he knew he could still retain his kingdom, but by the same hand I could make life difficult for him.

"I had the spring bearing temperatures checked when Shep . . . Mr. Sheppard mentioned it to me, and all the bearings were within the proper temperature range." I noticed the chief's failure to mention that we had just gotten under way from the repairs when he checked the temperatures. I let it go.

"We're on our way to WESTPAC, Chief," the captain said, then paused as he lit an already filled pipe. "We're taking the northern route, and I'd hate to have bearing problems up there. How long would it take to—whadaya call it—roll out the bearings to check them?"

"Well, Captain, if the ship were alongside the pier and the plant shut down so I could use most of my men, we could check all the bearings in say . . ." His eyes lifted and shifted to the right in calculation. "Oh, say eight hours for the check."

"XO?"

"I don't think the commodore would wait for us, which means we'd have to sail independently, which wouldn't be bad, but we've got a tanker laid on for tomorrow at first light. If we miss her we'd probably have to fuel at Dutch Harbor. That'd be a bitch."

"Whadaya recommend, XO?"

"We sail with the squadron, sir," he replied without hesitation.

"Chief?"

After a moment the chief said, "Sail, Captain. Dutch Harbor is a miserable place to refuel."

"How long to repair a spring bearing at sea?"

"Depending on the weather, of course, maybe three, four hours a bearing," the chief answered after thirty seconds of silence.

Finally, turning to me, his first recognition of my presence, the captain asked very formally, "Your opinion, Mr. Sheppard?"

What a dilemma the captain was in. Here, a junior officer with six days' experience as a chief engineer is obviously wanting to pull out of the squadron sail and check all the spring bearings in direct contradiction to a professional, well-experienced engineering chief who'd been doing the job for twenty years.

If the captain said yes to the inspection and we missed the squadron sail, he'd look bad. He'd look even worse if he suspected they might be bad and they were, and they failed at sea. In rough weather he'd still be left behind, and another ship would have to be used as an escort. The commodore had his dream set on his *full* squadron of *eight* destroyers steaming proudly into Tokyo Bay. It hadn't happened in a long time.

If I said we should inspect the spring bearings and the captain agreed with me, and the bearings were bad, it would injure the chief's pride and his position in the engineering department. A wise-ass ensign would have shown him up, thereby throwing into question his professional ability.

If I said don't sail and the bearings checked out okay, it would reinforce the opinion that officers stick together no matter how stupid the officers' actions might be.

If I said don't sail before a bearings check and we sailed anyway and the bearings failed, the captain's competence would be called into question by the crew. He would have been wrong, and the word gets around the fleet mighty fast.

On the other hand, if I said we should sail, thereby taking a chance of a failure and the bearings were okay, it would just show my inexperience and that I didn't really know what was going on. After all, I had been a chief engineer for only six days. There would be little harm done.

Captain, Captain . . . what is there for you to do?

If I said we should go, and the bearings failed, hell, we'd be no worse off. The work would be a little harder and the time a little longer. I wished I had mentioned the movie to the chief in private instead of in front of the whole damn main control crew. In my heart I knew the bearings should be checked. *Let me help you out, Captain, let me take the load.*

"Sail, Captain, I think they'll be okay," I answered as the ship whispered to me that I was wrong.

"Rejoin the squadron, XO. Report to the flagship all repairs completed," the captain ordered, looking at me in relief as if saying, I owe you one, Sheppard. He knew what I had done.

Spring Bearings

O n station in ready position one, a thousand yards astern of the oiler, we waited our turn to go along her starboard side. Another destroyer kept station a thousand yards behind us in waiting station two as the rest of the squadron steamed in ASW guarding stations three thousand yards around us. As soon as one ship completed refueling, it'd dash off to take one of the guarding stations. The rotation continued until all were refueled. Well choreographed but useless against quiet, high-speed Russian submarines if they wanted to attack us. The commodore did it by the book.

Our bow dug deep into the five-foot waves hitting from dead ahead. But this was the best course to steam when alongside at one hundred feet from a ship twice your size. It was my first refueling at sea. On the destroyer currently alongside I could make out the hapless 1st Division, the Deck Division, "deck apes," manning the lines of the refueling rigs in the cold rain of the North Pacific. Here the boatswain's mates reigned supreme and earned their pay.

I was on the bridge to observe. As we started alongside, I'd go below to main control ostensibly to ensure that the engineering plant didn't screw up while alongside. *For all the good I could do.* Chief Maclin was there as he always seemed to be. Neither of us had mentioned the spring bearing talk we had with the captain. I knew he felt I had backed down, and I sensed his scorn for my lack of conviction. This thing was all out of proportion.

Mr. Graffey and I stood next to the captain as he explained the fine points of going alongside an oiler. Mr. Graffey had the conn and was going to take us alongside under the stiff supervision of the captain. This was not a casual operation; disaster would be only a hundred feet away.

Mr. Bluing had the deck. Uneasiness tugged at my chest; my fingertips tingled. "Captain?" I said, but then I had nothing to say. A slight, almost imperceptible tremor rolled up through my feet. My eyes glanced from side to side in search of a reason. I met the captain's eyes; he nodded in recognition of feeling it too.

"What . . ." he started to ask.

"Number three spring bearing wiped and running hot. Main control requests permission to secure number one engine," the lee helmsman shouted. Mr. Graffey turned, looking at him. "What . . . what did you say?"

"This is Mr. Bluing," came the almost instant reply. "I have the conn . . . starboard engine stop," Mr. Bluing ordered in a voice just slightly louder than normal. The lee helmsman's hand was already on the starboard engine order telegraph handle and had it pulled back to stop by the time the "s" of starboard came from Mr. Bluing's lips.

Mr. Bluing ran to the port side bridge wing to check the area clear. It was clear. He shouted, "Left standard rudder—NO! belay that, left full rudder."

He had increased his rudder when he realized he needed more turning power to compensate for the dragging starboard screw, which tended to counteract his turn. In an emergency, ships in a column, such as we were, pulled out to port if you had an even number station, and to starboard if you had an odd. We were in waiting station one but were in fact the second ship in the refueling column. We hauled out to port.

Mr. Graffey continued standing next to the captain, his eyes wide in confusion over the rapid events. I walked over to the front of the bridge and picked up the ship-to-ship UHF radio microphone. "Captain? Report?" I questioned, scanning today's voice call status board. Mike Tango was our code name for today. It changed every twenty-four hours.

As the captain nodded yes, I spoke into the mike to the destroyer behind us. "X-Ray Romeo, this is Mike Tango. Have lost starboard engine. Pulling out to port. Out." Our voice call signs changed daily according to our standard operating plan, and it was a bitch keeping up with who was who. I looked again at the board, picking out the commodore's call sign. "Break. Break. Charlie Echo, you copy? Over," I asked the commodore's flag plot.

"This is Charlie Echo. Copy all. Out."

"Thank you, Don," Mr. Bluing said, rapidly passing me on his way to the starboard wing to check the other ships' positions. "Right standard rudder," I heard him order to get us out of the wicked trough of the waves and steaming back in the same direction as the squadron. With the captain's permission I left the bridge.

The bearing cap and top half of the four-foot-high number three spring bearing was almost removed by the time I got there. Chief Maclin stood next to it talking to Machinist Mate First Class Langston. The chief looked up at me as I approached, then he walked away. Two third-class machinist mates fought huge jacks in position to raise the shaft the few centimeters needed to slide the lower half of the eighty-pound bearing up around the shaft and out, and then slide a new one in.

Langston scrunched down to help the two third-class petty officers as he cursed the increased up and down hammering of the ship. "God-damnit," he yelled. "Get in there, you sonovabitch," he shouted to the jacks. The pitching ship seemed to grab tools out of the sailors' hands and toss them all about—always, of course, out of sight. The jacks refused to seat properly.

"I told him we shoulda did this in port," Langston complained, not saying who the "him" was. I waited fifteen minutes before he came up from under the shaft. "Those goddamned jacks are the shits to seat if you're tied up to a pier much less out here in this fuckin' ocean. We shoulda did it in port. I told him . . . I told him," Langston said to no one, his eyes squinting through the cold, dimly lit bilges, his arms covered with goose bumps punching up through the black smear of filth and grease.

Before a new bearing half could be rolled into place, it had to be painted with a bluing material and the shaft slowly turned within it by an electric motor hookup called the jacking gear. This slow rotation rubbed the bluing off the high points on the bearing. Then the bearing had to be rolled out again and shaved down with hard metal scrapers to bring the bearing half into perfect agreement with the shaft.

Being tossed around by the motion of the sea while using the sharp-edged scraper and pulling your hands across the sometimes protruding metal slivers cut your skin badly if you weren't careful—and it was impossible to be.

The main control messenger appeared at my side. "Excuse me, sir," he reported hesitantly, holding onto a railing to keep from being thrown around by the pitching ship. "Excuse me, sir, but the chief says to tell you that number two spring bearing on the port engine just wiped. He's on his way to repair it now."

"Thank you . . . ahh?"

"Philips, sir. Fireman Philips. M Division."

"Thank you, Philips. Does the bridge know?" What a stupid question; of course they did, and now we'd lost both engines. I felt the motion of the ship change from pitching as we drove into the seas to rolling as the high sea set us into the trough. *Shit, oh dear!*

The sharp shrill of the boatswain's pipe blasted over the 1MC, followed by: "Now hear this. Now hear this. Stand by to rig for towing. First Division, man your towing stations." The captain, to prevent us from wallowing in the trough, was having us towed, hopefully into the seas to lessen the roll, which was making our job almost impossible. Ah, good idea, I thought, but I had other things to do and didn't envy those poor bastards in 1st Division out there fighting the cold winds and high seas.

"Langston, how many spare spring bearings do we carry?"

"Three."

"Shit!"

"Yeah," he answered as I helped him manhandle the lower bearing half. My God, it was heavy, and its weight kept tossing us painfully against the protruding machinery and stanchions as we wrestled it out. Another machinist mate held on with one hand as he attempted to paint the new bearing half with bluing. The rolling ship caused him to spill the bluing over all of us, giving us the look of outer-space aliens.

I helped the third classes who had jacked up the shaft get out of the shaft alley bilges. They were filthy and wet, and shivering uncontrollably from their exposure to the cold water sloshing around them in the oil-slicked bilge.

The work became easier as we were apparently taken in tow, and the muscle-wrenching rolls were replaced by the more gentle but still vicious pitching. I wished I could have observed the towing setup. I'd only read about it in my *Conning a Destroyer* book. Oh, maybe one day.

After an hour of torturous work, we had the lower bearing half in place and "worked" in. We were just removing the jacks from the bilges when I looked at the time.

My God, I have the watch, I forgot. Screw it, let Mr. Bluing worry about that shit, I had work to do. But as soon as the messenger showed up again for a status report, I'd send my apologies.

The chief's gang on number two bearing worked faster than we did, and he reported finishing his lower half just as we were running in our upper half. And he had started forty-five minutes after we did. I guess an experienced chief could work a little faster than an ensign chief engineer with barely a weeks' experience. I appreciated his reporting to me. It was a good sign.

"Easy, easy, Langston," I coached as we mule-hauled the heavy top bearing cap onto the pedestal. From being just an observer, I'd taken charge of the job. Langston didn't seem to mind. Completion was near as I looked up to tell the messenger to let main control know we'd be ready in ten minutes. I saw the captain standing there.

"Sorry, sir, I forgot I had the watch. I've sent word to Mr. Bluing. Sorry, Captain."

He laughed, slapping me on the shoulder and bringing back a wet, greasy hand from my soaked and stained khakis. I tried not to shiver in front of him as Langston and I passed over the job to the two machinist mates helping us. Putting in the final bolts and torquing them down was the only thing left. I knew I looked most unmilitary in front of the captain and hoped my face wasn't as dirty or my lips as blue as those of the other men around me.

"Good job, men," the captain said, moving away from the splashing water in the bilge. He looked at me, his stoic face turning into a grin. "Good job, Don, good job," he said, extending his hand. I wiped mine on my trouser leg and noticed the blood as my hand went toward him. I drew it back but he reached forward, grasping it in his strong grip, and shook it. "I'm sorry, Don," he said, his face turning somber at the sight of the blood. He tried to recover but failed, turned, and walked away.

In twenty more minutes the tow was let go and we were under way on the starboard engine. In ten more minutes Chief Maclin finished his bearing and we were ahead standard on both. He arrived in main control looking as bedraggled as I was. Machinist Mate Second Class John L. Smallwood, USN, second in charge of the forward engine room under Machinist Mate First Class Langston, stood bleary eyed in front of the throttle board, nursing his heavily bandaged right hand. It was injured when the number two lower bearing half broke loose, smashing his hand against the bearing foundation.

Glassy eyed from the painkillers that Pharmacist Mate First Class Harold Jennings, USN, had given him, Smallwood held onto the throttle board, trying to keep his attention on the gauges. His head nodded. Chief Maclin sent him to his bunk. "I'm sorry, Smallwood," he said, helping him up the ladder. "Goddamn, I'm really sorry."

Chief Maclin turned to me, wiping a tear from his eye, and without word or expression offered his greasy, bloody hand. We shook, saying nothing, and I became one step closer to being the Prince of the Plant.

I returned to my stateroom and sat there for several minutes reviewing the recent events. My hands hurt and still bled, but I wanted a hot shower before having them dressed. I still shivered from the icy water. Corpsman Jennings had offered us tiny bottles of brandy but I'd refused mine. Contrary to navy tradition, and the myth, I knew that alcohol retarded warming, not aided it.

Should I have volunteered the way I had to help the machinist mates, or should I have stayed aloof and let them tend to their own work? Hell, I didn't know. What was done, was done.

I'd just stepped out of the shower when I felt the starboard engine stop. I reached for the phone as it rang. "We just lost another spring bearing, sir," Chief Maclin's strained, apologetic voice reported.

"Thank you, Chief. I'll be down in a minute."

Four hours later a perfectly seated bearing bore the weight of the spinning starboard shaft. The weather had grown mean. The wind blew, the waves heaved us about, and the heavy clouds smashed us with their drenching, ice-carried fury.

With bandaged hands I fought my way to the bridge to report to the captain. He looked at me in the dim red lights of the pilothouse, I couldn't tell whether in admiration or admonishment. I wanted to ask him if I'd done the right thing. But I couldn't. I was not mentally prepared for criticism. "Well done. You look beat, Don. What watch do you have?" It was okay. Three pounds lifted off my heart.

"The mid, sir," I answered, knowing he damn well knew which watch I had. He reached for his phone and told, I assume, Mr. Bluing to take me off the watch. I protested, but his frown told me not to question his decision.

Silently I stood there watching the waves grow higher and listening to the banshee winds. I watched with pleasure as the bridge team held onto anything to keep from being smashed about as I calmly flexed my body in concert with the sea's violent dance. I had no hint of seasickness, and I reveled in the pleasure of thinking about it without my stomach demanding restitution.

Detached with the USS *Haney* for refueling, we proceeded to Dutch Harbor, Alaska, about halfway down the Aleutian Islands chain from the mainland. Our course took us northwesterly into the land of ice and storms while our squadron mates steamed happily to the southwest and warmer climes. Small bits of ice already formed on our masts as we pitched and rolled in the unruly sea.

"Commodore pissed?" I hazarded, trying to make it sound casual. In answer, the captain handed me a message written on a flashing light message form. I took it clumsily in my bandaged hands and read.

BT
UNCLAS
R090718Z PRIORITY
TO: USS HENSHAW
FM: COMDESRON 13
INFO: USS HANEY
      COMDESDIV 132
      SUBJ: ENGINEERING READINESS

1. VIEW WITH ALARM YOUR WOEFUL LACK OF
FORESIGHT AND ENGINEERING READINESS.
2. YOU ARE DETACHED TO PROCEED DUTCH HARBOR
FOR FUELING.
3. MAKE BEST SPEED CONSISTENT WITH FUEL
AVAILABILITY AND ENGINEERING CAPABILITIES.

4. YOU HAVE DESTROYED THE PLAN, SUBMIT FULL
REPORT SOONEST.
5. FOR HANEY: DETACH AND ACCOMPANY
HENSHAW TO DUTCH HARBOR. SORRY YOU'LL
MISS THE PARTY.

UNCLAS
BT

I read it once and then again before handing it back to the stoic-faced
captain. "It doesn't seem so bad, sir."

The captain grinned, then broke out in laugher. "Not bad, Mr.
Sheppard? Not bad? It could be a bloody death knell," he chuckled, rising out of his chair and guiding me into his sea cabin.

"Captain left the bridge," the boatswain's obligatory shout penetrated
the icy wind howling around the bridge.

"Sit down, Don," the captain said. "I'm going to run through some
things OCS left out." He rang for a steward to bring up some coffee.
"Let's start off on why all this happened. The initial cause was I didn't
listen to the XO when he told me it wasn't a good idea to have someone named Roll being around depth charge racks. I think we all agree
now. But what would we have done with him? He was the leading torpedoman, and that's his station when we roll—sorry—drop depth charges.

"The second cause was that I didn't listen to you. But that would have
been a tough shot, with you being a fresh-caught chief engineer going up
against the word of a veteran like Maclin.

"And third, Don, you, you're a direct contributor." My face drooped.
What the hell's he talking about? I thought I was a hero. "If you thought
you were right—and you did think you were right—you should have put
up more opposition, not roll over dead because of the obvious resistance
of the three of us. I think, Don, that's the greatest lesson for you to learn
in this whole thing."

The captain stopped talking as the steward stumbled into the room
trying hard not to spill the "Cap'n's" coffee. As the steward started to fall
from a bad roll, the captain jumped up, catching him by the arm and saving both the steward and the coffee. The steward backed out with the
greatest of apologies as I struggled with the coffee cup between my en-
cumbered hands.

"I don't know if greater insistence from you would have made any difference to the XO or me. The commodore was rather adamant about us sailing into Tokyo Bay together. I think he still fancies himself a World War Two ensign on that damned PT boat of his that he always talks about.

"But I don't know, Don, it might have made a difference. Just keep it in mind. It's not a criticism of you. Hell, you've only been an officer for what . . . eleven months? I should have demanded more of you." *Demanded more of me?*

"Yes, sir," I answered, glad to be able to say something but confused on what I was saying yes sir to.

"Now, on the message from the commodore, which you didn't think was so bad. On the contrary, it was a stinger, but it won't hurt me much. The 'view with alarm' is the navy way of saying you're really pissed. 'Woeful' is used only when referring to such misdeeds as cowardliness under fire or crimes equal to the rape of the Virgin Mary.

"In the third item his reference to 'consistent with fuel availability' is standard and simply means a captain should consider his own ship's safety before mission accomplishment. That was a hard-fought new rule and stems back to World War Two when captains had to obey an order without regard to the consequence or his ship's safety. But to say consistent with 'engineering capabilities' is childish sarcasm.

"In item four, his saying 'you have destroyed the plan' would only show that he's some kind of megalomaniac.

"And to top the whole message, his statement to *Haney* and not to me, 'sorry you'll miss the party,' shows only an immaturity that I'm sure, once he realizes what he's said, he'll wish to hell he'd never heard of *Henshaw*. I wouldn't be surprised if we get another message canceling that one," he said, pointing at the message form on the desk.

"I don't know what to say, Captain."

"Don't say anything. This conversation is man to man. I do it only because I think you have potential. And another thing, as long as I'm giving you all the secrets of your high and mighty senior officers, it won't hurt me because I'm from the Potomac High—you know . . . Annapolis, Sodom on the Potomac—and the commodore is not. Mr. Bernard told me about the little talk you and he had. There is an Annapolis Protective Society, Don, and you've got to realize it." He picked up his standard, navy stock, handleless cup and took a deep swig, curling his face at the bitterness of its contents.

"Mustangs, no matter how good they are, are on the bottom of the unrestricted line officer chain and must be twice as good as an officer from Annapolis just to stay even. And there are people out there who'll put you down. Watch your six, Don, watch your six."

Watch your six, a fighter pilot's term for keeping an eye out behind you. I always do, Captain, I wanted to say but didn't.

Ice

<hr>

Although it was only early fall, it was god-awful cold. The gravity feed fueling at Dutch Harbor and the broken pipe heaters on the long fuel lines leading from the storage tanks on the top of the hill made for abominable delays. For two days we fueled while the sticky mass of bunkers crept down through the large fuel lines.

The storm that had plagued us on the journey here never let up. We fought the ice on the mast and superstructure with machinery cleaning steam lances. It seemed a losing battle, with the ice forming as fast as we melted it away. It was dangerous, backbreaking work to handle the steam lances with their heavy hoses. Finally we finished, and at 0300 on the third day *Henshaw* and *Haney* were under way.

The captain took *Henshaw* out through the treacherous Akutan Pass and rang up eighteen knots as we left Cape Sedanka on our starboard hand. He kept the sea on our starboard quarter as the best way to clear the area in the shortest time while still heading generally for Tokyo Bay. We rode fairly well for the first eight hours. The captain, being senior to the skipper of *Haney,* was in tactical command and put the ships in a loose column at two thousand yards. We had the sea to contend with and little time to worry about how sharp we looked to the occasional whale we might encounter.

The pitching and rolling left my stomach the slightest bit queasy but nothing my ego couldn't handle as I assumed the 1200 to 1600 watch. We were riding sluggishly now.

A destroyer is designed to have a very short roll period; that is, the natural time period of her roll from side to side is short and she'll recover quickly from the tilt. The ice forming on our mast made us top-heavy, negating the natural weight distribution. *Haney* had the same problem.

"Good thing we got a full load of fuel, Captain," I said to make conversation with the brooding man. He hadn't left the bridge since we'd gotten under way.

"Call the XO and Mr. Hethington up here," he answered.

I nodded to Mr. Rice, who walked over to the phone and pushed the button to the XO's stateroom. As he did we rolled to starboard and hung there, not snapping back as we should have. Forty-six degrees—easier to walk on the bulkheads than it was on the decks.

Ten seconds passed and we just hung there, then slowly, as the massive force of our underwater hull demanded, the ship righted itself. As the mast passed the vertical, it snapped down to the port side and held with a twenty-degree list for another ten seconds. Slowly back and forth we went, each time going further over, each time staying longer. Over—hold—back—over—hold—back. Further—longer—faster. The bow: up—down—up—down. My blood grew colder than the wind.

The windshield wipers strained valiantly to keep the forward bridge windows free, but the ice slowed the wipers—stopped them—then froze them in place.

"I don't like it, gentlemen," the captain started. "One of these times we won't come back. We gotta get that ice off the mast and it's a damn dangerous job. Suggestions?"

"We can't send men up that mast with steam hoses in this weather, sir," blurted Lt. (jg) John H. Hethington, USNR, the gunnery officer.

"What would you suggest, Mr. Hethington?" the captain replied, his cold voice lower by an octave. The XO said nothing. In a second, Mr. Hethington realized he'd made a stupid outburst.

"We should get the engineers up there with their steam hoses, sir."

"They might be a bit tired after three days of doing the same thing in Dutch Harbor, don't you think, Mr. Hethington?" the captain answered sarcastically, holding the back of his chair for support while we did the best we could on all the other available handholds. Then turning to the XO, the captain continued in a tone that frightened me, "Get the ice off, XO. Get the ice off." Turning to me, he said, "I'll take the deck, Mr. Sheppard . . . lay below."

The shrill of the boatswain's pipe calling attention sounded sharp over the clamor of the wind and ice-laced rain. "Now hear this, now here this. All officers and chief petty officers not actually on watch report to the wardroom. I say again, report to the wardroom."

"Gentlemen," the XO started as soon as the men assembled, "the ice has to be chopped and steamed away or none of us will see Thieves Alley in Yokosuka. The engineers are beat; they can't power the ship and steam off ice by themselves anymore. We're going to use the rest of the crew. That includes all hands. We're here to outline a plan."

In ten minutes the meeting concluded. The XO spoke with a purpose and authority I had never heard from him before. In another twenty minutes a jet of steam, manned by radarmen from combat, attacked the top of the mast. They took the honor of the first attempt. Only one man stayed on watch. The radar antennas were frozen solid and shut down anyway. Only two men, well belted in, could work on the upper mast. The safety precautions severely limited their effectiveness, and the cold wind demanded relief every fifteen minutes.

I could only guess at the severe psychological effect the men experienced hanging over the water as the ship hesitated at the end of each roll. What did they think as they looked down at the cold, choppy gray sea so close to them? I was glad I didn't have to find out and secretly pleased that the captain had forbidden me from going aloft with the unmistakable admonishment that I was an officer.

The deck force, also attached to safety lines and belts, mustered to chop away the ice on the main deck, which formed almost faster than they could chop it away. The spray instantly froze when it struck. The backbreaking work in the biting wind and the chance of being swept overboard ate away at them no less than those poor bastards aloft. The captain had discussed the matter with *Haney*'s CO, and they chose a course running with the storm to lessen the rolling and pitching.

I took the deck back from the captain and saw Mr. Graffey with his men on the fo'c'sle. It surprised me to see him there; he didn't seem that sort of man. I was wrong, and maybe the academy or someone had gotten the message to him that an officer doesn't stand under shelter when his men are getting wet.

Steaming with the storm exposed us to it longer, but the reduction to the ship's movement was more than worth it. The commodore was going to be pissed even more.

In the middle of the second day we started making headway on the ice. The shorter rolls didn't hang on as long. The seas smoothed a discernible amount and the wind's roar lessened. The men on the masts kept up their onerous task, shielded only by the inadequate foul-weather clothing. We should have had arctic gear but we didn't; this side trip to the Pacific was unplanned for.

The bulky steam lancing gloves offered little protection from the weather. They were designed only for handling hot steam lances and had their insulation in the palms with only thin canvas for the backs. Frostbite and the chills plagued every man on the ice detail.

Smashed hands, rope burns, and bruises from falling commonly appeared on the mess decks, with each man showing his wounds proudly as he came out of the "ring." Every man fought the elements with grace and elan, Mr. Graffey above all. Never did he complain and never did he neglect the well-being of the men assigned to him for the chopping detail.

Graffey entered the wardroom on the evening of the second day just before supper. We normally chopped and steam-lanced until dark. He shrugged off his foul-weather gear, shivering violently. He'd been supervising his teams all day and had that pale, far-off, I-don't-give-a-damn-anymore look of exhaustion.

We were alone and I brought him a cup of hot coffee. He accepted it, holding it in both hands, and stared at me as if looking into my soul. He furrowed his brow as if in deep thought. "You don't think I'm shit, do you, Mr. Sheppard?" he said in a muted, slow voice that monotoned out barely above a whisper. He'd taken to calling me Mr. Sheppard after I qualified as an OOD and he hadn't. And especially so since I became a department head before him even though he was many months senior to me.

"John"—I'd never called him anything but Mr. Graffey or just Graffey before. "Yeah John, I always thought you weren't worth a shit until this ice thing. You've done a magnificent job, and I'm proud of you." He tried to raise a smile across his blue lips. A tear came to his eyes. I walked into Mr. Bluing's stateroom, just forward of the wardroom, and yanked a spare blanket off the rack, then came back and put it around his shoulders.

"I . . . I'm so tired . . . I . . . so cold," he whispered. I took him by the shoulders and walked him out of the wardroom, picking up one of the supper sandwiches as we went. "I've got . . . the next watch," he said as

I led him to his bunk and helped him lie down. "Can't go . . . sleep, I've . . . got the next watch."

I took off his shoes and trousers and fed him the sandwich and held a cup of hot water for him to drink between bites. "It's okay, John . . . it's okay. I'll take your watch. You get some sleep. I'll take care of it, you get some sleep. There'll be ice to remove in the morning." He was asleep before I finished the sentence. Our period of courteous neutrality was over.

He stirred as I covered his shivering body with the spare blanket, and he muttered in his sleep, "Thank . . . thank you . . . Don."

At the end of the fourth day the seas abated and we turned southerly for Japan. In the morning the ice started melting; by noon we'd knocked off the removing detail, and by evening we were ahead standard. The weary crew stood tall. They'd fought and won against the wrathful elements, and no sailing clipper sailor rounding Cape Horn could have stood prouder.

All because a torpedoman had an odd name and we let it slide.

By 1900 we cleared the storm and were heading fair in near calm seas. The steak and lobster supper for the crew and the besting of the ice had put them in a festive mood. It permeated the ship and she sang for it. After supper—the first the captain had eaten in the wardroom since we put to sea—the captain relaxed. He handed me a Teletype message, his face barely controlling an I-told-you-so smirk.

BT
UNCLAS
R150945Z ROUTINE
TO: USS HENSHAW
FM: COMDESRON 13
INFO: USS HANEY
         COMDESDIV 132
SUBJ: OPERATIONAL PERFORMANCE
REF: A. MY MSG R090718Z

1. YOUR SITUATION REPORTS READ WITH INTEREST.
2. WELL DONE. CANCEL REFERENCE A.

UNCLAS
BT

Reference A was the message the commodore had sent to the captain chewing out his ass about engineering readiness. I handed back this message without comment. I was only an ensign. His smirk disappeared, replaced by a grin as he said, "And also, I have received authority to promote you to lieutenant junior grade."

I stared at him in awe, not believing what I heard. I hadn't known the captain recommended me for early promotion. I couldn't speak; I felt a moistness come to my eyes and a small lump form in my lower throat. "I . . . I, Captain . . ."

"I congratulate you, Don," the XO said, walking up to me and extending his hand. "Well done; you deserve it." Turning to the rest of the officers in the wardroom, the XO announced that I was being promoted early to lieutenant junior grade. There was a round of applause. Mr. Chadwick scowled. Ensign Graffey was the first to shake my hand.

We crossed the longitude 160 degrees east. The Western Pacific— WESTPAC.

Tokyo Bay filled my awareness. Huge junks plied their way across the wide bay with little attention to the large ships moving in and out. I studied the junks through binoculars with an interest only someone deathly afraid could muster.

The sun could not penetrate the low clouds hanging over the bay. Any minute I expected the roaring whine of a kamikaze to swoop out of the grayness and crash into our bridge, killing us all in revenge. *Why weren't we at general quarters?*

I feared the Japanese because I believed they wanted to kill me. I was a well-worked-over product of America's massive World War Two propaganda program that spewed its lies and half-truths throughout the country in the early 1940s. I had listened to the hype, the stories of bespectacled, bucktoothed, godless Nips bayoneting babies and raping young girls, nuns, and pregnant women. I found it difficult to believe, but would the American government lie to me?

The stories said the Japanese had to wear thick glasses because when they were babies their mothers carried them on their backs papoose style. Since their eyes could focus only on their mother's neck, they all became nearsighted.

And they were bucktoothed because they always had a false smile, and keeping the face in that unnatural position distorted the lower jaw, pulling it back so that the upper teeth protruded over the lower. Eating with chopsticks had the same effect, but it had never been explained to me why. I, of course, never used chopsticks. I saw all those war movies. These recollections amused me, but adulthood had not completely discredited them.

When I was a kid the best I could do in supporting the war was to buy war bonds. Everyone said this was important, but I never understood why the government needed money. Hell, I would often say to anyone who would listen—and few would—that if the government wanted money they could simply print up as much as they wanted. But no one listened to me, so I had to buy war bonds.

The $25 bond, the cheapest war bond, cost $18.75, and I never had that kind of money. Luckily for me the government invented the war stamp, which you could buy for a dime and could paste in a book until you had $18.70. With a nickel in cash you could turn in the book and get a real war bond. I had four war bonds and 136 stamps by the time the war was over. I knew, they knew, that my war bonds and stamps made a considerable impact on the funding of the Manhattan Project, which developed the atomic bomb that wiped out Hiroshima and Nagasaki.

One day, when I was in the seventh grade, four soldiers came to our school in two jeeps. If we bought a war stamp they would ride us once around the block. I borrowed money from anyone who would lend it to me and rode around the block six times. And for six times I was General MacArthur hurling back the Yellow Hordes at Bataan.

I laughed again at my childish thoughts as I went down the ladder to main control for the special sea and anchor detail. This was my station, and unless I had the conn this is where I was supposed to be. Chief Maclin was already there and welcomed me down with a smile.

"Congratulations on your promotion, sir. You're okay!"

"Thank you, Chief, I appreciate that."

Machinist Mate First Class Langston stole a glance at me as if we shared a great secret, and nodded. I smiled back at him and winked, not understanding but letting it slide. I'd talk to him later.

The engine order telegraph on the main throttle board chimed both engines back one-third. The throttle men answered and we shuddered to a standstill. Ahead one-third. Stop. "Moored," the 1MC announced, and we were in Japan.

"Must have been the skipper," Chief Maclin commented. "He's the only one I know who can make a two-bell landing. Probably showing off for the commodore."

I frowned at him as I thought about the horrible landing I'd made at the fuel dock at Point Loma. He smiled.

Yokosuka

Bone tired from lack of sleep and the pounding seas, Chief Maclin and I walked down the pier of the Naval Repair Facility, Yokosuka. I carried a list of jobs that the various departments needed done. I hadn't realized that the chief engineer was also the repair officer, but Chief Maclin thoughtfully reminded me when he handed me a list of engineering plant discrepancies two days out of Yokosuka.

"Get a list from all the other departments, sir, and we'll present them when we land." I hurried, working along with the chief late into the night around our watches, to put together a realistic package. He was with me now because I didn't have enough confidence to pull off a prerepair conference by myself.

Amid the bustle of the yard, we stopped by the CPO, or chief petty officers, club. He asked me to wait, he'd just be a moment. I figured he wanted a quick snort. In three minutes he came out with a package under his arm and a grin on his face. I questioned neither one. "This repair officer is an old mustang LDO and thinks he's hot shit," he volunteered, opening the package and showing me a bottle of Johnnie Walker Black. "He likes to play king shit and ignore you . . . give the appearance he's too busy. He has his little game of trying to be important by saving money at our expense." I didn't reply.

"I can handle him," Chief Maclin added, holding up the brown paper bag and winking at me. "Kiss his ass a little and liquor 'im up and we'll get about half of what we ask for," he instructed.

*   *   *

"You seagoing candy asses think money grows on trees, don't you? You want everything but you really don't need shit," snarled the fat, potbellied, thin-haired lieutenant junior grade, grabbing my repair request package and throwing it on his desk. "You're late. You don't get nothin'."

I grew cold; something snapped. My insides played back every smart-ass remark from every sonovabitch who had ever bullied me and given me a hard time for no good reason. My bile rose. Before I exploded, I asked Chief Maclin to wait outside. I locked the door behind him. Deliberately I turned and walked slowly back to the repair officer's desk. "When's the last time you've been to sea, Mr. Fat-Ass Repair Officer?" I demanded in a low, cold voice. I hoped my hands weren't shaking.

He didn't answer. His face turned white, apparently from the ten-foot appearance I made leaning over his desk with his tie knotted in my hand pulling him toward me, his face inches from mine. "Let me tell you . . . you probably haven't been to sea for ten years because your lard ass won't fit through a hatch anymore."

He gurgled. His hand clutched mine, fingernails digging in, pulling, trying to loosen my grip on his tie. "We've been in heavy seas or moored to a godforsaken frozen pier for more than twenty days and I'm not in any fuckin' mood to take any shit from a shoreside, feather merchant staffie who seems to have forgotten what the navy is all about," I snarled, trying to ignore the putrid garlic smell emanating from his mouth. "We don't exist so you can have some cushy shore billet and give us shit every time we ask you to do your job.

"And your job, ASSHOLE, is to repair our ships. My ship."

My stomach churned. I imagined seeing the pores on the back of my hands push out tiny globs of sweat. I tightened my grip, demanding, "You're going to authorize every one of those fucking repairs, Mister, and I don't give a shit how you do it.

"It's reasonable, and goddamn it we've spent more than eighty hours putting it together . . . and not for you to throw on your fuckin' desk. And not for you to bad-mouth an officer in front of his chief. You can fuck with me, shit-for-brains, but you don't fuck with my ship or my men. DO YOU UNDERSTAND THAT, ASSHOLE?"

"I . . . I . . . ," he tried to say as his hand crept across the desk trying for the phone. I grabbed it, yanking the cord out of the wall. *I'd always wanted to do that.*

"And add this to your repairs," I shouted, raising the phone as if to smash him in the head.

"Ahhh . . . O . . . okay! Okay!" he managed to get out. I was choking him too much.

I let him loose, straightened his tie, and patted his collar back in place. He breathed heavily, gasping and wheezing as sweat oozed around his blood red face. "My ship thanks you for that, sir, and I apologize.

"I'm sorry for the misunderstanding. Can I buy you a beer or something? It's almost lunchtime; can I buy you lunch?" I fussed, trying to straighten his tie and put order back to his desk.

"I really feel bad about all this . . . tired, I guess, just too goddamn tired," I said in a genuinely conciliatory voice.

Christ, I've just roughed up another naval officer. What's happening to me? I'd never done anything like that in my life before Clements. Wow! Am I becoming a real asshole, or what? They shouldn't mess with my ship.

"Ah . . . no, no beer . . . no, no lunch. I . . . I'll get on these repairs right away, sir," the shaken repair officer whimpered, trying to sneak back into his senatorial mantle.

"Thank you, sir," I said, moving toward the door. Then I turned and walked back toward his desk. He winced and jumped away. I picked up the brown paper bag with the Johnnie Walker Black in it. "You'll be too busy for this," I said with a chuckle, easing the door shut behind me.

"C'mon, Chief, we're done here," I said to the waiting Maclin. He did not reply until we were outside. I handed him the brown paper bag. "A present from the fat one."

"Done, sir? Present? It usually takes a couple hours of begging and whining to get your package through. Done?"

"Well, Chief, I guess he was in a good mood today," I answered, walking away from the repair office into the yard.

"He's known for being a real hard-ass, sir. He didn't give you any shit?"

"Ensigns take shit, JGs don't," I said with a laugh, continuing down the bustling street to the piers. "I've never been to Japan, Chief. You?" I commented, wanting to change the subject.

"Yes, sir, this is my third trip."

"Sorta scary. You know, World War Two and all," I said.

He laughed, touching me on the shoulder. "First time for me I got scared too. I got in at the end of the war and never made it over here until

I was a chief. Mostly I was on the East Coast. Going back there as soon as I can. Better than the Pacific, I think."

We passed the repair facility restaurant, where the chief said they served a good corned beef sandwich and Japanese beer. We went in and I tried my first Kirin, a delicious, strongly bitter brew. My feeling of disloyalty to Anheuser-Busch allowed me to have only one.

I marveled at the repair facility's scaffolding as we headed back to the ship. It was constructed only of thin bamboo rods tied together by rope. Ingenious and cheap. Safe?

The Japanese workmen all wore open-collared white shirts and baggy knickers with wraparound leggings below them. They all looked alike; so did we to them most likely. The few women I saw wore washed-out brown or black robes and had their hair pulled back. I wondered if it was true what they said about Oriental women.

Unnerving me most were the surgical masks the older people wore. It gave them an out-of-this-world, mysterious look. I worried about which one would stab me in the back.

At 1330 we waited at the foot of the gang plank as the liberty party flooded ashore, the simplistic lecture on how to conduct oneself in a foreign country completely forgotten. At 1400 the XO scheduled a meeting of department heads. I announced that all work requests had been approved and work would commence on the night shift.

The captain looked at the XO, who shrugged and asked, "Request permission to send the department heads on shore leave, sir." Enlisted men went on liberty; officers went on shore leave. The distinction escaped me.

The captain motioned me to stay as the others left. "Okay, Don, this has never happened before and certainly not in the short time you were gone. What happened?" he asked.

"Nothing, Captain. We were lucky."

"Don?"

"Well, ah . . . Captain . . . I had to be, sorta . . . persuasive. And . . . ah, things, well, things got a little out of hand. I'd rather not go into it. Is it really important that you know? Captain?" I hoped to end the matter before I had to explain assault and battery.

He looked at me. I stared him directly in the eye. I felt the sweat forming on the palms of my hands. He said nothing. I couldn't stand that and he knew it. He was trying to wear me down with silence. I was no match for him.

"I'm the only one involved. Chief Maclin is clear; the ship is clear. Please let me slide on this one, Captain."

More silence. I vowed not to speak again until he answered. In what seemed like thirty minutes but was probably only five, he got up from the wardroom table and walked to the starboard door. Halfway through he turned, shook his head, smiled, and left.

The night was cool and clear, and Thieves Alley was as gaudy as the old salts said it was. Junk toys filled bins in open-air stalls; cheap silk embroidered jackets and kimonos hung from makeshift racks; hawkers at each stand demanded in their singsong voices that we buy from them. They were the most honest and had the best merchandise and the best prices. Especially for us.

Some shops sold furniture; some sold clumsy, old-fashioned bicycles; some sold exotic dried foods. But all the stalls looked the same. All the noises sounded alike. Bewildering amalgamations of multicolored hanging lights, funny-looking people, and strange cacophonous babbling left me confused and frightened.

Maybe I'm missing something.

Mr. Bluing was with me. We'd come ashore together, him saying he couldn't stand any more of the "college kids'" bullshit about sex and booze. We strolled down the narrow street filled with shouting, hurrying sailors and marines from the ships in port. They were in uniform by regulation; we were in civilian clothes for the same reason.

We stopped at a pharmacy replete with indistinguishable, odd-looking bottles and herbs. He put his hand gently to my chest as I started to walk in with him. "No, Don, please wait out here." Through the window I saw him purchase a large bottle of what looked like pills. A woman who appeared to be well over a hundred pitter-pattered into the back, then returned and handed him a multicolored wrapped package. I didn't question his purchase as he came out of the store, relief painted in his smile and twinkling eyes.

We passed small restaurants where outdoor plastic food models in racks showed what was being served inside. The models looked pasty and strange and destroyed my appetite even though I was hungry. Weeks of pent-up emotions and boredom spilled into the cool night air as drunken Americans wove through the streets, downing swigs from large bottles of beer and shouting lewd remarks at the merchants and women.

The Japanese lowly merchant class smiled and bowed, as if accepting their lot in life. The Shore Patrol moved silently through the crowd, quieting down the men when things threatened to get out of hand. The sailors were having a fine time, and I could just imagine the tales to be told throughout their lives and in Hometown, USA, on how much they drank and what a grand place "Yoko" was. I found it wearisome.

"Wanna go back to the O club for dinner, then turn in?" Mr. Bluing asked, frowning at the obscenities. Tired and bored, I agreed. He looked relieved. It wouldn't have been cool if I'd suggested it myself—being the first time in the Orient and opting for the O club. O clubs were the same all over the world, and having dinner there on my first night on the beach didn't quite fill the image I held of myself as a rakish, devil-may-care destroyer officer.

We turned down a side street to walk back to the base. The sudden isolation, the darkness with its cold and its strange sounds conjured up sights of stubby Japanese soldiers marching through China in December 1937. The rape of Nanking. Fear iced through me. I walked closer to Mr. Bluing. They would ambush us in the dark, and I'd pay dearly for buying all those war bonds, for destroying Nagasaki and Hiroshima, for firebombing Tokyo.

But in a minute, as we turned another corner, we were in the red-light district—the willow world, as they called it—with sailors and marines drinking and shouting. Saved.

The ladies stood demurely outside their small hovels, smiling at the huge, big-nosed Americans while avoiding their eyes and their smell. The hawkers were the soul of politeness, humbly requesting if the fine gentlemen would like to be with a geisha girl, very young, very pretty. A virgin. When a choice was made, the madam took the yen and presented the young lady. The girl would giggle softly and bow gracefully and slowly shuffle, prisoner-like in her tight kimono, into the hovel. The madam always smiled, no matter what the sailors shouted.

The small women, appearing no older than high school girls, smiled through delicately carved faces with intriguing almond eyes. Their demure and softly spoken words stood in sharp contrast to the bawdy American youths trying to proposition them. I had never seen true Oriental young women before, and I stared at the beauty they radiated.

I felt a stirring in my loins. Were there officer houses? I wondered as we walked away.

Casualty Control

U nder way," echoed the 1MC as the screws churned and Japan slipped astern. Large white clouds formed to the south, and the strengthening breeze across Tokyo Bay chopped the water slightly. *Haney* steamed a thousand yards behind.

The spring bearings, having all been rolled out and checked by our friendly repair officer, hummed coolly as they embraced and supported the spinning shafts. New ones hung from the bulkheads in the engine rooms, replacing those we had used. The high-pressure steam coursing through the plant hissed sweetly to my ears. With a full load of fuel and topped off with water, we were ready. I was home; I was in a world I understood.

"Captain," I said as he settled in his chair after breakfast. I had the morning watch on this clear and beautiful day with only a hint of coldness in the air. "I need some time for damage control and casualty control drills." He didn't answer as he scanned the horizon with his battered, very old-fashioned, navy issue 7x50 binoculars.

"My grandfather's," he said, looking at them fondly, stroking them as he might a woman's breast. He held them at arms' length, turning them in the sunlight as if in some pagan ritual to the god of the sea. He dangled them in front of me, teasing me because I had none, as if the very sight of them would console me, cleanse my soul, and make me a better naval officer.

"Very nice, sir. Request permission to hold engineering casualty control drills this afternoon," I said, a little bored with his grandfather's binoculars routine.

He made one more scan of the empty sea to ensure that the binoculars had not failed him, then he set them delicately into their special rack by his chair and leaned back expansively, exhaling a relieving breath. You'd think they were as fragile as Dresden dolls the way he handled them.

"My grandfather took 'em when he was an ensign, used 'em for fifteen years," he said proudly. "My daddy used 'em for sixteen then gave 'em to me when I took command. Great glasses . . . been around the horn many a time. Don't make 'em like these anymore." He sighed, at peace with the world.

Trying to put some levity in the conversation so I could press home my request for engineering drills, I said, "Sir, does that make you guilty of accepting stolen goods and your admiral father equally guilty of the same act and your admiral grandfather more guilty because of his misappropriation of government property?" I finished with a grin, then added: "And does it make me guilty of a misprison of a felony because I haven't reported it to my commanding officer?"

He whirled, poised to strike; his astonished eyes, glaring focused hate, cut deep into my soul. I felt the furies of hell rip into me as his eyes narrowed to a brutal, cutting stare, his nostrils white, his lips bloodless. He gasped, roaring in air through his clenched teeth as his white knuckles gripped the sides of his chair.

Then slowly as his color returned he exhaled, letting the venomous air dissipate his momentary madness. *I'd gone too far with my little joke.* I tried to grin harder. Finally, after an eon of not breathing, he said with a forced smile, "Anyone ever tell you you're an asshole, Sheppard?"

"The XO, sir . . . alludes to that often."

"I don't know why I put up with you," he muttered, his hands shaking as he picked up the morning's message file.

"Sir, about the drills?" I hazarded.

He deliberately put down the message file, turned to me—disgust chiseled in his face—and said, "Mr. Sheppard, you must be a very slow learner. You know how I feel about engineering drills. How many times must I tell you, they do more damage than good. Everything is working okay; don't mess with the plant." His voice was controlled, flat with menace.

"Captain, with all due respect—" *God, how I hated people who said that.* "—we're very weak in casualty control. Oh, sure, we can normal steam and fix things when they break down, and we have damn few casualties because Chief Maclin runs a good plant, but overall we are unsatisfactory, and unless we can practice, we're going to be in deep shit one day."

I paused to muster up more courage. We'd had this conversation three times in the past, and each time I'd come out scathed. "Only Chief Maclin is any good at it. The other two engineering watch officers have never done it, and I need the practice myself."

"Are you lecturing me on how to run MY ship, Mr. Sheppard?" he bellowed, rising slowly from his chair, his head weaving like a charmer's snake out of a basket.

Oh, God. "No, sir. I . . . I just feel strongly about this. The ship needs it."

He flashed his cobra-hooded head to me, his eyes cold black, screaming, "GODDAMN YOU, SHEPPARD! DON'T GIVE ME THAT 'THE SHIP NEEDS IT' SHIT. I DETERMINE WHAT THIS SHIP NEEDS, NOT YOU. UNDERSTAND THAT, MISTER . . . UNDERSTAND THAT!" I recoiled from the shrieking attack.

"Yes, sir . . . yes, sir," I whimpered, slinking out to the open bridge.

Ten minutes passed in silence. The steward brought coffee up to the captain. He seemed to have mellowed a bit; at least he wasn't breathing hard anymore and his face had almost returned to its normal color. He was wrong, and he knew it. I spent my time on the open bridge as far away from him as I could get.

Haney, assigned station two thousand yards astern, was five hundred yards too close and fifteen degrees off to port. Most sloppy of her. Our captain being senior and in tactical command was responsible for both ships. This meant that the captain, and by extension the OOD, had to monitor the steaming formation and call the shots. "Captain, *Haney*'s way off station, sir."

"WAY OFF? Mr. Sheppard, what kind of report is that?"

"Sir, *Haney* is off station five hundred yards ahead and one thousand yards to port."

"WELL?" he snapped.

"Signalman," I shouted, "make to *Haney,* station." The signal flag went up, flapping in the wind. In seconds *Haney's* answering flag went halfway up. "Execute," I ordered, and our flag flashed to the cross arm on the signal mast, then flashed down before the word cleared my mouth. But even before I signaled execution, I could see *Haney*'s bow swing to starboard. They'd been caught napping, and the dreaded station signal— which meant you are off station, assume assigned station immediately— came as an insult to the sharpness of the ship and its captain.

In five minutes I heard the clicking of the signal light. In another minute the signalman handed the captain a filled-out flashing-light message form. He read it, responding, "Umph."

He handed the message to me as he got up and walked toward the door. It read: "Am exercising at engineering drills. Regret not informing you." The signal lamp started clicking again and the captain waited.

"Request permission to act independently to exercise crew at general drills," the overly formal message came in. I guess *Haney*'s captain smarted at us sending him a reprimand: not the best form when two captains of nearly the same seniority steamed alone. Commander David Baker wasn't normally so formal, and if I hadn't pissed him off maybe the whole thing would have been handled in a friendly manner via our ship-to-ship radio. I felt ashamed and confused. Maybe the captain hadn't intended for me to send a station message. *Shit!*

I watched the captain's strained face as the XO appeared. He told the XO told that *Haney* was conducting independent drills and would remain in radar range. "How about us?" the captain asked the XO a little too loudly. "You think we should muster up some drills?"

"We've got GQ scheduled for this afternoon and a few man-overboard drills for later this morning. We could get a few . . . ," he said, then hesitated. I was sure he knew of the captain's outburst, ". . . a few . . ." He looked out to sea away from the captain's face and almost whispered, ". . . engineering drills in if you'd like." *Thank you, thank you, XO.*

The captain paused, looking around the silent bridge, each sailor's head turning away as the captain's death-beamed eyes approached. "Yes . . . splendid idea, XO. Don, here, and I were just chatting about that," he said, looking at me where I stood close enough to eavesdrop. "Give the deck to Mr. Chadwick, Mr. Sheppard, and go below to set things up," he added, nodding to my JOOD. Mr. Chadwick had once been an OOD but had his qualification removed because—he knew, just knew—the captain didn't like Harvard graduates.

"If you please, sir," I answered, trying to sound like an officer doing his duty and not like a child begging for candy. "I'll need Mr. Chadwick to conduct damage control drills at the same time."

The captain's icy stare froze me to the spot and stopped the circulation of my blood. "I guess, Mr. Sheppard," he whispered—I had to lean over to hear his words—"you'd like general quarters too?"

"Yes . . . yes, sir."

"Get off my bridge, Mr. Sheppard."

At 0900 the first drill kicked off. "Water out of sight, number one boiler, securing boiler now!" came the report from the forward fire room. A water-out-of-sight situation in a boiler could easily happen if the "checkman" didn't pay attention to his water level. It was the checkman's duty to ensure that the water level in the boiler stayed within a narrow range on his sight glass.

The condensed steam water entered the boiler at 750 pounds of pressure. The slightest inattention of the checkman could cause either low water, in which case the boiler would melt down if not instantly secured, or high water, which would feed raw water through the steam lines, smashing against the turbine blades and destroying them almost immediately. Since the checkman couldn't tell if there was too much or too little water in the boiler, the casualty demanded one response: wrap up the boiler instantly by shutting off the fuel.

With the boiler fires out, the huge main and auxiliary steam valves, which opened the boiler steam to the turbines, had to be manhandled closed. This took two men in backbreaking torture to do it fast. The feed-water check valves, which in reality were just huge eighteen-inch faucets, had to be closed as fast as possible to keep the high-pressure water from filling up the steam drum and flooding out the turbines and main condensers.

"Cross connect the plant," Chief Maclin ordered quietly in the voice of a man who knew what he was doing. Engineers throughout all four of the huge engineering spaces hurriedly closed down the steam valves from the forward fire room while at the same time opening other huge valves that cut in steam from the aft fire room, connecting it to the turbines in the forward engine room.

The RPMs on the starboard engine increased as the turbines picked up the new steam. Number one main generator in the forward engine room faltered for a moment; the lights blinked once, then the generator jumped back to speed as the steam from aft cut in. I could see from the gauges that number three boiler steamed at a much higher rate to feed both of the main engines and their accessory pumps.

Chief Maclin winked at me. "Cross connected, sir."

I passed it on to the bridge, receiving a "well done" from the talker. I wondered if it had come from the captain as I turned back to Chief Maclin, saying, "Light off number one, Chief . . . split the plant."

He looked at me astonished that I'd given him a technical order. He paused for a moment, staring at me as if all my work in trying to take control of the main plant away from him had suddenly struck home. Looking him straight in the eye, I repeated the order. I wished I could have read his mind. "Aye . . . aye, aye, sir," he finally said, turning away in resignation.

It was my turn now. I had to show them I knew the plant and could perform as well as any of them. It was important to me. Hesitantly I said, "I'll run the next one, Chief. Please set it up." Then turning to the general quarters watch team, I announced, "Sheppard here, I've got the watch." Astonished faces looked at me, then to the chief. He nodded yes. It pissed me off. *I don't need your fuckin' endorsement. Goddamnit, I'm the chief engineer—not you.*

I saw in his face the subdued grin as he figured I'd screw up and he'd have to rescue me as he'd done a dozen young punk officers in the past.

"Make it easy, Chief. You know how we new kids are," I said, trying to calm my nerves. I hoped it hadn't sounded like a whimper. Frightened with the aspect of failing in front of my men, I prayed that the manuals I'd memorized on how to conduct these drills were true.

They'd all seemed so logical when I studied them, but I tried not to let logic impede reality as I ordered the chief to set up a drill to surprise me. My armpits gushed sweat; my eyes couldn't focus. I wanted to grab the note from my pocket on which I had written down the various steps to take for each type of casualty. I fingered it, hoping its knowledge would rub off onto my hands and find its way to my panicked brain.

The chief whispered something to Machinist Mate First Class Langston, who disappeared down to the lower level. My eyes strained to encompass every gauge on the throttle board. The throttle board here in main control duplicated the gauges in both fire rooms and in the after engine room. "Vacuum's dropping in number two main condenser," I said matter-of-factly to the chief. He gave no reply.

Seconds later the after engine room reported vacuum dropping and the second of their two air ejectors added on the line. But still the vacuum dropped. I reached for the handle on the engine order telegraph and rang port engine ahead flank, then rapidly pulled the handle back to port engine ahead one-third. This signaled the bridge that we had trouble, and ahead one-third on the port engine was the best bell we could answer. The starboard engine continued at ahead standard, fifteen knots.

"Number two main condenser has clogged strainers," Machinist Mate First Class Summers, in charge of the after engine room, reported over the phone. "Estimate three zero minutes to clear." The main condensers were large tanks about six feet high, ten feet wide, and twenty-four feet long; they took the remaining steam, after it passed through the main engine turbines, and, by the use of cold seawater running through thousands of small tubes inside them, condensed the steam to water.

With the strainers clogged, there wasn't enough cooling water to condense the steam that created the vacuum. Clogged strainers were simulated by closing down the massive seawater intake valves.

"Very well," I answered, "keep me informed."

"Who are you? Where's the chief?" Summers questioned over the 21MC.

"Sheppard. I'm running the drills."

"Oh?" came the reply just as, "Water out of sight, number three boiler . . . shutting down NOW," filled the air from the fireman, who was in constant communication with all the other engineering spaces via sound-powered phone.

I looked at number three boiler's falling steam gauge for what seemed an hour but was really only seconds before commanding, "Cross connect main steam." And to show the chief I knew what I was doing, I added, "Cross connect main feed, cross connect auxiliary steam, cross connect DA tank feed." For good measure, I said, "Cross connect main drains." *Who needed a crib sheet?* I looked at Chief Maclin, expecting to see him bow in respect, but all he did was point his first finger upward. *Shit, the bridge.*

"Inform the bridge we've lost number three boiler and are cross connecting now," I said to the throttle man connected to the lee helm on the bridge by sound-powered phone.

Chief Maclin picked up a phone, but I couldn't hear what he said. Then from the after engine room via the talker: "Number two main generator has kicked off the line. Losing all electrical power." I waited for the emergency diesel generator to automatically kick in, as it should do when power from the main generators failed. Nothing. I looked at the chief. He shrugged.

Shouting to the electrician on the main switchboard, I ordered him to pick up the electrical load from aft. In seconds we had power. "Number three boiler inspected satisfactory," came the report from the after fire room.

"Light off number three boiler and bring it on the line when ready. After engine room acknowledge," I added. In reality the boiler came off the line so fast that the steam pressure dropped very little, and it took only a short time to have it back on the line again. It took longer though as the men grew tired from the backbreaking effort of opening and closing the mammoth steam and feed-water valves.

The chief walked over to me and tapped me on the shoulder. I noticed his khakis were still perfectly starched and pressed, in sharp contrast to my bedraggled, sweat-stained clothes. He pointed upward again with his first finger. *Shit! I'd forgotten to call the bridge again.*

From the corner of my eye I saw the chief pick up the phone. I held up my hand. "Wait, Chief, let the plant settle down a bit first." He put the phone back, grinning as he nodded concurrence. "Chief, did the after emergency diesel generator kick in when we lost number two generator?"

"No, sir."

"You know why?"

"No, sir." He winked, noncommittal.

I asked the talker to have Mr. Chadwick report to me in main control. The talker passed the word, and in five minutes Chadwick casually arrived. "What drills are you holding?" I asked.

"Oh, we're giving lectures on various phases and contingencies of modern destroyer damage containment and control, sir," he answered, emphasizing the "sir" as if he were a new recruit in boot camp. I choked down my desire to smash him in the mouth for giving me such a trite and bullshit answer, but I ignored it. *Later.*

"Mr. Chadwick, when our main generators kick off the line, what's supposed to happen?" I asked sharply, pointing to number one main generator.

"Get dark?" he suggested with a chuckle.

I took a step toward him, fire in my eyes. Chief Maclin moved in between us, blocking my path as he brushed against me. "Oh, sorry, sir," he said, giving me a chance to recover.

"No, Mr. Chadwick, *your* emergency diesel generators are supposed to automatically start and pick up the load."

"I knew that, sir."

"When's the last time you witnessed them doing so, Mr. Chadwick?"

"Well, never actually, but the chief says . . ." I turned away from him, reaching over and hitting down the governor control on number one main generator. It kicked off the line, as it should have. We went dark; alarms squealed and in a second the battery-powered battle lanterns hanging in strategic locations around the engine room automatically came on, projecting an eerie, spotlighting effect. "Don't pick up power from aft," I shouted to the electrician on the board. We stood there.

"Steam pressure on number one is dropping, sir," the throttle man shouted. "I can't maintain speed." Chief Maclin reached up and rang the starboard engine order telegraph handle to flank and then to stop.

"They're shutting down number one boiler," the talker reported. "Loss of fuel oil pressure."

During the time we had waited for Mr. Chadwick, I had the chief tell the forward fire room to switch over to their electric fuel oil pump and not to use the steam-driven ones. He understood what I was doing. If we were using the steam pumps, the loss of electrical power would have no effect on the boiler. Letting the plant go dead would be a dramatic lesson for the DCA. I hoped.

I was betting that if number two diesel didn't start, there would be a high probability that number one wouldn't start either. Chief Maclin looked at me, shrugging as he nodded understanding.

Langston finally spoke in a hurried voice as if he had missed something. "Cross connect, sir, cross connect?"

"Negative," I shouted, imagining the captain going wild with the gyrocompass power-failure alarm screaming at him on the bridge and with no power and no radar and those hated drills continuing and continuing.

"Did you hear any emergency generators start up, Mr. Chadwick? Did the diesels kick over when the depth charge dropped and we lost the load?"

He looked around nervously for an ally, but only my spotlighted face glared at him. "No, sir," he answered, slumping back against the ladder to the main deck, his bravado seeping away.

"The boilers can't operate without electricity, Mr. Chadwick," I lied. "And because you're such a fuckup, Mr. Chadwick, if we were in battle and *your* generators didn't work, we could die. For want of a nail, Mr. Chadwick, want of a nail." He looked at me, looked around, then made a move to slink away. "STAY RIGHT THERE, MR. CHADWICK!" He jerked to a stop.

"Electrician, pick up the load from aft," I ordered as naturally as if I'd been doing it for years. Then, turning, I told Langston to bring the generator back on the line as soon as number one boiler was back up. I didn't want the engineers to go through another cross-connecting ordeal.

"You're dismissed, Mr. Chadwick." He looked at me venomously as he started up the ladder. The rest of us stood in strained silence for the fifteen minutes it took the forward plant to become operational.

I picked up the phone to the bridge. "Captain, we've completed the drills for today. Request permission to secure." I felt good, but as I started to leave, my eyes focused nervously on the huge, perhaps two feet in diameter, flange that connected the main steam line into number one turbine. The insulation lagging to hold in the heat made it look twice its size. *Odd, why should a steam flange make me feel uneasy?*

The 1MC blared out, "Set condition Yoke; I say again, set condition Yoke." We waited while the Z watertight doors and hatches were undogged and opened. Condition Zebra was the maximum watertight closure for the ship and was set at general quarters when ready to go to battle.

It was almost impossible to move around the ship with Zebra set; permission had to be obtained from the bridge every time you wanted to open a door. But it made the ship much harder to sink. The less restrictive condition Yoke was set for normal steaming—movement was tolerable at condition Yoke. In port, condition X-ray opened the ship almost completely. The old memorized ditty crossed my mind: "X by day, Y by night, Z when in the thick of fight."

My heart beat euphorically fast. I had the feeling of being in charge, of having won, of being the captain of this team.

It hadn't always been this way. My restless mind drifted back to the dull autumn skies of the Midwest and Mrs. Washington, my sixth-grade teacher at the Nameoki Grade School—bless her heart.

I shuddered at the ruthless memory. We were forming softball teams to play against other local schools. As always two of the biggest and most athletic boys won the elections for team captains. They chose up in turn. Each got to nine, with only Hector Miller and me remaining to be chosen.

Neither team captain nor their "chosen ones" wanted us. Hector Miller was crippled and walked with a severe limp. I was Fat Donny, the incompetent.

Mrs. Washington insisted we be chosen, but the teams argued adamantly against it. They couldn't possibly win *anything* if "Hector the Crip" and "Donny the Fat" were on their side. Mrs. Washington agreed with the wisdom but wrestled with the problem of what to do with us. She finally smiled with an idea and formed a third team, asking Hector and me to elect a captain.

I won by giving Hector half of my lunch. His family was so poor, his skimpy lunches never satisfied him. Then I chose up sides. I chose Hector but didn't want to. Mrs. Washington made me.

We were the third team, but we were never scheduled to play because Mrs. Washington was the head scheduler. At the end of the season, due to an anomaly in counting points, we came out ahead in the interschool competition. They counted how many games a team lost. We never played any, never lost any, therefore had the best "nonloss" record.

The school district awarded small trophy cups for each "winning" team member. Mrs. Washington, privately—may the gods smile on her—gave one to Hector and one to me. Hector kept his. I threw mine down a street drain, crying for the humiliation of it.

The chief and I sat in the engineering office, the thick smoke from his large cigar and my pungent pipe tobacco filling the small, austere log room–engineering office. I glanced around at the several technical books and blueprints, and the engineering logs from the spaces, as I tried settling down before going back up to the bridge to resume my watch. I didn't want to report to the captain, not quite yet. Nor did I want to talk to the chief. My outburst with Chadwick shamed me. Bad form to chew out a fellow officer in front of the men. Very bad form.

"Sir," Chief Maclin said, balancing his cup of coffee as the ship turned, heeling over to port. "I'd say you did real well on the drills today. I was really throwing the shit to you." His words sounded hollow.

"Thank you, Chief," I answered, pleased that he said anything at all. I reached over to close the door, giving me a few more seconds to recover from the Chadwick incident. "Chief, don't shit me. It was a piece of cake today. We were at general quarters and fully manned down below. You've obviously trained your men well and they knew exactly what to do. I noticed you had men stationed at every key valve, with backups at the cross connecters."

Chief Maclin, gazing at the glowing ash of his cigar, said nothing. "You set me up today, Chief. You wired this whole thing to make it look good and get me off the captain's ass to hold drills." I paused, relighting my pipe.

"I know, Chief, that drills are a pain in the ass and mighty hard on the troops. I know there's a high probability of damaging the plant when we're screwing around with it. I know the whole plant is a delicately balanced machine that takes steady steaming and dedication to get the best out of it. But . . . !"

I refused to look at the inch-and-a-half-long ash on his cigar. I could hardly breathe in the dense smoke. Maclin was playing that old, supposedly distracting trick of creating a diversionary scene of a too-long-to-be-natural cigar ash.

"But, Chief, we had the first team down there today, and rarely will the first team be on duty when the shit drops."

"You're right, sir. I know that, and you know that, but no one else seems to give a shit-damn about it, and the old man is dead set against drills.

"We heard about your little drama on the bridge this morning—actually a play-by-play description from the lee helm." He paused, knocking off the now two-inch-long ash into an ashtray. The scorched, straightened-out paper clip inserted to support the ash still glowed red at the burning end of the cigar. He looked at me, pissed that his trick hadn't worked. I smiled.

"Chief, I know I've got a problem with the old man, but I'll be able to take care of that—the diesel generators will be my opening. But let's say I get permission to hold more drills . . . what would you suggest?" The only thing he could suggest would be to run the drills against the watch sections on a surprise, random basis.

He paused, considering, then admitted, "I'd run the drills against the watch sections on a surprise, random basis." He grinned and excused himself. "Good luck, sir."

I'd won.

Casualty

I waited in my office for a few more minutes after the chief left. I reveled in my ability to hold the drills. I wanted to internalize my feelings before facing the captain lest my self-satisfaction burst forth in bragging. I ran a pipe cleaner through my pipe, then filled it again. I liked to watch the smoke curl up on the first two or three initial puffs. Smoking a pipe made me feel cool. I always wanted to be cool but never felt I carried it off very well.

I looked at the picture of the man for whom the ship was named—a dead hero, after whom all destroyers were named. *Major Henshaw, you were a marine. I was a marine once. A reserve.*

I chuckled at the thought. Private First Class Donald D. Sheppard, USMCR, defender of freedom, guardian of the peace and the Western concept of democracy. A sham. The marine reserve unit based in Venice, Illinois, just south of Granite City on the way to St. Louis, advertised in the high schools for volunteers—if you were seventeen. My buddy Bobby Manning and I joined, reasoning we'd get a uniform and a little extra money. And with the uniform and little extra money we could go to St. Louis, pick up girls, and get laid. Everyone knew that the big-city girls in St. Louis put out faster than the ones from Granite City and certainly faster than the prudes of Nameoki. Bobby and I wondered why it didn't work for us.

The bridge messenger popped his head into the engineering office, saying, "Mr. Bluing would like to know when you're coming back up on watch, sir."

Fuck Mr. Bluing. That asshole probably wants to get to his stateroom to rub his nose in private. "My respects to Mr. Bluing, please inform him I'll be up momentarily," I answered very formally. *Doesn't anyone understand the importance of a properly running plant?*

I returned to reminiscing. The marine reserve unit met every Tuesday night. We marched around the football field once, did the manual of arms for ten minutes, and then watched John Wayne movies until ten o'clock. Bobby and I, having been Civil Air Patrol "cadets" for several years, knew how to do all these things, so in a month we were promoted to PFC and squad leaders.

High-ranking squad leaders. Surely now we'd get laid. But no. Even smoking my pipe didn't help. To make up for it, we'd come back from our abortive trips to St. Louis via the "Valley," a red-light district under the "Free Bridge" in East St. Louis. Here, for a quarter, one could enjoy the delights of sex without bullshit. For twice that amount, precoital, oral services were available. Fifty cents and your right hand got a rest, and you slept well that night.

I left the office and met Langston just coming up the ladder from main control. "Sir . . . Mr. Sheppard, can I talk to you a moment?" he almost whispered, conspiratorially swinging his head slowly from side to side as if ensuring no one could overhear.

"Of course, Langston. Your boys did real well today. Thanks for your help. What can I do for you?"

"That's what I want to say . . . and," he glanced about again as if he'd be struck dead if caught talking to an officer, much less the chief engineer. "I . . . I never thought officers knew shit . . . excuse me, sir, anything about the plant, much less the drills. We—you know, me and my guys—well . . . we just wanna say you did well, you did okay."

My mind instantly told me not to dance a jig. Not to hug Langston. Be stoic. Do not smile. Be the iron man. Be cool. I couldn't answer for a moment, trying to control the wild excitement in my heart. I'd won their respect in their territory. The spring bearing incident hadn't been good enough; any fool can help change a spring bearing. But to control the plant—that's what they understood.

I offered my hand, smiling, playing it cool as I thanked him. But now, I could never do it again. It saddened me for an instant to realize I'd trapped myself in the leadership paradox. I'd done it and done it well, but it was their job and if I did it again I would be taking away from them. Too bad for me; I had enjoyed it.

"We're going to be running more drills with just the watch sections, Langston. Everyone will get a lot of practice. But please don't say anything until the chief can set it up. Okay?" He answered with a smile as he dropped back down into his magic world of heat, grease, and heartache.

I thought of Bobby Manning again as I headed up to the bridge. I joined the navy in 1948 and left the unit. Bobby stayed on and went to work at the steel mills. Then came the Korean War and the unit was activated with only a two-week summer session in Camp Lejeune, North Carolina, to pass as training. Bobby had written me on what a joke it was, saying they did nothing but watch movies and go on liberty when they weren't on KP.

After activation they had a month of advance infantry school at Camp Pendleton in California en route to the Chosen Reservoir, Korea.

Bobby came back a staff sergeant. Seventy-five percent of the unit came back dead. They died in the frozen waste around the reservoir and on the long retreat south. A high price for a uniform and a little extra money.

"I have the watch, sir." I saluted the agitated Mr. Bluing as he turned to inform the bridge crew. I repeated it to them that I had the watch and said it once again to the captain just as Mr. Bluing finished telling him the same thing. This ritual was necessary to ensure that everyone knew, without doubt, who was in charge. The JOOD, Mr. Chadwick, barely acknowledged my presence, his eyes avoiding mine. I'm sure he hated my guts.

"How'd it go?"

"Fine, Captain, thank you."

"Sir, signal from *Haney,* 'Request permission to rejoin,'" the talker from combat announced. I glanced at the captain; he nodded yes. I ordered it executed.

God, I'd love to be the captain of a destroyer and wear that hat with all the gold braid on it. Scrambled eggs, they call it. I want one.

"Request permission to light off superheaters, Captain?" I asked.

"Permission granted," he answered, and I nodded to Mr. Chadwick to pass the order to main control.

Standing on the open bridge, the captain and I watched *Haney* approaching from eight miles out. "Let's turn toward her and shorten the distance a bit, Mr. Sheppard. And bend on some speed so we can get this over with before lunch."

"Aye, sir. Mr. Chadwick, if you would, please make a course for *Haney*. Combat, make to *Haney* we're turning to shorten the distance; when we're two miles from her we'll come to new course of . . ." I looked at the captain questioningly; he smiled and said 210. ". . . 210," I repeated.

I glanced at Mr. Chadwick, who was doing nothing. "Mr. Chadwick, why aren't you turning?"

"SIR! I'm waiting for a recommended course from combat."

"Come out here, Mr. Chadwick. Do you see *Haney* there?" I said, pointing to the small dot hulling up on the horizon.

"Yes, sir, of course."

"Well, a good way to join up is to head for her and adjust as necessary as you get closer. Combat can't help you when both of us are moving in such an undefined way. Put your goddamned bow ahead of her and let's go."

His look chilled me as he ordered the rudder over standard and the talker reported, "Combat regrets cannot work out a course until one of us steadies up."

"Bridge concurs," I answered just as I heard Mr. Chadwick order ahead full on both engines. He was acting on the captain's previous statement of bending on some more speed. "Mr. Chadwick, has main control reported superheaters lit off yet?"

Mr. Chadwick glanced at the lee helm, who answered disgustedly, "No," then added, "No, SIR!"

"Fifteen knots, Mr. Chadwick," I admonished. He complied with a sheepish grin, and someone on the watch team snickered. In the last few minutes he'd made two bad mistakes: first, not turning immediately toward *Haney;* and second, kicking up the speed when the engineers were trying to light off superheaters.

At too high a speed, the pressurizing air being rammed into the boiler from outside would blow out the lighting-off torches, making it impossible for the superheater furnaces to be lit off. These were mistakes only brand-new ensigns fell prey too. Mr. Chadwick had been onboard for almost two years.

After *Haney* joined, the captain and I went down to lunch. He was in rare good spirits, and his mood permeated the wardroom as we ate his favorite dish of Filipino chicken adobe. The XO added to the jovial atmosphere, breaking his normal stoic and pessimistic outlook.

Yet something ellusive bothered me; I couldn't shake it. Excusing myself, I rose, looking around like a trapped animal; a slight shudder, a change in the sound of the ship echoed through my brain. The captain looked at me, then at the XO.

The captain's phone buzzed. It was the phone on the table leg at the captain's place at the head of table. The ship heeled over to starboard. "We've lost number one boiler; we're hauling out to starboard," I heard him repeat from the OOD as I hurried out of the wardroom. "They're wrapping up the forward plant . . ." followed my ears as I shut the door behind me.

An hour later I reported to a very unhappy captain. "Yes, sir . . . we've torqued down the flange bolts, and I'm reasonably sure it'll hold okay."

"What caused it?"

"I would say, sir, the drills . . . the rapid heating and cooling as we brought the boilers on the line and took them off probably distorted the flange enough that a small leak appeared." He stared at me with his horrible know-it-all sneer but said nothing.

"I'm sure once the superheaters got up to full temperature the flange would have expanded and sealed the leak, but I didn't want to take the chance that it would. That's why I asked to repair it now, before we join up with the squadron."

"Anyone hurt?"

"No, sir, but Fireman Philips almost got it. He was on top of the throttle board repairing a gauge line when it went."

"Could you have cross connected?"

"We did cross connect auxiliary steam and picked up the electrical load aft. But no, not the main steam, sir, because the leak turned out to be on the flange connecting straight to the turbines. We couldn't find it at first; you know how high-pressure steam acts—shoots out with a vicious cutting force and you can't see it until it vaporizes some distance from the leak, and you can't really tell where it's coming from. You can't see steam. Goddamned dangerous. That steam can cut through a four by four if it's in the way—"

"I do know a little about engineering plants, Mr. Chief Engineer," he interrupted, gritting his teeth.

"Yes, sir. But I'm afraid the situation was handled rather poorly, Captain. We didn't wrap up the plant fast enough because they wasted time looking for the leak. We could have lost that flange for good with a cut so deep that a new gasket wouldn't seal it. Then, only a shipyard or tender could have fixed it."

"Who had the watch?" he asked, cross-examining me. His face relaxed a little but not much.

"Langston, sir, but it's not his fault. He's never conducted casualty control drills before. Quite frankly, he screwed up by not shutting down the plant sooner and wrapping up number one boiler. He should have reduced pressure immediately and tracked the vapor trail as it fell back to the leak. It's rare that you'll find the exact location of a leak under full boiler pressure. It wasn't much of a leak."

I paused to catch my breath; I was talking too fast, trying to stave off the captain's anger. The XO and Mr. Bluing stood next to us on the open bridge, listening but not commenting.

"You say, Don—" *Don—he's not angry anymore.* "—that the drills could have caused it. How so?" the captain asked, lighting a cigarette and offering one to me. *How so? Didn't I just explain that?*

I shook my head no to the cigarette but wished my pipe were handy as I continued. "Well, sir, the way I see it, we steam normally all the time and the plant is warmed up and cooled slowly. When we were rapidly cutting the boilers in and out, the thermal shock to the system reached out for the weakest point, which was the flange in this case."

The captain glanced at the XO, who shrugged his shoulders, not knowing. Mr. Bluing listened only for the education. The phone talker called out, "From Chief Maclin for Mr. Sheppard, request permission to light off number one boiler in thirty minutes."

The captain's scowl near roasted my face. His most sarcastic tone whipped into me: "They now ask you, Mr. Sheppard—" *Shit, Mr. Sheppard again.* "—for permission to light off boilers when we're under way. Do you want my chair and maybe my sea cabin next?"

I knocked into the XO as I instinctively stepped back, stammering, "Well . . . well . . . no, sir, they're just a little confused down there right now. It's . . . it's the only real casualty they've had in a long time. They were just checking with me, sir, that's all, Captain."

He stood silently for a moment, then let out a sigh as his face mellowed, the awesome responsibility of command showing plainly as he asked, knowing full well what the answer would be, "What do you want to do, Mr. Sheppard?"

I paused, glancing at the XO, hoping for support. He shrugged, showing no change of expression. That was all the help I was going to get from him. Mr. Bluing didn't even give that much. Hesitantly, I answered, "We should hold drills by watch sections, not the full GQ team. That's probably when a casualty's going to happen anyway, and the watch officer must know how to handle it without waiting for Chief Maclin or me."

"Or—you?" the captain snapped. "How *much* experience do you have, Mr. Sheppard?"

"Well, Captain, very little. Some in Engineering Officer School and some today."

"Today? Who ran the drills today?" he asked, his tone rising slightly on the word "today."

"Except for the first one, Captain, I did."

He looked at the XO, then back to me. He opened his mouth but nothing came out. "You did, Mr. Sheppard?" the XO asked, more rhetorically than not.

"Well done, Don," the captain said with a smile.

The Chat

The confined stuffiness of the XO's stateroom churned my stomach, heralding the onslaught of seasickness, but I had to do it. My resolve to fire Chadwick wavered as I faced the XO in his paperwork kingdom. The XO ran the ship administratively and suffered the multifarious tasks that went with it. The captain fought the ship.

On all matters dealing with equipment and readiness, you went to the captain; on all others you went to the XO. But you'd damn well better keep the XO informed on what you tell the captain. I'd much rather deal with the captain, but this was the XO's responsibility, and it was up to him to take it to the old man.

Damage control didn't seem that important, sitting here in the midst of the administrative dragon the XO faced every minute of every day. Chadwick was a fun guy to be around, and socially I liked him. He organized the wardroom parties and was always ready with a laugh or a joke to cheer someone up. Though his jokes were mostly derogatory to the navy or to the captain or the XO, they were usually true, and I laughed with the rest of them.

Firing Chadwick would make me even less popular in the wardroom, but he had to go.

I wanted to belong in the wardroom, I wanted to be one of the boys, one of the carefree junior officers who talked about the good old college days and the parties. I wanted the academy officers to accept me as one of their own, not some old mustang who didn't know enough to care about anything but the ship and the navy.

I wanted a college degree so I could casually bring up esoteric theories or little-known historical facts during idle conversation. I wanted to have friends—friends just like Chadwick had, even though he was incompetent.

The ever-patient XO leaned back in his chair, tamping his favorite tobacco, Granger, into his pipe. He offered the pouch to me and sat silently as I filled my pipe. Heavy smoke clouded his stateroom, and I heard Mr. Bluing, a nonsmoker, cough from across the passageway. The XO, with a raised eyebrow, reached over and swung his door shut as I sat fidgeting on his couch, which converted to a bed.

The ship sounded different up here so far forward of the engine rooms; it unnerved me. I felt a loss of communication with my plant, with the ship. I felt alone. I wanted to make up some plausible reason for bothering the XO and leave. But I couldn't turn back now.

Withering under his silent stare, my mouth dry, I finally stammered, "XO, Mr. Chadwick . . . just isn't cutting it, and I want him out of damage control . . . and the engineering department," I said in a voice squeaking out too fast and at too high a pitch.

The XO took a long drag from his pipe, then tapped down the tobacco with an ornate tamper before he spoke. I hated his technique of not speaking immediately and making you sweat his reply. I resented him doing it to me as if I didn't know the tactic. I knew he thought his silence would draw forth further words from me. He was wrong.

My pipe burned down before he answered. His deep, resonant voice quivered a bit, showing his displeasure in having to deal with this, although I'm sure he knew it was coming. "How long, Don, has Mr. Chadwick been the DCA?"

"I don't know—six, maybe seven months," I answered, guessing at the number.

"How long have you been the chief engineer?"

"A little over a month," I replied, irritated at the cat and mouse game. The XO tapped his pipe out in an ashtray made from a five-inch brass shell casing. I'd admired it before and wanted one. It looked salty. He filled and lit his pipe again, this time not offering to share his Granger.

"Mr. Chadwick has been the DCA for more than a year. How do you think it would reflect on the captain and me if we fired him now? How about on your buddy Mr. Bernard? Relieving an officer for cause is enough to finish a man in the navy. To relieve an officer under any cloud, no matter how disguised, is enough to doom him to purgatory. Word gets out, you know."

"Yes, sir . . . but—"

"What's the matter with him?"

"He's lazy and doesn't give a shit for the ship. He lets his chief do all the work and doesn't even check on it."

"Much like any junior officer, I'd say," he replied as his eyes passed across my face as if he were trying to define what I was saying.

"He's been in the navy for almost two years. You can't really call him a *junior* officer anymore. Hell, he's not even an OOD yet."

"He used to be. A pretty good one, actually, but he made a bad mistake and the captain relieved him," the XO answered, fending off my thrust. "Have you tried working with him?"

"Well . . . no, I've been pretty busy with the main plant. I've sorta left him alone. But he should know his job."

"Have you tried to help him?"

"Well, no . . . the main plant—"

"Does Chief Maclin know his job?" he asked in his low, drawn-out voice that drove me crazy.

"Well, sure he does . . . oh, not as well as he could. I—"

"You're pretty fast to draw and shoot, Don. Is everyone incompetent in your book?"

I felt the lash. "No! Of course not, XO, but this is a special case. Damage control is very important. It needs—"

"It needs leadership and guidance, Mr. Sheppard. Something you have failed to give," he said, his voice barely above a whisper.

"Failed to give? What do you mean, failed to give?" I barked back as blood pumped to my skin and the hairs on my arms stood out. He ignored me, saying nothing as he filled and lit his pipe again, waiting for me to settle down. He blew a puff toward me, the sweet smell tingling my nostrils.

"Have you?"

"Well, no, XO . . . the main plant. I wanted—"

"Glory, Mr. Sheppard? Glory is what you wanted! There's nothing exciting about damage control, is there? There's no flash . . . no grandstand for you to play to. Is there?"

"XO, I—"

He cut me off again, his voice now louder, more clipped as he pointed a finger at me. "You're an awesome juggernaut of drive and efficiency. You make us mere mortals uncomfortable, even afraid. I've seen your enlisted service record . . . yeah, I know we're not supposed to, but I've got a friend at BUPERS. Youngest chief in the navy, huh? That took drive.

"What did you sacrifice for it? I read your commendation letters, the many for outstanding leadership, for splendid operational performance, for superb technical qualifications and indefatigable efforts. *Indefatigable*, no less."

He paused, his eyes boring into me like those of a pit viper ready to strike. My lips were sealed—welded together. I could say nothing. I didn't want to say anything.

"Cut us some slack, Don, cut us some slack."

A yellow pencil rolled across his desk as the ship gently swayed from side to side. I thought about being seasick as I watched the name on the pencil—Ticonderoga—first appear rolling clockwise, then counterclockwise. Back and forth, back and forth, filling my mind with all I wanted to think about. I could get up in a second and say excuse me and leave. I could just get up and leave—if I wanted to. If I could. I wished I'd brought my tobacco, but I wasn't going to ask him for any.

I couldn't look him in the eye. I glanced away to prevent it. In a few seconds when I could speak, I said, "Those letters don't mean anything, XO. I don't know why people write them. They don't mean anything." But I lied; they really did. I cherished each one as a priest cherishes his Bible.

He looked at me with saddened eyes. "Ease up, Don. Ease up! These people will be your friends . . . if you let them."

"XO, You don't—"

"Understand? But I do, Don, I do. You worked miracles with the ETs. They were a downtrodden lot, sloppy and irresponsible due to, I'm ashamed to admit, a lack of leadership and guidance . . . someone caring. You provided that, and when you contradicted the captain on it, we realized our shortcomings. You did that for them, Don. You did it for us. Can you offer any less to Mr. Chadwick?"

He offered his tobacco as he poured a cup of coffee for himself and me. It was cold. I didn't care and he pretended not to. He gave me a sugar cube. I didn't use cream anymore. "It's not important that you've never been to college." *How did he know that bugged me?* "Hell, Don, in a couple of years the navy'll send you to postgraduate school in Monterey for a bachelor's. Then you can go back a few years later and get a master's. It's easy, Don, just play it cool. I'll help you."

"XO, I—"

"Chief Maclin came to see me yesterday."

"Why?" I responded too quickly, instantly regretting it.

"There now, Don, it's part of my job to talk to the senior enlisted people," he answered, patronizing me. "He wanted to tell me how much he respects you for your work in the spaces. He's proud to see an officer getting his hands dirty. Yes, Don, Chief Machinist Mate Ernest B. Maclin, USN, with twenty-two years in this man's navy, is a Sheppard convert, along with the sonarmen and the ETs. And I might add the bridge team, who think you run a great watch—nice and easy, no bullshit, no yelling."

"Chief Maclin?"

"Yes. It impressed the hell out of him to see you trace out the steam lines and drain lines just like a new fireman would have to do when he comes aboard for duty. He said he'd never seen an officer do that before."

"Well, more should; the plant is very weak. In the bilges we have—"

"To settle down . . . all in good time, Don. And though Maclin says he doesn't know what happened at the Yoko repair facility between you and the repair officer, it sure impressed him."

"XO, I—"

"When do you sleep? You're a powerful influence for good on this ship. Don't burn out. My chief yeoman tells me you've checked out and read all the ship's regulations and all the tactical manuals. Commendable, Don. I must do that sometime. When's the last time you sat down with your brother officers and watched a movie or just shot the shit and made jokes about the captain and XO?"

"Well, I—"

"Now what was it, Mr. Sheppard, that you wanted to see me about?"

"Well, sir, I . . . I . . . just wanted to borrow some tobacco."

He tossed me an unopened pouch as I excused myself, backing out the door. He had bared my soul, cutting deep to where the goblins lived in the dark jungles of my mind. He was right, and I realized why I wanted Chadwick to leave in disgrace.

He represented what I had always wanted to be but never achieved.

Sheppard's boot camp class in 1948. (Author is in second row from top, second from right.) *Courtesy USN*

Deck hands from first division.

A destroyer with a staging over its side while painting at sea.

A destroyer digging in its bow. *Courtesy USN*

Sailors loading five-inch ammunition onto destroyer. *Courtesy USN*

Destroyers maneuvering at tactical drills.

Destroyers moored at Subic Bay,
Philippines.

On the bridge of a destroyer.

A destroyer in worsening seas.

Hungry sailors begin to gather in destroyer's galley.

A destroyer in a calm sea.

Destroyers maneuvering at tactical drills.

Reconciliation

I watched the movie that night, an insipid war adventure starring John Wayne. Afterward I stayed, forcing myself to talk about inane things and how great Yoko had been. Two of the guys who had been to WESTPAC before spoke of Subic Bay in the Philippines and of the sexual adventures awaiting us in the port city of Olongapo.

It hadn't been fun, and I knew I should have been inspecting the plant or at least getting some sleep. I had the four to eight in the morning and, using it as a reason, excused myself. The XO winked at me as I got up to leave.

I came to the bridge a little late. Mr. Chadwick was my JOOD and had the conn. *Haney,* the guide ship for tonight, stood out beautifully in the full moon, and from our station two thousand yards astern we could make out her every detail. "Mr. Chadwick, what do you think of letting combat conn the ship from CIC?"

He looked at me puzzled, not quite understanding. "The conn?"

"Sure, let them give the rudder and engine orders. Be good practice for them. Whadaya think?"

"You're the OOD, whatever you want," he answered defensively, as if I were laying some devious mustang trap for him.

"Okay, Chess," I said, using his nickname, "you go down there and I'll let the ship drift off station. You show 'em what to do to bring her back."

Chadwick looked at me curiously before answering, "But I've got the conn."

"I'll take it," I answered. He left as I explained the plan to the bridge team. They halfheartedly listened but weren't too interested. This was officer stuff. I told the boatswain's mate of the watch to have the helmsman drift us off station. "Take the conn, Boatswain's Mate," I ordered.

His eyes widened. His chin dropped. His mouth moved up and down but no words came out. I repeated the order. He looked at the helmsman, then back to me. In a hesitant voice he whispered, "Ah, this is the, ah . . . boatswain's mate of the . . . the watch. I, ah . . . got the conn."

The helmsman and lee helm answered and the quartermaster of the watch logged it in, as he logged in everything that happened on the bridge.

The boatswain's mate looked at me again, his face strained under the red lights of the bridge. I nodded my head to the left, and he ordered left twenty degrees left rudder. A little aggressive, I thought, but said nothing. "Drop five turns," he said to the lee helm without conviction.

His searching eyes asked me for approval. I pointed to the rudder, indicating for him to ease it by rapidly touching my thumb and first finger together. He smiled understandingly and reduced his rudder to left ten degrees. In a minute he said, "Steady as she goes." In a leap the mood on the bridge jumped from boredom to elation. I saw it on their faces: imagine, just imagine, we wretched enlisted men are conning the ship. The officer's holy of holies invaded this early morning in the South China Sea.

"Signalman," I whispered just in case the captain might be awake. "Make a light to *Haney,* OOD to OOD. 'Am exercising at ship handling drills. Will remain within two thousand yards of station.'"

When we were sufficiently off station, I passed the conn to combat. In five minutes the CIC talker said, "Combat recommends adding four turns and coming right fifteen degrees."

"No," I swiftly interrupted. "Combat has the conn; they don't recommend, they command."

Thirty seconds passed. "Combat says come left fifteen degrees and add four turns." The helmsman looked at me, his eyes asking for guidance. An enlisted man conning a destroyer was out of their realm of understanding; they had difficulty adjusting to it.

"Respond to combat as you would to any conning officer," I instructed. And they did. And they had fun. In about half an hour Mr. Chadwick returned to the bridge.

"They're eating it up down there, sir. This is a good idea."

We were all over the ocean for another half an hour until combat got the hang of it. The boatswain's mate of the watch kept a strong eye on what combat did. The minute they got on station, he'd have the helmsman drift us off and then he'd add or drop a few turns. They were doing okay.

Chadwick and I stood out on the starboard wing, letting the early-morning breeze from our passage wash across our faces. I had to talk with him, but I kept putting it off. I was never one for direct confrontations. Finally I said, "Don't you think, Mr. Chadwick, we can drop that 'sir' and 'Mr. Chadwick' shit? We've got to work together, and if you would, I'd rather you call me Don, and if you don't mind, I'd like to call you Chess."

He looked at me for a few moments. The skin on his moonlit face twisted, trying to find an appropriate expression. His glazed-over eyes harbored a lot of hate.

"The olive branch, Chess?" I said, offering my hand.

He hesitated like a frightened animal sniffing the air for predators. With his eyes cast to the deck he tried once to extend his hand but didn't get it too far before drawing it back. He looked up at my face again and then down to my still extended hand. His hand tentatively came forward, paused, then clasped mine as he stammered, "Do . . . Don?"

"Mind your helm," came a quick bark from the boatswain's mate of the watch to the helmsman. Chess and I looked into the pilothouse and then back at each other, grinning. I felt like a proud parent at a Little League game.

"I've ridden you pretty hard, Chess, and for no good reason except that I have this maniacal drive for perfection. I realize it's a fault; I fight it, but not very well."

A small shift of the wind came up from astern, bringing the harsh smell of stack gas. Words drifted out from the bridge. "Come left to course 145 degrees, aye."

"Wind's picking up a bit," Chess said, adding, "excuse me," and stepped into the bridge to check the radar repeater. He came back in a second, saying, "They're right on."

We stood in silence for a moment, both looking out to sea. He tried to speak once, but only his lips moved. Then finally with what appeared to be a Herculean effort, he said softly, "You make people nervous, sir . . . Don. We feel you're always testing us and we're wanting in the measure. And except with me, you don't complain, you just go ahead and try to fix it. It pisses people off. They don't trust you—you're in too tight with the captain. They, we, think you tell the CO every one of our faults, trying to make us look bad just so you can look good . . . except for Bob Rice, who thinks you're some kind of God. He says you took some real heat from the old man for him. He doesn't say why."

Chadwick paused, furrowed his brow, and glanced away, indicating he thought he might have gone too far.

His words stung. *Do I do that?* "Chess, I don't do that. I've never told the captain anything about another officer. Not even my perceived problem with you. It isn't true . . . it—"

"It doesn't matter, Don, if it's true or not. Truth is what people believe," he interrupted.

"Jesus, Chess, is that what the officers think of me?" He didn't answer but I knew he wasn't lying. I'd change. I hated the kind of person he described.

"Don, you're one hell of a guy and we could all learn from you. You're doing the wardroom a disservice with your holier than thou attitude. We admire you for what you've done—we know it's damn hard for someone to come up through the ranks and that only the best make it. Why damn, Don, at NROTC classes at Harvard we were told to hook up with a mustang if we could, and pay attention and we'd learn a helluva lot.

"They didn't tell us about a formidable character like you who can make us all feel . . . feel, well, inadequate." He mercifully ended as combat reported the carrier group just appearing at extreme range on their radar.

"Boatswain's Mate, belay drifting us off station. Tell combat to keep us in there tight," I ordered. Before I could ask them to give me a time to rendezvous, Chess had worked it out.

"Fifty-three minutes to join up, Mr. Sheppard," he said in a voice of authority I'd never heard him use before.

"Very well, Mr. Chadwick," I answered, walking over to the voice tube to the captain's sea cabin to report the sighting.

Just as I lifted the brass cover to the three-inch speaking tube that ended right over the captain's ear when he was in bed, combat reported, "Fifty-three minutes to join up. Interrogative station?"

The captain answered in a sleepy voice for me to inform him when we were assigned a station.

"Mr. Chadwick, take the conn. The old man could be out any minute."

"Aye, sir," he answered with confidence. We knew the formation was out there; we'd been detecting their surface search radars on our electronic sensing measure receivers (ESMs) in combat for the last half hour. The receivers could detect a transmitted radar signal about half again as far away as the emanating radar could transmit out and receive back. By the same method, the battle formation had probably detected our radar.

Chess moved over beside me, saying, "The XO, Don?" *My God, I'd forgotten.* The night orders clearly said to inform the XO when we located the formation. Proud of Chadwick and chagrined with myself for having let it slip my mind, I rang up the XO.

The still visible full moon held on as the morning sky lightened and the sun's warmth reached out. As the old hands say, a sailor is paid twice a day: once at sunrise, once at sunset. Both beautiful.

"Captain on the bridge." The nearest ship to us in the circular formation around the carrier started its flashing light.

"Combat reports formation coming to port. It'll shorten our time to station," came the talker. A pause, then, "Interrogative station?" combat asked again. They couldn't stand not knowing.

I keyed the 21MC, saying, "We don't know yet, combat, we'll keep you informed."

The captain sitting in his chair had barely said good morning since he'd come on the bridge fifteen minutes ago. He drank a cup of hot coffee from a pot that had been made in combat three hours ago. He seemed to like it.

"What are those idiots waiting for? Give us a station, Commodore," he said to no one in particular as Mr. Chadwick adjusted our course to meet the shortened distance the formation's port turn allowed. Lacking instructions, we headed for the carrier in the center of the formation. The captain hadn't commented when I informed him. The carrier hove into sight.

The flashing light from *Haney* blinked to us, and in a minute the signalman presented the message to the captain. "From CO to CO: Dave, thanks for tour of the sunny Aleutians. Always wanted to vacation there. Keep 'em rolling. I forgive you for the 'station.'" Signed, Mike.

The captain finally smiled as he handed me the message and the ship-to-ship radio sounded. "Charlie Whiskey, this is Papa Hotel, Quebec Tango five. I say again Quebec Tango five. Break, break, November Oscar . . . Sierra Golf seven. Over."

"From the commodore, Captain, take plane guard station one immediately," Chadwick answered swiftly, obviously having memorized the expected signals, beating me to it.

"Understood," the captain answered, nodding to the radio as he got up from his chair.

I picked up the mike and answered. "Papa Hotel, this is Charlie Whiskey, understand Quebec Tango five. WILCO. Out." WILCO meant I understand and will comply. This in contrast to ROGER, which meant only I understand. I heard Mr. Chadwick tell main control to stand by for twenty-five knots. *Well done, Chess!*

Over the 21MC combat blurted out: "From the commodore, take plane guard station one." Combat had all the same radio circuits we had on the bridge, and several of their own.

"Understood," I answered, looking at the captain for permission to take station. He nodded. I turned to Mr. Chadwick and said softly, "Go!" We didn't have a clear shot to station; one of the picket ships was in the way.

"For info, sir, *Haney*'s been assigned a picket station five miles ahead of the carrier," the combat talker added.

"Understood," the captain answered even though the message was for me. The officer of the deck informed the captain, not combat. Talking directly to the captain could easily, inadvertently, cut the OOD out of the picture. The skies promised a great day so I forgave him his breach of etiquette.

Mr. Chadwick swung the bow to a point just aft of the interfering ship's stern as he immediately responded to my instructions to go. In the same motion he cranked on twenty-five knots. The sea churned behind us as our bow sliced swiftly ahead. And without a puff of black smoke my boys jammed steam through the wide-open throttle valves into the hungry turbines. Even from the bridge I heard them sing in appreciation. We heeled over gracefully to starboard, rolling into the turn driven by the racing engines like a downhill skier in expert powder.

Lookin' good, Chess.

Quickly working out the maneuvering board solution, I recommended a course ten degrees more to starboard. He didn't react. Combat came up with a course eleven degrees to starboard and he took it. *Good job, Chess. Always take combat's recommendation when you can.* It's far too easy to get tied up with just the bridge and forget they're there to help you. It made 'em feel good to have their recommendation taken over that of an officer's. The talker kept them painfully well informed of the happenings on the bridge, as did all the talkers.

We raced by the stern of the picket ship, skirting it by two thousand yards as Mr. Chadwick came to port heading for the carrier's stern. Combat recommended a course. It agreed with mine. I concurred. At four miles to station, with a closing speed of twenty knots, the captain looked at me, questioning my intentions. He nodded me out to the open bridge. "You going to take her in to station?" he asked in his tough guy persona.

"With your permission, sir, I wish to let Mr. Chadwick do it," I answered, nervously keeping my eye on the rapid closing of the two ships. "I'll be right behind him to take over if it goes to hell . . . sir." *Sheppard, you egotistical asshole.*

With an outward sweep of his hand he motioned me back into the pilothouse and remained on the wing of the bridge shaking his head. I moved over beside Mr. Chadwick, his eyes asking me the same question the captain had. "You've got the conn, Chess," I whispered.

Help him, ship, he needs you. Listen, Chess, listen to the ship . . . she knows.

0648: Mr. Chadwick informed main control to stand by for a rapid drop in speed to fifteen knots.

0652: Mr. Chadwick informed the helmsman to stand by for left full rudder.

0653: Mr. Chadwick bent on left full rudder and dropped to fifteen knots.

0657: We settled perfectly into station.

0700: The signal lamp from the carrier flashed.

0701: The signalman handed the captain a message form.

0702: The captain smiled and gave it to the XO.

0703: The XO gave it to Mr. Chadwick. It read, "Bravo Zulu," well done!

0704: I finally had a friend.

Pilot Rescue Detail

C hess's jubilation at breakfast pleased me. "I was wrong about you, Don, and I'm sorry . . . Shit! You must have said something really big to the old man for him to let me take it in to station," he said, drinking his fourth cup of coffee.

"No, Chess, he just asked me if I was going to let you do it, and I said yes." Well, essentially it happened that way.

Chess's eyes held mine for five seconds before he said, "The captain doesn't think too much of me, I'm afraid. I used to be an OOD, but he caught me asleep in his chair once after I missed a turn. That was it. I wasn't even allowed on the bridge for a month.

"Stood most of my watches in combat and they didn't think much of me either. I love ship handling like you let me do this morning. Not the do this! do that! big brother lecture crap we usually get from old rub-adubnose."

He retold his ship handling story over and over as the officers came in for breakfast. The carrier's flight recovery operations had commenced and the roar of jets landing every few minutes provided his only pauses. "The ship talked to me, Don. I swear it . . . I swear to God, the ship actually talked to me. I've heard about it, but goddamned, I've never felt it before," he whispered to me.

"Ole Don, here, he did it for me," he'd say, patting me on the hand or lifting his coffee cup in a mock toast. The other officers put up with him, laughing with him, proud of his snippet of success. They included me in their banter and I felt good.

Warmed by the camaraderie, I finally realized that the college boys hadn't been making fun of me; they hadn't been putting me down. It was my own feeling of inferiority about not going to college that made me think so and act accordingly. I wondered if I could change.

An hour later in the engineering office, Chess was almost back to his old sullen behavior. "Chess, I know you've got it in you to be a great DCA, but you don't perform that way. What's the problem?"

"I'm not academy."

"Bullshit!"

"I'm sure you remember Roger Clements. I'm sure you do—you finished him off good, in just a week," he said bitterly. I winced. *Did everyone know the story?*

"You may find it hard to believe, but at one time he was a fine naval officer. He was even going to make it a career, until the system smashed him in the ass one too many times."

My face betrayed my disbelief as he continued more seriously than before. His eyelids narrowed over his blue eyes until they were barely slits. His brow furrowed, making his handsome face ugly, foreboding. "You don't think you were the first to discover we didn't have enough spare parts for the electronics equipment, do you?"

I thought I was.

"When Clements tried to do something about it, Bluing cut him to pieces. Clements wasn't strong enough to go over Bluing's head or clever enough to pull off the stunt you and Jenkins did."

Blood rushed to my face as if to explode my head. His words hit me like a Mack truck careening down a tunnel of shock. He stopped to let me think as he leaned his chair back against the bulkhead. I pushed the door closed. His somber face gave way to a questioning look, then to a diabolic, conspiratorial grin. "C'mon, Don, a destroyer is a small place. Nothing happens without someone knowing about it. Jenkins was so jazzed about you, he had to tell someone. He told me."

My pulse settled somewhere between two to three times normal as I squeaked, "Who . . . who else knows?"

"Just ole Bobby Jenkins and me. We're from the same hometown."

Beads of sweat trickled down my body and collected in my sodden shoes. "Chess, I know you don't like me; how come you . . . you never told anyone?"

"Because I was proud of you."

I looked at him for several seconds, my mind a jumble of fear, before I could calm myself enough to mutter, "Thank you, Chess." He didn't answer—what could he say?—as I sat there thinking of the dumb stunt Jenkins and I had pulled soon after I first came aboard. The lack of repair parts was a critical problem, and I had figured we needed something dramatic to shock Mr. Bluing into action and to give me access to the captain's ear.

On that day—I remember well as the day I publicly contradicted the captain on his criticism of the ETs—I knew fog was likely in the afternoon. I had the watch and I knew the captain would be on the bridge. I instructed Jenkins to simulate a failure of the surface search radar, and then all I had to do was wait long enough for the fog to roll in. With the excuse that even the air search radar had been cannibalized, I knew something would happen. Luckily for me, it worked out okay. But even now if the captain found out about it, he could destroy me. It had been stupid; simply put, it was sabotage.

"What . . . what about you, Chess, what happened to you?" I stammered, trying to recover enough to continue the purpose of this meeting.

"Same thing. I wanted to be a good naval officer, but the harder I tried the harder it became. Status quo seemed to be the watchword. I wanted to hold drills, I wanted to shore up bulkheads, I wanted to send my men off to fire-fighting school and do all the things DCA school taught me to do. But Rich Bernard stopped me, just as the captain stopped him. Lectures were the best I could do.

"You're quite familiar with the captain's feelings about engineering and damage control drills. He's petrified of screwing things up and looking bad. I can only imagine the private hell he lives in, hoping nothing happens while he's in command."

I couldn't figure it. The captain just didn't seem like that kind of man. "Well, in any case, Chess, where do we go from here?"

He continued, ignoring my question. "Clements handled it with his smart mouth and cruel outlook. I just checked out. I did the least I had to do and counted the days before I could get off this ship. I got a year to go, Don—I'd like it to be productive."

"What do you suggest, Chess? I'll give you all the support you need."

He looked at me, his lips curling in a sardonic grin. "I need your drag with the old man and the XO."

"I'm not sure how tight I am with the XO, but what do we need?"

"You've lived in an ivory tower here, Don," he said in his typical sarcastic way. I didn't question what he meant; I didn't want to know the answer. He was starting to piss me off with his insufferable lecturing, and I guess my face showed it. He changed his tone, but not much. "As you probably know, each division furnishes so many of their men on a continuous basis to the three damage control parties, and quite naturally they send the ones who are the latest screwups in their own divisions.

"The others in the damage control parties, and their petty officers in charge from R Division, know this and consequently do not make any great effort to train them. They know the guy will be yanked out as soon as one of his division mates screws up worse than he did. We can't get any stability, and the men haven't learned to trust one another. Morale? There is none. The only good thing about being in a damage control party is you can sleep during general quarters."

I knew this from Engineering Officer School. They warned us that damage control was always an afterthought on destroyers. They even gave the same reasons as Chess.

"I'll talk to the XO. What else?"

"Let me use some of our precious damage control equipment to run drills and actually do something with them, and don't bitch about the cost of buying extras so we can keep a practice supply on hand." He finished, waiting for my reply as he drummed his fingers on my minidesk.

My God, the kid's fired up.

"You got it, Chess."

"When do we start?"

"I'll talk to the XO."

"When?"

"Today!"

"Thanks . . . great, but remember Repair Five is yours. They're the main engineering spaces repair party. You control and train them, not me. Repair One, forward, and Repair Three, aft, are my babies," he said, getting up and offering his hand, and shaking it as if we'd concluded a mammoth financial deal. He whistled "Anchors Aweigh" as he walked down the passageway to see, I'm sure, Chief Damage Controlman Burton.

I sat back, listening to the jets roaring in as I fought down my embarrassment about Repair Five. In my grandstanding—as the XO called it—I had forgotten they were my responsibility. Chief Maclin probably hadn't forgotten. I hoped he hadn't.

That night as we steamed with our squadron mates in a bent-line ASW screen formation ahead of the carrier, I thought how silly it was. In my mind, it was a foolhardy theory that destroyers running ahead of the carrier each within sonar range of the other could stop a submarine from penetrating the screen to get to the carrier. It worked in World War Two when surface ships were faster than the submarines. But not now. Hell, a submarine could lay in wait and after we in the screen steamed by it could go for a tail shot on the carrier. No one seemed willing to admit that Russian subs could outrun us.

I knew they could. I'd tracked one at 43 knots for several hours in the Atlantic not too long ago and was duly sworn to secrecy about it.

At daybreak we took station off the carrier's port beam at five thousand yards. A boring station. At least in plane guard one, you had the close station keeping to remain busy. But out here, nothing.

I strolled along the main deck, inspecting watertight doors while trying to get up the courage to approach the XO on the damage control drills, when the 1MC blared out, "Away the pilot rescue detail. Man the motor whaleboat. Away the pilot rescue detail on the double."

Rushing to the boat for no good reason except being nosy, I heard the XO report over the 1MC that two planes had a midair collision and the pilot of one had bailed out. I looked up and saw the burning plane fall into the sea. I saw the parachute open as the ship heeled over, racing for the area.

Mr. Graffey, the first lieutenant, whose job it was to lead the pilot rescue detail, wasn't here. He had the watch, I recalled. No other officer was here. "Away the motor whaleboat," came the order over the 1MC loudspeakers. The talker to the bridge, just suited up with his phones, repeated the order. At the last minute, just as the boat was at the rail ready to go into the water at the captain's command, I jumped in and took charge. There was no deck officer around.

Shit! I shouldn't be doing this.

At that precise moment the ship backed down full; the turbines screaming as their backing blades sucked up the steam jamming into them. We shuddered and groaned to five knots from twenty-five just one hundred yards from where the pilot was about to go in.

The whaleboat hit the water with its prop at high speed. The stern sank and we sped for the pilot. The XO on the bridge, using a loud hailer, ordered us to pick up the pilot.

Of course, XO, what do you think we're out here for?

The helo was just launching from the carrier. I could hear the god-awful shriek of our boiler safeties as the engineers hand lifted them to keep a sufficient flow of steam through the superheaters so they wouldn't melt down.

That's where I should be, not in this bloody boat. I've done it again.

We were just lifting the pilot into the motor whaleboat when the helo appeared right over us, its downdraft violently filling the parachute canopy and yanking the pilot out of our grasp. The helo hovered as the downed pilot, with his parachute wrapped around himself, fought his way into the helo's lifting sling. But as they tried to lift him, his fouled parachute filled with water and the helo couldn't pull him up. They surely must have heard his screams as they tried to rack him in two. "BACK OFF, BACK OFF!" I screamed and screamed. "WE'LL RESCUE, WE'LL RESCUE!"

They paid no attention. *Maybe they couldn't hear me.*

All the boat crew was now shouting as they dumped him back into the water. He wiggled out of the sling and swam toward us, his face grotesque in fear and anguish.

We headed for him. "GODDAMN YOU!" I shouted at the helo as it came right back in, its downdraft once more blowing us away. Shark fins circled about fifty feet out and closing. The gunner's mate with his M1 Garand rifle fired into them.

One more time the now feeble pilot managed to attach himself to the lifting ring, and once more the helo's screaming engine couldn't lift him without pulling him apart.

What were the idiots thinking? What could they do if they could get him to the helo? What could they do about the fouled parachute around him—cut it away in the air?

They dumped him again and moved to a hover a hundred yards downwind. The seas picked up, chopping the water around us. I saw the fear on the pilot's pale white face as we moved in again. "Help me," he pleaded as we closed. His hands, bloody from trying to tear off his harness, ripped at his body in confusion and fear. His face, unrecognizable from blood and horror, sent waves of revulsion through me.

His glazed eyes locked onto mine, penetrating into me, until a wave passed over him and buried him out of our sight. He popped up again four feet from our reaching hands, his arms stretching out for us. He lay face up in his yellow Mae West inflated life vest, the waves washing over him as we pulled alongside.

A flash of a fin. The firing of the Garand. His body yanked violently down into the water. Blood. More fins. More firing. A new clip. He popped up; his face showed no expression and his lips tried to speak but only a "TH—" came out as we lifted him into the motor whaleboat, trying to cut away the shroud lines that entangled, enslaved his body.

His left leg was gone.

Four other slimy black shark fins cut through the water no more than ten feet away. A fifth joined as they circled our boat. We barely got the pilot in when a fin flashed where the pilot's right leg had been two seconds before.

The shark tangled itself in the cut-off parachute canopy, thrashing violently in its demonic fight to free itself. The gunner's mate opened fire, killing two of the huge bastards only three yards from us. The others attacked their brothers. A huge froth of blood stained the sea red as we pulled away in disgust from their feeding frenzy.

"He's dead, sir!" the corpsman, Petty Officer First Class Jennings, blurted out, screaming, "Those stupid bastards in the helo . . . they killed him . . . my God! They killed him. Why didn't they let us in?"

"NO! Try, try more . . . we can save him," I pleaded, bending over the pilot, giving him mouth-to-mouth resuscitation, desperately trying to force life back into his corpse. Five minutes crept into ten as we plodded back to the ship. But my effort was to no avail—he was dead.

Blessedly, Jennings pulled me away.

Chaplain

The carrier flew continuous sorties, but I never knew where they went or what they did when they got there. The captain knew very little more. We'd joined the operation late and missed the initial briefing and didn't even have the exercise's operation plan. For the first day, Mr. Bluing tried to piece things together by listening to the radio traffic and reading the Teletype messages, but they were all classified secret and we didn't have the codes. He was unsuccessful until Sunday morning, two days after we joined.

We'd just been relieved of plane guard duty after the last aircraft recovered and flight ops secured, the foxtrot flag hauled down. The captain had been up most of the night. He always stayed on the bridge during flight ops when we were on plane guard duty. I ordered left full rudder, pulling out of station, and when he was satisfied I was doing the right thing, he went below for breakfast.

A minute after he left, the pilothouse radio crackled out a string of code letters. I recognized our call sign and the commodore's. Mr. Rice hurriedly set to decoding it, trying to beat combat in the continuing competition between the bridge crew and the radarmen. They won as the talker announced: "From the flagship, sir, the commodore orders us to come alongside to embark the chaplain soonest." I glanced at Mr. Rice; he nodded yes.

"Give 'em a WILCO," I answered and called the captain in the wardroom after I told main control we'd stay at twenty-five knots for a little while.

"How soon until we catch up to her?" he demanded in a gruff voice, as if it were my fault his breakfast had been interrupted. But right away he added, "I'm sorry, Don, I'm just bloody tired and I hate to disturb the crew on a Sunday morning. And the chaplain . . . damn." I'd never heard him complain before.

"We're still at twenty-five knots, Captain; she's about five miles fine off our port bow. A signal came in seconds ago slowing the task group down to fifteen knots. We can be alongside in about half an hour. With your permission, I'm heading for her now."

"Go! What's our fuel look like?"

"We're sounding the tanks now, sir, but I estimate we're about fifty percent."

"Shit! Means we'll have to go alongside the carrier this afternoon for refueling," he said with the gruffness back in his voice. Steaming at high speeds as we had been doing with the carrier ate up prodigious amounts of fuel. And our tanks hadn't had a drink since leaving Yokosuka.

The phone remained silent as the radio hissed a plain worded message asking for our ETA, estimated time of arrival, alongside. I started to repeat it to the captain. "I heard the goddamned thing," he shouted. "Let's go with it. I'll be up in a minute or two, as soon as I finish my breakfast. I'll need a full stomach for the chaplain." *Why?*

The shrill sound of the boatswain's pipe filled the ship, followed by the 1MC blaring, "Now hear this. Now hear this. Set the high line detail. Set the high line detail. Port side to." I could almost hear the moans from the mess decks as half the crew left breakfast half finished to man their stations. My station was in main control. I gave the conn to Mr. Rice to make the initial approach. Mr. Bluing would be up in minutes to take the watch.

The XO appeared, nonchalantly saying, "Mr. Bluing is sick in bed, Don. The captain said you're to take her alongside." My insides collapsed. I felt as if dry ice had engulfed my bowels.

"Where's the captain?" I blurted, panic choking my throat. "I've never done this before, XO." I managed to get out in a more subdued, controlled voice, "I've only watched twice."

"Piece of cake, Don," the XO replied, putting his arm around my shoulder and walking me to the bridge wings. "You approach about one hundred fifty feet off her starboard side with three knots faster speed than she's doing. When your bow passes her stern, you drop the three knots and you'll be right beside her bridge to bridge when you reach her speed. Then you slowly work your way in to one hundred feet."

"I know all that. Where's the captain? The captain?"

He ignored my question. "Easy enough if you remember her starboard screw is creating a low-pressure area at her stern and your port screw is creating a low-pressure area at your stern. These effects combined want to pull the two sterns in to collide. At the same time the bow waves from each ship are forcing both bows out, amplifying the pulling together of the sterns."

I had trouble breathing. Seeing.

"Just keep in mind to give only courses to steer and not rudder orders. Sometimes, the helmsman will have full rudder on to keep the sterns apart. If you think of it, you'll panic with full rudder on into the ship you're alongside. Just don't think of it. And for God's sake, don't worry about the rest of the ship. Just keep us alongside. We'll take care of everything else. The captain will be right behind you; he won't let anything bad happen."

"Oh . . . good." I felt better.

XO, you sly sonovabitch, you're psyching me up. You're one cool bastard, XO.

I looked at him, smiling. The con artist was being conned.

The XO took the deck from me and gave it to Mr. Chadwick when he came on the bridge three minutes later. I relieved Mr. Rice of the conn. I placed my hands on the port side bulwark of the open bridge. I felt the ship's vibration. I felt the ship's assurance. I felt the oneness. I was ready. My sweat-soaked body dried. The odor remained.

At five hundred yards I reduced my speed to eighteen knots, three knots faster than the flagship. The seas grew choppier. I steered 150 yards to the starboard of her wake. I sensed the activity around me of the high line detail preparing their lines and equipment. I tried to ignore the activity as the captain softly said from behind me, "Don't pay attention to what's happening on the ship. Just keep us alongside. The XO is taking care of everything else." I didn't even know the captain was behind me. I smiled an appreciative aye, aye, sir.

I felt the pull of the flagship's low-pressure area as we crossed her stern, and I ordered fifteen knots. The speed change echoed in my mind as I felt the engine slowing. I concerned myself about the plant but cast out the thought immediately. Chief Maclin was down there. He knew that no matter what the casualty was, he was not to pull any equipment off the line without the bridge ordering it so.

If we lost a bearing, he had to keep the engine going the best he could. If we lost a boiler, he had to cross connect in seconds. He could not make any changes without the bridge's permission. The results could be catastrophic when alongside another ship, particularly the same size ship, at only one hundred feet separation.

I started easing in before we'd reached our bridge-to-bridge alignment. I knew what I was doing now. "Don't get cocky, Sheppard," I felt more than heard from the captain behind me.

Did he say it?

At what looked like one hundred feet—I couldn't really tell, but it looked awfully close—I heard, "On *Rollard,* stand by for shot line forward!" I heard a whistle blow. I heard the forward station fire its line throwing gun to just forward of *Rollard*'s bridge. In minutes the distance line went over. Eighty feet—wow, too close. I eased my course to starboard to pull away. Too much; we lurched out to 120 feet. I pulled us back in, slower now.

Bright pieces of colored cloth tied onto the distance line showed how far I was away. Each color represented twenty feet. I remembered my *Conning a Destroyer* book. Rub Your Belly With Grease: red, twenty feet; yellow, forty feet; blue, sixty feet; white, eighty feet; and green, one hundred feet. I was on the white as the line pulled taut.

We fell behind. "Add three turns," I ordered. In three minutes we came abreast of the other ship's bridge. I dropped two turns and there we held as the after station got the high line equipment across. The wind increased and the seas grew choppier. It was more difficult to hold her.

We drifted in to ninety feet. I came right one degree. A large bag came over first; it contained movies to swap and messages for the captain. We sent our old movies back. One nice thing about going alongside another ship—you got new movies. Our bow waves grew larger as the wave heights increased.

A leather civilian suitcase came over next. I fought down the urge to look astern to see how things were going. "Add one turn." Next came a man in the metal high line chair . . . this was the most crucial time. Some would say the movie exchange was the most important. My feet accepted the hum of the ship telling me we were doing okay.

Suddenly a huge rolling swell of water hit our bows, driving them apart and forcing our sterns closer together. The high line slackened as if it had been let go, and the chair and the man dipped into the churning sea before the sailors could take up the tension. As quick as the swell came, it passed, throwing the sterns apart as it did. The high line snapped taut, twanging in anger before the sailors could slacken the line again. The ships settled as the chaplain landed safely on the fantail.

I came right again as we closed to eighty feet. "Add two turns."

A sound-powered phone line had been passed with the distance line, and I could see the commodore talking to our captain. The captain didn't look happy. I noticed the signalmen passing messages by semaphore just using their arms without using flags. I knew these to be personal messages, signalman to signalman. I would have enjoyed reading them, but I fought down the urge.

Just keep it alongside.

"Take in the lines," I heard the XO order, and I detected the activity. I got a little nervous when the distance line came back to us. It was my crutch.

"After lines will be free in two minutes," I heard the phone talker repeat.

I turned my head into the pilothouse, yelling in, "Tell main control to stand by for—"

"MR. SHEPPARD, belay that," the captain interrupted, ensuring in a loud voice to the bridge that he was speaking only to me and not taking the conn by giving an order that automatically gave him the conn. "Don't even think about it," he scowled. "Announce you have the conn."

"This is Mr. Sheppard, I have the conn."

Ten seconds later, the XO reported to the captain and me, "All lines clear."

"Slow and easy, Don," the captain whispered as the XO secured the high line detail. This meant everyone but the engineers. They stayed on until we cleared the other vessel.

"Add ten turns," I ordered and came right four degrees. We eased ahead and slowly away to starboard. Five minutes later we were in the clear. "Tell main control to stand by for twenty-five knots," I ordered, looking sheepishly at the captain for assurance. He smiled. How did he know I was stupidly thinking about a high-speed breakaway from the flagship?

"Combat . . . course to station at twenty-five knots." I was already heading in the general direction as I cranked on the twenty-five knots, but I was a bit confused, having lost most of the big picture with my undivided attention to the conn while alongside. The carrier was there dead on our bow at four and a half miles. I knew for sure that one never crossed a carrier's bow any closer than five miles, or ten thousand yards. I bent on right standard rudder to ensure I passed well behind the carrier's stern.

Our station was on the other side of her at five miles off her starboard quarter. The captain hadn't said a word. Combat's course took us on a dogleg one mile astern of the carrier. I asked them for a new solution to clear the carrier's stern by two miles—a greater comfort zone for the captain. They immediately gave me a course more to starboard. They'd already had it figured.

The chief boatswain's mate—the bosun, we called him—escorted the still dripping chaplain to the bridge door, looked at him once, curled a lip, and marched back out.

"Praise the lord . . . praise the lord, he has delivered me from the depth. Praise the lord, my son, my captain, he has placed me safely unto your hands," the tall, thin, wiry man of about twenty-five chanted, slinking more than walking onto the bridge. His skinny arms extended over his protruding beer belly as if to embrace someone. He headed toward the XO.

"Captain," he shrilled, his fear-ridden face the clammy white of a man who might be in shock or knew he was about to die.

The pilot, before he died, looked that way.

The XO, with a disgusted sneer, jerked his thumb toward the captain. The chaplain turned to his left in confusion, then bolted for the captain's chair.

"My captain, my savior, the sea engulfed me. You are my savior, my savior," he shouted, slobber dripping from his mouth.

I heard Mr. Rice's whispered voice, "Mind the helm, sir."

"Mind your helm," I ordered to the helmsman, not knowing or even checking if he was off course. "Boatswain's Mate, get this bridge cleaned up," I barked, taking out my bewilderment on the bridge crew.

"Aye, aye, sir," the boatswain yelled, jumping into action, doing nothing but moving around rapidly while he did it.

The captain's right arm shot out at the approaching man. "Stop!" he ordered, his extended forefinger inches from the man's advancing nose. The chaplain's head moved back while the rest of his body arched forward. The boatswain's mate, rushing back and forth on the bridge in his feigned effort to get things cleaned up, thrust out his arm to support the chaplain's back, keeping him from tumbling backward.

"XO! GET THIS MAN OFF MY BRIDGE!"

Silently we made the port turn around the carrier's stern. As we headed for our wide open station five miles away, the skipper's face burst into a broad grin. "Fuckin' navy!" he muttered between fits of loud laughter. "This fuckin' navy . . ." And he went into his sea cabin. I was astonished. I'd rarely heard him use the word before and certainly never seen him rude to a guest on our ship, especially to someone on the squadron commodore's staff.

In two minutes he appeared back on the bridge, pointing a finger at me. "And you, Mister . . . Mister Hotshot, for even thinking about a high speed breakaway, you'll have him for a roommate, and he'll be aboard for a long time," he said laughingly, then returned to his sea cabin.

The smiling bridge crew stared at me in silence. I shrugged, not understanding. I gave the conn to Mr. Rice as I keyed the 21MC to the signal shack. "Gaines," I called to the lead signalman, "come up here, please."

"Gaines, what were you and the guy on the flagship saying to each other?"

"Why nothing, suh—you know, just signalman to signalman jawboning," he replied sheepishly, trying to suppress a smile.

"Come on, Gaines, what did they say?"

"I thought you could read semaphore, suh."

"You might not have noticed, young man, but I was a tad busy at the time you were sending *illegal* messages to the flagship."

Gaines frowned in his endearing, down-home way. "Why, suh, I plum didn't know them messages was illegal. Why, my ole pappy back in Tennessee would be downright miffed with me if he kneowd I did anything like that. I'll never do that again, suh, not in a coon's age I won't."

I kept my eyes locked on him until he finally *volunteered*, "I think they said the chaplain was a royal pain in the ass, and the commodore, suh, was downright miffed at him."

"Thank you, Leading Signalman Gaines. I downright plum appreciate this here jawboning," I answered.

"Why, suh, that's right nice of you to say. As my good ole division officer, here, Mr. Rice, says, this here signal gang we got on ole *Henshaw* is the best in the fleet, and we're right proud to serve the fine Oh-Oh-Dees we got." And PO1c. Jefferson Davis Gaines, USN, from Tulla-homa, Tennessee, believed it with a passion.

The ship heeled over to port as Mr. Rice turned onto station and re-duced our speed to fifteen knots. "Tell the captain we're on station," I said just as the OOD's phone on the forward bulkhead of the pilothouse buzzed. I picked it up. It was the XO.

He spoke. "Aye, aye, sir," I answered.

Mr. Rice was smiling. "What?" I asked.

"Captain wants to know why I called him instead of you and are you pissed at him?" Mr. Rice shrugged. "Ah . . . he laughed—it sounded like he was joking."

I walked over to the voice tube and said, "Captain, the XO called me. He wants to hold church call at 1000 . . . if it's okay with you, sir."

Silence. "Sir?" I asked again.

"The XO wants to hold church call at 1000?" the captain repeated.

"Yes, sir. That's what he says."

"What's the fuel state?"

"Just got it, sir. We're at forty-seven percent. Recommend we go alongside the carrier for refueling."

Silence.

"Sir?"

"So you can make a high-speed breakaway?"

"Captain, I wasn't going to do it . . . really, I was just thinking about it. Anyway, the physics were all on our side."

"Yeah!" he whispered, his tone demeaning me.

"Church services, sir?"

"Where's he going to get a chaplain?" he replied with a snicker in his voice, then laughed as if it were a huge joke. I didn't get it.

"I reckon, sir, he'll use Chaplain Layman."

"Tell the XO, Mr. Sheppard," irony dripping from the captain's mouth like saliva, "to proceed at best worship consistent with crew safety."

Lookin' Good, Dave

===

Well, we finally know now what this exercise is all about, XO," I heard the captain saying as I walked into the wardroom for lunch. They had just sat down. I apologized for my lateness as I took my proper place at the table—up near the captain, as my status as a department head allowed.

"I've been relieved by Mr. Graffey; he has the watch, sir." The captain nodded as he continued his conversation with the XO and a pale-faced Mr. Bluing. We'd received the op orders along with the chaplain and the new movies.

The door to the wardroom opened and a young, apprehensive sailor marched in and stood next to the captain's chair. He swayed from the sea's movement as he stammered out in the tradition of the sea and the sailing ships, "Ah . . . Captain, the officer of the deck reports twelve noon . . . NOON. All of the chronometers wound and compared. Request permission to strike eight bells on time." He stood there seemingly not knowing what to do next. I was sure he had no idea of what he had just requested.

The captain looked up at him and smiled. "Make it so," he replied with the traditional answer and accepted the noon position sheet from the quartermaster and the fuel and water report I had signed moments before.

"Thank you, sir," the much-relieved boy said, then hastily exited this bastion of officer prerogative. The captain looked at me.

"Any word on refueling?" he asked rhetorically. If there had been, I would have reported it immediately. He knew this and picked up his phone to the bridge before I could answer. "Mr. Graffey, make a message to the commodore: 'Present fuel state forty-eight percent. Interrogative refueling.'" No destroyer captain ever wanted to go below 75 percent. Too many things could go wrong at sea.

Earlier, before he came down for lunch, the captain had reluctantly given me permission to take us alongside the carrier for fuel, even though he was still pissed at me for thinking of making a high-speed breakaway from the flagship. I couldn't figure how he knew. Maybe it was like a mother knows what her children are thinking when they are young.

As the captain raised his first spoonful of soup, he said matter-of-factly, "It's a SIOP exercise."

Mr. Bluing turned even paler as he cast a furtive glance toward the pass-through window to the wardroom pantry, where the Filipino stewards prepared the officers' meals. "Now, Mr. Bluing, the word 'SIOP' is not classified." We all nodded in agreement even though I doubted that many of the officers knew what it meant. I didn't.

"Captain . . . please," the voice of the chaplain whined as he saw the soup spoon enter the captain's mouth. "I must insist we say grace and praise the lord before we partake of this most bountiful feast."

Before the captain could answer, the ferret-faced chaplain belted out a full three minutes' worth of thanking and praising, ending with: "And Lord, please forgive the captain and his Mr. Sheppard for almost drowning your humbly faithful servant in your most vicious sea. Forgive them; they knew not what they did. Amen! Let us partake, my children."

The wardroom stared at the chaplain in open-mouthed surprise. All eyes turned from the skinny man with the potbellied stomach toward the captain. The captain slowly rose, his face a burning crimson. A steward came in with silver trays of bread; detecting the mood, he stepped gingerly back out to the pantry. We stared. I was pissed. The captain's eyes swept the table at a glance, stopping for a second on mine, then locked onto the chaplain's. The chaplain sat there slurping his soup, seemingly oblivious to the havoc his words had brought.

None of us dared speak or eat. The captain, now fully standing, towered in rage over the rest of us. He threw his napkin on the table and stomped to the door. With his hand on the knob, he turned slowly and laughed, but the cold steel of his eyes frightened those of us who had felt his temper before.

"We knew not what we did, eh? Well, when we send you back, Reverend Dicky Layman, I suggest you wear a bathing suit and have God with you." He slammed the door behind him.

The XO looked at Mr. Bluing. He looked at me, then shifted his eyes to Mr. Hethington, the gunnery officer. "Excuse me," the XO said in a most courteous tone as he rose from the table. We department heads followed him out, hearing the chaplain say, "What'd he mean by that? What's going . . . where are they going?"

I took my hunger with me as I stopped at the engineering office, now Refueling Central. The oil king, BT2c. Jose Martinez, USN, and BT1c. Roger Chandler, USN, the leading BT in charge of both fire rooms, leaned over plastic diagrams of the fuel tankage system, making marks on it with grease pencils. "How's it going?" I asked.

Martinez looked up at me nervously. It was his first refueling at sea. "Okay, Mr. Sheppard, but I'm a little scared I'll fu—, I mean screw things up."

Behind him Boiler Tender First Class Chandler shook his head no.

Only the most trustworthy boiler tenders, BTs, could aspire to become an oil king. Martinez had become the oil king when Chandler made first class and was put in charge of the fire rooms just before we left San Diego. The oil king was responsible for the proper management of the fuel oil onboard. He stood no watches, had no other duties but to ensure that the center-line, ready-service tanks remained topped off at all times and that the fuel remaining in the storage tanks was properly distributed to the lowest tanks available and evenly split throughout the ship. Chandler had been the oil king for a year before his promotion to first class and leading boilerman. We didn't have a chief assigned, though we rated one.

Fuel oil tanks took up one-third of a destroyer's space. Fuel oil management kept the ship on an even keel, contributing significantly to the ship's stability.

Of course both Chief Maclin and Boiler Tender First Class Chandler kept an eye on the fuel status and with their experience knew when something wasn't quite right. I had not yet developed this sense.

"I'm taking her alongside," I said, bragging a little, hoping to impress them.

Barely looking up, Chandler answered, as if he gave a damn about what officers did, "Oh, that's nice, sir."

Leaving them to their task of preparing the ship for refueling, and after dropping down to main control to have a look-see, I returned to my stateroom to eat a can of peanuts and stretch out in my bunk to rest before returning to the bridge. But I couldn't rest, because Lt. (jg) Richard Jordan Layman, USNR, Chaplain Corps, was lying in the lower bunk. My bunk.

"You're in my bunk, Chaplain."

"God wants me to have this bunk."

"You're in my bunk, Chaplain!"

"God commands, my son. Man proposes, God disposes," he said, pointing upward and looking at me sadly with all the piousness of the Pope.

I untied my desk chair from its secured-for-sea status, sat down, and opened the can of peanuts. I tried to read as I finished the peanuts. I stood up and walked over to the small sink in the room and got a glass of water. "One for me, my son," he said. I brought a glass over to him. He finished it in one gulp, dripping a bit over his shirt.

He didn't say thank you as he handed the empty glass back to me. He didn't even look at me as he extended his hand with the empty glass in it, as if I were his dutiful servant. My body shook as I returned the glass to its holder. As a department head, I rated a stateroom to myself, if it were possible, and it irked me just to be sharing with anyone, much less this guy. He'd already cost me a lunch.

Trying to be friendly, I asked, "I understand we're going to be roommates for quite a while. What do you prefer I call you—Dick, Richard . . . what?"

He looked at me with the innocence of the lamb. "Why you can call me 'Your Reverence,' 'My Father,' or simply 'Chaplain'—whatever pleases you, my son."

My heart pounded as I tried to control myself by filling and lighting my pipe. The first good drag settled me a bit until I heard, "God does not want you to smoke around me."

I lost it.

My chair flew backward as I leaped for his feet; yanked them up and pulling him out of my rack. My hands were at his shirt collar as I lifted him and threw him toward the chair. His face whitened as he gasped for breath.

"I'm going to call you by your first name—Dick. And I may even use your middle name—Head. Now, you just stay out of my way. Stay out of my bunk. And don't keep telling me what God wants. The captain is god on this ship, and don't you bloody well ever forget it," I vented, dropping him back into the chair.

Undaunted and through his heavy breathing, he said softly, "The captain is master only under God, my son."

"Don't call me 'my son'; call me Mr. Sheppard," I said breathlessly, thinking nothing good can come of this conversation. I offered him my outstretched hand in friendship. He took it, unfazed, as if it were his due.

I walked back to the fantail, trying to settle myself. We were in a loose waiting station two miles astern of the carrier. Another destroyer was alongside and another headed our way for what appeared to be a waiting station behind us. The rest of the ships formed into a bent-line, ASW screen.

"Well, Mr. Sheppard, is your new roommate settling in okay? I hope it's not too much of an inconvenience for you," the captain said, smirking as I came onto the bridge.

"No, sir, anything to serve my ship, sir. Dick and I are the best of friends."

"Dick?"

Mr. Hethington had the deck, and I could see he was anxious to get below to supervise his rigging crews. We hadn't refueled from a carrier in a long time. "Mr. Bluing still sick, Captain?"

"I think so. The XO will be up in a few moments. The chaplain wanted to talk to him for some reason. You know anything about that?"

"No. Shall I take the deck, sir?" I asked, noticing the captain's uneasiness over Mr. Hethington's anxiety.

As I stood on the starboard wing keeping station, the captain strolled over and pointed to the carrier. "She's a lot easier to go alongside than another destroyer. Her screws are deep, and you'll get very little suction effect. We'll be far enough aft of her bow wave that you'll not even notice it unless a huge wave comes jamming through. Piece of cake, as you always say. Fueling course is directly into the wind at due north, 000."

I looked at him; he wasn't being sarcastic. In a few minutes the XO came to the bridge, scowled at me, and motioned the captain into the pilothouse. I feared that their whispered conversation might concern my conduct with the chaplain. The captain frowned, looked my way, then burst out laughing. The XO remained serious as he walked over, and I briefed him on our status before he relieved me of the deck. "I've got the conn," I reported just to ensure that no confusion existed because the XO had the deck.

The oil king came over to me saluting, reporting the engineering department ready in all respects to receive fuel from alongside. "We'll be taking on about three hundred twenty-five tons, approximately ninety thousand gallons, sir." Fully loaded we carried six hundred fifty tons of fuel.

If there had been any threat of bad weather, we'd have been in trouble. You could already feel the sluggishness caused by our higher center of gravity, much like the ice had caused but not nearly as bad.

The captain came over and I reported the oil king's comments while the oil king stood beside me. Martinez smiled, saluting the captain as the captain said, "Good job, Petty Officer Martinez . . . make your boss look good."

How nice of you to say that, Captain.

When we were alone the captain said, "Good naval officers never lose their temper, Don."

Puzzled, I looked at him. He smiled. "Yes, sir, I've noticed that," I answered.

He frowned, his eyes narrowed, and his lips curled into a sly grin. "Consider yourself verbally admonished."

"Yes, sir, so considered." And I didn't have to ask for what. A verbal admonishment was the least punishment a captain could give. There was no record kept of it, and it ranked between an ass chewing and a letter of admonishment, which became a part of your service jacket.

Flags fluttered up from the carrier's signal racks. I pointed to the lee helm; he had my instructions, which he passed to main control to stand by for twenty-five knots. "Take waiting station one for refueling my starboard side. Fueling course 000."

"UNDERSTOOD!" I yelled with too much nervousness in my voice, pointing again to the lee helm, who again passed my message. We were going to look good.

"Execute!" Gaines yelled, and I kicked the engines ahead to twenty knots, with just a trace of black smoke pushing out of the stacks and the dip of the stern showing the action.

Before we reached waiting station, the carrier's flags fluttered up again. "Come along my starboard side for fuel," Signalman Gaines yelled out.

"Understood," I yelled. The captain nodded. The XO had set the refueling party twenty minutes ago and the men waited at their stations, ready.

"Can I take her in at twenty-five knots, Captain?" He touched the bulwark and a slight grin formed as the wind whipped our faces.

"Yes, but come in a little wider, maybe two hundred feet or more."

"Captain?"

"Okay, asshole, one hundred twenty-five."

We passed the carrier's stern with our ten knot speed advantage; it seemed very fast. She was so big. I wanted to shout out to reduce speed, but I was committed to this foolish deed. I heard the captain's heavy breathing behind me. This wasn't dangerous; all that could happen is that we'd lunge too far ahead of station, then have to jockey back to get into position. It wasn't dangerous, but if we failed our heroic approach, we'd look bad.

Wait . . . wait, I cautioned myself. Steady, listen to the ship. Steady, don't chicken out. I waited for what seemed a millennium, then yelled into the pilothouse, "Tell main control to stand by for fifteen knots; watch the smoke." Ten seconds, five seconds. The sheer cliff of the carrier loomed by us at a sickeningly high speed. "Left to 358." We were too far out. Five more seconds seemed to stretch to hours. Then: "All engines ahead standard; make turns for fifteen knots," I yelled over the screaming wind. I sensed I'd waited too long. We were going to roar right through station. "Stand by for five knots . . . stand by! STAND BY!"

"AYE, SIR!" the lee helmsman shouted.

"Superheaters, Don?"

"It's okay, Captain . . . it's okay . . . okay . . . it's worked out."

Five seconds. One second. We weren't going to make it. "All engines ahead one-third; make turns for five knots." In a second it was as if a giant hand grabbed us and pulled us to a stop. The ship vibrated and slowed. An embarrassing puff of black smoke shot out. I'd asked too much of my boys.

One second, two seconds crept by. The sweat on my body, chilled by our speed and the twenty-knot wind blowing from dead ahead, froze in my pores. I felt the tingle. Now! "All engines ahead standard; make turns for fifteen knots." One second. Three seconds. Five. Ten.

We were dead on station. "On *Henshaw,* stand by for shot line forward," a bullhorn somewhere on the carrier roared out. A whistle blew, and in a second their twelve-guage line throwing gun landed its three-inch plastic float just aft of mount 52, just where it was supposed to land. The sailors hauled in the thin, stringlike line connected to successively larger lines until finally the distance line came across.

A signal lamp blinked from the admiral's flag bridge perhaps one hundred feet above us. I forced myself not to read it. In a minute, Gaines, with a broad grin, handed the message to the captain.

"Stand by for shot line aft." I heard a line throwing shotgun firing, and with a glance I saw the weighted, oblong, three-inch by nine-inch plastic float with its trailing twelve-inch steel firing rod attached arch over the water between us and land somewhere on the fantail.

The distance line pulled taut with the white rag fluttering just at our side. Eighty feet. Too close. "Right to 004."

The huge, nine-inch hoses came over—one aft, one forward. The forward hose snaked across just below me, and a quick look showed the boatswain's mates jamming the hose into an oblong fitting rising vertically from the deck and quickly tying it down. I heard the ready-to-take-on-fuel report passed up from Mr. Hethington aft and Mr. Graffey forward, followed by the oil king requesting permission to take on fuel.

Don't listen, conn the ship, don't concern yourself.

"Add one turn. Steer 000." We had our best man, QM3c. Bobby J. Morton, USN, at the helm with the JOOD behind him keeping constant watch to ensure he followed the helm orders from the conning officer. We had our best men on the throttles down below and our best men manning the boilers. Destroyers did not take chances when alongside. But it was easy.

I soon discovered that the heavy, fuel-laden hoses kept us just about at the right alignment fore and aft, and that keeping the bow cocked out two or three degrees from the carrier created a funnel effect that worked in conjunction with the weight of the hose to keep us pretty well out to the correct distance. Very few rudder commands had to be given.

I stood there bored after the first half hour. Ten more minutes passed before I gave an engine order. "Add one turn." Ten more minutes passed. The sea freshened.

"Mr. Rice," the captain shouted. "Take the conn, Mr. Rice; spell Mr. Sheppard for half an hour or so." I welcomed the relief, realizing, as the captain did, that boredom could become a formidable enemy.

"Thank you, Captain," I said after briefing Mr. Rice for a few seconds and stepping away from the raised conning platform just aft of the port pelorus. I took off my sunglasses, rubbed my nose hard, and sucked in a huge breath of fresh sea air.

God, how I love this.

The captain handed me the message he'd received from the flag bridge just as we settled on station.

"Lookin' good, Dave," it read.

"Nice message, sir," I said, handing it back.

"The admiral's a friend of my father," he said with a chuckle.

"Yes, sir," I answered, then walked into the pilothouse. Mr. Bluing had managed to come to the bridge and had taken Mr. Rice's place behind the helmsman. The chaplain smiled at me as he passed through the door to the port bridge wing. I turned and watched him lift his camera as he shoved himself in front of Mr. Rice.

"What the hell?" Rice yelled, almost falling off the conning platform.

"Not hell, my son, heaven. God wants these pictures," the chaplain shouted above the wind in his squeaky, high-pitched voice, advancing the film and snapping the camera shutter release as fast as he could.

"XO!" the captain screamed.

The astonished XO raced to the wing, grabbed the chaplain by the arm, and spun him around and down off the conning platform.

The captain looked at me, looked into the pilothouse, turned back to me, and said, "Cancel that verbal admonishment, Mr. Sheppard."

With nothing to do, I listened to the sound-powered phone circuit connecting our "Refueling Central" to the carrier's. Constant chatter went back and forth: "Reduce pressure . . . start pumping again . . . start . . . stop . . . more pressure . . . less . . . wait . . ." It seemed too much, seemed too slow; it went on for thirty minutes while I listened. "Ten-minute standby to stop pumping," I heard the oil king report to the carrier. Then the phone talker to the bridge from main control said the same thing.

As I stood next to the captain reorienting myself before taking the conn, he said, "There's gotta be a faster way. Can you just imagine how vulnerable we are sitting here next to a huge, fat carrier with neither one of us able to maneuver for at least five minutes while we go through an emergency breakaway situation? It's scary, Don."

I took back the conn from a disappointed Mr. Rice. He must have thought I'd forgotten.

Tsk, tsk; ensigns will be ensigns.

"What's your plan, Don?" the captain asked.

I looked at him shame-faced. "Twenty-five knots, sir!" Without a change of expression, he nodded yes.

"All lines clear," the talker shouted, and I ordered twenty-five knots before his words died out. We leaped ahead with just a trace of black smoke showing as we sped past the carrier's mammoth gray steel sides— sides higher than our mainmast with its rotating radar antennas.

I eased out a little to 004, waited thirty seconds, and eased more to the right with a course of 006. Our beautiful rapierlike bow gently moved away, slowly increasing the distance between us. I could see the carrier's crewmen leaning over the sides clapping, watching us in our destroyer derring-do.

As our stern passed the carrier's bow we got a slight kick from her bow wave, and I ordered right standard rudder. With the bit in our teeth we raced to station in the bent-line screen. I looked to the captain for praise. "You committed a cardinal sin," he said, passing me on his way back into the pilothouse.

I followed him in, slinking like a puppy dog with its tail between its legs after being whipped for peeing on the carpet. "What, Captain?" I almost pleaded, walking toward him. The XO took me by the arm before I covered the distance to the captain's chair.

"Always glance at the lines yourself after a talker or anyone else tells you they're clear. This is especially true during UNREPs, underway replenishments, but also when you're leaving a pier. That's what he meant; he checked—you might not have noticed."

"Thanks, XO."

SIOP

===============================

"hen we get the signal 'Blue Thunder,' we'll know the launch is on and the exercise war has started," Mr. Bluing finished. "This brief, I say again, is classified secret and the targets are top secret. Of course, we don't know the targets and neither do the pilots until the last stages of an alert."

Mr. Bluing thrived in his element now. He wasn't a hardware man or a people lover. His was the sterile world of plans, charts, and thoughts. He had little use for the execution phases. He didn't rub his nose very much during the long brief and generally seemed in a much better mood since we left Yoko. Maybe the bottle of stuff he bought in Thieves Alley helped.

"Our only mission in this entire exercise is to guard the carrier after the launch as she turns and runs toward the Red China coast."

"This is incredible," Mr. Hethington uttered, his jaw quivering. A bit of weak coffee spilled from his shaking hands down his shirt front, blending in nicely with the khaki color. He never seemed to be an imaginative man, but he was steady; he could be depended upon to do his duty.

I don't think Mr. Hethington ever had an independent thought in his life. He personified the bookman and hid behind his knowledge as if it were a shield. If it wasn't in the book, it didn't exist and therefore could not be done; the last bulwark of the incompetent.

The military needed men such as Mr. Hethington. Too many iconoclasts led to confusion, disarray, and, at worst, anarchy. From the captain's attitude toward him, I got the impression that Mr. Hethington wasn't one of his boys even though he belonged to the "Protective Society." We never became good friends; I heard he thought I was too gung-ho and too critical.

"What does SIOP stand for again?" I asked, pronouncing it "syop" as Mr. Bluing had. I was just as puzzled as Mr. Hethington.

"SIOP, single integrated operations plan," Mr. Bluing answered in that insufferable lecturing tone he used when he knew he had the upper hand. "It's simple, gentlemen; when the balloon goes up and the carrier can't receive clear instructions from higher headquarters, they assume that our national command structure has broken down or has been destroyed. Therefore, a state of war exists, and they launch.

"Each carrier, depending on where it is in WESTPAC, has targeting information it hands out to the attack pilots. The pilots study the information, and when they're within the maximum one-way range, they launch. Simple, gentlemen," Mr. Bluing finished, leaning smugly back in his chair. He pointed silently at each one of us with a long yellow pencil as if he were taking roll, then stuck it between his teeth and tightened his jaws around it. I hoped he'd bite it in two.

"One-way range . . . that's a suicide mission," Mr. Hethington blurted, starting to rise from his chair. "Americans don't do that. Goddamn it, we're not kamikazes, we're Americans."

The captain pointed a finger at Mr. Hethington, then said in a dry, sterile voice, "Sit down, Mr. Hethington. Think about the big picture. When the SIOP is executed, it means all communications have failed. Neither the president nor anyone else is in command. What would you have us do? SAC has the same mission. So do the TAC bases stationed over here. Nuclear war is under way: should we just wait and let the carriers be sunk by Soviet submarines?

"And, Mr. Hethington, if we were guarding the carrier and a torpedo headed for her, and we could intercept it, taking the torpedo hit ourselves, would that be suicide or would that be for the greater good of the navy and the country?"

"Well . . . yes, sir . . . no, sir, but, I mean, it seems a lot to ask of the pilots to launch under these conditions," he said haughtily as if it were a definitive answer. He ignored the second question.

Wonder if I'd do it—follow the order.

The captain, not changing his expression or tone, answered, "No one is asking *you* to launch, Mr. Hethington." It tolled the end of Mr. Hethington's participation.

Wow, these guys are talking war and death, and I'm bugging the captain about a few engineering drills.

After a moment of silence to let Mr. Hethington recover from the captain's subtle attack, Mr. Bluing spoke again. "Once the carrier launches and starts her run to the coast to recover any pilots who might make it out, our job is to steam the best we can trying to keep up. But she'll be doing more than thirty knots, and to even try to keep up will suck us and the rest of the destroyers dry in less than eighteen hours. But we'll do what we can, probably twenty knots; it's our best compromise speed," Mr. Bluing stated as if there were to be no more questions. He was referring to the cube-of-the-speed, fuel-consumption curves.

At our best economical speed of fifteen knots, we could steam for about three thousand miles. At four boilers and thirty knots, we'd last only about eighteen hours—five hundred miles. Destroyers rarely steamed at thirty knots. It was just too delicate of an operation. The slightest inattention or one small mistake could spell disaster.

"Anyway," the captain said with a yawn, leaning back in his chair and balancing on its back legs, "the Commmie subs would probably put a spread of fish into the carrier before we even knew there was an emergency situation." He sounded resigned to the superiority of the submarine advantage. "Their boats always try to follow our carriers in WESTPAC."

"There's one out there now," I volunteered, instantly regretting my remark.

"How do you know?" the XO blurted. All eyes looked at me.

"I can just feel it."

"Bullshit!" both the XO and Mr. Bluing snapped back.

"Yes, sirs," I answered, noticing the captain smile. We had discussed the same feeling earlier this morning. He felt it too.

The captain reached for his phone, I swear, before it buzzed. He listened for a few moments and said, "Acknowledge the transmission." He turned to us as he stood. "Blue Thunder. The carrier's coming into the wind to launch. The screen's been ordered widely dispersed and to take up a westerly heading at twenty knots," he explained as he passed through the wardroom door.

*   *   *

Later, as I took the watch at 0345, we were alone at twenty knots heading west. No destroyers could be seen, and I knew that the carrier must be miles and miles ahead of us by now. An uneasiness added to the chill of the early-morning air. I keyed the 29MC to Sonar. "Sheppard here, who's got the watch?"

"Jarvis, sir, good morning," came the cheery reply. Jarvis and I had become friends after that ASW exercise off San Diego. He thought I was magic.

"When's the last time you made a bathy drop, Jarvis?" I asked. To detect the thermo layers in the sea, we dropped a bathythermograph instrument into the water. As it sank it measured and sent back to us the various temperatures at different depths. This told us where thermocline layers existed and gave us some idea of where a submarine might hide and a rough figure of sonar performance. Thermoclines refracted sonar beams just as water does when you view a stick in it.

"Twenty-three hours ago . . . not much help. Your sonar worth a damn at this speed?" I knew it wasn't.

"No, sir, but I gotta vague feeling." Since that San Diego incident, Jarvis and I periodically played chess, and I used the opportunity to encourage him to tune his mind in on submarines. It'd worked for him a couple of times and made him a hero among his peers.

From the log I knew that the captain hadn't gone into his sea cabin until 0115 and had been asleep for only a few hours. Should I wake him on a feeling, a hunch? Should I cut my speed, make a bathy drop, and go active with our sonar? If I reduced speed slow enough, the sub might not notice and we could gain contact before he realized it.

Surface ship sonars were no good at speeds greater than about thirteen knots; too much own ship distortion caused by the water rushing past us. It was 0430, the time when men's energy and attentiveness were at their lowest ebb. If anyone had been tracking us for any length of time, they'd be complacent.

Call the captain? Yes!

I lifted the cover to the voice tube that ended right over his sleeping head. "Captain . . . OOD here, request permission to slow and make a bathy drop and take a couple of sonar pings. I think there may be a sub on us." I heard him mumble but received no answer. I repeated my request.

Is he awake?

Thirty seconds passed. "Uhhh . . . okay, Don. Sub?" And I heard his snore as I closed the cover. This wasn't a big thing, yet if I'd been sure, I would have insisted that he understand.

"Combat, I think we got a sub out there. Clear off the DRT and get it going. I'll let you know." Under nonuse, the DRT became a flat-surface catchall that accumulated books and junk that combat seemed to attract. One decent roll usually cleared it for them.

I called Jarvis in Sonar and told him my plan. He suggested I slow as fast as possible because the submarine, if there were a submarine, would be tracking us on passive—we'd heard no pings—and would know instantly when our screw count changed. Even if they weren't alert, the screw count change, which was simply a change in RPMs, would be noticeable. "Right, thank you, Jarvis."

I called main control. Machinist Mate First Class Langston had the watch. I explained my plan. "When I ring up ten knots, I want you to slow as fast as possible. While you're cranking down the ahead throttle, open up the astern. Start lowering superheat now. I want our speed down before he knows it."

"Who is he, sir?"

"Oh, I'm sorry, Langston, we're going after a Russian submarine."

"Oh," came the startled reply. "Yes, sir."

"We'll wait until you're ready. Everything depends on how fast you can dump ten knots." I wanted to say get Chief Maclin to main control, but it would have shown a lack of confidence in Langston. Langston knew what to do and would alert all spaces on what was happening. I'd bet, though, that the messenger was on his way to the chief's quarters as we spoke.

"What?" came a sleepy growl as I rang up the XO and told him I thought there was a sub tracking us. "What?" he asked again. I said it again.

"Can you come up here, sir?"

"I . . . I'll be right up," he answered.

Combat reported the DRT manned and ready. Sonar reported the stacks and gear manned and ready to go active. We'd been steaming with the sonar on standby just to make it more difficult for a submarine to track us at a greater distance. And, besides, tracking was useless at this speed anyway. Fifteen agonizing minutes passed. Main control reported manned and ready; it was Chief Maclin's voice. I said good morning.

I looked at Mr. Rice in the dim red lights of the pilothouse brightened by the full moon and cloudless skies. No wind rippled the glassy water. The feeling was too strong, no time for a BT drop. "All engines ahead two-thirds; make turns for ten knots!"

We seemed to jolt to a stop. Our powerful ping slapped into our ears. I followed it out in my mind, waiting for the positive report from Jarvis. I worried about the superheater furnaces at this low speed. Had the temperature been lowered enough? Were the furnaces getting enough steam flow to keep them from melting down?

Several days before, I had discussed with Chief Maclin and Boiler Tender First Class Chandler the idea of opening the astern throttles, letting them suck up steam to the astern blading while adding more ahead steam than normally necessary to compensate for the drag of the astern turbines. We could thereby maintain enough steam flow through the superheaters to protect them from melting down.

They hadn't thought much of the idea, saying we needed the OODs to think ahead a little more. "And it probably wouldn't work anyway," Chandler had said, ending his part of the conversation. He didn't take to new things well. Chief Maclin had allowed it would work, but his boys would have to be on their toes, and the OOD had better give plenty of warning time.

That's why I wasn't worried when I slowed to five knots alongside the carrier. I wished I'd told the captain about it beforehand. He got mighty pissed when I told him later.

"XO's in combat," the talker reported. *Good.*

"Sonar contact bearing 165, three thousand yards, echo quality sharp, classified possible submarine. Designate Sierra One," came Jarvis's clarion call. I knew combat plotted it. Sierra One meant a sonar contact, first for the day. It carried this designation until termination of the exercise or until the sub sank us or we destroyed it.

"Range clear," Mr. Rice shouted, indicating no surface ships on that bearing. The bridge hummed with excitement; each man stood taller.

"We got him, Captain," I yelled into the voice tube, not waiting for acknowledgment as I rushed for the 21MC. He didn't answer. "I'm here," he said, walking out of his sea cabin.

"Captain on the bridge," came the report from the boatswain's mate of the watch.

I keyed the 21MC to main control and combat. "Beautiful job, Langston; we got the bastard. Combat, mark datum." Datum, singular of data, was a mark on the DRT showing the last contact position.

"GQ, Captain?" He nodded. I turned to the boatswain's mate of the watch, who was standing at attention with his hand on the 1MC keying knob. He knew his part. I nodded.

The announcing system blared out in the early calm morning. "NOW HEAR THIS, now hear this, general quarters . . . general quarters. All hands man your 1AS stations. Now general quarters. Set the 1AS team. General quarters, set the 1AS team." The 1AS team was ASW combat.

The pings continued. Sonar had their microphones cut into the pilot-house speakers. "Sonar contact bearing 169, twenty-eight hundred yards, echo quality sharp, course 273, speed twenty knots, up Doppler, classified possible submarine." Drumbeats and bugle calls danced through my mind.

"Left standard rudder, steer course 180. All engines ahead standard; make turns for thirteen knots. Main control, what's my minimum speed?" It depended on the superheater temperature.

"Ten knots," came the instant reply.

"Secure the superheaters as soon as possible! Belay turn indicators; we'll just use the telegraph and go for the speeds indicated."

"Sonar, I'm going to slow in a minute or two. When I do, go passive and try to ident that mother."

"Zero Doppler," Sonar reported, indicating that the submarine was neither moving away from us nor toward us.

"Main control, I need to slow to at least one-third . . . how long?"

Chief Maclin's voice answered, "Any speed you want, sir. We got a system, remember?" I'd forgotten in my haste over the sub contact.

"Jarvis," I yelled into the 29MC. "In a minute or so, as soon as the superheaters are secured, I'm going to back her down and come to a stop. I want you passive. As soon as you get a good recording of his noises, I'm kicking ass out of here to come in from behind him."

In two minutes I ordered, "All engines back two-thirds." We shuddered and came to a halt. "All stop."

An agonizing five minutes passed. "Got it!" Jarvis yelled.

"All engines ahead full . . . right full rudder." The stern dug in and we heeled to starboard as the ship obeyed the pounding steam and the laws of physics. I knew I created large swirling knuckles in the water from the radical screw change and the hard turns. These could impede our attack by showing false targets, but I had to do it. A stopped destroyer is dead meat to a torpedo. And my radical maneuvers would surely confuse the sub. The searching pings from below started again as I eased my turn and reduced my speed.

"Sonar contact bearing 180, one thousand yards, speed five knots, up Doppler. Classify as positive submarine. I say again positive submarine."

"Jarvis, *positive* submarine?" the captain asked as calmly as if he were questioning a steward about what was in the soup.

"She's gone active."

Active—unheard of!

"Ident, Jarvis?" I asked.

"A . . . little . . . a little confusing, sir," Jarvis answered. His uncharacteristic hesitation unnerved me. He was one of our coolest heads. Meanwhile the sub headed directly for us. "Sir, can you come down here for a minute?"

"Jarvis, I've got the deck. Can you tell me anything?" I answered, looking at the captain.

"Mr. Sheppard, remember your story of the S2F chase and the MAD gear testing you told me about? Same. Same," said Jarvis.

"Bridge, combat . . . 1AS team set and tracking."

"Bridge, main control. Manned and ready except for the chief engineer."

Except for the chief engineer? Never heard on this bridge before. Except for the chief engineer? I was considered part of the team.

My heart sang. The captain glanced at me, smiling, as he keyed the 21MC to main control.

"Chief engineer's on the bridge running a Russian submarine to ground, Chief Maclin. He'll be down later," the captain said, missing nothing. A poor choice of metaphor, but I loved him for it.

"Right ten degrees rudder," came the request/order from the 1AS team headed by the XO. I glanced at the captain and he nodded yes. I relinquished control. It was the XO's show now. Mr. Bluing arrived on the bridge and relieved me. He didn't look good; even in this flattering light of dawn, he didn't look good.

I walked over to report my relief to the captain. "What was Jarvis talking about?" he asked. I had told the captain the story of my lucky encounter with that forty-three-knot Russian sub when I was flying in S2Fs.

"He thinks it's a Russian nuclear submarine," I whispered. "I guess he didn't want to discuss it over the phone circuits . . . it might still be secret. I don't know."

"Oh!" he answered, rising from his chair. "Mr. Bluing, I'll be in combat."

"Captain left the bridge."

Kaohsiung

The submarine played with us for about an hour. Then, seeming to grow tired of the game, turned north and pulled away from us at thirty knots, cavitating so badly we could almost hear it with our naked ears.

Cavitation occurs when the turning propellor blades cause tiny bubbles of air to form as the blades cut through the water. These bubbles make a loud, chirping whine as they collapse against the blades. Only above a certain speed, determined by the prop and hull design, does cavitation occur. It is easy to track when passive. Of course surface ships cavitate too, but they are so loud that the extra noise doesn't make a helluva lot of difference.

We never once got in a position good enough to simulate a depth charge drop. It was just a game that we weren't qualified to play. He was too fast, too maneuverable. He just toyed with us.

I bemoaned the lack of more modern weapons such as the Mark (MK) 44 or MK 46 antisubmarine, homing torpedoes. The carrier was too far away to support us with her helos or ASW aircraft, and the other destroyers just couldn't make it over to us in time—for all the good they could have done anyway. We wondered why he did it. Surely he could have kept on tracking us on passive and we'd never have known about it—except for a hunch. Maybe he was just bored.

For two days we were on our own, maintaining a station away position in a box fifty miles by fifty miles. The weather here on the northern border of the South China Sea remained calm and warm. Boredom ate away at us. I pushed the captain for drills, to which he reluctantly agreed. I gave Chess his head, and his drills became meaningful and fun as he pitted Repair Three against Repair One for speed and quality.

While Chess ran his drills, I exercised the main spaces by watch section. They did well as the watch officers—Chief Maclin and Machinist Mates First Class Langston and Summers—picked it up, competing with their watches against the clock and each other. We became almost as good with the watch sections as we were with the GQ teams.

Chief Maclin even got the little-used Repair Five into the game by calling a casualty in a space, then announcing that all hands were dead and calling Repair Five to man the space. Repair Five consisted of engineers from all four spaces, and they did remarkably well.

At the end of the second day, we'd had enough and went back to our regular watches. My biggest supporter, Chief Maclin, drove the men a little too hard, I thought, but I wasn't going to intervene. He had the fever.

I reveled in fire fighting. It had fascinated me since I was a kid, and I drove the men relentlessly to become the absolute best. Chess built fire main mock-ups on the main deck and put gashes in them. With fire main pressure applied, he required the men to go in under the high-velocity water to repair the mains. He made the men wear oxygen-breathing apparatus, OBA, during all inside ship drills so they could learn to function in the OBA's cumbersome bulk.

But after two days Chess was ready to back off and give *his* men a rest.

I reported taking over the watch that evening when the captain called me out to the open bridge. Chess had the conn. "The XO brought Petty Officer Chandler up to see me yesterday evening," the captain said, taking an overly long time to light a cigarette. "Chandler doesn't seem to be one of your fans, Mr. Sheppard."

The world darkened from my narrowed eyes, a pain shot through my jaws as they tightened, my hands balled into fists. I instantly tried to mask my feelings, but I wasn't fast enough. The captain had noticed.

"He didn't come through me, Captain," I said softly over the wind. "I'll have his ass for this!" I whispered to myself. He heard me.

"No, you won't," he said sharply, then took a deep puff on his cigarette.

My blood pressure surged. Betrayed, betrayed by one of my own men, one of my leaders. The thought of revenge pounded through me. I couldn't speak and berated myself for the stupid statement I'd just made about having his ass.

"He came to the XO saying you were ruining the boilers and driving his men to exhaustion."

His men, I almost shouted but kept quiet. I didn't want to make another asinine outburst. I measured my breathing.

"I see that bothers you, but remember, if the men don't have an outlet for their frustration—someone who'll listen—things could get really bad. The men on this ship know they can talk to me or the XO anytime they want without permission of their division officers or their department heads. It's a good policy, and from what I hear, you do the same thing in the engineering department and Chief Maclin gets pissed. Is there any difference?"

"No, sir, but—"

"But nothing, Don. Chandler has every right to see me. This isn't the navy of two hundred years ago."

"Yes, sir." I truly agreed, but it still pissed me off.

He looked out to sea for several seconds, then turned back to me. "Are you ruining the boilers?" he asked with all seriousness.

I got pissed again but answered calmly, "No, sir. They're a lot tougher than people think they are, and if we spring a leak in a tube, we'll go in and roll it out."

"Chandler mentioned your plan to go to one-third ahead with a full head of superheat. He told me it could be disastrous. Is that so?"

"Yes, sir, if you don't know what you're doing, but it's been all worked out with both him and Chief Maclin and at the time he said he could hack it. Maclin thought it was a good idea. Why is Chandler disagreeing now? Goddamnit, Captain, the practice is as sound as hell, and I don't know why people haven't used it in the past. They probably have but didn't report it because the 'book' didn't say anything about it. It's simply a matter of training and information from the bridge."

Lieutenant Junior Grade Chadwick put his head out the door to the open bridge, announcing reluctantly, knowing the conversation between the captain and me was far from social, "We're at the north end of our box, Mr. Sheppard. Time to turn."

"Very well, make it so." The ship heeled to starboard under the force of the standard fifteen degrees right rudder. "We're coming around to 180, Captain, to the southern leg of our box," I reported by reflex.

"Very well," he answered with the same reflex.

He stood awkwardly. I realized he was caught in the leadership dilemma, seemingly finding it difficult to put it in words. Each leader was responsible for developing his men; they were the future of the family, tribe, clan, regiment, ship, business, or whatever. The good leader had to encourage innovative thinking and action; he had to give the good men their head.

The words I heard him say to the XO on the first day I came aboard and fixed those UHF transceivers with ballpoint pens came back to me. "Well, XO, it looks like we finally got us a live one." I wondered at the time what he meant. I understood now.

Initiative is a rare commodity among human beings, and he recognized mine. Not many men measured up, and when one was finally found, a good leader had to give him sufficient room to maneuver. But it was scary.

The captain flipped his cigarette over the side—a forbidden thing to do since the burning tip could land back aboard the ship and start a fire. He looked at me sheepishly for his sin, then said, "Have you ever heard the true story on why they called Admiral Arleigh Burke, Thirty-one Knot Burke?"

He continued before I could answer. "It wasn't that he dashed around the Pacific at thirty-one knots with his eight destroyers hammering the Japanese whenever he could, it was because he pushed his ships so hard with their newfangled superheaters that he burned them out. His destroyers were designed for thirty-five or thirty-six knots, but they could do only thirty-one because of his sloppy use of them. It was a cut, Don, a constant censure for not taking care of his superheaters."

I wanted to say, "So?" but I didn't. He thought he was being wise, teaching me a lesson in his best Socratic manner. I knew the story of Thirty-one Knot Burke. "Yes, sir," I said, then mumbled, "What he really needed was a sharp chief engineer." I hoped he hadn't heard me over the wind out here on the wing of the bridge.

We just stood there. I wondered if I was supposed to say something. He couldn't hold out any longer and added, "Chief Maclin came up to see me an hour later."

Oh, my God, Maclin too?

I prayed for Chess to come up with something demanding my attention. There was no place to run.

"Do you want to know what he said?"

"Yes, sir."

"Why don't you ask me, then?"

"Because you're the captain."

He thought that over in silence for a minute, then started for the door. *Shit, I'd lost the game.* "Captain?"

He turned with a smirk. "He said, Chandler was a cunt."

"Captain, you've got to know the whole story," I almost demanded. "Chandler's pissed because I told him he had to learn to be an engineering watch officer like the other first classes in the main spaces. He thought once he became the leading BT he wouldn't have to stand watches. I guess being the oil king for so long spoiled him. I was told he was going to get even with me. I guess he thought talking to the XO would fix me."

The captain's face tried a smile but failed. "Umph?" he answered, flipping his head and walking away.

Two days later the carrier returned and we steamed in formation toward Hong Kong. The old-timers of our jubilant crew told fabulous stories of the shopping bargains, cheap liquor, and luscious Chinese girls. *Ah, Hong Kong.*

The sound of a whining church service and the horrible smell of vomit greeted me as I stepped into officer's country. In my stateroom, the chaplain lay in the upper bunk, preaching into a tape recorder. The small sink in the corner contained his rotting lunch. He gave me one of his pathetic smiles, motioning me not to speak.

I reached over, yanked the tape recorder cord from the receptacle, and tossed it over his chest.

He jumped up, almost smashing into the overhead. "This is God's work, my son," he screeched, his beady eyes wide in astonishment.

"What's that in the sink? God's puke?"

"God did not deem that I retain his bountiful offering," he said, meekly bending over and trying to replug his tape recorder. I shook my head disgustedly. I couldn't stand the smell, and I knew I could never get this guy to clean it up. *Shit!* I cleaned the sink, something I had a lot of practice at, and felt sorry for the weak stomach of God's messenger lying there finishing his fire and brimstone sermon into the tiny microphone.

"What do you do with the taped sermons, Dick?" I asked, cleaning up the last of the vomit from the bulkhead around the sink. I took off my khakis and got ready to lie down for a few minutes.

"I make copies of them, and every Sunday we go from ship to ship and pass them out."

"Pass them out? You mean we take all the trouble to go alongside all eight destroyers just so you can pass out taped sermons?"

"Not all eight, my son. The chaplains from the carrier sometimes fly over by helo or go over by high line. We deliver God's word to only three or four."

"Shouldn't you go over by high line too? Wouldn't your flock rather have the message delivered by God's own representative himself?"

"It is God's will," he answered, ignoring the sarcasm.

"Is it God's will that the carrier chaplains put their ass on the line for helo transfers and high lines?"

"It is God's will."

"And your yellow streak," I muttered, pulling up my khakis as I left. I couldn't take any more.

We were the guide ship; the flagship was to come alongside our starboard side. Our only duty and responsibility was to maintain course and speed; the approaching ship did all the maneuvering. My station in main control cut me off from most of the happenings on the ship. I couldn't stand not knowing what was going on. I sneaked up to the main deck just above the hatch to main control. Chief Maclin was down there; it was his world.

The flagship made her approach slow and wide. She must have been two hundred feet out as she overshot her alignment and eased back, then crept in toward our side. *Not too sharp.*

In ten minutes she was in position—it should have taken three. The forward distance line came across, and in minutes her deck crew had rigged a small line for the taped sermon transfer. At least they were sharp. I saw the signalmen exchange their waving arm messages.

I read their weaving semaphoric hands discussing our impending trip to Hong Kong and the lewd things they were going to do. Leading Signalman Gaines did not participate. The signalmen thought no one could read their very fast and abbreviated messages. I saw the captain talking to the commodore over the bridge-to-bridge sound-powered phone circuit. I wished I knew what they were talking about.

I saw the chaplain standing on the signal bridge extending his arms out and hands down in blessing, but no one on the flagship paid any attention to him.

After a phlegmatic breakaway, and we were back on station, the captain called the department heads together in the wardroom. "Formosa

Patrol, gentlemen. We've lost out on the trip to Hong Kong; the destroyer assigned to the patrol lost a boiler. Melted down a superheater, I understand." He looked at me. "We have to take her place for a couple of weeks. We'll fuel this evening from the carrier and be on our way. I'll announce it to the crew."

The approach to the carrier was textbook perfect. Mr. Chadwick had the conn. I had all but begged the captain to give him a chance even though it was a night refueling. I concerned myself with taking on fuel with the captain's edict in mind to find a way to do it faster. In Refueling Central, my engineering office, the log room, I paid strict attention while the Boiler Tender Second Class Martinez, the oil king, received soundings from the tanks being filled. Each tank had two men assigned to sound the tanks through a sounding tube.

They called in on their tapes the number of feet wetted by the fuel as their tanks filled up. A call for pressure reduction went to the carrier as a tank reached close to its maximum, and we waited nervously while the tank was topped off. We then switched tanks and went through the whole cumbersome procedure again.

I went forward and down to the operations berthing compartment. We were currently filling the tank below it. Two firemen knelt over its three-inch sounding tube. The caustic rush of air screeching up through the tube clanked the snakelike metal sounding tape as the firemen tried to force it down.

"It's the air being pushed out of the tank by the fuel, sir," one of the firemen explained.

"Damn hard to get the tape down this mother," the other fireman volunteered.

The biting smell of whooshing bunkers caused shots of pain to careen off the inside of my skull. "A bitch, eh?" the first fireman volunteered, his face scrunched up behind the bandanna he wore uselessly over his lower face as if to protect him from the smell.

"Close . . . close. Stand by for pressure reduction," the first fireman yelled into his sound-powered phones to Refueling Central.

"STOP! STOP!" the first fireman shouted as his extracted tape showed almost full. The whoosh of air stopped. The tape went into the sounding tube again.

"Shit! Not enough, gimme more . . . LOW pressure, Martinez," he said. In three minutes, a smaller whoosh threw beads of fuel oil out the top of the tube, splattering around them, the bulkheads, the bunks, the deck, and their clothes with never-to-be-gotten-out black stains.

"Frightening shit, eh? Mr. Sheppard," the first fireman puffed, his lightning swift hands winding up the tape as fast as he could. He wiped it with a disgusting-looking rag, and unwound the tape down the sounding tube again.

"LOWER PRESSURE! LOWER," he shouted in three minutes over the now screaming sounding tube. "Damn, can't get this tape down the tube fast enough. Air's pushing it back up to me . . . fuck it. STOP PUMPING. STOP PUMPING!"

A final sounding. "Shit, sir, missed it . . . only ninety percent full. Shit, Chandler will have my ass, but it's so damn hard to sound at the end. Sorry, sir."

That's the key, the final soundings. How can we speed them up?

"How could we do this faster, you guys?" I asked as they twisted on the sounding tube cap and wiped their faces of the offending goo.

They looked at each other, shrugging their shoulders, then looked back to me. "Don't know, sir," the first fireman answered.

"Well . . ." the second fireman offered, his lips pursed, his eyes narrowed in concentration, "I guess if we took off the manhole covers, we could see the fuel coming in and wouldn't have to sound. With any luck we could bring the fuel right to the top. Dangerous though. If we screwed up or the pressure wasn't cut fast enough, we'd be swimming in it."

Open manhole covers, eh? Dangerous. We could drench this place. I'd need accurate data on filling rates. And balls . . . too dangerous.

The Chinese Nationalist island of Taiwan used to be called by its Portuguese name, Formosa. And the 120-mile strait between them and mainland China used to be called the Formosa Strait. In 1949, warlord Chiang Kai-shek escaped from the Communists in mainland China with many of his soldiers, settled on Formosa, and adopted the Chinese name Taiwan.

The Chinese Communists, CHICOMS, didn't like the Nationalists so close and so strong, and for many years they mounted small, harassing raids against the island. The United States vowed to protect Formosa and kept a large contingent of aircraft there and a couple of destroyers patrolling in the strait to hold off any invasion until the air force could arrive.

The old hands, with their secret knowledge gained from other cruises, said the opposite: we were there to keep the Chinese Nationalists, the CHINATS, from invading mainland China. Who knew for sure? Who trusted governments anyway? Certainly not me. I was the chief engineer; let the captain and XO worry about grand strategy. I had a plant to run.

On the mainland, across from about the center of Formosa, two small islands called Matsu and Quemoy still held out against the CHICOMS. It didn't bother the Commies that much, for if it had they would have invaded them and been done with it. But the CHICOMS were having troubles elsewhere and only harassed them with shell fire now and then. One job of the Formosa Patrol was to run escort when the islands were resupplied. Every destroyer on its WESTPAC tour got its turn on patrol; ours was just coming earlier in our tour.

The crew didn't care that much. Liberty was good in the southern port city of Kaohsiung, and the women, the crew reported, were the most beautiful in the world. Mr. Bluing had the watch as we entered the narrow, hundred-foot-wide entrance gap bordered by sheer cliffs on each side. Hundreds of fishing junks and small sampans hindered us. The Chinese pilot said to ignore them; they'd get out of our way. We had precious little maneuvering room as the captain heroically followed his advice. My first glimpse of the Orient. Japan was an anomaly; it wasn't the *real* Orient. It existed as a class unto itself.

We tied up alongside the Formosa Defense Force flagship for briefings and special arming of .50-caliber machine guns. The crew anxiously awaited liberty. So did I. The bumboats, small junks or large sampans, pulled alongside our fantail. Our specially placed guards kept them at a distance. Charged, high-pressure fire hoses were laid out to repel the more adventurous ones. They sold anything you might want, from exotic fruits to rare Chinese treasures to the use of their sisters. It was fascinating to me—a simple country boy from Nameoki.

They fought for our garbage. If we'd been there long enough, they would have painted our sides for it. *Were we that rich of a country that others would work just for our garbage?*

Half the crew had liberty the first night, the other half the next night. I opted for the second night, taking the command duty officer, CDO, watch for Mr. Hethington, a bachelor. Both the XO and captain and the other officers not on duty went ashore to a modest drinking party given by the harbormaster. It was the thing to do.

The CDO has complete charge of the ship when no senior officer with the authority to relieve him is present. In theory, the CDO could take the ship to sea and fight her if the occasion arose. It had arisen in many cases on 7 December 1941, the day the Japanese attacked Pearl Harbor.

As I watched the setting sun over the fantail, I fantasized catastrophic events ashore and my daring dash for the narrow channel as I brought my guns to bear on the invading Commie fleet. "Saving the island," *Time* magazine would say as the president placed the white-starred blue sash of the Medal of Honor over my head.

Custom and good sense, however, demanded that the CDO try to contact the XO and CO before getting under way, but according to the emergency, you had to use your best judgment. In my fantasies I'd shout his name twice over the water, then shove off.

Nothing happened, but I stayed awake most of the night checking on the armed sentries we had posted every fifty feet. Pirates abounded in these waters. Many a merchant ship experienced raiding parties but never a U.S. Navy ship. I wore a .45 automatic pistol with four extra clips slung low on my right hip, gunslinger style. Its weight comforted me like a warm blanket on a winter night.

I went ashore the next evening to a smaller party given for those officers who couldn't make it ashore the first night. The women were beautiful—devastatingly beautiful—in their cheongsams clinging to their small, lithe bodies. I stared but they graciously ignored it, probably having witnessed it from the officers of every newly arriving ship since 1949. Now it was the beginning of 1960.

Engineer

===============

A slight chop rode atop long, rolling swells in the Strait. It wasn't violent, it wasn't calm, just an agonizingly slow roll that heeled the ship over eight to nine degrees at a time. I had the watch, tired and sad about leaving Kaohsiung so soon. The visions of the childlike woman with her enchanting, singsong voice still pirouetted through my memory. A thousand thoughts of her waltzed joyously through my mind, each striving for ascendancy. I felt as if I were sixteen and she was my prom date.

The official greeter, surreptitiously using a card when he thought no one was looking, had introduced me as the chief engineer. Mai Ling, the harbormaster's youngest daughter, smiled broadly when she heard it— not the normal receiving line, pasted-on smile but rather one of genuine pleasure, or she was damn good at this sort of thing. I thought no more about it until she singled me out after all the officers and dignitaries had arrived. "May we talk, sir?" she whispered, tapping me on the shoulder.

"I am an engineer too," she said in her lilting tone, bowing her head as if she were ashamed of it. "May we talk about engineering? It will honor me," she cooed.

"Of course," I answered, thinking she was just being nice to the "big noses."

She offered me her glass of plum wine and sharply ordered a waiter to bring another. The wine was too sweet but I drank it anyway. I would have preferred a beer. She led me by the hand to a far corner of the not-

196

too-large reception room. We sat next to each other at a small table as the waiter brought her wine and a small bowl of what looked like peanuts. The high cut of her cheongsam skirt revealed a gorgeous thigh. I tried not to gawk.

She offered a toast but our glasses didn't touch, only our fingers holding them. Breathing became difficult. "I understand you have separately fired superheater furnaces," she said in opening, bowing her head again, avoiding my eyes. Her statement startled me; I hadn't thought she was serious. When I didn't answer right away she added, "It must be inconvenient for a ship. On land, with its near constant load, it really wouldn't be a problem. Do you agree?"

She *was* an engineer. And, as I regained my composure, we talked about entropy, weight-bearing surfaces, fuel purification, and a hundred subjects her mind absorbed, catalogued, and questioned. We talked about *Henshaw* and the problems we encountered running the plant and my passion for drills and training. She listened eagerly, commenting on proper steam flow balance and the interdependence of all elements and the obvious difficulty of running four boilers at a time. She knew what she was talking about.

She was no longer just a consumingly beautiful woman but rather a fellow engineer with a ravenous appetite for knowledge and technical companionship. Waiters and servants brought continuous wine and goodies. We paid scant attention. When she emphasized a point she touched my hand and no longer shifted her eyes away from mine. Her father came over once but she dismissed him as if he were an annoying fly. He backed off angrily.

I told her of my problem of refueling at sea and the final sounding dilemma. "Do you know the flow of the incoming fuel. Can you control it?" she asked.

When I answered yes, she stood, took my hand, and led me to a side door. "Come with me," she whispered, back now in her Chinese-lady voice. She led me through a garden toward the back of the huge white house and up a flight of outdoor stairs. "This is my workroom," she said, pushing the door open. I hesitated; she smiled, touched my arm with her right hand, and with a sweep of her left hand motioned me in.

Engineering books filled the shelves lining the walls. Slide rules, abacuses, and a mechanical Marchant calculator lay randomly on the messy desk. A full drafting setup occupied the far corner. A small bed covered with papers, books, and prints took up one side of the wall, and a huge banner from the University of Southern California hung over a small, paper-scattered table. She let me gaze for a minute. "This is my work-room," she said again. "I am designing a new steam generation plant for the city."

I stared; she laughed. "You are the only American who has seen this room. You do me great honor by discussing your dreams with me. My dream is this new steam generation plant. It will bring great fortune to our city," she said picking up a set of drawings and unrolling them while pointing to further prints thumbtacked to the wall.

Her Chinese-lady deference disappeared as she went over the blue-prints with me. I didn't know much about shoreside plants, but the theory was the same and I admired the strength and cleanliness of her design.

"USC—you must be very wise," I commented, noting and pointing to a plaque she uncovered while shifting the drawings. Mai Ling had gradu-ated with a doctorate, summa cum laude.

She lowered her eyes, bowed her head, and whispered, "It is nothing. I am embarrassed, sir, I am just a woman." Her tone was so low I had to move closer to hear her.

"Just a woman . . . shit, you're a brilliant engineer," I crudely ex-claimed, laughing as I raised her head.

She was trying to be serious but couldn't. "It sounds like I'm in Cali-fornia again," she said, giggling, and on impulse took my hand and squeezed it. I looked at her, she looked at me; then, as if a dark memory passed through her mind, she bowed, lowering her head again.

I put my hand under her chin and gently lifted her face. Her eyes, moist and radiant, met mine. Neither of us spoke. Her eyes stayed locked on mine as she moved to me. My arms went around her. I lowered my head. We kissed. She pulled her body into mine; her fragrance like sun-light engulfed and warmed me. Her hands on the back of my head drove my lips into hers.

Taking me by the hand as if I were a child, she led me to the small bed and with a wave of her arm brushed papers, books, and prints to the floor and slowly began undoing the buttons on her cheongsam.

She was so small. So delicate. A tiger.

Later, drained, the afterglow drifting away, I stammered, "For . . . give me, Mai Ling."

"It is my fault . . . forgive me," she said, running her fingers lightly through my hair and over my chest. We both laughed.

As we dressed she said, "I know from my visits to your ships that each tank has a—what do you call it?—a person hole . . . to inspect the tanks."

"Manhole."

"Yes, manhole . . . woman not allowed I guess," she commented wryly. "Why not remove the manhole covers and sound the tanks visually while the fuel flows in?"

That's what the fireman had suggested.

"Very dangerous. What if the men are too slow and the fuel gushes out through the open manhole? Much more would come out than if just a sounding tube overflowed," I answered, instantly ashamed of my negativity.

She looked at me in dismay, frowning as she said, "Train your men. How important is it that you refuel rapidly?"

Train my men, of course—don't take counsel of your fears.

I answered, embarrassed. "Very important, if you're in hostile waters."

"Then you must take the chance; there is nothing you can't do if it is important enough. Will it give you merit?"

"Merit? Yes, probably . . . if it works," I answered, my words coming out in a whine.

"We all strive for merit. Is—what is your saying?—is the risk worth the gain?"

"To me it is. I crave merit."

"As do I. I will help you," she cooed, moving toward me again. Her tiny hands grasped my chin, slowly pulling me down to her. Her scent—that of a thousand night-blooming jasmine—engulfed me as a wave inundating the shore. She kissed me with the slight hint of her tongue penetrating my lips. "That is my merit for you."

For the next half hour she dredged my mind for tank capacities and fuel flows and distance between valves and speed of communications. Then silently she worked out equations for tank filling rates, communications lags, and myriad other factors that would determine for each tank when the inflow valve must be closed, and the safety margin. As she sat down at her desk, she again undid the delicate buttons on the high mandarin collar of her cheongsam. She sighed in relief, turning around and smiling at me for approval.

In thirty minutes more, she showed me a paper of numbers written in delicate scrolls. I saw that it contained a fill-in-the-blanks form of tank capacity, size, piping flow, and a dozen other factors to determine exactly when a man, viewing the rising oil in his tank through the open manhole, should cut off the flow. It boiled down to one number: given the incoming pressure, and we always knew that, how high can the oil in the tank get, how close to the top can it be, before the sounder closes his incoming valve?

Simple. Simple. I had a uniform equation I could use on any tank. My admiration for her soared, and as she handed the paper to me with its delicate equations her hand lingered on it. Her head bowed and she whispered with a hint of a tear in her eyes, "You have given me great honor. When you return, we must, if it pleases you, discuss this humble paper more."

"It would please me to see you again, Mai Ling, and I would be proud to visit your steam generation plant—if it is permitted."

Her hand remained on the paper as I held the other end. Her reluctance to let it go showed clearly in her dark, sad eyes. With my other hand I pulled her toward me gently, kissing her eyes, the tip of her nose, and lightly on her lips. "That was my merit for you."

She looked at me with her almond eyes almost closed in concentration, the question in her mind begging a solution. I knew what she was thinking: the eternal question of ships passing in the night. She ran her hand slowly through her hair and then down my chest, pulling on each button as she did. "We'll probably never see each other again," she said. "Please don't think ill of me, my friend. It has been so long, and I hungered for a man of your stature."

I opened my mouth to speak. She touched it with her fingertips. "No, please, say nothing. We must go, Engineer. The party is almost over . . . your friends will miss you."

We walked slowly in silence back to the reception room. With reluctance and a heavy heart, I kissed the palm of her hand and released it just before we entered. My absence had not gone unnoticed, and the sly looks of my fellow officers told me they thought I'd been rolling in the hay with the beautiful youngest daughter of the harbormaster. The harbormaster, of course, knew better; he knew I was an engineer, and engineering was the only passion his daughter understood.

I lingered, fumbling around so I could be the last into the cars waiting to take us back to the landing. I looked at her again. Her chest, her small breasts confined under the tight-fitting cheongsam, heaved ever so slightly as she shamelessly toyed with the loose buttons on her mandarin collar. Her tongue brushed out of her lips almost imperceptibly as she bent no more than a quarter of an inch in a parting bow. I could still feel the warmth of her kiss as I clung longingly to the perfumed paper she had given me, as if by holding it, a part of her remained.

We steamed at condition two—half the crew on watch, the other half sleeping or carrying out essential ship's work. Watch and watch, it was called. In condition three, our normal steaming condition, a third of the crew was on watch. It really wasn't a half or a third; the cooks and supply people and administrative people went about their normal business of keeping the ship functioning while the operating groups stood watch and watch, on for four, off for four. Grueling, but we didn't know if the CHICOMs would attack or not. We had to be ready. These were hostile seas.

One gun mount, with live ammunition in its ready service racks, was prepared to fire on a few minutes' notice. The fire control men, in their director high over the bridge, were ready to designate and track targets for the guns. The torpedomen stood ready to roll—no! launch—depth charges.

An officer was assigned to CIC, and the repair parties stood, I should say lay, around ready for action with skeleton crews. It was an inefficient way to steam, but it allowed us to fight the ship in minutes. A modified condition Yoke was set, making access through the ship difficult, but less so than with a full Zebra.

In condition one, general quarters, every door was bolted down and everything and everybody stood manned and ready. Condition two was simply a half-assed general quarters, but we could stay on it forever. General quarters could be maintained only for a very limited time. All ship's business stopped and the tension exhausted the crew.

"The CHICOM navy is nowhere equal to ours," the briefing officer had told us, "but don't discount it." I had listened intently. To me, it sounded like a bugle call as I pictured myself getting ready for the Battle of Midway.

"The big threat is from their submarines," he continued. "We think they've got about twenty-five of 'em, nothing new or modern but still formidable. Hitler did a lot more with far fewer boats in the beginning," the briefer droned on as if giving us a history lesson. He must have given this brief a hundred times. *Lucky bastard stationed here on the flagship and going ashore every night.* The thought made me jealous of not being able to see Mai Ling again. I hated him. The captain and XO listened with rapt attention. Most of the junior officers just wanted to get ashore.

"Of the submarines, the whiskey-class, which they got from the Russians, or the couple they built themselves, will be your biggest headache. They're old but damned good. Pay attention to your sonars. A Whiskey is a noisy boat and they have trouble getting close without being heard.

"Go passive as much as you can, and for Christ's sake do it on an unscheduled basis. And do it often. I tell this to all the destroyers coming on station here, but few listen. They go about pinging up the ocean for a hundred miles around themselves. And the CHICOMS just sit back and listen knowing exactly where we are. They're better at this than we are.

"Anytime they want to, they can put a torpedo up your ass and you won't have a clue until you're in the water. Hell, in World War Two, the Germans sank more than four hundred merchies right off our East Coast and we couldn't stop them—and their boats were a lot less sophisticated than the Whiskeys. Sorry to be so blunt, gentlemen, but that's the way it is." The captain glanced at the XO and shook his head.

"The subs are out there, we know that, but we're just too cocky to listen. Give it a go and you'll get some free ASW time. Submerged, those Whiskeys can do fifteen knots. We've detected only two in the last four years and have never surfaced one. It'd make your day and your career if you did.

"They've got a snorkel and long legs. Shit! They've got a radius of sixteen thousand miles, so they can stay in the Strait a lot longer than you guys." He stopped, and with disdain, looked around at the bored faces.

The constant cigarettes the captain smoked and the continual puffing of the XO's pipe showed they didn't care for the smart-ass attitude of the briefing lieutenant commander, even though they both knew *Henshaw* steamed with her sonar on active and rarely went passive. Though the briefing officer seemed conscious of how the captain felt, he didn't seem to give a damn. I guess he'd given this lecture too many times, to too many officers who just didn't care. He knew they just wanted to go ashore for a beer and a good time. It was Kaohsiung.

I was the CIC watch officer; I didn't like it—I'd rather be on the bridge—but this was my condition two station. Combat watches were boring but easier to tolerate; you could at least sit down and read technical manuals on naval warfare. I enjoyed that and had read every one on-board.

To pass the time, I invented games for the radarmen. They didn't like it much; it made them work on something they already knew how to do: who could do the fastest plot of a closest point of approach, the CPA, on a vessel heading toward us; who could decode a made-up signal the fastest; who could do this, who could do that. Speed, speed and accuracy I demanded. But there wasn't much shipping or aircraft traffic on the lethargic Formosa Patrol, and the games quickly grew burdensome and no longer fun.

On the second day out, as we approached the Chinese coast, I related the briefing we'd received in Kaohsiung to *my* watch section. All radarmen held secret clearances. "So I guess the biggest worry is the whiskey-class boats. They got fifteen or more other ones but they're mostly junk and not much of a threat. They've got four ex-Russian Gordy-class destroyers, which aren't too bad, and several captured ex-Japanese gunboats.

"They also have four Riga-class, Russian-designed escorts they built themselves, but they're lightly armored and wouldn't be much of a threat to us." I paused to light my pipe. The radarmen didn't move their eyes from me.

"If the CHICOMs want to hit us, and some say they do, the Whiskeys will probably do the attacking. They're the ones we want to find. The mother has to snorkel and we know they keep an eye on us. It's hide-and-seek and we're 'it.'

"We're going to get one because you guys are going to spot the snorkel on radar . . . no bullshit. You guys are going to spot one because you're the best. And we're going to beat Jarvis and his big ears down there." The radarmen nodded their heads in acknowledgment, smiling.

"I want the ESM receivers manned and scanning for the search radar of the Whiskeys. If he turns that hummer on, I want us to know about it and we'll snare him. And do you know what? I've got five bucks that says I'll find him first." I walked over and taped a five dollar bill to the status board.

The four men looked at me in amazement. "What?" I asked.

Radarman First Class Roland B. Garvin, USN, the leading radarman, spoke first. "No one has ever laid out our duties as well as this before, sir. Nor has anyone given a briefing like you just did. And no one has ever told us what was going on in detail. We never had a pep talk unless we screwed up. Hell, most officers on watch down here read pocket novels while they sit on their asses, or whine until the watch is over."

Bluing screwed up, damn him and his insufferable superiority bullshit.

"Is that good or bad, Garvin?" I said with a laugh.

"Well, I guess it's good; it keeps them out of our hair so we can get our job done," Garvin answered after thinking for a moment. Officers weren't to be trusted when a fellow officer was being criticized by an enlisted man.

I just shook my head and started walking over to the ESM gear. "Sir," Garvin called out. I turned. "We'll get that Whiskey for you, sir."

"Not for me, Garvin, not for you, not for anybody, but for the ship. You should've seen that smart-ass briefing officer. I'd like to jam a whiskey class straight up his sanctimonious ass."

"Sir?" Garvin asked.

"What?"

"Oh, nothing."

"Then get your ass in gear and find that sub."

"They were right!" Garvin said, raising his voice slightly over the hum of the ventilation fans.

"Right, who?"

"The engineers. They're right when they say you're one pushin' mother, Lieutenant."

"Hah!" I laughed. "What the hell do engineers know anyway?" And we manned our stations.

In about half an hour Garvin came up to me with an odd smile.

"What, you get anything?"

"Sir, begging your pardon, sir."

"Goddamnit, Garvin, you sound like someone straight out of *Mutiny on the Bounty.* Are there weevils in the hardtack? Were you shorted on your rum tot or something?"

Garvin, unfazed, said it again in an old English seaman's accent, "Beggin' your pardon, sorr, but some of the boys, some of the top gallant boys, sorr, you know how it is, sorr, have been wantin' to know if . . . did you really make it with the harbormaster's youngest daughter, sorr? With all due respect, sorr."

I smiled as I shouted back in mock anger, "No, goddamnit, I didn't. Watch your fucking radars or I'll have you kissing the gunner's daughter. We're looking for a sub not sea stories."

"He did," the man on the ESM set said to the man on the surface search radar repeater, loud enough for me to hear. "He did, he did, I can tell by how he answered."

We steamed at ten knots to take maximum advantage of our pinging sonar; we hadn't gone passive yet. My radarmen stayed glued to their scopes to detect the slightest target that could be a snorkel tube sticking out of the water. The approximately two-foot-diameter pipe with a hood on top stood above the surface by about four feet. It trailed a slight wake behind itself as it sucked in the oxygen for the sub's diesels and drained off the exhaust while the sub charged its batteries underwater.

I'd ensured that Electronics Technician First Class Jenkins had our surface search up to peak efficiency, maximum performance. Surreptitiously, I kept my hand in the electronics of the ship, even though I had no responsibility there. It was wrong, I knew it, but I did it anyway and enjoyed those times they asked me for advice. The ETs had come a long way, and I didn't want their efforts destroyed. Ensign Rice was a good enough officer, but he needed guidance. Mr. Bluing didn't give advice— at least to my satisfaction he didn't. In the press of everyday operations, the navy woefully neglected leadership training.

I had the IC men, the interior communications gang, who did work for me through the DCA, run a special wire from the bridge to an extra speaker in combat so I could listen in on the sonar circuit for the sub. The IC men took care of all equipment that had wires going in or coming out of it, except for the electronics equipment and the main power lines.

They also took care of the gyrocompass and, most importantly, the movie projectors and the movies. They're the ones who bartered and bribed for good movies from one ship to another and from the lethargic naval stations who didn't care what movies the ships got. They were in

R Division, the Repair Division, under Chess Chadwick, who was Mr. Hethington's JOOD during condition two steaming.

Jarvis, the leading sonarman, who by no stretch of the imagination worked for me, gave special attention to peaking up the sonar after I informed him of the Whiskey threat and the words of the briefing officer. The captain had told all of us to brief our men well on what we could expect. I reckon that Lieutenant Junior Grade Banning, USN, USNA, must have forgotten to give them the full picture. He was my opposite number in combat during condition two. Jarvis told me that all Banning said was there could be some old Russian submarines around and to pay attention.

We'd been under way now for four days, and no meal could pass without someone commenting about me "getting it on" with the harbormaster's youngest daughter. Of course, it was never said in the presence of the captain or the XO. At first I tried to deny it, telling them we just talked about engineering, but the more I said it, the more it sounded like a lie.

The beauty and unattainability of the harbormaster's youngest daughter was legendary in Kaohsiung. The story spread throughout the ship on what a stud I was and "you shoulda seen the girl." In the main spaces, I couldn't show up without some engineer giving a low whistle of admiration. My ego grew to like it, and I offered sly innuendos that it might be true but that I was too much of a gentleman to discuss it. I hated myself every time I said it, swearing each time I'd not say it again.

The XO called me to his stateroom after my watch. The chaplain sat there as I entered. "ASK HIM!" Layman shouted, pointing an accusing finger at me as I walked in and took a seat on the couch. The XO just looked at me, not saying a word. "ASK HIM!" the chaplain's squeaky voice demanded again. The XO still didn't say anything, trying to suppress a smile while busying himself with his pipe.

"Ask me what, Dicky?" I said calmly, not using his middle name.

"SEE, LIEUTENANT COMMANDER, HE CALLS ME THAT NAME. HE CALLS ME DICK HEAD. May God forgive me for saying it."

"Now listen, Chaplain," the XO answered, keeping his coolly modulated voice intact above the screaming. It was as if he were talking to a child. "I didn't hear him call you Dick Head; he called you Dicky. What's the matter with that? And for your information, I am not addressed by my rank of lieutenant commander. You call the XO of a ship either commander or XO."

"Ask me what?" I snapped, trying to stare the chaplain down.

"Are you an adulterer? Have you sinned with a heathen Chinese woman?" he shouted, his right fist stretched toward me, his extended fore-finger wavering inches from my face.

My pulse jumped, my shoulders straightened, and the hairs on my arms bristled. I started to rise with a murderous glaze on my face. The XO's scowl and strong hand on my arm brought me under control. In a moment when I regained my composure, I asked in a voice bleeding with sarcasm, "Do you meaneth, Dicky Boy, have I cometh in some woman's pussy other than that of my wife's?"

The XO burst out laughing as the chaplain bellowed uncontrollably that I'd rot in hell and suffer eternal damnation. He kept screaming it over and over as the XO shoved me out the door, slamming it behind me.

I tried hard, really hard to keep a smirk off my face.

Whiskey-Class

I dragged myself to my midwatch early; we changed watches every four hours and I found sleeping difficult. The Formosa Strait jitters, the old hands called it. I'd get used to it they said. I could only imagine what several weeks of condition two watches would do to the morale and efficiency of the crew. "Don't worry," said the old salts, "After a few more days of boredom, the old man will go back to condition three." The Strait was the closest we could get to a warlike state in our quiescent, peacetime navy.

The clock over the DRT showed 2330. I listened to the passive sonar speaker spewing out the soft rumble of multiple diesel engines superimposed over the hissing murmur of the sea. The sea itself embracing the clicking, snapping, and whoosh of marine life and flowing waters. We were fifty miles off the coast of China.

The radarscopes painted a confusion of feathery, intermittent contacts. I went up to the bridge and saw the makeshift running lights of a fishing fleet stretching out to the dim, moonlit horizon. They had been with us since the previous day, surrounding us as we plodded along at five knots. We had no specific place to go; just being here was our duty. We steamed slow for optimum use of our passive sonar. The captain had listened when the briefer at COMFORPATFOR, Commander Formosa Patrol Force, had said, "Go slow, go passive."

"Common enough sight," John Hethington said, dismissing the fishing fleet with a contemptuous wave of his hand. "This is my third patrol,

Don. It's always the same—boring, just plain boring. Those guys are out there fishing, making a living, and we try to stay out of their way the best we can, but sometimes there are just too many of them. I'm sure we've cut a lot of nets."

"Yes, sir, but haven't they been with us a long time? They were here this morning. Isn't that odd, you know, to stay with us so long?"

"No, they don't seem to mind, don't complain," he said with a chuckle. He lit a cigarette, cupping the lighter in his hands so he wouldn't lose too much of his night vision.

Doesn't seem right. Back in combat I had Garvin activate the DRT. "I want those fishing junks plotted. We'll track every one of them. Let's see if they have a pattern."

"But Mr. Sheppard, that's almost impossible. Christ almighty, there must be fifty to sixty of 'em out there."

"So?"

"Aye, aye . . . ah . . . sir," he replied without enthusiasm, almost forgetting the mandatory "sir," probably thinking, goddamn officers.

Three radarmen, RDs they were called, commenced plotting while another stayed glued to the ESM receivers. The ESM gear was no more than a regular radio tuned to much higher frequencies. It had a direction finding capability and we could record what we heard for later analysis. Since manning the sets was the most boring job in combat, the sets were rarely used. I insisted they be manned for the entire watch. We shifted men in and out of the position every fifteen minutes to fight the monotony.

The tedious plotting, accompanied by subtle complaints, continued, and by 0130 we had a decent picture of the junks around us. They followed our slow speed of five knots, which seemed to be a bit fast for net fishing, but my unfamiliarity with the Chinese fishing patterns did not allow me to give it any significance. The RDs were quite sure by now that standing watches with Sheppard wasn't so much fun anymore.

To the fire control director, high above us atop the pilothouse, we called out targets too weak for the RDs to track and report. The fire control radar had a much better target definition than our AN/SPS-10, surface search radar, and could pinpoint a target to feet—even inches, the fire control men liked to brag.

The director housing the fire control radar was a small gun turret–looking object with protruding arms for visual range finding. It laid out our gun target lines and ranges to target. This information, after being fed to our mechanical fire control computer, trained and elevated the guns, and gave a signal to fire when all was ready. Ensign Rice, manning the fire control director during our watch, enthusiastically joined in our game.

The ship's slow roll at five knots sapped our strength, nibbled at our initiative. We needed a better course to ride comfortably, but it was difficult for us to move with so many fishing junks around. I asked Mr. Hethington to increase to seven knots to see what the fishing junks would do. He reluctantly complied.

They fell behind for five minutes, then increased their speed. They kept up with us. *Why?* But I soon became bored with the game and flipped through the *Radar Identification* book for something useful to do. "How'd they know we changed speeds so fast, Garvin?" I asked more rhetorically than not.

"Maybe they got radar, sir, I doubt it, though; they're a scraggly looking bunch."

Radar? I turned to the commercial radar section. *Yes!* "Garvin," I said, walking over to the ESM receivers. "Garvin, you may be right. Good thinking; check the commercial bands—the low-power navigation kind. Here, here are the frequencies and characteristics," I explained, handing him the book.

Ten more minutes. "Something, sir, bearing 201. Strong signal . . . shut down after two sweeps. Lucky I got it."

I called Mr. Hethington to report. He wasn't interested, saying, "There's a thousand of those small commercial radars around; most merchies carry them. Doesn't mean a thing."

"But it was strong, John, and we don't hold any merchantmen on our screens. Shouldn't we call the old man?"

"Nah! It's nothing. I've got a helluva mess up here trying to stay out of the way of these goddamned junks. They seem to be all over the place. I can't seem to shake 'em."

"That's because they're following us."

"Bullshit, why'd they want to do that?"

"I don't know."

"You sure?" he asked.

"You mean am I sure I don't know?" I answered, being contrite.

"No, asshole, are you sure they're following us?"

"Looks that way from our plot," I replied, trying to sound official.

"You plotting all those junks?" he questioned.

"Yes, sir."

"Waste of time—too many of them. Go back to sleep down there."

"Is that an official order from the bridge, sir?"

"Yes, but just for you—so you can dream of the harbormaster's beautiful youngest daughter and leave us real sailors on the bridge alone." He laughed and the phone went dead.

Standing watches in combat was considered inferior to standing watches on the bridge because the bridge was in command, though in situations such as this one, combat had a much better picture of what was going on. But tradition dies hard, and for centuries ships were fought from the bridge or quarterdeck where one could see the enemy and smell the gunpowder and see the broadsides take effect.

Okay for then, but now the separation of the captain on the bridge from the information available in combat was unacceptable. Now there were long-range strike aircraft and fast submarines and the electronic battles with radar and ECM, electronic countermeasure equipment, such as our ESM gear, jamming and generating false signals, and the newer missiles coming on-line.

"Good morning, sir," Jarvis's voice came over the 29MC from Sonar. "How's it going up there?"

"It's interesting, Jarvis. What do you make of your listening on passive?"

"You been listening, sir?"

"Yeah."

"You . . . ah . . . hear anything strange?" he asked, a stuttering hesitation in his voice.

"It's difficult to draw any conclusions, Jarvis. My ear isn't as good as yours. Whadaya getting at?" I answered, wondering what he was trying to say.

Sonarmen in the fleet were notoriously conservative; far too many times they'd been wrongly criticized for bad calls, and they wanted a fine margin of assurance before they called a contact. They knew that the whole ship or the entire fleet could act on their calls.

It was easy to make a mistake; the sea produced many confusing noises, and many things gave an echo or a sound that seemed like, but had nothing to do with, a submarine. The sonarmen wanted to be sure

before commitment. Because of this, we probably missed many opportunities. I knew from my ASW flying days that their work was hard—
damn hard.

"Odd, sir."

"What, Jarvis, what?" I answered, trying to hold back my impatience.

"I don't know, sir, a little tingle maybe. Lemme get back to you,
okay?" and he hung up.

Staring at the plot on the DRT bewildered me. So many lines crossing
and turning, getting close then moving away. One plotter wore sound-
powered phones to the radar operator and another to the fire control director. Between the two, the plot grew more complex by the minute.
Lines started from nowhere and some ended in the same place.

"This one, sir, is different," Garvin said, pointing to a relatively
straight line plot. "It—"

"Got the signal again, sir," the young man on the ESM gear shouted.
"Same radar now bearing 220 degrees. Strong signal, only two sweeps."

"Got it," I yelled, turning back to Garvin. "What do—" But before
I had time to finish I saw his finger on one plot line now outlined in
red. It was almost a straight line trailing off to our left at about two
thousand yards, generally pulling to the right as if it were trying to
overtake and parallel us. All the other plots moved in random patterns
around us.

"Jarvis," I said over the phone, "look at—"

"At 221, sir?" he interrupted.

"Yeah, whadaya got?"

"I've got our searchlight mode on. Listen to it with earphones. Hear
anything strange?"

I listened but detected nothing until he said, "I'll switch to another
junk . . . listen." I strained my ears in concentration. "Now back,
sir . . . listen." And it was almost obvious. The signal from the one at 220
had a confused sound like a diesel engine with the whir of an electric
motor superimposed over it, whereas the other one was purely a small
diesel engine, clear and distinct.

"Whadaya think, sir?" he asked, his uneasiness barely controlled.

"Goddamnit, Jarvis, you're the expert. What the fuck do you think?"

A second's pause, then, "I think a submarine is hiding under that
junk's diesel engine."

"So do I, Jarvis . . . so do I. It's had a straight track for an hour, whereas the other junks are random. I think it is, Jarvis. Do not, do not go active until ordered. Got it?"

I briefed Mr. Hethington, requesting permission to call the XO, who was our ASW man for combat. He said no, it was my imagination. I said I would call him anyway, miffed that he so cavalierly dismissed our findings. He said, "Okay, call the XO." I recommended he call the captain. He said no. I said I'd call him. I suspected that Mr. Hethington knew if we obtained contact, he'd be up the rest of the night. With his anger undisguised, he said he'd call the captain.

The twenty-four-hour clock read 0312 as the XO arrived. I started to brief him when a sleepy-eyed captain in his shorts came in, saying, "Take it from the top." Neither one seemed happy; neither one had been to bed before midnight.

They both looked at the plot; both heard the commercial radar recording and both ran through the sonar listening. They looked at each other, then at me. Neither looked groggy anymore. "So you think it's a submarine trailing us, Mr. Sheppard," the XO said, more a statement than a question.

"Yes, sir, and as you can see from the plot, it appears he's slowly moving in to parallel us. That just started, by the way," I said, lecturing; they could plainly see from the plot what was happening.

"Why?" the captain asked.

I looked at him; my heart beat a little faster and I gripped the corner of the DRT for support. *Why? I hadn't considered why.* I took a deep breath. The captain looked over to the XO; the XO raised an eyebrow. They knew something I didn't. *Shit!*

"Well . . . ah . . ." I sucked in another breath of the smoky air. "One, ah . . . possible scenario, Captain, is he's moving into position off our port side so he can turn and put a torpedo into us broadside." The XO winced, then forced a nonchalant face. The captain lit the cigarette that a radarman offered him and scratched his groin through his underwear.

"Possibility," I continued, "they could be practicing this technique for future use." Neither of the two changed their expression. I took it as a signal to continue my postulations. I berated myself for not considering why it was happening before I called them. *I'm not much of a naval officer; I'm shooting from the hip.*

"It could be a damaged boat and the junks are just escorting her in. But that seems a little far-fetched, since their course isn't taking them any closer to China." I looked at the captain, then to the XO. "Christ, Captain . . . I don't know. I'm sorry."

The captain turned to the lead radarman. "Garvin, at present conditions, how soon will he be in position off our port beam?" Garvin, who had been listening to us in rapt attention, jumped to the DRT as if a red-hot poker was jammed up his ass. Twenty-three minutes popped into my mind.

Garvin rudely pushed aside the men doing the plotting, bent over the DRT, and worked furiously with a parallel ruler and a set of dividers to come up with a solution. We waited in silence. The man on the ESM gear shouted, "Got it again, Captain, bearing 230. Strong, two sweeps."

The sub, I knew it was a sub, was adjusting, moving into position.

"Twenty-four minutes, Captain," Garvin reported, and the plotters went back to their work.

"Come with me," the captain said, and the XO and I followed him into his sea cabin. He started dressing as he said, "Don, we had another briefing, a top secret one, at COMFORPATFOR that you weren't privy to. I'm sure you enjoyed your lady friend much more." I flushed; he smiled, then continued, "Rumor says the CHICOMS are expected to launch some kind of provocative action very soon. This may be it. I think your first evaluation was the most plausible."

"GQ, Captain?" the XO asked, getting up and heading toward the door.

"Silently, XO. I don't want to alert the sub of any change, and banging the doors closed would do just that."

The XO looked at his watch. "It's 0330. Most of the ship is awake now changing the watch. We'll pass GQ by word of mouth, and tell them to close the doors gently."

"If I may make a suggestion, Captain," I said, standing to leave. "Why don't we blow tubes. That's noisy enough to mask any clanking going on." He nodded yes.

The XO left as I reached for the telephone, asking the captain with my eyes if I could use it. He nodded yes again. "Main control, this is Mr. Sheppard. Oh, Langston, good morning . . . yes, thank you. Get ready to blow tubes as fast as you can. We got a situation up here, and blowing tubes will help. Lemme know right away when you're ready. I'll be in combat. Langston, by the way, we're going to GQ now—but silently. No banging around down there. Keep it quiet, okay? We got a CHICOM sub who may want to play with us. I'll be down as soon as I can. And Langston, inform Chief Maclin and pass the word to the spaces and the damage control parties. Thanks . . . oh, you're ready to blow tubes now?" I looked at the captain for permission.

"Are you the OOD?" he asked, raising one eyebrow. *No, of course I wasn't.* I felt like a fool.

"Sorry, Captain. Wait, Langston, I've got to brief the OOD."

Returning to combat, I heard the clattering, whooshing sound of blackened steam from the stacks penetrating the steel bulkheads. Built-in steam piping inside the boilers shot high-pressure steam into the fireboxes. The steam, hitting the outside of the tubes, blew away the soot that formed around them. If the wind wasn't right, the soot and the steam spewed out of the stacks, covering everything topside with a tenaciously clinging, powdery black mess.

We usually maneuvered so the wind blew athwartships—across our decks. This lessened the mess, but the deckhands in 1st Division always hated the engineers for making their lives more difficult. We were lucky tonight; we couldn't maneuver but the winds blew across us. Most of the soot blew into the Strait and, I'm sure, into many of the fishing junks. It was particularly messy this morning because our low-speed steaming had sooted up the tubes very badly.

The soot forming around the tubes in the fireboxes insulated them from the flame, which reduced our heat transfer efficiency. We had to use more fuel to compensate. We engineers wanted to blow tubes every four hours, but no one else on the ship did, especially the Deck Division.

As I walked into combat, the XO had his ASW team assembled. He motioned me over. "Don, if you want, you can take it. You discovered the sub; he's yours to prosecute," he said, magnanimously handing me his sound-powered phones. I slipped them on. My first prosecution. *Stand by Communists; the Nameoki Kid is in the saddle. High fucking noon.*

"Thanks, XO." But I noticed him putting on another set. "Jarvis, Sheppard here. It's you and me, baby. This one's for real. Keep a good ear for hydrophone effects, torpedo in the water noise." I shuddered at the word torpedo as it dawned on me that I had forgotten all about torpedo evasion maneuvering. *What was it? Yeah, turn thirty degrees off their inward path . . . was it thirty? And then turn into the path to offer a smaller target . . . is that right? Will that work? Shit! I can't ask anyone now. Hell I'm an OOD, I should know these things. Christ!*

"XO?" I asked in a few minutes, as if it were just for conversation. "XO . . . you really think it works to turn into the torpedoes when you detect them coming?"

I lit my pipe as if I really didn't care what the answer was. "That's what doctrine says, Don, that's what I would do."

"Yeah," I answered, bending over the plot and cuddling my sound-powered phones tighter over my ears. *Whew!*

Twenty minutes passed and we were at full general quarters, 1AS, ASW condition, with the ship buttoned up and all hands on station. Except for continuing the course to draw closer to our broadside, the junk and the sub gave no indications of knowing we were ready. Their commercial radar shinned out every ten minutes, right on schedule each time. Two bathy drops had been made in the last ten minutes; we knew the thermoclines. There were none—we had a level playing field. Four minutes until he could be in position to fire.

"Plan, Don?" the captain asked over the phone. He must have known that the XO had turned it over to me. What confidence they had to let this wise-ass punk kid prosecute a real threat.

"In about a minute, sir, with your permission, I'm going to turn into him and hit him with one fully focused sonar blast. After that, Captain, I'll have to wait and see what he does."

"XO, you concur?" the captain asked.

"Yes, sir . . . we've chatted."

"Ahh . . . Captain," I asked, "will you alert main control? I . . . we will need them to answer the bells quite smartly . . . if you would, sir."

"You worry about the prosecution, I'll take care of everything else. But if it makes you more comfortable to know, I've talked to Maclin and *your* engineers already. Okay? We know what to do, son." I felt foolish again. *Son?*

I keyed the mouthpiece of my phones. "Stand by, Jarvis, we're going to turn into him now to make any torpedo shot a little more difficult for him. Ready? The junk's out there at eighteen hundred yards, bearing 247. You got the picture, just like we talked about—one blast full on, then listen. Stand by! Jarvis, stand by, we're coming around. NOW! NOW! Hit it!"

The lights dimmed as the highly concentrated beam of sound slashed out from the transducer deep under our hull. I could only imagine the effect in the sub when it hit. It was deafening, I knew. The loudspeaker in combat passed the returning ping to us in clarion quality.

"Sonar contact bearing 247, range seventeen hundred twenty yards, echo quality sharp, up Doppler, classified possible submarine, designate Sierra One," came Jarvis's report. A smile crossed the XO's face. I wondered how Mr. Hethington felt about this. His verbal opposition to a possible submarine was widely known on the bridge and in combat. This wouldn't make him like me any better.

"Bearing has junks surrounding it," reported Mr. Bluing, on the bridge at his GQ station, as he was required to do on all sonar contacts to ensure the contact wasn't a ship.

"Stay passive, Jarvis," I cautioned. I knew that his urge to go active must have been driving him crazy.

"Mark datum, designate Datum One," I casually told the DRT team as I tried to maintain my cool. They'd already marked it lightly until official confirmation came from the ASW team leader. All datum meant was a mark on the DRT table showing last contact.

"He's increased speed and is pulling away," Jarvis reported uselessly; we could hear it on the speaker. I glanced at the XO, hoping for some guidance. He seemed to read my thoughts.

"You've got it, Don."

"He's a Whiskey, Mr. Sheppard . . . positive ident."

Sonar had tapes of the submerged sounds of most of the world's submarine classes and practiced continually in their identifications. We could even compare the sounds side by side with our tape recorders.

"Sonar, go active." We had him; I felt great.

For an hour he ran at twelve knots northwest toward China. How long he had been submerged before we detected him, I didn't know. I asked Garvin how long we'd been with the fishing fleet. How long could he stay submerged at twelve knots? Not too much longer, I reckoned. He'd have to snorkel soon. Or he could turn and attack or, more simply, fire out of his stern tubes. He could carry at least twenty torpedoes if he were attack configured, far fewer if he were a minelayer. He didn't try to maneuver; he ran dead for the coast of China.

This wasn't much fun; we'd have to make him surface to score a point, or, of course, sink him if he took hostile action. I hoped we could sink him; a Whiskey is a creditable enemy. But if the seas grew choppy and mixed the water, we'd get thermoclines and the sub could probably get away.

The plotting paper on the DRT contained my notes on the chase. It became a legal document once we started prosecution. I felt the chase as if I were a primordial hunter running a mammoth to ground. Over and over I asked myself what action I would take if he turned on us to fire or fired at us from his stern tubes. I kept a close watch on his stern angle; when it even got close to the proper launch angle, I turned radically.

When the captain dropped down to combat for a look at the chart, he handed the XO a message. In a few seconds, the XO handed it to me. It came from COMFORPATFOR, saying, generally, to try to surface the sub using reasonable efforts and, if we were attacked, to defend ourselves.

"I don't understand what *reasonable efforts* are," I said, handing the message back to the captain.

The captain laughed. "Neither do I. If things go to hell, a court of inquiry in Hawaii would have to determine that on Monday morning. They'll be critical in their starched whites with their proclivity to eat their young."

PINNNNG . . . ping. PINNNNG . . . ping.

"Sierra One slowing, sir, and turning to starboard."

"All engines ahead one-third; make turns for ten knots," I ordered over the sound-powered phones. The ASW team leader effectively had the conn while prosecuting a contact. The bridge would obey his orders unless a collision or close call might result. I saw the engine order telegraph repeater over the DRT drop to one-third.

"Up Doppler; combat, we're closing; echo quality still sharp . . . he's tracking good."

At 0523 the XO handed me a cup of coffee, asking, "You want me to take it for a while?" *Is he kidding?*

"Oh, thank you, but no, XO, I'm okay." I reached for the phone circuit to main control.

Chief Maclin answered. "You having fun up there while we sweat our balls off down here, sir?"

"Yeah, Chief, but it looks like we're going to have some more. The sub's slowed and is heading for us. All he can see now is a bow shot, but he always had that opportunity with his stern tubes. We don't understand why he's doing this, but you guys will have to be bloody fast on the bells if he gets ornery."

"How big are those boats, sir?"

"About sixteen hundred tons displacement submerged, and he comes in at two hundred feet long . . . big! He's got two big diesels at four thousand horsepower each. And he can stay under a long time."

"From what I hear, he's been down a long time. Won't he have to snorkel soon?"

"I would think so, Chief." I knew he'd pass this information to all the spaces; he was good at sharing the word. I always told him as much as I could. Other people I've dealt with just hinted at how much they knew, using it as a power tool to achieve status when not deserved. I never told this kind of guy anything.

"Sierra One has slowed to three knots, range one thousand yards, echo quality sharp, up Doppler," Sonar reported.

The reports were now abbreviated. We could see it on the DRT plotting paper as someone in Sonar passed the info directly to the radarmen plotting the locations on the DRT plotter. The XO had left combat twenty minutes before to arrange breakfast for the crew. He had broken the cooks and mess cooks away from their battle stations and sent them to the galley. I dialed the captain. "Captain, could you come down here a minute? I think something's going to happen." As the captain entered, I heard the word passed for the XO to report to combat. The captain had shaved and put on clean, starched khakis. The XO came in thirty seconds later.

"He's getting too close. I think he wants to snuggle up and raise his snorkel. I don't know how he's stayed down so long anyway at the speeds he's been making. I'd like to use gertrude, sir." Gertrude was our underwater loudspeaker system. It was called an underwater telephone but it was more like an underwater loud hailer. The captain nodded yes.

"Uncle Joe . . . Uncle Joe . . . do you hear me? Over." Sonar sent out into the water. Uncle Joe was the standard hailing call for Russian submarines. I didn't know if it worked for the Chinese. Maybe we should have called Uncle Mao. In any case they didn't answer. It wouldn't have made any difference if they had; we had no one on board who understood Chinese. It was all part of the game.

"Combat, he's turning again, coming to port. He's at three knots . . . still turning to port. No speed increase. He's running parallel to our course now . . . range one thousand yards off the starboard beam."

"Bridge, combat, we think he's going to snorkel. Keep an eye peeled off the starboard beam," I passed to the OOD, Mr. Bluing. I wondered what the sub's skipper was thinking. This had to be embarrassing. His turning into us at this close range and running parallel could only mean he had no hostile intent. *Yeah?* We'd just made two more bathy drops, and the water stayed in our favor.

Five minutes passed. Those men who had eaten breakfast were now back on their GQ stations. They were tense; you could feel it. It permeated the ship like vomit in a closed car.

The captain kept the ship briefed over the 1MC throughout the chase. He briefed them again, ending with, "It is our intention to surface that sub. It doesn't happen that often. Once he surfaces, and everyone who wants to gets a picture, the chase is over."

"Combat, he's blowing ballast. He's coming up, zero Doppler," Jarvis reported with a slightly higher voice than normal. "UP! UP!"

"Periscope broad off the starboard beam," the starboard lookout yelled so loud that we heard it in combat one deck below. We had the doors open so the captain could get to the bridge fast. He and the XO ran topside. In three minutes they returned.

"Mr. Sheppard, ahead standard and come to port if you would," the captain ordered. I passed the command to the bridge, then looked at him for guidance. "Go out to two thousand yards ahead of him and drop a depth charge across his course." I briefed Sonar and main control.

"Don't worry, sir," Chief Maclin replied with uncharacteristic mirth. "We've got plenty of fresh spring bearings aboard."

The water erupted as the depth charge, set shallow, threw tons of water into the air. We'd dropped while making twenty knots and were well away when it exploded. I swung wide and headed back toward the sub. His periscope and snorkel disappeared. He got the message.

Station keeping on his two-knot speed was a nightmare of rudder and engine orders. Destroyers were much more maneuverable at high speeds. At two knots, each slight roll intensified to a heavy sea. We handled it well, and those who hadn't eaten yet went to breakfast. I ate at the DRT. No one was going to take this chase away from me. The XO, finally realizing this, made no more suggestions for a relief. This sub was mine.

He ran shallow in the calm sea, but the weather was freshening and pretty soon he'd have to go deeper. The increased wind made station keeping more difficult. His periscope appeared again. We ran out ahead and dropped another depth charge, this time at fifteen hundred yards in front of him. He dove again. It was 0958 when his periscope broke the surface for the third time. His snorkel popped up, and we heard his die-sels start.

We went through the depth charge drop again at thirteen hundred yards, but he didn't react. *This Chinese skipper must have balls of iron.* If it were Chinese. "Suggestions, gentlemen?" the captain asked.

I shrugged my shoulders in despair; the sub had called our bluff. The XO said nothing. "What if he thinks we'll ram him?" the captain asked as if we were discussing what kind of charcoal to use at a barbecue.

I came in at ten knots, heading directly for his periscope. I now had the conn on the bridge, and the XO had the ASW job in combat. My magnificent captain was letting me play this one out. Bless his heart. His nervousness showed in his hands holding each other as if trying to stop them from doing something, something stupid. One thousand yards, closing. I could see the eye of the periscope. What must they think of a destroyer barreling down on them, attempting a collision? It would hurt them a hellova lot more than us. The sub's skipper knew this.

As I saw the periscope start down and heard the check valve on the snorkel tube clank shut, I came around hard to port, missing by one hundred yards the swirling water where the scope had a minute ago dis-appeared. The captain leaned against the bulwark, all color drained from his face as if he were in shock. He looked out to sea to conceal it. I doubted we'd try that one again. "I cut that just a little too close; sorry, Captain."

Back in combat, we continued tracking the sub. Deeper now at two hundred feet, the sub continued its crawl to China. Often he'd stop and we'd circle until he moved. We hung on tenaciously. It must be foul down there. The seas grew smoother, and our last bathy drop showed thermoclines forming. How long can that guy stay below? We moved forward of him again. In direct violation of international law, and an act of war, we rolled another depth charge, this time set deep, to explode a thousand yards in front of him. It had to shake them up a little.

It did.

Sonar reported, "He's blowing ballast, he's coming up . . . he's com-ing up." At 1042 the sub surfaced and two men ignobly appeared on the top of the conning tower hoisting the People's Republic of China flag. We dipped our flag in salute, trained the guns forward, and steamed around him twice to take pictures. We dipped our flag once more, then like the conquering hero rode off into the mythical sunset.

We'd made our coup. It was 1115; I'd have to be on watch again in thirty minutes.

Garvin took down the five dollar bill I'd taped up four days ago. "Jarvis won . . . sir!" he said, smiling.

We pulled into Kaohsiung three days later for replenishment and fuel. Since surfacing the Whiskey, everything else paled. The old hands had been right; we went back to condition three, modified in that one skeleton director and one gun crew stayed manned up. The rest of us were on one in three again with the four to eight in the afternoon dogged, that is, two two-hour watches instead of one four, so the watch standers could rotate. I returned to the bridge from CIC.

Doctor Mai Ling was in the city of Keelung, to the north, when we returned for replenishment, and it made me sad. I did, however, have a short talk with her father. He seemed pleased to see me go, and I'm sure Mai Ling was never told of my visit.

Two more weeks on the Strait left us drained. We didn't hold drills for fear of a breakdown out here all by ourselves. We had settled into a quiet routine of boredom and near apathy. On the second to the last day of our patrol, an early-morning fog demanded we steam slower than normal. We still used mostly passive sonar.

Having just gotten off the four to eight in the morning, I talked to the captain about our freshwater problem. The evaporators weren't working too well and our store of freshwater grew smaller every day. We had one big evaporator and one small one. We couldn't find the trouble in the big one even though it was a simple system.

It worked by heating seawater with high-pressure steam from the boilers. We then ran the seawater-generated steam through a series of cooling tubes to condense it into freshwater and pumped the remaining brine overboard. By the same method we collected the condensate from the steam we used to heat the seawater. We wasted nothing at sea. The evaporators were our only source of feed water for the boilers and galley, for drinking, and for showers. No one had taken a shower for a week.

With "water hours" declared—that is, water available only at specified times—woe be unto anyone caught violating them. Sickening, dank body odors permeated every nook of the ship. The situation became critical, almost to a point where we might have to return to Kaohsiung early, but we had only two more days on station; we could scrape by until then, I hoped. After Kaohsiung, we were off to Subic Bay for a repair period and liberty in Olongapo.

To my chagrin, we had to quit blowing tubes because that steam was blown out of the stacks and consequently lost. Our fuel consumption grew at an alarming rate as the increasing soot insulated our thickly encrusted fire tubes. Cold sandwiches were the norm because they used far less water than the regular meals, and not as many trays and silverware had to be used and washed.

The clear sound of small-arms gunfire carried over the misty water from our port side. Two weak radar returns had been detected from that direction about ten minutes previously. They appeared to be two fishing junks merging into one blip. We thought nothing of it; it happened frequently and they were moving away, out of our way. Eyes strained to see the source. Three more shots cracked in our ears. "Man the fifties," the captain spoke softly as we turned left to track the shooting. "All stop!" the captain whispered, taking the conn. Shouts came out of the fog. A scream.

"Ahead one-third, turns for three knots." Laughter, harsh and crude, just ahead of us.

"Contact lost in close range, Captain," both the JOOD and combat reported.

A whispered, "All stop." A woman's scream. Another shot. A cry. A curse. Guttural laughter. Very close.

The fog cleared just a little as we coasted forward, rolling gently in the lazy sea. Chinese voices demanding, Chinese voices pleading came from close on the port bow.

"Clear the fog watch off the fo'c'sle," the captain whispered. A messenger leaped to obey. The XO appeared with a .45-caliber automatic pistol strapped around his waist. He handed one to the captain and motioned three gunner's mates, each with a Garand rifle, to spread out along the walkway aft to the signal bridge.

We waited. Drifting. The voices grew louder. We stayed deathly silent. Women sobbing, harsh voices demanding. A scream. "One long blast, if you please, Boatswain's Mate," the captain ordered softly.

A huge roar of steam erupted from our whistle, designed to be heard more than over a mile away. I foolishly thought of the feed water this was taking. Six seconds of deafening blast must have sounded like the call to hell to the unsuspecting Chinese. Shouting, cries, confusion. An engine started. Running feet. Harsh oaths. A diesel engine fading away. Clearing fog. A scrape of wood against our port side just aft of the anchor. A clear view—a fishing junk.

We made her fast amidships as the XO and Corpsman Jennings went over the side, two of the gunner's mates preceding them. "A fishing junk, pirates. We scared them off," the captain recited to no one.

The chaplain, standing midships with his foot-long cross to fend me off if I appeared, did nothing, just looked at the junk, shaking his head, mumbling something I couldn't hear from the signal bridge. I noticed the XO motioning him into the junk, but the chaplain's violently shaking head indicated no as he scurried away.

Twenty minutes later the XO signaled to the captain from the main deck midships. The captain picked up a phone; they talked. "I can't take them with us into Kaohsiung," is all I heard of the conversation. The junk's lines were slipped three minutes later and she drifted away, trying to start her engine. The captain backed down one-third to give her clearance, waited until we had stern way on, opposed the engines to twist away, and rang up ahead two-thirds for the slow steam to Kaohsiung for fuel, water, and debriefing.

"One woman raped, one man dead, one woman shot in the leg, not too badly. Three men and one young boy about ten severely beaten, and several things stolen—I couldn't tell what. One old man spoke a little English," the XO dispassionately reported. "We dressed their wounds, gave 'em some food, and wished them well. They were Red Chinese, more afraid of us than of the pirates."

I couldn't go ashore; we'd be here for only three hours, and we had to refuel and take on water. My heart ached, like a schoolboy's first romance, to see Mai Ling again. *Grow up, Sheppard.*

As I left COMFORPATFOR's flagship, I slipped a letter and a package to one of the young officers, asking him to deliver it *personally* to the harbormaster's youngest daughter. He winked knowingly. I guess the story had gotten around the flagship. I had betrayed Mai Ling. He accepted the mission gladly. He knew of her and welcomed the opportunity to meet her.

The letter expressed my thanks again and told her I hadn't had a chance to test her system but would write to her when we did. The package contained the greatest gift I could give, an operating manual for our plant. It wasn't classified; we'd given them out with our gift of destroyers to half a dozen foreign governments. I wished I could have seen her—touched her. *A fantasy—did it even happen?*

Jungle Jim

The radar painted a soothing yellow-orange picture of the Philippines as we steamed south down her mountainous west coast. Pictures of World War Two limped in and out of my mind. The Japanese had devastated the islands not too many years ago. We turned east, then northeast as we entered Subic Bay and headed for the large U.S. Naval Repair Facility located there.

Bataan Peninsula passed down our starboard side as we headed in for the port city of Olongapo. I imagined the desperate fight the Americans had endured with the intense Japanese shelling, the creeping starvation, as the fanatical hordes of the Land of the Rising Sun stormed inexorably down the peninsula.

My mind saw Gen. Douglas MacArthur escaping on the PT boats and the fifty-nine-year-old Brig. Gen. Jonathan Mayhew Wainright, U.S. Army, taking command, keeping the futile fight going.

A thousand ghosts screamed at me: ghosts without faces, without uniforms—gaunt men in steel helmets begging me for help. I thought of Corregidor, that hopelessly lost island at the mouth of Manila Bay, and the bloody defensive battle waged there.

I thought of the infamous seventy-mile death march from Bataan—the thousands of Filipinos and Americans dying at the hands of the oppressively cruel Japanese. The goal of the march was Camp O'Donnel, an idyllic-sounding place that soon came to mean forced labor, constant agony, and finally death.

"Let it go, Don," Mr. Bluing said, seeming to detect my feelings as we stood next to each other on the signal bridge. The crystal-clear light blue bay and the white sand and the thick jungle on each side left me awe-struck. A gentle breeze teasing the palms, and small fishing boats slowly trolling and netting, denied that any man-made disturbance could exist juxtaposed to such tranquillity.

"Moored."

"All stop . . . double up all lines. Main control, secure main engines," Mr. Bluing ordered in rapid succession. He'd made a superb, two-bell landing, as his ship-handling skill demanded. He was good.

It was 0930. A small band of navy chiefs and officers and Filipino customs officials came aboard as soon as the brow went over. Two dozen sailors in gleaming whites shuffled around the quarterdeck waiting for customs clearance and liberty call. I didn't know how they managed to get there so fast. Hell, we'd just secured the special sea and anchor de-tail five minutes ago.

Customs clearance consisted of the XO saying, "Nothing to declare."

"Liberty call. Liberty call. Liberty for the crew sections one and three. Liberty call," passed over the 1MC. The early birds, money in their pock-ets and lust in their hearts, headed for the sin city of the Orient, Olongapo.

The XO knew from experience he'd have a dozen requests for mar-riage-to-a-foreign-national forms by 0900 tomorrow.

Earlier we'd sent our more urgent requests ahead by Teletype to the repair facility, the evaps being our most critical. We'd managed to get it up to about half capability, but that wasn't enough.

That morning, while still at sea, the XO eased the water restrictions so we wouldn't smell so bad when we arrived in port. I didn't think it was a good idea because, until we were alongside the piers, we could still have been called upon for a mission. I, we, just wouldn't have enough feed water to remain at sea if all the crew took showers. I voiced strong objections to deaf ears. The captain sided with the XO, but I showed them—I didn't take a shower.

The repair facility took all our jobs, adding a few of their own that BUSHIPS had authorized as class upgrades. This wasn't at all like Yoko-suka and their parsimonious ways. Olongapo was fine duty, and the per-sonnel assigned wanted the reputation of being the best and the cheapest in the world. They were. The lieutenant commander, the repair officer himself, was in the boarding party and told us he'd take care of everything and he didn't need the crew to help. "Service," he said, "is why I'm here and service is what you'll get."

After the initial briefing by the repair officer, the department heads met separately with their counterparts in the boarding party. The engineering meeting, held in a corner of the mess decks, revealed they'd clean all four boilers, an onerous task, and renew any insulation lagging that needed it. "Leaks?" they asked. "Point 'em out and we'll fix 'em." All too good to be true.

Next came a team from their Welfare and Recreation Department describing to the crew the many facilities and activities they could attend. Getting laid in Olongapo never came up. The facility commander, a full captain and a good Christian, wanted to offer enough things to do so the sailors wouldn't be bored or enticed to sin. "Good clean activity to renew the body and cleanse the soul," he preached to the men responsible for the welfare and recreation of their "guest ships."

A wild-game dinner scheduled by welfare and rec Wednesday night needed more meat, so a couple of hunting parties were being organized to get the game. I wanted to go but felt I should remain onboard to supervise the repairs. I mentioned this to the XO, who was planning to go. He said I wasn't needed and I'd just get in the way. "The Subic Bay repair facility is the best in the world. Leave them alone to do their job," he remonstrated, ordering me to go.

At the last minute the XO canceled out, leaving only Ensign Rice, Jarvis, Jenkins, and me to go. We left late Monday afternoon under the supervision of a chief petty officer and three small Negrito pygmies. "They know what they're doing, sir," the welfare and rec chief said when he saw the looks on our faces. "Trust 'em."

An old navy pickup truck trundled along rutted, narrow roads the jungle raced to reclaim as we drove deeper and deeper into the tangled bush. The chief hummed show tunes from the thirties as we bounced along. "Good duty here, sir," he said to me sitting next to him in the cab, then resumed his humming. Sailors either hate a place or love it. When time to transfer, they'd always say the next duty assignment was going to be the best and the one they were leaving was always the worst. I wondered if it held true for Subic Bay.

After forty minutes, the chief pulled up in a clearing. Here the road ended in a tangle of vines and large trees. "Wild boar hunting is best here," he said, swinging out of the closed-bed pickup. He opened the tailgate, motioning the sailors and pygmies out. The hunting party didn't look so good; the small black, and I mean black, pygmies hadn't spoken a word during the entire trip, and the temperature in the closed pickup bed had drained them all.

"Just do as they tell you. They don't speak English but they can get their message across," the chief said, adding that he'd be back tomorrow at 0900. Two of the pygmies picked up our food and packs and quickly set off into the jungle. Their leader jerked his head for us to follow them. We hugged our twelve-gauge shotguns loaded with buckshot and looked around at each other. We shrugged and walked into the jungle.

I'd hated shotguns ever since I saw Mr. Brown, a neighbor in Nameoki, put a double-barreled shotgun under his chin and pull both triggers. I was eight years old.

The four-foot-tall pygmies set a quick pace. I felt as if I were in some Tarzan movie. The realization that I was heading deeper into an unknown and frightening element made my breath come harder. Maybe it was the heat that made my knees buckle, or maybe it was the undergrowth. I could see that my mates felt the same way, but none of us macho men would dare admit it.

We stopped after twenty minutes and watched the worker pygmies clear a spot for us to sit while the lead man opened up a sack, producing lunch for us courtesy of the Subic Bay Welfare and Recreation Department.

He didn't say a word as he passed out the box lunches. We opened them: an apple and two wilted, heavily mayonnaised bologna sandwiches. The navy called bologna horse cock in deference to the uncut loaf's shape. The lead pygmy moved over to sit by his men. They ate some strange root that one of the men chopped off a tree. He offered us a bite but we politely refused. *God, it's hot.*

The leader, wearing a bone in his hair and a loincloth for clothes, said, *"Wego."* The two men policed up the area and we followed them deeper into the jungle.

"You know they're headhunters, don't you, sir?" Jarvis laboriously puffed out. He weighed more than 250 pounds. He shouldn't have been here in this sweltering jungle.

"No, I didn't know they were headhunters," Rice answered. "But surely welfare and rec wouldn't put us out here with wild men, would they?"

"Well, I hear," Jarvis said, "that the base security guys were having problems with thieves climbing over or cutting the fences and robbing the place blind every night . . ." He stopped in midsentence, looking around as if searching for a noise—he had phenomenally sensitive ears—

then rubbed his profusely sweating face with a towel, adding, "Well, the story goes they hired these Negritos to patrol the fence. In the morning after the first night, ten heads, stuck on top of the fence poles, greeted the facility and they haven't had any trouble since." We just looked at him.

I clutched my shotgun tighter against the ever-thickening jungle. Vines reached out, grabbing us with their slimy tentacles. I couldn't scream; I was an officer. Our feet stuck in the glob of the rotting undergrowth, making a sucking squish as we pulled them free. We forced ourselves to smile when we furtively glanced at each other.

Mr. Rice's face was pale, drawn. Jarvis puffed, his ambling walk slowing us with each step. The lead man, who liked to be called Jungle Jim, the chief had told me, prodded Jarvis with a stick. It pissed me off, but I said nothing. What could I say? I didn't want him pissed off at us.

The occasional snake slithered on the ground in front of us; we could see others in the overhanging tree branches. I pointed these out to Jungle Jim. He shrugged and flashed me an ominous smile.

In a little less than an hour we came to another clearing. Jarvis's weight and the heat exertion had taken their toll. He slumped to the ground like a dropped egg the second we passed the tree line. Jungle Jim looked at him disdainfully, speaking in soft tones to his men. I'm sure it wasn't complimentary.

The two pygmies smirked and disappeared back into the jungle. They were out of sight in ten seconds. I refused myself the pleasure of sitting down like the others were doing. I hadn't missed Jungle Jim's message. It didn't matter to them that Jarvis was perhaps the finest sonarman in the fleet, thereby aiding in keeping his country free of Communists.

Toughing it out, I motioned for us to leave, lifting my shotgun into the air like a defiant American Indian. Jungle Jim smiled, shaking his head no. I snuck the shotgun down. In ten minutes his two men appeared carrying red fruit. They offered it to us, laughing like schoolboys. Neither of them wore shoes, but each carried a machete in a rope belt.

Jarvis took one of the bright red, apple-sized melons, looking at it with his nose turned up. The smallest pygmy, three inches shorter than the others, laughed, taking his machete and slicing one of the fruits into two. He put one of the pieces into his mouth, muttering ummmm, and gave the other half to Jenkins. Jenkins took a hesitant bite. His eyes flashed into the jungle, then back at the fruit. He smiled, looked perplexed for a moment, then eagerly jammed the rest of it into his mouth. "Good," he slobbered through crunching teeth. I tried it.

"Great, sweet," I managed to get out as I greedily munched the one handed to me.

I leaned over and gave some to the panting Jarvis. He gobbled it up and asked for more. The pygmies finally sat. So did we. I offered them cigarettes. They puffed furiously, blowing out smoke rings in the still, hot, muggy air. The rings held their shape amazingly well for minutes before breaking up. I'd never seen that; it must have been the oppressive humidity.

Jungle Jim stood up dramatically and stomped out his cigarette with his bare foot, miming to us that we could no longer smoke. Then he got on all fours, moving back and forth, rooting the ground. He raised his head and sniffed, picking up the cigarette to his nose, then pretended to run away from us. "Got it Jungle Jim, the wild boar will smell the smoke and run away," I said and the others agreed. "We understand." Jungle Jim got up, smiling through his broken, blackened, sharp-pointed teeth.

A roar like a lion's broke through the jungle we'd just traversed. I looked in fear to my companions and we all looked at Jungle Jim. He screwed up his face, nodding his head back and forth, and waved his hands to dismiss it. *Dismiss it, bullshit. Nothing in Nameoki, Illinois, ever sounded like that.*

As soon as Jarvis's chest let him breathe again, we continued across the clearing. "I'm going to lose weight . . . motherfuck . . . I tell you, sir, I'm going to lose weight," Jarvis puffed as we followed the scraggly haired Negritos. The high grass of the clearing made walking easier compared to the undergrowth, but I couldn't put out of my mind public televison's stories of lions liking this high grass type of terrain. I didn't think there were lions in the Philippines, but maybe tigers or leopards. *Shit!*

Beyond the end of the clearing about twenty yards into the undergrowth, we stopped as Jungle Jim pointed out a slow, gurgling stream perhaps ten feet across. On the other side, a small clearing showed itself, and I recognized the hoofprints of pigs. Jungle Jim turned and showed us a shallow hole under a tree right across from the watering place. He pointed to the sun, and with his hands in a ball showed it lifting from the ground. "Pig . . . come," he grunted. He took one of our flashlights and made a snorting noise, then put the flashlight in front of his face as he squealed. He dropped the flashlight, jumped up and acted as though he had a gun, and yelled, "Bang bang."

"Got it, Jungle Jim," Mr. Rice answered. The lead Negrito, slobbering a black juice out the side of his mouth from chewing tobacco, pointed to the small pygmy and then to our left. We nodded. He pointed to the other Negrito and to our right. We nodded. Pushing a finger to his own nose, he made a general sweep around the area with his arms. "Got it, Jungle Jim."

Then pointing to the sun again, he formed his hands into a ball and bent them to the ground. Pausing for a moment in that position to ensure we were all looking, he brought his circled hands up, then repeated it. "Pigs come . . . bang bang!" As he was leaving he made a cigarette smoking gesture, shaking his head no. Then he put his hands pressed together to the side of his face, bent his head sideways, and closed his eyes, indicating sleep. "Okay? Okay?" he said, then squealed out again, "Pigs come."

"We got it, Jungle Jim," Jarvis puffed. Jungle Jim knelt, starting to go through the bit with the sun again.

"Goddamnit, we got it, Jungle Jim, we got it! Get the fuck out of here," Mr. Rice burst out in frustration, then looked to me in apology. I smiled that it was okay.

The Negrito pygmies left. We didn't know where they went, and it felt a little lonely out here. Finally we settled into the shallow hole—our accommodations for the night—with our shotguns leaning over the top toward the watering hole. I was hungry and wanted to light my pipe. I didn't. We tried to get comfortable as the sun disappeared. No twilight; it just disappeared. Strange jungle-movie noises filled the humid air. It was dark, god-awful dark. The occasional slither caused my pulse to quicken and skip. "I'm scared shitless," I declared to no one.

"This whole thing is fucking stupid, Jarvis. Why'd I let you talk me into coming the shit out here?" Jenkins blurted out. I'd never heard him say so much of a cussword as damn before.

"Hell, we could be getting laid right now by one of those hot Filipino girls . . . right now, Jenkins, and here we are in this godforsaken jungle about to be eaten up by tigers."

"I don't think it's that bad, Jarvis," Mr. Rice offered. "Look, we'll be bringing back some wild boar for the feast tomorrow, and all the guys will really appreciate what we've done for them. Everything will work out great," Mr. Rice said in the tone copied from some war movie where the commandant of the lost battalion is cheering up his men before they die. "You'll see, you'll just see." I suppressed a giggle, thinking how Jenkins and Jarvis, both with IQs over 135, were taking this patronizing, officer bullshit. They just looked at him, glanced at me, then looked back at each other.

We took turns sleeping, none of us really comfortable. I wanted to pee—had to pee but was too scared to get out of the hole. It was midnight by the time I finally dropped into a fretful, bladder-burdened sleep, praying I wouldn't snore. Jarvis took the watch, saying he couldn't sleep anyway. In what seemed like minutes, although my watch registered 0324, I felt a hand shake me. I jumped up but a hand steadied me. "Listen," Jarvis whispered. I heard nothing but shook Jenkins awake at my side. Mr. Rice stirred once, then I felt him sit up.

"Wha . . . what?" he mumbled.

"Listen . . . over us in the tree," Jarvis with his powerful ears said, muting his words.

A slight rustle of leaves came through. But there was no wind, not even the slightest hint of one. My blood rushed through my veins. I felt my skin flush, my bowels constrict. I no longer had to pee. "Whadaya think, Mr. Sheppard?" Mr. Rice asked.

What do I think? I don't think jack shit. Let's knock off this senior officer crap. I don't know dick about what's going on here. I'm bone-assed scared.

But I answered calmly, "I don't know, Mr. Rice. You guys got any ideas? My mind's in neutral."

I could sense Jarvis's concentration. "It sounds like a huge snake . . . same sounds I heard on the way in here."

"Could it be a tiger?" Jenkins asked through clenched teeth.

"I don't hear any breathing up there. Do snakes breathe?" Mr. Rice asked, his voice an octave higher.

"Hey, can you guys be quiet? I'm trying to listen," Jarvis snarled.

"Yeah, it's a huge motherfucking snake," Jarvis declared. "What'll we do? Come on, you guys, think of something. I discovered the bastard."

"He's going to eat us up," Jenkins answered, his voice all but a whimper.

"Now, Jarvis, snakes don't eat people up, you know that," Mr. Rice came on again in his let's-comfort-the-men voice. I wanted to kick him in the balls.

"Let's shoot him," Jenkins's high-pitched whisper offered, and without further comment we each reached for our shotguns. My senior officer status came to play again as I said for each of us to point our guns up over us. *Now that's a logical step.*

"When I give the word, we'll all shoot," I said, trying to sound confident.

"What then?" Jarvis uttered so low that I had to ask him what he said. "What then?" he repeated. *Shit, I don't know. Where had OCS failed me?*

"Let's run for the clearing," Jenkins contributed.

"Sounds like a plan to me," Mr. Rice said coolly.

"Okay, which way is the clearing?" Jarvis asked.

Silence.

"Anybody got an idea?" I muttered wishing I could turn on my flashlight but knowing it would be of no use in this undergrowth, and it might spook that demon above us to attack. I knew that the clearing was twenty yards away from us in one direction and the dense jungle in all others. "Anybody?" We couldn't even see each other in this hole and kept reaching out to touch one another to ensure each other's nearness.

Silence, then Jarvis spoke. "You guys feel my hand. It's pointing toward the clearing." I wondered how he knew. We reached out, groping for him. "Each of you keep a hand on me," he instructed. "With the other point your shotgun up, and when I say fire, fire and run with me."

"Ready?" I asked, answered by three grunts. "Give the word, Jarvis."

"FIRE!" and four shotguns unloosed their destructive impact against the tree and its lurking monster. Branches fell and hot pieces of slimy meat covered us as we bolted out of the hellhole, dropping our shotguns as we ran, stumbling, smashing into trees, falling, crawling, tumbling, in our panic.

I ended up alone, with my arms around a tree. I could hear the others cry out, separated now, lost in the undergrowth. Stranded, which way to move? I sure the hell wasn't staying here.

"Hey. Hey you guys," Jarvis yelled an angelic call for us. "I'm in the clearing. Hey you guys, come over to me, I'm in the clearing," he continued.

I followed his voice. "Over here," Jarvis repeated again and again as I homed in on his beautiful, bright call. After what seemed an hour, I touched him. Jenkins was already with him. I started yelling for Mr. Rice. He yelled back, each time closer and closer.

We were together, holding hands, spinning around, laughing as if we were first graders on recess. But it ended in seconds as the relief of seeing everyone passed. Euphoria turned to fear of the jungle.

We settled in for the night, huddled together as we waited the insufferably long hours until dawn.

I cursed the welfare and recreation officer for his stupid programs for keeping the troops occupied. We were occupied all right, occupied keeping our hearts from being clawed out by some mammoth fuckin' jungle cat or from being bitten to death by a deadly jungle viper. I'd seen jungle movies, but you can bet your ass I'd never watch another. That is, if I ever got the chance.

We didn't dare separate or even lie down. We sat there tired and scared. At the first hint of dawn we made out Jungle Jim walking, almost meandering toward us. But we weren't about to give him the satisfaction of looking happy to see him.

We heard pigs rooting at the water hole on the other side of the stream. I heard a pig squeal in agony and the hoofbeats of several others. Jungle Jim squeaked, for what could have passed as a laugh, then took my hand and led us back into the undergrowth. I heard his men shout. He stopped, looked around, and then, seemingly satisfied, led us to last night's hole, pointing down at our blood-soaked equipment in it.

Scattered grotesquely among our gear and shotguns, and hanging sloppily from the tree branches above, were hundreds of pounds of shredded mammoth snake. Our shotgun blasts had splattered its long, slimy body in a ten-foot radius.

Jungle Jim smiled, dancing around, his ugly-toothed mouth squealing like a child's chant, "Goo hnt . . . Goo hnt."

Remembering our moments of hell, we stared into the shallow hole without comment.

The two worker pygmies carried a small wild boar across the stream on a long pole with the ends resting on their shoulders, a spear hole in its neck still dripping muddy blood. We gathered our equipment and washed it off in the stream as best we could.

We didn't care about the boar.

Women

S ailors at sea count the days until they get to port. Once there,
they count the days until they get under way again, anticipation destroying itself in the light of fulfillment. I itched to get
back to sea; two weeks seemed a long time to be in one place.
Here at Subic we had little to do because the repair facility took care of
everything. Time passed slowly, even though the CO of the base had an
aggressive sports program and, even in the hot sun, teams were formed
and games were played. The sailors had long since run out of money
buying drinks and women.

On the last night I decided I should at least see Olongapo, so along
with John Hethington and Chess Chadwick, I ventured into town. At a
wooden bridge over a moatlike strip of black, filth-polluted water, a sign
warned sailors to stay in groups of at least four. WATCH YOUR WAL-
LET was prominently blazoned on three other signs.

A dead dog lay festering and partially decomposed in the still, rancid
water, with only half a body left. A cat floated by, only its back showing.
Two boys of about eight leaned over on the muddy bank, laughing as
they beat the cat with sticks. They didn't seem to mind the stench or the
flies buzzing around or the mosquitoes or the emaciated dogs and the
dead rats being eaten by their brothers.

Two drunken sailors sang as they wove onto the bridge in front of us.
One held his stomach and moaned for God to help him as he banged into
a stanchion, drops of blood dripping from his forehead from the crash.
His mate put his arm around him, guided him, saying that everything was

going to be okay. The young seaman screamed "AGHHH," broke loose, flung himself to the rail, and vomited on the two young boys below him.

Carnival Row they called Main Street, and justifiably so. Madness: the neon lights, the rock music, the laughter, the hawkers, the crowds. Young boys chanted, "You want plenty boom boom, sailor boy . . . my sister very pretty good boom boom for you, she virgin plenty pretty for you, sailor boy."

We ignored them; it was the fastest way to get mugged in an alley leading to where his "plenty pretty sister" supposedly waited with open virginal thighs. But we couldn't ignore the stench, the flies, and the swarming mosquitoes hitting our faces and sucking at our necks.

We shuffled down the streets amongst the multitude of Filipino policemen and Shore Patrol, hoping their presence was enough to keep some kind of order. Hell, they were from the same ships as the guys they were watching. Outside the door of each bar, a gargantuan, garishly dressed man stood wide legged, calling us in. They were all named Tiny Tim. At each door beautiful young women enticed us in to buy a drink and have plenty boom boom with them.

We stopped at a yelling crowd gathered around a muddy pool, shallow and about thirty feet in diameter. We worked our way in, Mr. Hethington saying we'd really enjoy this one. Shocked, I stepped back in disgust as I saw sailors screaming, laughing as they threw live baby ducks toward the huge open jaws of four large alligators.

The sport seemed to be who could make the alligators contort the most, crawling over each other and swimming the fastest for the panicked ducklings. Vendors sold small boxes of ducks, just like grain is sold for children at a petting zoo in the States. The enraptured, participating sailors reveled in this bloody death orgy. Have we advanced none at all from the Dark Ages? I thought of Donald Duck's nephews Huey, Dewey, and Louie. I wanted to throw up.

Hell, it's Olongapo, what do I expect?

We finally went into a bar. VD movies shown to us in boot camp played before my mind in sobering clarity. The graphic colored shots of advanced gonorrhea and tertiary syphilis still rendered me impotent when I thought of them. The myth that girls who didn't have VD wore white socks to show they were clean came to mind as I looked at the young Filipino girls . . . many sporting white socks.

Since we were in civilian clothes, and therefore obviously officers with plenty of money, we got immediate access to an alcove hidden by a tawdry green curtain. "Hey, this place smells like stale urine," Mr. Hethington grunted, turning up his nose.

"Yeah!" Chess replied. "They should get some fresh urine in here."

Mr. Hethington looked at him, a questioning frown crossing his face. "Yeah," he answered, not sure it was the correct response.

In seconds, three stunningly beautiful girls, with delicate features and long raven hair expertly coiffed, slinked sinuously through the curtain. They were tiny and wore short, tight dresses and spoke in soft melodious whispers. I could easily see why so many of our men fell in love with them. So far, the XO had received forty-three request forms for marriage to foreign nationals.

They sat beside us, their hands resting on our legs. "You buy me drink, Officer. I be very very nice to you if you buy your honey drink for me," each whispered into our ears. "My" girl slipped her hands to my genitals and squeezed. "Oh! so big officer boom boom. You fuckee me for five dollar, Giant Boom Boom Officer?" I removed her hand and she feigned a pout, making her even more beautiful.

Without us ordering, a surly waiter, an ugly giant of a man, brought in three small glasses of "whiskey," in reality, cold tea, for the girls. His name was Tiny Tim. "What?" he grunted, looking at each of us individually.

"San Miguel," we answered and he ducked his head out. San Miguel was a delicious Filipino beer boasting a helluva kick after three or four. It was nothing at all like the washed-out American product we had in the States.

Awkward, meaningless conversation filled the interval until Tiny Tim returned, sloshing the drinks noisily on the small table. My girl, Bambi, nibbled on my earlobe as she constantly told me how much she loved me and how handsome I was and how big a boom boom I had. "Please, you not hurt Bambi when you fuckee me in little while. You buy me nother drink, Big-Boom-Boom-Officer-Man?" A solid sales tool, I thought, always go for the trial close early in the negotiations.

We ordered another round. I slugged down my beer and announced I was leaving. John and Chess tried talking me out of it, but this wasn't my thing. "You think Bambi ugly . . . you no like Bambi," she pleaded, her hands rubbing my face and playing with my ear. "You stay, stay, Donald, Bambi give you one big suckee suckee for free. Bambi love Donald. Bambi good girl very very clean. Please Big-Boom-Boom, you stay, okay? You love Bambi?"

It was a powerful plea sounding compassionately and compellingly true. Looking into the enchanting face, glimpsing her astounding figure and body motions, and taking in the fragrance of her enticing perfume, I could easily delude myself into believing her plaintive lament. I could see how the young sailors could succumb—it was masterfully presented. True love, Olongapo style.

I rose, shamefully erected. She changed. From a fluffy little kitty cat, she transformed into an absolute bitch, screaming, "You queer, fag man, you much little boom boom, sonbitch. I no fuckee you one million dollar . . . you suckee Tiny Tim over over . . . all you good for."

Tiny Tim's massive head burst through the curtain as he yanked it open. A clean-faced young shore patrolman's head followed. "It's okay," I immediately said, holding my hands palms forward to them.

"He hurt you, Bambi?" Tiny Tim bellowed.

"NO! He not hurt Bambi . . . he just not want fuckee fuckee Bambi," she answered in a much softer tone. I looked at the astonished faces of John and Chess as I tried to hide behind a sheepish smile.

"You guys stay here. I'm okay . . . have a drink on me," I said, tossing a ten dollar bill on the greasy, oilcloth table covering. "See ya back at the ship," I yelled above the din of the rock music as I passed through the curtain.

Bambi, who had stood up with me, took my arm and followed me out. She looked up at me smiling. "No problem, sir," she said in perfect English with no trace of an accent. "It's showbiz, sir, just plain show business. Please forgive me for embarrassing you." And she disappeared in the crowd, leaving me standing there in awe of her verbal transformation.

I squirmed my way out of the bar into the relatively quiet street, thinking of the many whorehouses I'd heard about. I contrasted tonight's display with the demurely gracious Japanese establishments in Yokosuka.

In Spain, Portugal, and Italy the mass market was different; they used the "shape up" technique. One went into the "house" and sat on one side of a huge room while the ladies sat on the other. You inspected them across the room while they made their sly, enticing movements. Once you chose by indicating to the madam, she took the girl and brought her across to you. The girl took your hand and led you out of the reception room into her chambers. You paid the girl in advance and she left for a few minutes.

Havana and Mexico were just about the same. In England, the streetwalker prevailed—but still, many steps removed from the Japanese method I witnessed in Yokosuka.

Except for the call girls and streetwalkers I'd heard of, I never knew much about prostitution in the United States, except for Honolulu during World War Two. The U.S. Army policed the whorehouses on Hotel Street in downtown Honolulu. They controlled and managed the mile-long lines of servicemen, keeping order and ensuring that the men behaved themselves en route to the assembly line efficiency of each house.

A serviceman in back of the line could expect to wait six to seven hours before he even got to a house, much less serviced. It was rumored that more than a hundred girls were in production night and day, around the clock. I guess you'd have to want a piece of ass pretty badly to put up with that. The army even provided prophylactic stations, I've heard, so the participants could "clean" themselves up afterward.

I guess, if I had to chose, the bar girl method seems to be the most natural, with its boy meets girl quasirapport established before coupling. As I crossed the bridge to a quieter world, I buried the enigma of Bambi's cultural shift into a deep pocket of my mind. *Interesting.*

We steamed fifty miles off the coast of Red China on our way to meet our squadron coming out of Hong Kong. I was in combat preparing to go on the first dogwatch, the 1600 to 1800. I liked to stop in combat before going on the bridge. Their status boards showed a much better and easier-to-understand picture of the tactical situation, and I felt it made me better prepared to take over the watch.

I sat there for a while looking at the electronic threat map of the China coast. We'd been tasked with monitoring their radars as a secondary mission on our steam toward Hong Kong to rendezvous with our carrier group. We verified all the known sites and detected a few new coastal search radars, but nothing significant.

I listened to the ESM search without a helluva lot of interest. A radar identifies itself by the frequency of its transmission and its pulse length and width. These parameters change with the radar's purpose. A high-definition, short-range navigation radar will have a high-frequency carrier wave and a short, very rapid pulse. A radar designed for long-range air search will be just the opposite—low carrier frequency and a long, slow pulse rate.

"Nothing new," I said casually, scanning the bands of the surface search. Then an unfamiliar sound grabbed my attention with its high frequency but slow, short pulse rate. This isn't supposed to happen. I called Garvin over to listen. He wasn't on watch and was just lolling around in combat because it was air conditioned. Combat, sonar, and the radio shack were the only spaces air conditioned on the ship. Electronic equipment efficiency must come first.

"New to me," he said, straining to identify it. He reached over and switched on the tape recorder. "Shit, it's crapped out. Get Jenkins up here right away," he yelled to a radarman on watch. "Fuck, our first new intercept and the goddamn recorder's out."

"I'll get one," I shouted, scurrying out the door and almost banging into the XO. He was making his way to the bridge with a stack of paper for the captain's signature.

"What's the problem?" he said, frowning and trying to straighten his papers. The XO hated to see people run; it made him nervous that something might be wrong with the ship.

"See Garvin, sir," I yelled, heading for my stateroom.

The chaplain was asleep as I ran in. He had conducted only one service since he'd been aboard and that was the first day and only the XO had attended. The men wouldn't talk to him about anything. I wondered if the captain's attitude had anything to do with it. *Nah, he's a phony.*

"Whadaya doing, Sheppard?" he yelled as I picked up the tape recorder. "That's mine, whadaya doing with it?"

"We got a strange radar signal in combat and our tape recorder is broken. I need this to record it," I answered, moving out of the stateroom.

"No," he shouted. "It's for God's work only, you may not take it for killing."

"I'm not going to kill anyone with it, I'm only going to record a radar signal and I don't have much time."

He jumped out of the upper bunk with an agility I'd never seen. As he landed he lurched for me. I sidestepped and he fell over the chair. I left him sprawled on the deck, crying that God had forsaken him.

I raced up to combat, too late; the signal had gone off the air. I had the bridge messenger take the tape recorder back to the chaplain, not wanting to face him again, and told the captain the story just in case the chaplain might say I hit him. He only shook his head and told me to write up as much as I knew about the signal. Garvin had already done so and we sent it off to the Electronic Intelligence Center; ELINT, (in Japan) info copy, of course, went to the commodore. We had to show we were doing something out here.

A good movie was due to be shown that night, *The Enemy Below,* about hunting submarines. I'd seen it three times but enjoyed it more each time I saw it and got its message: tenacity and dedication pay off. After supper, waiting for the movie to start and not wanting to go back to my stateroom, I inspected all the main spaces, chatting with the men— just "shooting the shit," it was called.

In this guise, though I fooled no one, I inspected the condition of the plant. Getting down on the deck plates was the only true way to know the plant, to know anything actually, for sure. Though reports may be honest and well intentioned, each had to filter through the speaker's mind, taking on his own bias and agenda; and as a report trickled up, it could be changed inadvertently in the telling. I liked to take the pulse of the men myself.

In the after engine room, I stopped at number three main feed pump. These huge pumps jammed feed water directly into the high-pressure steam drums. This was the flow of water the checkmen controlled to keep the water level within range. The pumps were crucial. As I listened to number three pump, it didn't seem right although all pressures and temperatures were okay and the pump looked good. Something was wrong. I called Machinist Mate First Class Summers over to listen. He was in charge of the after engine room and was there for lack of anything else to do.

"Sounds okay to me," he stated in his New York twang.

"Will you tell the chief I think something's wrong with the bearings?"

"Well, okay, you're the boss, but there ain't nothing wrong with it. Shit, sir, tearing down that pump is a four-hour job. Chief ain't gonna like it."

"Humor me, Summers."

The chaplain sat gazing at the bulkhead as I walked into the stateroom to get some tobacco before going up to the wardroom for the movie. His red-eyed, puffy-cheeked face annoyed me as I reached into a drawer for some peanuts to take with me. "I'm a fraud, Mr. Sheppard. I don't even know God and God doesn't care about me," he sobbed.

I didn't answer; I hated this sanctimonious bastard and his recorded sermons. Whatever was on his mind now, I didn't want to hear. He grabbed my arm. I turned ready to yank away as he started crying. "What?" I demanded.

"Have you no compassion for me?" he pleaded, his eyes begging me to stay.

"Dicky, you're an asshole."

"I know, but I don't mean to be. My wife left me, my children won't talk to me . . . none of the men will even look me in the eye when they pass. Your captain won't let me on the bridge and insists I eat at second sitting in the wardroom. My home diocese won't communicate with me. I'm all alone in this world."

I said nothing as his whiney voice squeaked out more loudly. "I'm seasick all the time and no one cares but you, Mr. Sheppard. You care, don't you?" Again I didn't answer, his face now paler, his body shaking more. "And I've treated you so badly . . . forgive me. Oh God, please forgive me." He looked like a skinny cat wet in a rainstorm.

"What can I do, Chaplain?" *Shit! There goes the movie.*

"Can you imagine a preacher with the last name of Layman? It just isn't right. All my life I wanted to be a man of God, but I was thwarted at every turn. I got bad grades in school and none of the other kids would play with me because I looked so funny.

"I cheated to enter seminary college and lied my way through. I couldn't get a church of my own or even an assistant's position." He hesitated, then tried to continue. "I . . ." He stopped again, reaching out to touch me as if I could work a miracle just by listening to him.

"What do you do? Everyone respects you as much as they hate me. Tell me, does God direct you? Does God—"

"First of all, Dick, knock off calling people son. They don't like it. Makes you seem pompous. Also, quit referring to God every other word. People get tired of it and don't believe it anyway."

"Don't believe in God? Why I . . . God, we—"

"Knock off the God bit," I repeated more forcibly. "Be a man first." I lowered my voice so much that he had to bend to hear me. "Do things because you're a man and let God worry about how you're doing. We've got enough to do without worrying about *Him* all the time. Do Dick Layman's work for a change, and if it coincides with God's, that's great. If it doesn't, well, maybe He'll let you know—like maybe right now."

I heard another feed pump being run up to speed; the pumps were right under my stateroom. I heard the slight pounding sound the pumps made when brought on parallel with each other—the outflows banging the check valves in competition until the new one took supremacy and the old one shut down.

I envisioned, thirty feet below me, pissed-off engineers getting ready to tear down a perfectly sound main feed pump because Sheppard wanted it done. I could imagine them saying, "Doesn't he realize we're tired from getting all that ass in the big O, the city of love? Well, you know how officers are always trying to shove their shit around."

"I'm being tested . . . I'm failing," the pathetic chaplain groaned.

I grabbed him by the shoulders, shaking him. "Goddamnit, Dick, you're a loser because you want to be a loser. Shuck it off, boy. Become a winner for a change," I yelled.

"First of all, take hold of yourself. Have faith in you. Second, you must hold church services and talk of good things, not hell and damnation. You must speak from your heart, not a book. You must speak as Dick Layman, fellow human being, not as a messenger for someone else. God is in you too, Dick Layman! Act on it. Do you understand?"

Silence crowded the room. I felt his body quiver under my hands. "Well . . . but no one will come if I hold services. I don't even know how anymore," he sobbed.

"Have you so little faith? All you need is Dick Layman. Dick Layman can do it! I'll help you." My words tumbled out. "But you'll have to do it on your own. Come with me to where the men are. Don't hide yourself in this stateroom." I took him by the hand but stopped by the door and spun him around.

"Wait. Don't you have any clean khakis? Those are a mess—you sleep in them? And another thing, hold in your gut." I scrounged in his drawer, the smell offending me, and pulled out his remaining set. I pinned his cross and lieutenant junior grade bar on his collar. I ran a brush over his shoes while he dressed. "Even though you're a chaplain, you're a naval officer and you must dress the part. The men won't respect you if you don't. You're an officer, remember that. You've got to know the men. They have to know you . . . it's not a free ride."

"Yes, sir."

"A chaplain is supposed to be a link between the officers and the men. But they gotta trust you first. To trust you, they gotta know you. Get your ass out there in the trenches, Dicky Boy. And we're going to start right now."

"But—"

"But shit, c'mon." I took him by the arm to the after engine room.

"Damn, Mr. Sheppard, why're we tearing down this pump? Everything looks good on it; bearing temperatures are great," a machinist mate second class complained, untorquing the main rotor housing with a young striker handing him the tools.

"I think it might wipe pretty soon, and with all the unreps we're getting, we can't afford the danger of losing an engine." His eyebrows raised, the doubt on his face saying clearly that he thought I was crazy or power mad. It didn't make any difference now. We'd find out soon enough.

"You met the chaplain yet?" I asked, sparing him further comment.

"Well, ah, well, I seen him around."

"Chaplain Layman, this is Petty Officer Chavez," I said. Chavez wiped his right hand with a rag and extended it. Layman's quivering arm went out to the machinist mate's hand almost as if he were afraid to touch it.

"That, uh . . . that looks like hard work, Petty Officer Chavez."

"Yes, sir, Chaplain, it is," he answered, sweeping a cold glance at me, then going back to grunting the main rotor housing free.

We went to the other main spaces. I introduced Layman around and tried to stimulate conversation. He wasn't good at it. We went to Sonar. Jarvis was there occupying most of the space. Layman seemed more comfortable here talking to Jarvis about how the sonar worked. As we were about to leave, the fat sonarman glanced at the chaplain's skinny body, then to me. "Sir, Chaplain, ah, will . . . will you help me lose weight?" he asked, slurring over his words.

"Why, yes, my son, God will—" My right hand shot around Layman's upper arm, my fingers digging into the bare skin below his short-sleeve shirt. He suppressed a yelp. "Of course I will help you, Petty Officer Jarvis. Of course I will help you."

We toured every manned space on the 2000 to 2400 watch. It became easier for him. "Dick, I have to get some sleep now before my watch at 0400. On every watch you have to make an appearance. Every watch, you understand?" He nodded yes. "And don't mention God, not even once. And don't call anyone son. Go to every space that we went to tonight. Stay away from the captain and the bridge for now. Keep out of combat. The captain spends a lot of time there. In all the other places, talk to the guys . . . they'll listen. I'll know, Dick, if you don't. It's up to you."

Cursing myself for getting into this thing, I went to see the XO after breakfast and told him the story. The gentleman in him suppressed a grin, but not very well. "So what I'm asking, XO, is that you schedule church services for next Sunday morning, and that you go. Okay?"

"Have you told the captain any of this?"

"No, I'd rather not, sir, unless, of course, you advise me to. I really don't want to. I'm not sure he would be as understanding as you, XO."

"Don't give me that bullshit. Is this one of your scams, Sheppard?"

"XO . . . ?"

His eyes searched me up and down as if I were carrying a concealed weapon. After a few moments—long moments—he answered, "Okay," his jaws clamping around the word.

I wished I'd never started this campaign as I hunted up Jenkins, Jarvis, and Garvin that afternoon. They all owed me big time for making them look good. I extracted a promise from each that they'd do their best to get their men to the church call in four days. And, yes, they'd go themselves. I asked Chess and Mr. Rice; they agreed. Mr. Graffey said yes. I ask Mr. Bluing and John Hethington; they said no. Jefferson Davis Gaines, our leading signalman, said he'd be mighty proud to have himself and his God-fearing boys at church call.

I ran across Chief Maclin in the engineering office at 0900 as he laid three main feed pump bearings, just on the microscopic edge of wiping, on my desk. "Summers sends his apologies and his thanks, Mr. Sheppard. How did you know?"

"The ship talks to me. Maybe a lucky guess? But I need a big favor, Chief, and I'll owe ya . . ."

Dick Layman faithfully followed my instructions. On his own, he talked to the cooks and asked their advice on Jarvis losing weight. They said they would help.

Throughout the ship, at all hours of the day and night, Layman could be seen wandering around, talking to the men, laughing with them. I talked to the laundry guys, and sure, they'd do a special run on his filthy khakis. And would-be Chaplain Layman walked a little taller and held his gut in a little more and his voice had less of a squeak.

Sunday morning, 0900. Layman looked out the open porthole in our stateroom, his body slumped, his hands vibrating like a hummingbird's wings as he held his prepared notes, reading them over and over in his now again high-pitched, squeaky voice. I sat there, saying nothing, watching the sweat soak through his khakis. He clutched his Bible to his breast, demanding it help him, demanding God help.

I stood, yanking his notes away from his death-gripped hands. I tossed them out the porthole. He turned to me, his wide eyes blank, white, his pupils driven deep up into his forehead. "You can do it, Dick. You can do it." My arms went around him. I hugged him to me.

"I can do it," he whispered back.

Sunday morning, 1000. Four bells sounded on the morning watch. Fifty-three men sat reluctantly on the mess decks as the preacher, ignobly called Layman, shuffled to the lectern. He stood over it for a moment, hugging it as if it were a crutch. His mouth moved. Nothing came out.

He glanced at me sitting in the front row. I mouthed, "Do it." His eyes darted around at the silent men. He looked like a man facing a firing squad. The humming vent fans and the smooth sea flowing under our hull were the only sounds.

A tingle washed over me. *The ship? No!* He flinched, glanced around in question, then lifted himself from the lectern. His shoulders pulled back. The sound of the sea disappeared and a burning light glistened in his eyes.

He tossed his Bible on the table next to him.

His first words got our attention: "Men, this is a no-shitter."

By 1030, five bells on the morning watch, twenty more men had joined. By 1100, six bells on the morning watch, eighty-one men crowded the space as Dick Layman stepped away from the lectern to the wild clapping of hands.

He had not spoken of some nebulous God nor of the church nor of a savior or an afterlife. His low, measured voice spoke of men, men like ourselves, and the good within us. He spoke of the ship and the glory of what we did. And he spoke that all of us were Gods into ourselves.

The men listened and understood, and Lt. (jg) Richard H. Layman, USNR, Chaplain Corps, became a chaplain.

FRAM

A murky Sunday morning's haze hung over us as we loitered three miles off the coast of China waiting for the carrier task group to steam out of Hong Kong harbor. Three destroyers came first, sweeping the area with their sonars. The carrier followed two thousand yards astern with a destroyer on each of her beams. Two other destroyers took station to her rear. As the group majestically cleared, they formed a circular screen with the after slot open.

We headed for the empty slot as our signal lamp clicked its request to the commodore's flagship. "Interrogative station?"

A reply followed almost immediately, "Remain outside the screen and await instructions." We came left, paralleling the carrier group at ten thousand yards, and waited while China sank below the horizon astern.

Thirty-two minutes ground by while we waited, feeling neglected, unwanted as if we were a stray animal begging to join the herd. I was there to take the watch, but Mr. Bluing wouldn't hear of it as he ambled from bridge wing to bridge wing, his eyes on the deck as if looking for an idea he had dropped and couldn't find.

"This shouldn't be," he kept mumbling, his head occasionally coming up from the deck to look contemptuously at the carrier's small silhouette on the horizon. "Surely they'll give us a station."

The captain's hand went out to Mr. Bluing's arm as he passed too closely to the captain's chair. "Settle down, Mr. Bluing . . . no big thing," the captain said soothingly like a father to his son as they awaited the birth of the fifth grandchild.

"Captain, we don't even have an op order. Again we're out of sync, always chasing about away from the group. Always sucking hind tit. It isn't right. Sheppard and his damned spring bearings caused all this."

"That's quite enough, Mr. Bluing," the captain said, rising from his chair. He paused. "You're completely out of line. The spring bearings were my fault, my fault alone. Understand that, Mr. Bluing, and we'll get along quite nicely. And stop that infernal pacing or leave the bridge." He plopped into his chair again, glancing over to me as if in apology of his senior watch officer.

"Ah, sorry, sir . . . my apologies, sir."

"Not to me, Mr. Bluing. Apologize to Mr. Sheppard, standing there behind you waiting to take the watch for the last half an hour. What's the matter with you anyway?"

"Nothing, sir . . . sorry, sir." He turned to me, his face blank, his skin pale. He grasped his hands together to keep the shake from showing. I could see the blood vessels pumping in his temples, red in contrast to his pallor. "My apologies, Mr. Sheppard. Are you ready to take the deck?"

"Ready to relieve you, sir," I answered, shocked that Mr. Bluing blamed me for the spring bearings fiasco.

A little faster action on the bridge in Seattle Bay, Mr. Bluing, by avoiding that sailboat earlier, might have prevented all that from happening.

He started the ritual of bringing me up to speed on the plant setup and the tactical situation and any contacts in the area when a flashing light winked at us from the flagship.

Gaines cleared his throat, not liking to see officers "afightn'," and drawled from his position on the signal lamp, "Ya all stand by for high line transfer of commodore to this 'ere ship. They'll make the approach."

"Damnit, Gaines!" Mr. Bluing snapped. "I'm sure that message didn't start out with 'ya all' in front of it. Do it right, Gaines, goddamnit, do it right."

"Yes, sir, right sorry, sir, yes, sir!" Gaines answered mournfully, shame painting his hound-dog face.

The chaplain, now a person in the captain's eyes, could come on the bridge whenever he wanted. "Captain, may I transfer to the other ships to hold services?" The captain looked at him for a moment, then glanced at the XO and then to me. The captain knew all about our minidrama and the change in Dick Layman.

"Signalman, make to the commodore, 'Request transfer chaplain to squadron flagship for church services.'"

Ten minutes passed as the flagship maneuvered to astern of us. "Say again, request clarification," the flashing light blinked. The captain nodded and Gaines repeated the signal.

Mr. Chadwick, now an OOD again, relieved me and had the conn as the flagship ease up along our port side. They looked good with a new coat of paint, making us look shabby in comparison. I stood at the after station with Dick Layman offering him moral support. I'd asked the captain if I could leave my station to be with him.

His hands shook, and even though the day was cool and a fresh wind blew over the deck, small beads of sweat formed on his furrowed face. High lines frightened him. I spoke soft words of encouragement as he white-knuckled his small prayer book and chaplain's kit. "It's okay, Dick, I'm right here with you," I whispered, touching his shoulder in support.

"Thank you, Don," he replied, looking at me as if I were the Pope. Smiles and frowns chased each other across his face.

Five large mail sacks came over first, followed back by old movies. Our mail had been sparse since we'd separated from the squadron on our gypsy missions. Normally mail followed the ships quite accurately, if the mail routers knew where you were going to be. If you deviated from your mail routing message, the mail in the pipeline got delayed as they tried to reroute it. They had done a good job following us through the Strait and at Subic, but still a lot of mail went to the carrier group.

The routers were good at what they did. If they knew you were going to unrep from a certain oiler or supply ship, they'd place your mail on a ship going to that ship. If they knew you were joining a carrier, they'd route your mail to it.

After the mail and our old movies came their movies, then the commodore. The commodore shook hands with the chaplain and watched as he swung over the side in a perfect, dry-feet transfer. Dick waved back as sailors broke the high line and hauled it in. I stood back as the commodore came aboard. I didn't want to explain why the chief engineer was out on deck instead of in main control when making a high line transfer.

The instant the commodore's feet touched our deck, his squadron flag, his pennant, was unfurled and hoisted quickly to the forearm. Gaines was good. They called it "breaking the flag."

The XO greeted the commodore, giving him the obligatory statement that the captain awaited his pleasure on the bridge, then he led him to the pilothouse.

We wheeled about, heading for the commodore's blank station off the port beam of the carrier. His ex-flagship, *Rollard,* headed for the empty station astern. We belonged; we had a station, and Mr. Bluing's world snapped back into place.

The captain and XO met with the commodore behind the closed doors of the captain's in-port cabin for more than an hour while the rest of us sweated out why he was aboard. After a congenial lunch, the XO asked all department heads to remain, thus giving the signal for the rest of the officers to leave.

The five foot nine inches of the commodore, in contrast to the captain's six-foot frame, left me oddly nervous. Caveman mentality that size equals prowess, I guess. The commodore trained his eyes on each of us as if using a stereo-optic gun sight to locate our souls before he started. "I haven't had much of a chance to be aboard *Henshaw,* but I welcome this opportunity to talk to you. There isn't any big mystery as to why I'm here, just visiting my ships, getting on the deck plates, so to speak."

We all smiled. "That's it, and I have a bit of news for you." He cleared his throat and looked at each one of us in turn. When his eyes met mine, my stomach curled into a knot.

"You haven't been with us much," he continued, and I noticed the captain wince as if it were a rebuke.

"First, with the captain's permission, I'd like each of you to brief me on the status of your department."

"Yes," the captain said, almost cutting off the commodore, "I want each of you to give an honest and detailed account of where you stand."

Of course, and woe be unto us department heads if we say something he doesn't already know.

"Mr. Bluing, our ops officer," the XO said, formally introducing Mr. Bluing as if it were their first meeting.

"I understand you're one of the finest ship handlers in the squadron, Mr. Bluing," the commodore said, taking a sip of coffee.

Mr. Bluing flushed. "Well . . . well, thank you, sir," he blurted out, momentarily taking his hand away from his nose. "I'm really just average," he answered modestly. "We're in pretty good shape, Commodore. About a year ago we had problems with our electronics gear, but after Mr. Sheppard came aboard it got squared away."

My God, he's giving me credit.

"So I understand. He's the ballpoint pen expert, isn't he?" the commodore answered, not taking his eyes off Mr. Bluing. It was my turn to flush. I noticed a smirk on the XO's face.

"We've not had as many AAW [anti–air warfare] drills as I'd like to see," continued Mr. Bluing, "so we're quite rusty there. Our state of training is up on everything else. My OPTAR gets a little weak during the last month of the quarter, but I reckon everyone else's does too. Our air search radar isn't worth a damn—oh, excuse me, sir—darn, even though we have it tuned to max efficiency. Outside of that we're in pretty good shape, sir," he finished, taking a surreptitious look at the captain, which the commodore had grace enough not to notice.

"Our gunnery officer, Mr. Hethington, Commodore," the XO said, waving his hand toward the pencil-fumbling lieutenant junior grade.

Silence followed the XO's introduction. I didn't think it right for a department head to talk directly to the commodore about ship's problems. That was the captain's job.

"I guess," Hethington finally gurgled, "I have the same problems as ops has on the OPTAR thing, and . . ." He paused, seemingly trying to give the correct response. Mr. Hethington didn't do well in unfamiliar, unrehearsed situations. He snuck an obvious look at the XO, not daring to look the commodore in the face.

"Go ahead, Mr. Hethington. And what?" the XO encouraged.

"We haven't fired the guns in months," he blurted as if, by not talking fast enough, the words wouldn't come out. "The crews lack training in actual firing even though we go through dry runs as often as possible. It just isn't the same, and I'm sorry to say . . ." He looked again at the XO, hoping for a sign to continue. Yes, the XO nodded again, trying to hide his annoyance with Mr. Hethington's timidity. "They . . . they have a lackadaisical attitude about it," he said as if he'd just betrayed his captain.

"And also, our torpedoes are old and poorly maintained because of the dwindling availability of repair parts and technicians in the repair

facilities to work on them. We spend a lot of time on preventive maintenance, but it all seems in vain to the frustrated torpedomen. And at this
moment, I don't trust the launch tubes to even kick one of 'em out. Sorry,
sir, but that's the truth," he finished, leaning back as if the burden of
Atlas had just been lifted off his shoulders.

"Mr. Hethington, I appreciate your problem and your honesty. If it
makes you feel any better, some ships aren't even trying to maintain
them anymore. Throwing good money after bad you could say." The
commodore chuckled over his inanity as we smiled like nice little naval officers. "I have some news later that'll take care of your, our, problem. Very candid report, thank you," the commodore answered, swaying his chair back and forth in cadence with the slight pitching of the
ship. He lit a cigar and poured himself another cup of coffee from the
sterling silver pot.

Lieutenant Junior Grade Roger B. Wachifsky, USNR, Supply Corps,
our new supply and fiscal officer who had just come aboard before we
sailed from San Diego, answered next. I wondered why the XO had introduced him before me; I was next senior to the gunnery officer.

In staccato calmness Wachifsky reported: "We're okay across the
board, Commodore. Our material condition is excellent. We only have
one oven out awaiting a new element. Everything else is working, you
know. We're at eighty-three percent of repair parts overall, and of the remaining, everything else is on order. The OPTAR—barring any untoward
demand—will make it okay just under the wire.

"Our food budget is slightly over target, but I can 'belly rob' by serving
fewer steak dinners and adjust before the end of the quarter." He smiled,
seemingly proud of himself for injecting navy jargon into his statement.

A supply officer has a budget of a given cost per man per meal per
day. He can look good on the books and serve cheap meals to a grumbling crew and be called a belly robber, or he can be a great guy and
serve expensive meals and go over his budget. We didn't have to pay for
the food, but it was his job to control it. Being slightly over budget was
the accepted norm.

Wachifsky spoke with the practiced ease of an orator, not at all
flustered by the magnificence of the exalted commodore sitting across
from him.

"With my limited experience, Commodore." Wachifsky stopped and
smiled, looking at each of us as if to confirm his modesty, then he rapidly

continued. "I'd say we're doing quite well," he finished, then glancing at me with a sly smile added, "That is, sir, if Mr. Sheppard can keep his evaps working," he jested good-naturedly.

I shuddered at the accusation of poor maintenance, but I couldn't fault him. He was new and a nice guy and didn't know, or care, that something like that should never be said in front of a commodore. And he was, of course, only a staff officer.

"And, oh yes," he continued, "almost slipped my mind. You know, we have a great corpsman, and the sick bay is in fine shape . . . or at least I think it is. I keep forgetting I'm responsible for that too, but I'm really not qualified to judge. A team from Subic inspected Jennings and his pills while we were there and the report was 4.0."

The commodore and the captain smiled at each other over his professional, though honest, naivete.

"Excellent report, Mr. Wachifsky. MBA, Princeton, Phi Beta Kappa, I understand."

"Yes, sir," he answered matter-of-factly.

"Me too," the commodore replied just as nonchalantly.

"Yes, sir, I know." And they grinned their secret grin at each other.

Assholes. Can't shake it, can you, Sheppard?

"Mr. Sheppard, our chief engineer, Commodore."

I cleared my throat, cursing myself for having to do it.

How honest does the captain really want us to be? Damn him, he should have briefed us.

"Well, sir, in the short run we're okay. We've been out of overhaul for a long time and this ship is fifteen years old. Subic Bay did a phenomenal job for us, and though everything is working now, we spend an inordinate amount of time and money on maintenance, and our fuel consumption is excessive.

"I exceed my OPTAR every quarter and have to borrow from the captain. I don't like to do that, but I have to. I hope it's not just my poor management." I paused for a moment, glancing at the captain, hoping for some sign of encouragement. None came.

"Our state of training is good. Casualty control drills, carried out by the watch sections on a weekly basis, are quite successful. They do a creditable job." The commodore's blank expression gave no indication of interest, just rock-hard indifference.

"My . . . our . . . weakest area is damage control. I had a little problem getting a grip on it in the beginning, but with the XO's help, I think I . . . we . . . have a handle on it."

The commodore drew a long drag on his cigar, filling the wardroom with its gray haze. The abnormally long ash on the tip was now an inch and a half. The old paper clip thing. *Were we that simple?* Only Wachifsky seemed to notice.

"You're a mustang, aren't you, Mr. Sheppard?" the commodore asked.

"Yes . . . yes, sir," I answered, nervous over the change in direction of the conversation.

"Well done; it's a tough way to do it. We could use a few more mustangs in this man's navy," he answered, looking to the captain for concurrence. The captain politically nodded yes as the commodore continued. "How are the men with pneumonia doing now?" he asked. Only the greatest will kept me from diving under the table in shame.

"Ahh, they're all okay now, sir. I sincerely regret the incident. I—"

"What are the details?" he broke in.

How the hell did he even know about it? It happened more than three months ago and was pretty well hushed up by the captain and XO.

I hesitated, not even having the courage to look at the captain for help. "Well, sir, I, ah, I had a great deal of trouble having the damage control teams wear their OBAs. The second a petty officer walked away from the men, they'd take off the masks. And the captain wouldn't authorize flogging," I answered, trying to inject levity into my statement. The commodore frowned. It didn't work.

"Well, sir, one day when three of them were in a containment drill in a small, closed compartment, I figured they probably weren't wearing their masks. I opened the door and threw in a red smoke grenade. Well, they weren't wearing them, and unfortunately before I could get the men out, they developed pneumonia. They're okay now, sir."

Strained silence inundated the wardroom table. I wanted to continue but I needed some sign. My navy career was over; I knew it. Why would he ask if it weren't? The captain had not made much of the incident, though the XO had a huge chunk of my ass. I hoped a boiler would melt down so I'd have an excuse to run out and hide in a fire room.

"Do you have any problem with them wearing OBAs now?" he asked.

"No, sir, I don't."

"Cheap lesson then, Mr. Sheppard. Might save a ship someday," he said. I knew my career was still safe, at least until I did something else equally stupid.

"The hull, sir," I continued, "is weakening in places, and though we keep a good eye out for cracks and such and weld them up as soon as we find them, overall, Commodore, the hull could be in better shape."

"Good report, Mr. Sheppard. How are your bulkhead mounted spares?" he asked, referring to the big bearings and large pump rotors we kept mounted on the bulkheads of the spaces.

"We're at a hundred percent, sir."

"Spring bearings?" he asked, chuckling.

"One hundred thirty percent. We managed to pick up an extra one in Yokosuka," I answered, not thinking it was so funny.

"I've heard the whole story from the captain, Mr. Sheppard, and I apologize for my overemphasis on all ships staying together, which caused you and Captain Baker to act against your better judgment. Sorry!"

My respect for him soared. A commodore apologizing to a lieutenant junior grade was unheard of. But it plummeted as I realized he'd censured our captain in front of his department heads in the same breath. He probably didn't even realize it. A furtive glance showed the XO's eyes narrow. I didn't dare look at the captain. "I also understand from the XO, Mr. Sheppard, that you have an uncanny ability to locate submarines. Is that true?"

"I . . . I've just had some good luck, sir," I answered nervously. His attempt at camaraderie was getting on my nerves. Did he think we were schoolboys waiting for a pat on the head? *Yes! Obviously.* I looked at the captain; his expression hadn't changed during the entire patronizing conversation. I knew him well enough to know he was barely tolerating this pompous ROTC man, this Philistine, as he had referred to him a few times.

"Well, Mr. Sheppard, we'll see if we can put your luck to good use." Then with a wide grin he focused on all of us with a sweep of his head. "Your captain and XO gave me just about the same reports, gentlemen, but I like to talk to the department heads themselves. Sort of a high-level deck plate thing," he said again, chuckling, and we all sycophantically joined in.

"But I have news for you; you're scheduled to go into FRAM a couple of months after you get back. That'll take care of your material problems."

FRAM, what the hell was a FRAM? And the meeting ended.

A half hour later, over the ship-to-ship UHF radio, a stern voice blurted, "Quebec Tango, this is Kilo Mike break Alpha Romeo."

"From the carrier, sir, take up plane guard station one immediately," Mr. Banning, my JOOD, hurriedly deciphered, yelling it to everyone on the bridge. Combat instantly verified the message text.

We were on picket station five miles broad off the carrier's port bow. The overcast skies gloomed the day, and periodic rain squalls kept everything wet. Plane guard station one lay fifteen hundred yards, fifteen degrees off the carrier's port quarter. Their mission was to pick up pilots who crashed into the water and to offer station a reference point for aircraft making their final approach.

Sounded great, but a rescue helo was always in the air during flight ops, and they could supposedly get to any downed aircraft much faster and more efficiently than we could, although my one experience with a downed pilot didn't validate that. And no pilot in his right mind would use a destroyer for a reference point when coming in for a carrier landing, not with the new automated landing systems and the LSOs. The landing signal officers, all aviators, were professionals at that sort of thing, not us black shoes.

We were running an electronic silence exercise—EMCON, or emission control—with all radars shut down. I had just gotten a visual on the carrier's range and bearing before the transmission and ran a quick course and speed calculation in my head. I looked at the captain; he nodded approval. "Right full rudder, all engines ahead flank, make turns for twenty-five knots," I ordered.

We surged ahead as the huge screws bit harder and deeper into the amber blue of the South China Sea. We heeled over to starboard as the full rudder kicked our stern around. The froth boiled behind us, and we settled on course heading for where the carrier's stern would be when I made my final turn to port to take up station.

Rain started, lightly at first, as Mr. Banning computed a more precise course on the maneuvering board; combat concurred. I made the minor course changes that their more exact calculations offered, then I waited.

We headed to station with a closing speed between the carrier and us of fifty knots. I figured it would take eleven and a half minutes to be on station. Combat concurred. It was a simple evolution destroyers did as a matter of course.

Then the blinding rain came in.

The captain sat in his chair caressing his grandfather's binoculars. As time progressed, he caressed harder, his knuckles turning white.

The soaked commodore walked in from the port wing and stood hovering over his shoulder. The captain hated his being that close. The commodore adjusted his sunglasses up and down his nose, over and over. There was no sun. It was raining. His widened eyes tried to reach his hairline via his washboarded brow. The hissing air sucking into his lungs rivaled the whoosh of our bow wave pushing out as we raced to the carrier—where we thought it was. And the commodore couldn't say a word. But he wanted to, and his lips moved up and down as if he were practicing the words to relieve the captain of command.

"Sheppard's good, Commodore . . . piece of cake. Not to worry, sir."

The commodore looked at him and his face straightened. "Of course, Captain, all my squadron conning officers are good . . . not to concern yourself."

"Thank you, sir," the captain answered as the commodore disappeared into combat.

"Commodore left the bridge," the boatswain's mate of the watch reported.

But in a second he was back. "I'll just watch from out here," he said. "I need the fresh air."

"Commodore on the bridge."

The dull black squall line polluting the horizon approached us like ten million locusts, their numbers multiplying, their height increasing, their bodies growing darker. I felt the slap of the wind on my face. I felt the excitement of the ship, the power under my command. I ticked off the minutes until I had to come around to port and slow the engines to match the speed of the mammoth carrier. The seconds rushed by; I tried to be nonchalant as the JOOD called off the minutes to station.

The captain's strained look of confidence was pure showmanship for this non-Annapolis commodore. We raced on. I felt the ship sing in appreciation of my trust in her.

"Thirty seconds," the JOOD called out, his squeaky voice betraying his fear. I could see the carrier in my mind's eye. The ship told me where she was; I could feel it, I knew where she was. The captain rose from his chair, his rain slicker squishing as he walked out to the open bridge to stand next to me. He touched my shoulder. It felt good.

"Time zero!" the JOOD screamed. It wasn't right yet. It didn't feel right. Better to turn late than early. The carrier was still too far away. I could, I thought, just make out her image in the pelting rain as I alerted main control to stand by for fifteen knots.

I waited twenty more seconds; the captain touched my shoulder again. He too knew where the carrier was. We smiled at each other as the rain lessened, and I confidently ordered, "Left full rudder, all engines ahead standard, make turns for fifteen knots."

The fogging rain thinned and there we were off the carrier's port quarter, range 1,450 yards. Close enough. "On station, Captain," I stoically reported, trying to suppress a shit-eating grin. He winked at me as he turned to report the obvious to the near-catatonic commodore.

Wow! The old man had guts. Would I have the courage to let a junior officer take a destroyer in against a carrier in reduced visibility like this when I'm a CO? No! I just ain't got the balls of ole Cap'n Dave.

I hoped the captain's brown shoe buddy had seen us pull off that maneuver. I'm sure he did, along with the admiral friend of his father. The ring knockers, the Canoe U. boys, were a tight community, as quick to fault as they were to praise.

The navy called aviators brown shoes and all other officers black shoes. It stemmed from before World War Two when aviators wore khaki uniforms with brown shoes to fly and lounge in. Since nonaviators didn't wear khakis, they didn't wear brown shoes, only black ones with their gray or blue uniforms. Now all officers and chiefs wear khakis and brown shoes, but the name remains.

High Line

==

I'm sorry, Don," Roger Wachifsky said, standing next to me on the bridge. "The XO told me I might have embarrassed you in front of the commodore with that crack about the evaps."

"It's okay, Roger, I'm sure he took it as a joke. It's just that you have to be careful what you say around senior officers. They have so much on their minds, they sometimes hear only a snatch of a comment and take it as gospel, out of context. No harm done," I replied with a tinge of sarcasm that Roger seemed to have missed.

"What's FRAM mean anyway?" he asked, his eyes darting around the bridge as if not wanting to miss anything. He enjoyed being on the bridge. He'd told me he really wanted to be an aviator or a surface line officer, but his weak eyes denied him the opportunity and his NROTC adviser had insisted he go supply.

"I don't know, and I haven't had a chance to talk to the captain or XO yet. If you find out let me know. Okay?"

"Barometer's dropped to 29.9, sir," interrupted Morton, the quartermaster of the watch.

"Very well," I answered, and I passed the information to the captain sitting in his chair.

He grunted, saying, "Tell the commodore." With the commodore onboard we were ipso facto the flagship even though the commodore's staff was on another vessel. We had to report all external happenings to him.

"Does that mean the weather will get worse?" Wachifsky asked, bending down in the pilothouse so he could see out the upper part of the window. His tailor-made khakis fit well on his athletic five-foot-eleven frame.

"It's a good indicator," I shouted as an F-4 fighter jet screamed down our starboard side onto the carrier's flight deck and wrenched to a dramatic stop as its tail hook caught the number two wire. Another F-4 came in low behind him, and another followed him.

The captain in his chair tallied the takeoffs and recoveries and didn't seem content until all the aircraft landed. This responsibility he took unto himself even though he had no authority or control over it. Most COs, I understood, cared only about maintaining station and looking good. The launch and recovery frequencies, patched into a speaker over the captain's head, allowed him to monitor the status. He stayed on the bridge as long as any aircraft were in the air. He took plane guard station one very seriously.

I couldn't muster the same feelings. The carrier was in charge, and the helos—the angels, they were called—were always airborne during flight ops. I really didn't know what good we could do; I guess that's why he was the captain and I wasn't.

In eleven minutes the last Phantom recovered, and as it did the captain rose ponderously out of his chair and stretched his huge frame like a cat awakening. "Ease back to two thousand yards, Mr. Sheppard," he said with a yawn.

An uncomfortable roll announced the freshening sea wasn't done with us yet. The admiral reduced the carrier group's speed to ten knots as dark clouds formed on the horizon. The commodore came on to the bridge with a weather message and offered it to the captain. He'd been in combat talking to his staff over the radio. "It's going to get a bit choppy, Dave. Prepare to transfer me back to the flagship."

We couldn't do that, I thought pedantically, because where the commodore was, was the flagship, but I wisely kept my mouth shut.

The XO passed the word for all departments to rig for heavy weather. Theoretically this should mean very little. A ship at sea was always supposed to be ready for heavy weather. But we humans get sloppy as good weather lulls us into complacency. The best inspection by the officers and leading hands could only encourage us to think we were ready for heavy weather. The smashing seas would tell us for sure.

*　*　*

We waited a thousand yards fine on the starboard quarter of the USS *Rollard,* the "real" flagship, as Chess tried to gauge her pitching movement. We'd chosen a course that minimized the roll but increased the pitching—a safer thing to do. *Haney* took a rescue station just aft of our port quarter; five hundred yards behind *Rollard.*

It was 1615, and Mr. Chadwick had the conn. Mr. Bluing was sick, and the captain asked me to keep the deck while Chadwick took us alongside. I should have been off watch, but I started the evolution at 1530 and the captain's doctrine said: if you start, you finish—except for landings, which he took mostly for himself. This was the fault of various admirals who judged how good a captain was by how good the ship looked coming in for a landing.

All captains wanted to look good in the admiral's eye; consequently, they made the landings themselves, to the detriment of their officers. Even on the rare occasion when a junior officer was making the landing and it turned out poorly, the captain would be blamed for not training his men well enough. My theory, backed up by watching Captain Baker, was that the captain should never have the conn.

Chess took us in wide and slow and paralleled us out at two hundred feet. Screwing up his courage, he started easing over.

I had QM3c. Bobby J. Morton, USN, on the helm; he was our best. I'd talked to Chief Maclin, telling him I'd be on the bridge and to play it tight; things were ugly up here. I wished Lieutenant Bluing had the conn. He was much better than any of us at this.

Our rolls synchronized as we got in closer. The wind rose to forty knots, gusting to fifty. It was stupid to attempt a high line in these seas. Why couldn't the goddamned commodore stay aboard with us? Bluing should be up here doing this, not me. I was the chief engineer.

What's the worry? Chadwick had the conn. He's okay. The captain is right beside him. What's an OOD without the conn supposed to do?

The wind's frightful wail raised goose bumps across my body. They prickled through my shirt as the wind plastered it against me. The skin of the captain's face flapped in angry defiance, moisture streaming from his eyes. Chadwick's face lost its handsomeness in wind-whipped distortion.

"On *Rollard,* stand by for shot line forward," came Hethington's splintered voice over a bullhorn from our forward station. The crack of a shotgun. Our first shot line, fired at 150 feet. Too far. The plastic float dropped into the churning water between us. *Rollard* fired hers at 120. It carried astern halfway over. I tried to keep knowledge of everything going on around me. I'd never been the OOD on a high line transfer, I had just had the conn. *Where was the XO?*

Like two dancers our masts swayed together, first left, then right in a wind-torn, aquatic ballet. My hands clutched the bulwark, holding me from spilling to the deck. With the grip, I tried to talk to the ship. It wouldn't answer. I wasn't a player here.

The inside of my mouth felt like a desert. One hundred feet. Chadwick steadied as best he could. The huge waves racing between us amplified in fury as we drew closer to *Rollard*.

Another shot line gun fired and I heard failure in a distant, panicked yell. At a freak moment, *Rollard* started a roll to starboard as we heeled to port. Chadwick screamed above the wind for a twenty-degree course change to starboard. Morton spun his helm to the right—not soon enough. The rudder barely answered as our mast tops touched lightly, like a maiden aunt's kiss, and arched away. He steadied again at 120 feet, more for himself than for the ship.

"Steady now . . . piece of cake," the captain yelled, the wind thrashing his words as they carried aft. The captain reached forward and squeezed Chadwick's shoulder. Chadwick's grip on the bulwark eased, his body loosened. He turned around to the captain's caricatured face and smiled. Everything was okay.

One hundred feet. The shotgun's blast pierced the wind. The float fired out, fighting its way toward us. The wind laughed and tumbled it astern. Eighty feet. Fire. The shot line float flew out again. Failed. Another shot. A cheer.

We pounded and rolled, each man on deck tethered as our bows dug deep into the crashing waves, bringing frothing green water all the way up to my conning station. On the first one, Chadwick's reflexes pulled him down for a second, but he fought his way up through the smashing water as the wave cleared over us, running dangerously astern.

I huddled in the pilothouse.

Haney held tenaciously to station behind us, her motor whaleboat rigged out in anticipation of plucking the downed commodore out of the water if we failed. My anger grew at the stupidity of this maneuver. The high line came across with a dummy load, drenching itself for more than a fourth of the way on its journey. The sickening, putrid smell of vomit jammed out from the pilothouse.

A high line was just that: a two-inch manila line running from one ship to another, secured to two small masts high on each ship and made tight by men holding the ends of the line. The men had to tighten or loosen the high line according to the roll of the ship or to the distance between the two ships. They tried to keep it tight.

To this high line a large pulley was attached with a one-inch line to each end of it, tended on each ship by another crew of sailors. The pulley was attached to an aluminum chair with flotation gear around it. Once a man was strapped into the chair, the receiving ship pulled him in while the delivering ship eased out on their end—a simple enough maneuver in calm seas. But rolling, pitching ships complicated the operation immensely.

Chadwick eased out to one hundred feet as our masts almost touched again. "He's on his way," came a report from somewhere to someone. I passed it to the captain and went outside and aft the few feet to the signal bridge to watch. The commodore went full into the water, the entire high line chair disappearing between us.

There was nothing I could do. I could only hold on and pray as the thirty or so men on each high line crew pulled the line tight, then slackened it as the commodore popped up. Both ships were working together, using pure brute strength to tend the lines. They were doing it well.

Another glance showed the commodore being yanked out of the water straight up as the line went instantly from slack to screaming, gut-wrenching taut. The transfer chair twisted, swaying violently from the sudden yank and the increasing wind. The fury of the men slackening the line could be felt even this far from the after transfer station.

Into the water, out. In, out. Then the line pulled tight and the chair swung up, dripping onto the other ship.

Four men grabbed it as all lines slackened so as not to pull the chair away. A huge wave breasted between us. We were going to be bodily thrust apart. There was nothing I could do. The boatswain's mates on each ship saw it coming before they could be told.

Two men yanked the safety belt off the commodore and dragged him out of the chair and away as hand axes on both ships flashed against the rigging. For a split second the tangled manila line remained taut, then crinkled back onto itself, forming a tangled ball catching the wind and lifting high, flying out and away in the rain-filled, darkened skies. We were free, and I uttered my thanks to the ship as Chadwick slowly eased away from *Rollard.*

"The commodore's got balls," I yelled breathlessly over the wind screaming through the pilothouse.

"He's got shit for brains. That was the most stupid thing I've ever done in my life," the captain said calmly into my ear, his voice flat, drained of all feelings and emotions as we cleared *Rollard.* Wachifsky watched us in amazement.

"From the commodore, sir," a drenched signalman reported, handing a wet message sheet to the captain. "He sends, 'Bravo Zulu.'" The captain looked at Mr. Chadwick, then broke out laughing.

We indeed had not been ready for heavy weather, even though we thought we were. Tied-down typewriters and equipment fell crashing to the decks, and storeroom shelves toppled their contents. Tools clanked around in the bilges, and combat looked like a paper-shredding mill. The engineers slaved to keep their water levels proper as the seas shook their machines, trying to pull them off their foundations. The delicate evaporators, with their demands for fine tuning, were beginning to fail us again.

By sunset the next day, if there had been a sun, the wind abated, but not much. The glass crept up, heralding the end of the storm, but we hadn't noticed it yet. Lieutenant Junior Grade Wachifsky fought his way across the bridge to the captain and me. "Well," he managed to get out between deep breaths, "This'll take care of my food budget overage. No one's eating anything, you know—just a few sandwiches now and then. Hell, Captain, we can have steak every day until the end of the quarter if you'd like."

The captain looked at him with a weak smile. The captain hadn't left the bridge, except to use the head, for thirty-six hours. The storm spread out our carrier group over two hundred miles of ocean as each ship fought on its own for survival. "How about the wardroom?" the captain asked, his voice low, strained from lack of sleep and the sheer exhaustion of his responsibility for the ship, for his men. He tried to show some interest in the supply officer for making his way up to the bridge to report what the captain knew as obvious.

"Should have a lower mess bill, Captain—no takers there either," he answered, looking out at the wind-torn maelstrom. His eyes opened wide as he stared at the boiling turmoil of the seas around us.

Lower mess bill—that'd be nice, I thought. While under way the mess bill grew very large. With all officers aboard and eating, we generally had to pay about $60 every month. We received only $47.50 per month to buy food. We bought it ashore or from the general mess. Stewards were assigned to cook the meals and serve them. Our stewards were good and prepared fine meals at a low cost. Only with the good management of a sharp, leading steward or a conscientious mess caterer could the bills be kept in check.

When back in the States and the officers going home every night, only the duty officers ate aboard, and the mess bills ran about $20 to $30. One had to be watchful, though, that an overzealous caterer or leading steward didn't "borrow" food from the general mess and "forget" to pay for it—a not infrequent occurrence aboard "other" ships but "never" here on *Henshaw*. The supply officer, by law, was the mess treasurer, with the job of overseeing the wardroom accounts.

We all thought that supply officers had a good deal going; they didn't stand watches at sea or the duty in port. They never had that gaunt, tired look we watch officers had from lack of sleep. We resented it, but Wachifsky was a good guy and had even volunteered to stand watches, but we had a full complement of officers and I guess the captain figured that the line officers needed the experience more than the supply officer.

I watched Lieutenant Junior Grade Wachifsky scrutinize each man on the bridge as if judging him. His fascinated eyes glanced continually back to the heaving sea, and he hung on like a veteran. Of course he had experienced ice storms in Alaska, which, I guess, made him a true sailor. Few seamen have experienced the mind-numbing fear of ice storms in the North Pacific.

I mused over his name. Wachifsky. I almost had that name and a different life. It depended on who in the family told the story. My paternal grandfather was a Russian nobleman, or a highwayman. In one version, he fell from grace with the czar and had to flee the country as royal guards pursued him. The other version said he'd been caught robbing coaches on the highways and had to flee the country with the criminal police chasing him.

In either case he and his family arrived in London around the year 1914. The exact year was always hazy. My grandfather became a professional gambler at an exclusive, men-only club. My father and his older sister used to wait at the entrance until he'd finally come out, and they'd beg money from him for rent and food.

My father, Abraham Wachifsky, earned money playing piano at local pubs but not enough for the family to live on. He took up boxing to supplement the begging from his father, calling himself, dramatically, "Kid Sheppard" when he fought. Slowly the family saved enough money to send a younger brother to America. With some of the money he sent back, and with the boxing and the cleaning of houses and taking in laundry and a little begging, an elder sister came over.

Then another sister came, then the mother, and finally my father, who now called himself Al. Each got on the ship at Liverpool as a "Wachifsky" and each got off at Ellis Island deliberately named "Sheppard."

I thought of being a kid again in Nameoki as the wind whistled through the supposedly watertight doors of the pilothouse. And I thought of Lincoln Place—on the other side of town, on the other side of the tracks—where foreigners lived in their tight-knit community. I thought of how they acted differently than we did.

I never knew how they acted differently except the high school boys always seemed a little tougher, and the girls—with their long black hair—seemed a little prettier. But everyone said they were different. Not better or worse, just different. I thought of how their lives wove a different kind of cloth because of a name suffix and two parallel sets of tracks. I never did understand what it was all about. It had been in the late forties. They all worked at the steel mills.

"Fleet Rehabilitation and Modernization."

"What, Captain?" I asked to his mumbled statement over the noise.

"Fleet Rehabilitation and Modernization," he answered a bit more clearly. "That's what FRAM means. They tear down the whole ship and rebuild her from the hull up and install the newest equipment. I'm glad I won't be aboard for that. I've got my orders."

Orders? Christ! Orders? A new captain. My throat constricted. I sucked in a gallon of wet air. My eyes couldn't focus.

A new captain? I didn't want a new captain. Would a new captain like me?

"When, Captain?

"The commodore brought them. I'm heading for the Pentagon. Great orders."

"No, Captain, when will you be leaving?" I asked, knowing it was none of my business.

"Soon, I suspect," he mumbled, looking out to sea. He didn't appear all that pleased.

Maybe it was the storm. But hell, what do we mere lieutenant junior grades know about the feelings of a captain?

I couldn't think for a minute. My stomach tried to rid itself of breakfast but I sternly fought it down. Those days were over, thank God. I had come to terms with it.

My mind had greater things to do than worry about being seasick. My mind was to work on the greater problems of life, not worry about the body. My body could take care of itself and was to call on me only when something more was needed. It had taken me more than a year to completely bring it under control. But I had, and I no longer concerned myself with it. I automatically lifted my feet when crossing transoms, and ugly dark scars remained on my shins for the hard lesson learned. Several pairs of khaki trousers shamed me with their unremovable blood stains, but I was too cheap to throw them away.

"Glass is steady, sir, for the last hour, holding at 29.6."

Open Manholes

We ran with the storm for another day, the wind and seas slackening each hour. My muscles accepted the flexing strain of the ship as they automatically adjusted themselves to the pitching and rolling.

As storms go, this one hadn't been bad, but it doesn't take much to toss around a destroyer. We searched for any other ship to rendezvous with but nothing showed on our radars. Each ship steamed independently during the storm, and we had soon become well dispersed. And no other ship could be reached by radio through the storm-hampered ether.

Prior to the year 1945, the officer in tactical command, the OTC, determined which storm evasion tactics to use. In one case, this policy had cost the navy three sunken ships, nine severely damaged, and twenty others limping about. Almost 150 planes suffered loss or damage beyond repair, and nearly eight hundred men were lost or killed.

On 18 December 1944, the Third Fleet, off the Philippines supporting General MacArthur's planned invasion, encountered heavy weather leading into a typhoon. Vice Admiral W. F. "Bull" Halsey kept his fleet together, thinking they'd offer mutual support while trying to maintain the course and speed of the formation. It hadn't worked. Each ship had its own characteristics, each riding the wind and the waves differently. What was good for one wasn't good for all. This keeping the fleet together added drastically to the damage suffered.

Since that time, doctrine changed and now the OTC must detach his ships to proceed independently as early as possible. This wisely left the captain of each ship to be the best judge of how to ride out the storm. The message: the safety of the ship is paramount to the mission assigned. None of the three ships lost in 1944 had ballasted.

Our exhausted crew welcomed the calming seas. Their burning muscles relaxed; they no longer had to cling fearfully to something, anything to keep from being thrashed about. It had been like three days in a carnival's tossing-floor ride. We could now untie the safety lines from the lookouts without fear of losing them overboard.

About 2200 the carrier's position came in over the Fox Schedules and we set an estimated course for her, 230 miles away. That is if our own position was correct, which it wasn't; neither, probably, was the carrier's.

We hadn't been able to take a navigational fix since the storm overtook us, and we ran on a dead-reckoned course, which wasn't worth the pencil lead it took to write it down. The next morning at 0612 the XO cut a celestial fix and crossed five stars in a two-mile box. Good fix, and the sun appeared, and all seemed fine with the world—except for our fuel state: 41 percent.

Such a drastically low fuel state degraded our stability. The captain and I had discussed ballasting twice but both times decided to wait. Putting seawater into empty fuel tanks was dangerous and cumbersome even if it did improve stability. It would take weeks of steady steaming to flush out all the saltwater residue, and while we were doing it, we always faced the dilemma of a slug of water in the fuel dowsing the boiler fires.

And surely it would happen at the most critical time, such as coming alongside a pier or another vessel. No captain made the decision to ballast lightly. It was always the last resort. We didn't do it and we made it.

The carrier's new position and ours put us 175 miles apart. Fuel, water, and damage states filled the radio waves between the destroyers and carrier. The carrier adjusted her PIM, plan of intended movement, to minimize the steaming distances between her and the largest number of small boys, as they called us. Our fuel state was not the lowest; actually we were among the highest. But all of us were down around 20 percent on water. It could be used now only for drinking and the boilers. And if it got worse, only for the boilers.

The vibration increased in the engineering office, where sounding through open manholes was being discussed by Martinez, the oil king;

Chandler, the leading boiler tender; Chief Maclin; and I. The phone rang. "Captain wants you on the bridge right away, sir," Chandler said, not looking at me. I still smarted from his going over my head to the captain and he knew it.

"Maybe he wants to talk to you about doing something new. Don't think Chandler has had a chance to sneak up and rat on us yet," Chief Maclin said, looking disdainfully at Chandler. Chandler blanched. He'd gone over Maclin's head too, and Chief Maclin had taken it a lot more personally than I had.

"Enough, Chief, let's drop it. You guys work this out again just as we've done ten times before."

Why the increase in speed? I wondered. The captain knows it'll suck us dry much faster. We used power—and that meant fuel—as the cube of the speed. We could steam at twenty-seven knots using only two boilers. To gain four more knots, we had to double the boiler power by bringing two more on the line.

As I walked into the pilothouse the captain handed me a message from the admiral classified "top secret." It was addressed to our commodore for action, and for information to all the ships in the carrier task group, as well as the carrier's boss and the commander of the Seventh Fleet and his boss, the commander in chief of the Pacific Fleet.

BT
TOP SECRET
O112300Z IMMEDIATE
FROM: CTG 77.1
TO: CTU 77.1.1
INFO: TG 77.1
       CTF 77
       COMSEVENTHFLT
       CINCPACFLT
SUBJ: TASK GROUP OPERATIONS (C)
1. CARRIER IS UNACCEPTABLY OFF SIOP STATION
AND MUST RETURN AT BEST SPEED.
2. SUBJECT YOUR CONCURRENCE WILL FUEL FOUR
CLOSEST SMALL BOYS AS SOON AS POSSIBLE ASSUMING
THEY CAN REACH US IN NO MORE THAN THREE HOURS
AND BE ALONG SIDE FOR LESS THAN AN HOUR EACH.

3. HAVE ORDERED TANKER TO YOU FOR SERVICES
TOMORROW APPROXIMATELY 1900.
4. ASSUME YOU'LL TOKEN-FUEL OTHER SMALL BOYS
FROM THE FOUR WE SERVICE.
5. REGRET INCONVENIENCE. ADVISE SOONEST.
TOP SECRET
BT

I read it once and then again. What a beautiful message; he lays the whole bag on the commodore. I looked up at the captain. He said nothing. I glanced at the engine order telegraph; it indicated twenty knots rung up. "How far away?" I asked, knowing the captain's next question.

"Eighty-three miles."

My mind did some quick mathematical and political calculations. "Could I recommend twenty-seven knots, sir?" I replied.

"Mr. Chadwick, twenty-seven knots if you please," the captain ordered, smiling. "Figured you'd say that. Squeeze us in there. What state on arrival?"

"Maybe twenty percent. We'll use less fuel now that we're so light."

"An hour alongside. How much can we take?"

"One hundred percent, sir." He looked at me, furrowing his brow, as I added, "If you approve of sounding through the manholes." He knew we had a chance here to really look good. Under a conventional fueling we'd barely get up to 50, maybe 55 percent in an hour.

"Is that what you were telling me about? The secret equations from your Chinese fairy princess?" he said with twinkling eyes.

"Captain!" I flushed from the snickering of the watch crew. "We talked engineering. Really, Captain, we did, that's all." *Well, we did touch—just a little bit.*

"Of course you talked engineering, Mr. Sheppard, and I'm sure the crew appreciates your sacrifice as much as I do."

Louder snickering. A few laughs.

He started walking across the bridge when Leading Signal Gaines drawled, "Suh, us boys in the signal gang sure do believe you. We know that officers never do nothin' like that. Why my Pappy—"

"Thank you, Gaines," I snapped, cutting him off.

As I turned to walk away, the captain's now jovial voice said in mock seriousness, "Mr. Sheppard, don't fuck up!"

In two hours and forty minutes we were alongside with the first hose ready to pump fuel at maximum pressure. We had every manhole watched by two men. Martinez and I had personally instructed each team and made damn sure they understood what was going on. They did.

By the sound-powered phone line to the carrier's fueling central that came over with the hoses, I asked to talk to the chief engineer, a full commander, EDO, named Bloodsoe. He admired my plan and guaranteed he'd personally monitor the refueling and he himself would close the pumps down when I requested it. No margin for error, I emphasized. Sarcastically he ensured me they could handle it.

"Commence pumping!"

The first five tanks went well. On the sixth and seventh we overflowed five or so gallons onto the decks in a berthing compartment. A cleanup team moved in rapidly to contain the mess. Forty agonizing minutes passed. I lost a drop of sweat for every drop of fuel. The XO uncharacteristically bugged me on the progress.

I tried to be nice. I understood his concern for the potential screwing up of the berthing compartments where most of the manholes were located. But he had to leave me alone and let me concentrate on the soundings. We were trodding dangerous ground. I needed no distractions. I finally told him, very nicely, "XO, for God's sake, I just can't talk to you now. Believe me, it'll be okay."

Angrily he yelled, "You'd better not fuck up, Sheppard, or I'll have your smart ass in hack for a month."

"Yes, sir, I understand." All I needed was negative vibes from the XO. He sounded really uptight. I couldn't blame him; if we screwed up, there'd be a lot of sailors with no place to sleep tonight.

I watched with fascination as the soundings came in and were marked on the board by Martinez. Chandler was out encouraging each manhole team. He'd finally gotten caught up in the excitement and threw himself into it with a fervor. Chief Maclin periodically peered out of main control to check the progress.

I could swear I felt the ship sink deeper into the water as the tanks took on their weight. Venting during a normal refueling was always a problem—air just couldn't escape from the sounding tubes fast enough. Open manhole covers eliminated the problem forever.

The water king had the carrier's precious water flowing into his tanks at the max pressure of a two-inch fire hose, and Chief Maclin reported 80 percent onboard. The machinist mates were sounding their water tanks through the manhole covers too. A spill here was only wasteful since most of the tank tops were in the main spaces anyway. I didn't think of taking on water this way, but Chief Maclin came through again.

I reported 95 percent to the bridge and to Commander Bloodsoe on the carrier. He was keeping his word. "Five-minute standby," I reported. Fifty-one minutes alongside so far. "Stand by three minutes; keep the pressure up," I passed to all stations. Commander Bloodsoe acknowledged standing by.

Three minutes passed. Martinez's colored grease-pencil markings on the fuel status board went higher and higher as we approached completion. "Two more minutes," I said over the phones, a little embarrassed for the miscalculations. "STAND BY, STAND BY . . . ONE MINUTE," I yelled, then waited one minute, then two. Almost full, almost. NOW! shouted in my brain. I twitched as I yelled over the phones, "CEASE PUMPING, CEASE PUMPING, STOP! STOP! STOP!"

Instantly the immense whooshing rush through the tanks stopped. The pounding of my heart replaced it. An elation passed through me I didn't think existed, a feeling I didn't think possible.

Thank you, Mai Ling. Thank you, my little angel. May your power station serve you as well.

The last line went back and the vibration of a twenty-five-knot bell told me a fast breakaway was our finale.

The phone rang; I picked it up. "Chief engineer?" came the captain's voice.

"Yes, sir."

"Percent?"

"Ninety-nine point four, sir."

"You told me we could take on a hundred. You blew it," he said with a chuckle. "Water?"

"One hundred five, if you count the bilges."

"We won't. Good job, son, damn good job." *Son?* I loved it when he called me son.

"How many minutes alongside, sir?"

"Fifty-eight . . . goddamn, only fifty-eight minutes. That's got to be a record. Thank you, Don."

"Not me, Captain. The engineers did it. I just watched."

"Sure, Don, sure." And he hung up.

The click of the 1MC key and the boatswain's pipe calling all hands to attention boomed throughout the ship. "This is the captain speaking. We have just received a message from the carrier group admiral that reads, 'Your handling alongside superb. The speed of your refueling magnificent. Please accept my personal Bravo Zulu!' End of message. This was a team effort, men, and I thank each of you for a job well done."

Lookin' good, Dave.

In two hours we were alongside *Rollard* sluggishly pumping fuel and water into her. The hoses had been passed via a jury-rigged high line, and our fuel transfer pumps—designed only to move fuel oil from storage tanks to the ready service tanks—strained to give her but a trickle, but enough to ensure she could ride out a moderate storm. In five hours we'd transferred 15 percent fuel and 15 percent water. The BTs and deck crew were dead on their asses, and we had another destroyer to fuel when we finished here.

The captain never left the conning station on the wing of the bridge for the entire five hours. He ate while he stood behind the conning officers and assigned a relief every hour to ensure alertness. His gaunt face showed eyes the color of blood, worry lines at the depth of a much older man, and the frighteningly blank stare that lack of sleep wipes over a man's face. But he never left, not even to go to the head. Iron Man Baker!

I faulted him for this. Surely his mind suffered from fatigue. We had competent, responsible conning officers aboard; Mr. Bluing and the XO were without peer, even if he might consider the rest of us too inexperienced for the job. I knew he'd been awake for more than thirty hours except for fitfully dozing in his chair on the two-hour run to rendezvous with *Rollard.*

I guess he figured he could sleep on the plane going home and didn't want to ruin his career at the eleventh hour with a collision at sea.

On the emotional level, I marveled and admired his stamina as we completed the token refueling of another destroyer and formed up steaming toward the carrier running away from us to the west.

Submarines and Targets

Submarines are named after fish. *Cat Fish* is the name of this one, and I tried to look coordinated as I sloppily scrambled up the submarine's wet rounded side holding onto a lifeline and my small bag of clothing.

"Request permission to come aboard, sir," I snapped out, saluting as I climbed up to the submarine's navigational deck atop the conning tower.

"Permission granted. I'm Doug Fowler," said the lieutenant commander captain, USN, USNA, extending his hand. "Go below, Mr. Sheppard, we're diving in a minute or two."

I caught a glance of a man in khakis going over the side to our waiting motor whaleboat as I dropped through the hatch into the smelly submarine. The stench of body odor mingling with the sweet smell of lubricating oil and diesel fumes insulted my nostrils.

"DIVE! DIVE!" echoed through the sub followed by the UUGAA! UUGAA! of a blaring Klaxon horn. I'd seen enough movies to know to keep out of the way while a submarine is diving. The young lieutenant XO sat me down in the wardroom. "Wait here!" he said with a sneer, then disappeared out the curtained doorway.

Creaking, metallic noises snapped out of the sweating bulkheads. I could swear I saw the steel sides moving in from the pressure as we dove. The wardroom closed in around me, strangling me. I knew, just knew, we were in an uncontrollable dive to oblivion. Why wasn't I being dashed forward from the acute down angle that I just knew we had?

Captain Fowler had lost control. He looked too young anyway to be a captain. The Nameoki Kid is about to die. I had to pee. A man shouldn't have to pee when he's about to die.

A sonar ping crashed into my ears. Another. *Shit!* I waited for the crash of the depth charges, for the lights to dim, for the leaks to spew out, for the crew to contain them with rags, for the seawater to get to the batteries, for the deadly chlorine gas. *Don't roll, Roll.*

The pundits were wrong. My life wasn't playing out before my eyes. For ten minutes I dehydrated as my sweat gushed through my khakis. Captain Fowler and the XO came in and sat down next to me in their tiny wardroom. I was relieved; they'd saved the boat.

"So, Mr. Sheppard . . . Don," Captain Fowler said, leaning back and trying to get comfortable on the narrow bench. "You're the first of an exchange program your commodore wants us to participate in as long as we're together."

I heard the screws and the melodic ping of a speeding destroyer pass over us. "That's the last one of those you'll hear before you get off," the XO said, pouring a cup of coffee and handing it to me.

"Yes, sir . . . thank you, sir."

"We're not all that formal here, Don. Lighten up."

"Yes . . . yes, sir."

"What would you like to learn aboard *Cat Fish?*"

"Well . . ." I hesitated. "Well, my captain told me to watch very closely how you always manage to escape on those few occasions that we do acquire you." A smirk passed across both their arrogant faces.

"Do you know why you were chosen to be the first?" Doug Fowler asked.

"Guess I'm the least needed in the ASW exercise we're going into. Not much for a chief engineer to do during ASW." They looked at each other questioningly as if trying to decide if I were for real or just another surface navy bullshit artist.

"You're the chief engineer?" the XO asked a little too loudly. "The captain asked for the sharpest ASW man in the squadron to be first, and it turns out the commodore sends a chief engineer! Wow, can you believe it?"

"Now, XO, don't be such an asshole. Sorry, Don, the XO has some pretty strong feelings about the inadequacies of the surface navy, which, I admit, I share. What the XO probably means is that if you're the best they have, you should have an active part in the squadron ASW role. You should probably be assigned to his staff, since the destroyer's primary role is to protect the carrier from submarines. Does that make sense to you?"

"Well, Captain . . . XO, I'm damned surprised to hear I'm the best ASW man in the squadron, and that's scary because I have so little to do with it."

"From your bio the commodore sent over, you surfaced a Whiskey in the Formosa Strait and you detected a Russian nuc during the last SIOP exercise and you registered a kill on one of us off San Diego last summer. Are these things true?" Captain Fowler asked.

I tried to catch my jaw before it bounced off my neck. "Ah . . . the events are true, but I can hardly take credit for the action of the whole ship," I answered, rubbing my palms on my trouser legs, hoping the sweat stains wouldn't show when I stood.

"Umph? A couple of years ago the whole ASW fleet in WESTLANT went looking for a Russian nuc boat. After the drill had been secured, a Chief Sheppard, as I recall from the reports, in one of the S2F squadrons flushed him. Any relation?" the XO asked.

The hull creaked. The phone rang. The captain picked it up and grunted in answer. "We're at one hundred fifty feet, speed ten knots, course 095 outbound from the screen," he announced to no one in particular. The slight ping of active destroyer sonars bounced off the hull, giving me an eerie feeling of being attacked from outside as well as from these two submariners.

They both looked at me, waiting for an answer. "Well . . . yes, that was me. I was commissioned later, but it was just pure luck I found it. I've never read anything on what it was, nor did I hear much about it when it was all over."

"Didn't you find it odd that a submarine could do forty knots?" the captain asked.

"Forty-three actually . . . well, yes . . . yes, sir, I did. I figured it had to be a nuclear submarine but no one would talk to me about it—I was only an enlisted puke—so I just shined it on." The XO's glance to the captain indicated how stupid it was that the incident hadn't gotten wide circulation in the fleet.

"Do you think a destroyer is an effective weapon against a submarine, Don?"

"No, sir, I don't."

"Why not?" the captain asked. I imagined the pressure on the sub's hull at this depth of one hundred fifty feet; but more, I felt the pressure of these two men questioning me. I didn't like it. I had figured this trip would be a nice rest for me. I wondered if the exchange officer on *Henshaw* was getting the same treatment from my captain and XO. I doubted it. Mr. Bluing would probably be taking care of him—most likely, ignoring his presence.

"We stay active most of the time and rarely have a submarine to play with. Our weapons system is no better than what we had in World War One. When we can get time on the simulator—the Attack Teacher—at the ASW School in San Diego, only the ASW crew goes. The captain and XO are always too busy, I understand. It's more of a lark than anything worthwhile, I think. I've never been to the Attack Teacher. The theory of hunting subs is simple, but it just doesn't work for us."

"It is simple. The only problem for you is that we know where you are and you don't even know we're there," the XO offered. "And we get a lot of practice; we track everything around and run simulated torpedo attacks. We know you guys ping like mad, and we can pick up your slop so far away from you that you'd never have a chance to get close. If we wanted to, we could go right under you, protected by the thermocline layers. We get constant readings on them, whereas you have to slow to make a bathy drop. You guys are a piece of cake," the XO lectured, shrugging his shoulders and throwing his hands into the air in a sign of resignation.

I flushed more with each word. He was right. "Cut him some slack, XO. It's not his fault that the surface navy just hasn't evolved yet. None of us have; the airedales don't use us the way they should and the surface folks don't either. You know, Don, a carrier attack group should have submarines assigned just like they do destroyers and ASW aircraft and helos. A sub is the most efficient ASW weapon we have; we can get down to where the action is and kill the sub in its own environment. A level playing field. The day will come soon when we don't have three separate navies, five if you count the amphibs and the auxiliaries."

I could only answer, "Yes, sir." I hadn't thought about the bigger scheme of things as he had.

"Another few items, Don, on why we're so great as to turn out megalomaniacs like the XO here," he smiled, tossing a cigarette to the XO, who seemed undaunted by the statement.

"First, we go to submarine school after commissioning, not right to a ship without knowing anything. And our white hats also graduate sub school before being assigned to a boat. Once onboard everyone must do further qualifications before earning their dolphins. Having your dolphins awarded is a big thing. We take that seriously. An ensign coming aboard his first boat is almost qualified to take the watch. He's been well trained and can run a decent torpedo attack on the first try.

"Second, we get extra pay, submarine pay, which usually attracts a higher percentage of the good ones."

Fat Donny squeezed himself free, slithering out of his cave into my body like a malaria demanding its toll of sweat and pain, chills and weakness. I squirmed, feeling inadequate, unwanted.

"Third, we have a constant tender availability when we're in port, and we take advantage of it by releasing the men to go to classes or the attack trainer to hone his skills. And we treat our sonarmen like gods; they're the kingpins of our existence.

"And the last couple of things, before we bore you to tears, is that we never have drills. Everything is done for real except firing the torpedoes. I might add, we get a chance to do that a lot on the Hawaii Range.

"We're very often inspected by control teams to ensure that our readiness is topnotch. And we use the senior enlisted man as chief of the boat to keep a constant channel open between the men and the XO and me. They never feel they've got no one to talk to."

The captain stood, offering me his hand. "The XO and I figured if we were going to participate in this cross training, we wanted to level with you on how we felt. I hope you understand." I shook his hand, expressing my thanks.

"Oh! One more thing, Mr. Sheppard. We consider there are only two kinds of ships: submarines and targets." He chuckled as he passed through the curtain to the passageway.

For the next few hours the XO led me through the boat. He wasn't a bad guy one on one and congenially explained the inner workings of the submarine, freely answering the multitude of questions I asked. Most important, I learned to use the pressurized heads. I'd never given any thought to how submariners flushed their toilets when they were submerged. They blew it out with compressed air.

That was a far cry from the early days of sailing when the head actually meant the head of the ship, the bow. To facilitate defecation, a small platform extended down from the bulwarks. A man stepped over the rail and squatted to eliminate into the sea. Few men bothered to wipe themselves, and I imagined a friendly wave splashing up to do it for them.

Some of the bigger ships had boxes mounted inboard of the bulwarks with chutes to the sea—certainly safer but not as exciting. Eventually the location on the ship took on the meaning, and to this day sailors call latrines, toilets, johns, privies, and so forth the "head."

Later, I paid strict attention as the XO briefed his watch officers over the plotting table. "A standard penetration exercise for us, gentlemen, and for Mr. Sheppard, here, to see." He had already introduced me. "We'll start ten miles in front of the screen; our target is the carrier. We'll get within one thousand yards of her and pop a smoke."

He looked around at the bored officers, cleared his throat, and continued. "I know, I know, it's old hat and we've done it a dozen times, but this time we want to show Mr. Sheppard how it's done." A few chuckles.

"How would you do it, Don?" the captain asked, standing in the background.

I thought for a moment, uncomfortably looking at the five officers standing around the table. "They'll be conducting flight ops this afternoon. Winds aren't very strong today; everyone will be steaming at least twenty knots or more to get enough wind across the carrier's deck. They'll be making turns and probably zigzagging, and everyone will have their surface search radars on. You can track them on your ESM receivers if you wanna put up an antenna.

"But you probably don't even have to do that; they'll be pinging away and I'm sure you can track that on passive much farther out than their range can be, just like radars can be detected out to more than one and a half times their detection capability. If I recall, when I got off watch this morning, there was a two-hundred-foot or so thermocline down here, and you can hide under it until the screen passes. Hell, just put your bow to them and you'll be a smaller target. Our sonars aren't worth shit anyway, especially at twenty knots."

The captain stared at me as the XO nodded his agreement. The other officers glanced at one another. Encouraged, I shot a dose of chemotherapy against the insidiously lurking cancer of Fat Donny.

"A different plan might be to swing wide of the screen and come up from behind. They'll be using a bent-line screen, you know, with all the destroyers in somewhat of a semicircle around the carrier's heading.

Maybe they'll have one destroyer in the rear, but he'll be pinging away and going too fast to be effective on passive. None of our sonars are worth a damn on passive.

"Once around the screen, ease in at top speed. Hell, no one will be listening, and ASW helos will probably still be on the carrier's deck and not available to dip their sonar balls into the water. Make all the noise you want.

"Or," I added, "you can come up behind the rear ship and stay in her screw wake, her baffles—we can't detect anything there—and you can go right under her and pop your smoke as you come free of her bow. She'll certainly be in plane guard station one; if not, she'll probably not detect you anyway under the layer."

No one spoke as I finished. I felt like a fool lecturing college professors on their specialties. "How fast can you go submerged and all out?" I asked nervously just to break the silence.

"About twenty knots," the captain answered. "Which of the three methods would you choose, Mr. Sheppard?"

I paused for a moment. *Can they be patronizing me? Shit, I don't care. Yes I do; I admire these people.*

"I'd choose the feint to the north and come around the port side of the screen, then make a high-speed run to the carrier. The commodore always puts *Haney* out there because her sonar is the worst in the squadron. You can shave her pretty close without fear."

"XO?" the captain asked. The XO nodded.

"Mr. Weathers?" the captain asked, turning to a young, almost childish-looking, very tall JG. "You're scheduled to run the attack. Whadaya think?"

"What I think, Captain, is we should feint to the north and come around the port side of the screen, then make a high-speed run in to the carrier. And I'd shave the outboard destroyer pretty close."

"He's our resident smart-ass, Don, just like I hear you are." *How did he know that?* "But he's good. Mr. Weathers, come north to skirt the screen," the captain ordered, then turning back to me asked, "What depth do you suggest, Mr. Sheppard?"

"What are the layer depths, sir?"

"We got a layer at two hundred fifty feet—you were right about that— and it extends down to two ninety. Several more go much deeper," the XO answered without a moment's hesitation.

"Then I'd go in at around three hundred feet."

"Why not go in the layer area?"

"Ducting," I answered too fast, knowing now he was testing me. My smart-ass mouth continued, "As you know, Captain, one of those destroyers might get lucky, and if his sonar beam got caught within the layer it might bounce along for a pretty long way, and I—*I?*—don't want to take the chance of a long-range, second-pulse detection."

The captain winced, opened his mouth to say something, paused as if thinking for a minute, then said with a smile in his voice, "*You* don't want to take the chance, Mr. Sheppard?"

"Sorry, Captain, I didn't mean anything by it. I just have this nasty habit of internalizing everything around me."

"Understood. Go on."

"Well," I started again, deflated, "running under the layer could distort, or refract, the sonar beam twice—once when it hit the top of the layer and again as it hit the bottom. That should cause sufficient confusion to the operators. Most of them are somewhat lackadaisical anyway because of lack of practice and the lack of recognition for what they do. It's a big problem on destroyers."

They listened silently as I spoke. I guess they never heard from a guy from the other side.

Doug Fowler looked at his XO. The XO raised his eyebrows. "Well, it's your idea, Don. You take us in," the captain said, looking at Mr. Weathers with a nod and an apology.

The 311-foot submarine turned broad around the end destroyer on the port side of the screen and, when clear, made a run in to the carrier at a two-hundred-foot depth. All eighty-five or so officers and men carried out their tasks in silence, and I had the "make-believe" conn. I gave "instructions" through the OOD; I told him what I wanted to do and he gave the orders. The captain watched like a father seeing his young daughter on a bicycle for the first time. It had been comically easy to come around the screen.

"Prepare to release smoke," I ordered as if I were truly the conning officer. "What range, Captain?" I asked, berating myself for not asking sooner. I thought of the six torpedo tubes in the forward torpedo room pointed toward the carrier. I got caught up in the excitement of the chase. For a stupid moment I wanted to fire them.

I knew now what the captain meant when he said there were just two kinds of ships, submarines and targets. The carrier represented a target to me—not something to protect but something to kill. I shuddered, thinking how it must affect these men over the years.

"Wait," the captain said "Set a course to pass under her amidships . . . we'll snap a picture."

From the passive data sonar sent to the attack director, I worked out a quick intercept. "Come left to course 170."

"Left to course 170, aye, sir," the helmsman repeated, putting his wheel over before he realized I only had the play conn. Mr. Weathers quickly repeated the order, much to the comfort of the helmsman.

"Recommend a speed, Mr. Weathers, if you would. I don't have a feel for it."

"I'd drop to twelve knots. That should give you a safe course," he answered, and the captain grinned.

I—we—ordered twelve knots and we came a bit farther to the left. Nodding that my course and speed looked good, the XO told the messenger to pass the word silently that we were going under the carrier. In a few minutes I knew why; the wamp, wamp, wamp of the carrier's huge turning screws felt like the devil himself beating on the door.

"Up scope," the captain said.

"Up scope," I ordered.

"No, Mr. Sheppard, I get to do that."

"Sorry."

"Camera ready, Captain," someone said.

As we passed underneath the carrier just aft of midships, the screw noise pounded us all the harder, but I seemed to be the only one noticing it. "When we're about two hundred yards on the other side, pop the smoke, Mr. Weathers, and come to periscope depth."

I looked in confusion to Mr. Weathers. Surreptitiously he extended all his fingers and thumbs upward, clinched them back, and extended his right first finger upward and nodded his head. "Up ten degrees bow," I ordered.

"Up ten degrees," he repeated with a grin.

"Take over, Mr. Weathers," the captain ordered, noticing my discomfort. I breathed in relief. I didn't know what to do and was feeling like a ventriloquist's dummy trying to pretend I did. I watched closely. I'd know next time.

A whooshing sound passed almost silently through the control room. "Smoke away," someone said.

The captain peered into the periscope. "Here, Don, take a look." I wished I had a billed hat I could turn around like the ones the Nazi U-boat captains in the movies had. But I didn't and looked in with both hands gripping the handles, as I'd seen it done. There was the carrier, so large I could see only part of her. "Swing it around and take a look," he offered.

I looked at the screen; they were breaking up in panic to find us after we'd so easily penetrated them. I could imagine Captain Baker silently cursing on the bridge as Sonar passed up their regrets. I could see the XO shaking his head impotently. "Spot *Henshaw?*" the captain asked.

"Yes, sir," I answered after a moment of searching back and forth. My ship, my home, seemed so small, so vulnerable to this undersea killer. She came about in a tight turn to starboard.

"Camera ready," the captain ordered to someone. "We'll take some pictures for your captain, Don." He took back the scope. "There's so much confusion out there with all their turning and increased speeds and all the bubbles they're making, they'll never spot our scope." But he pulled it down anyway. Five minutes passed; constant reports from Sonar filled the control station. The sub officers knew what they all meant; I could catch only a few. Five minutes passed.

"Now," the captain whispered. The scope went up. He put his eyes to it, ordered a small course change, waited forty seconds while snapping the lens of an unseen camera, then said casually, "Got it. Take her down under the layers." Two hundred fifty feet. I felt the bow go down. How wretchedly easy this had been for the submarine.

I wanted to command one. I wanted to be like Doug Fowler, a great white knight destroying the surface dragons. I was ashamed of the surface navy and ambivalently hated these cocky bastards and their layers and their marvelous machines.

The pictures showed *Henshaw* beautifully; the light was right and the exposure near perfect. I hated them. The carrier's bottom showed a great deal of fouling; she'd been out of dry dock quite a while. "We'll send these over so she can use them for yard overhaul planning," the XO said with a snicker as he tossed the pictures to me.

For the next two days I studied; I studied hard using their own qualification book as a guide. I had fun learning new things, trying to compress a six-month course into two days. I didn't get much sleep, but I wasn't here to get much sleep. I felt a need to impress these guys. That

old feeling of inferiority gripped my throat again, like an emotional cancer that lay dormant, waiting to flair up, to cloud my mind, to stifle my
feeling of self-worth, to destroy my productivity. *Go away, Fat Donny.*

I learned to make dummy torpedo runs using three merchantmen
steaming through the area. I reveled in truant joy. It was ridiculously
simple, not much different than destroyer torpedo runs. On the first one
I missed because of impatience and overconfidence. I guess my face
showed my disappointment. The CO said, "'Tis better to have tried and
failed than not to have tried at all." I returned an insipid smile.

On the next one I got to use active sonar—a rare luxury, Mr. Weathers
insisted as he graded me "sat." On the last merchy it was all visual, just
like World War Two, as I played the wolf pack commander on secret
orders from the fuehrer himself. My mathematical torpedo would have
hit her dead center.

The next exercise with the carrier group required that we initiate contact if they didn't detect us in the first twenty minutes. The captain let
them catch us in eighteen—"to give them some feeling of confidence,"
he said, laughing, to the XO. "They should be able to 'kill' us this time,"
he told me in a briefing tone. "They've got some S2Fs and some helos
with dipping sonar. It'll actually be tough to get away if they can get all
those assets locked in on us. We're required to reinstate contact if they
lose us for more than ten minutes. A real tough mental exercise for
us . . . you know, initiating contact."

And he was right. Once a destroyer locked in on us, he called in another destroyer and the helos and S2Fs. They got us the first time in
twenty-two minutes with a simulated drop of an MK 44 ASW torpedo
launched from an S2F. We surfaced to acknowledge.

Our periscope was barely wet on the way down when the helos attacked. "Not quite up to the rules, but shit," Doug Fowler said, "gotta
give 'em something." The S2Fs laid a sonobuoy pattern around their datum and went into MAD trapping circles until we went below 250 feet
and they lost us or, the captain assumed, the destroyers came bounding in
with their sonars beating up the water.

The layer had deteriorated and they got us. The sound of the hand grenades simulating depth charges scared me but didn't faze the crew, although they couldn't have heard them too often. A tough lot.

The OOD stood his watch in the control station. I was on the bridge as
the JOOD with the captain and two lookouts. The honor to be trusted by

him on this small concession bathed my ego as he talked to me. "Our vulnerability is those damned batteries. We have to surface eventually, and that's when they can get us." He hadn't defined the "they." "We can only cruise ten thousand miles at ten knots and then our diesel tanks suck dry. Soon, Don, we'll all be nuclear, and then watch out. No more snorkeling or cruising on the surface to charge our batteries. We'll truly be submarines. I'm on my way to nuc school in Idaho after this deployment and then hopefully a nuc command."

"Good luck, sir," is all I could answer.

"All lights bright lights," the lookouts gave their mandatory report on the half hour. Not any different than a destroyer, I thought, when we were equalized, as on night steaming.

Doug Fowler, with his binoculars to his eyes, continued talking to me. "The navy insists that all officers and men assigned to nuclear subs be nuclear engineering qualified. Pretty expensive and time consuming, but I guess they know what they're doing; the school's about a year long," he mused, then turned silent.

The starlight, unhindered by clouds or mist, shone thousands of beams of brilliance across the water. The moon poked its crescent over the horizon as Doug Fowler spoke again. "Don, you've done okay aboard *Cat Fish,* and to a man we're pretty impressed with what you've learned in such a short time."

I didn't answer for a minute, then to my surprise I said, "Captain, thank you, but I lied about getting those submarines you mentioned when I first came aboard. It wasn't luck, sir."

"I know," he answered, his binoculars to his eyes again, searching out over the sea. The carrier group, unseen over our low height of eye, night steamed ten miles off our starboard side at 090, relative. The small surface search antenna turning slowly above us gave me a soothing purr of confidence.

"I would get these feelings, these impressions. I knew they were there, but only my gut feeling told me. I—"

"I know, Mr. Sheppard, you got it early. Usually only captains and mothers develop it fully," he answered not taking his eyes from his 7x50 navy issue binoculars. I felt his hand touch my shoulder. "You'll make a helluva skipper one day. Too bad it couldn't be in submarines."

"Yes, sir," I replied. The oncoming watch requesting permission to come up to the bridge broke any further comment. "Request permission to go below," formed my answer.

In the morning, *Henshaw*'s motor whaleboat came across the five hundred yards separating us. The exchange submarine officer stood amidships appearing bored. Her bow wave churned up the water as she approached, looking very impressive in this dead calm sea and early-morning sun. At the precise moment the coxswain rang his bell signaling the engineer to back her down, the man in the bow, the bow hook, threw a line over. A perfect landing. *Thank you.*

Lieutenant Commander Fowler stood in silence on the main deck with me. "Request permission to leave the ship, sir, and I thank you for all your help," I said, snapping up a salute. He returned it and handed me a small box with his left hand.

"From the wardroom . . . open it." As I lifted the lid, sunlight glistened off the gold submariner's dolphins. "I—"

"Permission granted to leave the ship, sir," he answered, patting me on the shoulder.

"I . . ." But no other words came out; the lump in my throat prevented it. The gentle wind on my face swiftly dried the forming tear. "I—"

"Stand by to dive," he ordered, swinging around, agilely climbing the ladder to the conning station.

"Shove off, Coxswain," I said. "Make *Henshaw*," I added as we backed away smartly.

The submarine's bow dipped under first, then the water engulfed midships, then aft, and finally the conning tower. The periscope leveled out, the eyepiece turning in my direction for a second. I saluted. The periscope disappeared.

Win Some, Lose Some

A damned audacious bunch, Captain," I answered his question on how I liked the submarine. "I learned a lot. They think we're incompetent and that we don't really give a shit." I handed him the pictures of *Henshaw.* He winced.

"Those cocky bastards," he shuddered, probably thinking—as I had—what if they had been a Russian sub?

I said nothing while he stared at the photographs, passing them over to the XO, who frowned, handed them back to the captain, and grunted. "XO," I asked, "how long to go on the ASW exercise?"

"One more run this afternoon and then another tonight."

I dramatically shifted my eyes around the wardroom as if checking for bugs. "If I may suggest, we might try this—" And in communications with the commodore over a conference net, we laid out the plan as if it were coming from the captain himself. I knew it would work.

At lunch only Mr. Chadwick and Mr. Banning, the ASW officer, asked any questions about my visit to the sub. And when I tried to tell them, Mr. Bluing spoke up on how lazy the sub officer, my counterpart, had been and how he showed no interest and only wanted to sleep and watch the movies. "I gave him plenty of opportunity to ask me questions but he didn't seem to give a damn." *I'll bet.*

Four o'clock, 1600. COMEX. We steamed five hundred yards behind *Rollard* in the center screen station. I'd figured Captain Fowler would assume I told our commodore of the last attack and on skirting the port side of the screen and how it was a deception that we popped the smoke on the starboard side of the carrier to have us figure he'd approached from that direction. I figured he'd discount the screen wings this time and go for a down-the-throat approach. Their next port call was Hong Kong, and I knew they were anxious to put an end to these "useless" ASW drills.

The commodore and the admiral had approved our plan of steaming behind *Rollard* on passive and hopefully catching the sub coming through the center. *Haney,* with her weak sonar, was not on the wing. Doug Fowler would have bet on that. I knew the sub could not tell if a destroyer was behind the carrier. It wasn't; we were the "off" destroyer ready to catch him as he penetrated the screen.

We dropped back to fifteen hundred yards behind the screen, figuring he couldn't detect us through the noise of the pinging and the racket the carrier put out. The captain oscillated from bridge wing to bridge wing, each time through demanding the range to the behemoth behind us at only thirty-five hundred yards. Each time through he scowled at me. If he was nervous, I should be panicked.

"Never! Never get closer than five thousand yards in front of a carrier," he kept mumbling the time-honored law of safety, but the admiral had the bit in his teeth, and the commodore wanted a clean kill, not a stage play as they had yesterday from that cocky submarine lieutenant commander.

The S2Fs and helos circled our location, ready to join the destroyers at first sign of detection. The layer extended from 120 to 230 feet. I knew they'd be there. And to help, the seas were freshening, mixing the surface water and extending down to break up the layer.

The first half hour went uneventfully. Standing next to Leading Sonarman Jarvis in Sonar, I encouraged him to concentrate through the noise of our sister ships. *Cat Fish* was old for a submarine; he'd been commissioned in 1944, more than a year before we were. And he was as noisy as his XO complained. He hadn't had an overhaul for quite a while and was due for FRAM just as we were. Jarvis's eyes glazed, taking on a distant stare. His body went rigid as he passed into a trance, communicating with the sea.

The sub would be an easy target, I had assured Jarvis and the hovering Mr. Banning. "Shush," Jarvis commanded. "I think . . . yes, I hear something dead ahead." We fell silent, watching as Jarvis's wrinkled face concentrated on the sound. "Yes . . . yes . . . it is dead ahead. Very faint, sir. Very faint. Oh, God, Mr. Sheppard, I hope desire isn't overriding reality. I know it's him."

I nudged Mr. Banning, motioning him to phone the bridge and CIC. We waited. "He's . . . yes, closer now. I can hear a little better. I can feel it . . . it's hard, so goddamn much noise from the screen," Jarvis lamented.

I heard the captain ask the commodore over our open net to ensure the helos didn't dip their sonar ball, and I prayed the S2Fs didn't drop any sonobouys. A sharp sub, which they all seemed to be, could tell when sonobouys splashed into the water over them.

"He's coming through the center, Captain, dead slow," I whispered over the phone.

"Commodore's been informed," he murmured.

Jarvis, with his still grossly overweight body, despite his avowed statements in the Philipine jungle and the efforts of Chaplain Layman, sat jammed into his chair. Rolls of fat hung over the armrests. He was the kingpin, numero uno, and he knew it. The sweat on his face betrayed the calm he tried to affect. His wonderful ears alone had to carry this day for my ego.

"I think he's inside the screen now, Mr. Sheppard."

"C'mon, Willie," I said with the rare use of his nickname, "you can do it, baby. Do it, Willie, feel the sonovabitch . . . get the tingle, Willie. Feel him," I encouraged. I felt nothing. *Why?*

"He's there!" Jarvis pointed to a splotch on his large scope. "He's penetrated the screen."

I slapped him on the back. "Good show, boy," I yelled, then shouted over my phones to combat, "Got 'em, got 'em. Execute."

I heard the XO's voice over the tactical net. "Romeo Sierra, this is Uniform Yankee. Execute Charlie. I say again, execute Charlie. Out."

As prearranged, all sonars went passive as the screen slowed to ten knots; superheat had been secured an hour ago. The carrier veered off hard to port and kicked up speed. The outer two destroyers wheeled around to box in the sub. The S2Fs dropped a sonobuoy pattern. The helos dipped their sonar balls deep and reported contact. "Mark datum one," I heard the XO's voice over the sound-powered phones.

Rollard turned sharply to join in and circled the datum at one thousand yards. "Go active, Lifeblood," came over the tactical net. The flagship screwed up using our stateside call sign; they should have used Uniform Yankee, our code call sign for the day.

"Sonar contact, bearing 110, range one thousand yards, echo quality sharp, up Doppler, classified as possible submarine. Classify Sierra One," Jarvis reported in his textbook response, now assured, now confident.

"Mark datum two, Sierra One," the XO announced calmly, though I knew from his clipped words his heart pounded with excitement. "Echo Bravo, take the fence," he ordered. The ship in contact took tactical command of the hunt. Once the contact was lost, the senior of the two skippers took command. We, the captain that is, was junior to *Rollard,* but we had contact.

"Losing contact; he's breaking up," Jarvis whined.

"Sonar contact," *Rollard* reported. "Uniform Yankee, take the fence. Mark datum three, Sierra One."

"Sonar contact," Jarvis reported again. We stayed on the fence, circling our prey while *Rollard* ran in to drop. She dropped and ordered us in as she heeled over and pulled away to starboard. I heard her hand grenades explode.

I've betrayed you, Cat fish. Forgive me.

Torpedoman Roll chucked a half-dozen concussion grenades over the side as we passed over the sub.

The S2Fs and helos took over; the carrier returned to PIM and slowly overtook us. I hurried to the bridge to watch.

"Mad man . . . mad man," spewed loudly over the radio from the S2Fs. "Drop . . . drop . . . drop," he reported, saying he put a simulated MK 44 homing torpedo into the water. "Up his ass," he added for emphasis.

Thirty seconds later: "Sonar contact," a helo reported as she launched a simulated MK 44 attack.

An object popped out of the water a thousand or so yards off our beam, followed by a column of black smoke rising in the choppy sea. We turned east to our retirement course away from the submarine as he signaled his intention to surface.

His ominous conning tower came awash, pulling up the rest of the long, sleek hull. Once he surfaced and his conning tower manned, the S2Fs made a low pass over him, then winged up and buzzed our mast by no more than one hundred feet as they wiggled their wings in appreciation of the hunt. They were feelin' good. The two helos momentarily hovered next to us fifty feet out. The pilots saluted and pulled away.

A handheld aldis signal lamp blinked from the sub to *Rollard*. We were close enough in the line of sight to read the message to the commodore. "Good tactic, good coordination. Well done."

The light turned to us, blinking so fast I couldn't read it. Jefferson Davis Gaines ran over to the captain with a message form. "Confusing, suh—that there submarine says: 'For Sheppard, well done, it's not too late to join us. CO sends.'"

The captain looked at me with that rippling grin of his slowly forming across his face. "Mr. Sheppard?"

"Yes, sir . . . Gaines, send, 'Thank you.' And on the attack please remember, ''tis better to have tried and failed than not to have tried at all.'"

"Another light, suh; it says . . . excuse me, suh, it says: 'Smart-ass. XO sends.' They shouldn't be a'cussing over the light, suh. Ain't right."

"Gentlemen, station ship, Hong Kong, is where we're heading," the XO casually mentioned as we finished lunch and he lit a cigar, not one of his for-new-ensigns ones.

"Hong Kong, hot damn!" Rog Wachifsky shouted at the announcement. "What's 'station ship' mean though?"

"It means we anchor close in to the beach and get another liberty boat and we're responsible for the mail and we become the central movie exchange for the fleet. We'll run the Shore Patrol and work with the Brits and local police. But mostly, I guess—if I understand properly—we must stay there no matter what," replied the XO.

"Why?" I asked while Mr. Bluing noisily stirred his coffee, glaring at the XO.

"The instructions say simply, and I quote, 'Remain on station under all conditions and at all times to render aid and support to U.S. government diplomatic personnel as required and necessary. Orders will be taken from the senior State Department representative present.' End quote. Read that as evacuation if the CHICOMS come over the hill."

"How do you know all that?" Mr. Bluing asked, rubbing his nose, his eyes slightly closed, obviously miffed that the XO had the word before he did. "Where'd you get that information? We have any instructions yet?"

"Just before lunch, flashing light from the commodore; and, yes, we have instructions in the WESTPAC Guide," the XO answered sharply, a snip in his voice. Mr. Bluing was becoming mighty grouchy lately and spent far too much time in the rack.

"My ship," the XO continued, ignoring the nearly bedridden ops officer with the itchy nose, "had it once when I was a junior officer. Actually, we worked our asses off and didn't get much liberty. But my XO had been an asshole, not a good guy like yours."

Some junior officer at the end of the wardroom table hazarded a groan. Chuckles rippled through the camaraderie. We were high on the successful sub kill and the accolades of the admiral and commodore. I nursed my guilt at having used what I had learned to defeat them. I couldn't rationalize it away.

"What about you, Captain?" Mr. Graffey asked. "Have you ever had the duty?"

"No, but I tell you this, I'm going to sleep and shop and walk the streets seeing the sights. This one's the XO's and Mr. Bluing's. I'm going to be on R and R and you can just call me when you're ready to leave. I'll be back when you set the sea and anchor detail."

According to the pilot charts we studied, this constant ten-to-fifteen-knot wind from the north was rare for this time of year, but the weather reports showed nothing untoward. The barometer held nice and steady at 30.24 inches. Not too shabby even though the seas were increasing slightly, and a fine chop periodically formed.

Finishing an excellent dessert of apple pie and the last of the ice cream, the captain pushed back expansively in his chair. "A little business, gentlemen, if you'll forgive me talking shop at the table."

It was unusual for the captain to break his sacrosanct rule. "You've all been briefed on the upcoming FRAM, but I feel we must do more than let the yardbirds do all our planning for us. We must help them. This applies only to below the main deck; the entire superstructure will be removed and replaced. But below deck we must discover and record every discrepancy. Don, especially you. Big overhauls like this tend to run out of money about three-quarters of the way through, and the yard starts taking shortcuts. Make your lists—everyone—and give them to the XO for typing."

Four bells on the evening watch danced their soft rhythm throughout the ship: 2000. The glass still read 30.24 inches. The seas rolled in uncharacteristically from the south against the wind as we sat tensely at our 1AS stations waiting to "kill" the sub again.

The long-gone twilight let the moon rise in the east. Jarvis, his sonar on passive, dropped huge beads of sweat from his straining face onto his control board as he leaned forward in his seat, probably thinking that if he were closer to the set he'd hear it better. Nothing!

I had no idea how *Cat Fish* would attack. I tried projecting myself into the sub, to hear the thoughts, detect their thinking. Nothing!

Four destroyers steamed in a bent-line screen two thousand yards ahead of the carrier. We were on her starboard beam at two thousand yards and *Rollard* was on her port. The remaining two cans were two thousand yards off the carrier's port and starboard quarters. A tight net of ships to penetrate.

This unorthodox screen might confuse the sub, but I doubted it. The four destroyers in the bent-line screen pinged away while the rest of us listened. This would tell the sub we were someplace else. It amused me that I had transitioned back to the surface fleet and now thought of *Cat Fish* as a sub, not Doug Fowler's boat.

The roughening seas had eliminated the thermocline at one hundred feet, and the water seemed "clean" down to six hundred. "Looks like something coming up astern, coming up through the baffles, very slight . . . Mr. Banning, coming fast, coming up fast. It's . . . it's him, it's him! I think," Jarvis yelled unprofessionally.

"Two flares off our port beam," I heard over the sound-powered phone.

"Port beam? Can't be," I shouted, bounding out of the sonar shack for the bridge. "Those sons of bitches are between us and the carrier!"

The flares sputtered into the water as *Cat Fish*'s sleek form broke the surface. A blinking light winked at the carrier as I stepped onto the bridge to an angry captain.

From our position we just barely made out what the carrier blinked back to the sub: "Thank you for your services. Proceed on mission assigned."

Then the sub's aldis lamp turned to us over the seven-hundred-yard separation, flashing: "If at first you don't succeed . . ."

The clank of his closing conning tower hatch shot over the swelling sea between us. I heard his Klaxon sounding the dive. I saw the froth of his bow digging into the waves, all in the painful clarity of our failure.

"Captain, they knew which one we were," I whined, crying out my impotent frustration. "They knew, Captain. Goddamn them, how could they know which one we were? And surfacing between us and the carrier with so little room, they rubbed our noses in it, Captain." The captain did not reply. I watched the sub disappear into the sea as my heart raged.

I was ten years old again: Roland Stepovich held me down while his thirteen-year-old buddy "Tiger" Trampowski tore at my pockets, searching for my lunch money. He found it. He ripped the pocket apart. He yanked out the two coins. He kicked me in the stomach. He yelled: "You better not tell anyone or I'll stomp the shit out of you."

Rage.

Hong Kong

ong, heavy swells pushed us from astern as we made our way
west for Hong Kong. Strangely, the wind chopped the sea from
the north, as if fighting the swells to see which could make us
the most uncomfortable.

Two days later Mr. Bluing threaded his way through the hundreds
of junks and merchantmen sailing in and out of Hong Kong harbor. I
thought Kaohsiung was "junk madness"; here, the junks paid no attention to the ships as they scurried about, crossing our bow by mere
feet with a death-wish nonchalance. The clean white buildings appearing through the mist on both sides of the harbor stood in sharp
contrast to the squalor of the sampans and junks gathering around us
and following us in. The difference between a junk and a sampan is
size. If a water buffalo could stand athwartships in the vessel, it is a
junk; if it couldn't, it is a sampan.

Rog Wachifsky stood next to me outside the watertight door leading to
the hatch down into main control. I couldn't stand being down there
when something new was happening. Rog lectured me, giving me a running commentary on the geography as we slowly steamed in.

"The low-lying mainland side jutting into the harbor is called
Kowloon. It has nine small hills, you know," he said, pointing them out,
"nine dragons, or *Kau-lung* in Chinese. I guess *'Kau-lung'* sounds close
to 'Kowloon.'"

I was more interested in the myriad junks trying to ruin the captain's career than I was in a geography lesson. "How do you know all this?" I asked, not really caring.

"I read up on it, of course . . . didn't you?"

"Afraid I was a bit busy over the last few days, Rog," I said without rancor. The north wind remained constant, but clear skies belied the impending storm that goes with a drastic change in the normal wind direction.

"This is a textbook port. Supply Officer School in Athens, Georgia, uses it as an example of how an SO can ruin his life," Rog said, turning away from me. I barely heard him.

"How so? Ruin your life?"

"Money exchange."

"Goddamnit, Rog, what are you talking about?"

"Money exchange . . . Filipino pesos for dollars, you know."

"No, I don't know," I said testily, more concerned with the erratic junk I was watching swinging in too close. It crunched into us midships and slid down our port side under the sound of grinding wood against our thin gray paint. I leaned over to inspect as the junk bounced away after staying with us for about thirty seconds.

"NO DAMAGE," I yelled to the captain's peering head from the signal bridge.

"Wow!" Rog said, then continued. "Exchange rate, you know, two pesos to a dollar in the Philippines. You can get ten for a dollar here in Hong Kong on the black market. Mighty tempting if your schedule's right, you know."

His use of the interjection "you know" bugged me when I was uptight. "Where the hell you from anyway, Rog?" I asked the question that I knew had to be asked one day. I was sufficiently pissed at the junk squalor that I didn't care about the answer, but I still hoped he wouldn't say Granite City, Illinois.

"Why, New York City," he replied, sounding surprised I'd even ask such a dumb question.

"What about the exchange rate, for Christ's sake?"

"Well, figure it out. A supply officer brings, say, fifty thousand dollars here, just before he sails, and buys five hundred thousand pesos for a dime apiece. When he gets to the Philippines he exchanges money for the crew. You know we have to do that to save the sailors from paying an exchange fee."

Overseas, the safe in the supply office held a couple hundred thousand dollars in cash for this purpose and for any other hard money needs we might run into.

"The local officials bring their money onboard and we buy it at the standard rate of exchange. So, say he buys another fifty thousand dollars worth, a hundred thousand pesos. Not uncommon I understand when you pull into a big city like Manila."

"Yeah?"

"Don't you see how beautiful it is? He's got pesos he's bought for a dime and sells them to the sailors for fifty cents, you know, two for one—two pesos for a dollar." He paused, looking at me as if I were a recalcitrant student who wouldn't learn his lessons.

"I can follow you, Rog." *And you can stick that Princeton Phi Beta Kappa key up your ass, too, Mr. "You Know" Wachifsky.*

"So, he makes forty cents on every peso. If he can pass all five hundred thousand he'll make a cool twenty thousand dollars. Just before he leaves, he buys back the unused pesos from the sailors at two for one and in turn exchanges them back with the Filipino officials at the same rate. The only thing that can go wrong is if the locals get back too many pesos.

"They might just wonder why the sailors didn't spend many pesos. They try, you know, to keep the exchange rate artificially low. Therefore, buying pesos on the local black market, which I understand is going for eight to one, is a jailing offense."

"Why didn't it work for your friend?"

"Not my friend, Don. I told you I heard about it at SO school," he answered, walking over to the lifeline and peering into the filthy harbor.

"Okay, why didn't it work for the guy the school told you about?"

"Three hours out of Manila they were diverted to Japan and he was stuck with fifty thousand dollars in pesos. Therefore, he didn't have enough cash in his safe to buy yen for the sailors. I reckon it embarrassed him a trifle."

"What happened to him?"

"Five years in the military prison at Leavenworth, the federal prison in Kansas, and a dishonorable discharge. I guess that's why they tell us the story."

The falling anchor chain clattering through the hawse pipe rumbled throughout the ship. The hiss of steam as the engines backed to set the anchor followed seconds later. "Moored," blasted over the 1MC. Forward again for a minute, then I felt the ship turn and heard the opposed engines twist us around. Another clattering, another backing. The other anchor went out. I guess the north wind bothered the captain too.

But the engines continued to maneuver. I called down to Chief Maclin. "Second anchor's fouled," he shouted up.

On the fo'c'sle, Mr. Hethington and Mr. Graffey stared at the slack port anchor chain as I walked up, not minding my own business again. "Looks bad," the chief boatswain's mate mumbled without emotion or care in his voice as he looked blankly to Mr. Hethington for orders.

I knew he didn't much like the autocratic way Mr. Hethington ran the gunnery department, which included the 1st Division—the Deck Division—under Mr. Graffey. He wasn't about to offer any advice unless he had to. The chief boatswain's mate used to be a fine man, but he had lost his initiative because of our poor leadership and our lack of understanding and communication.

He never complained outside of chief's quarters except at the Chief's Club in Subic, where I had gone with Maclin for a drink one night. I sympathized with him, but unfortunately there was nothing overt I could do about it. From my enlisted days I knew that most sailors felt their officers were grossly incompetent and haughtily overbearing.

Now, as an officer, I knew it to be mostly true. At least on this destroyer. The captain and the XO were notable exceptions, as were Chess Chadwick and Rog Wachifsky. John Graffey tried, but working for Mr. Hethington was too much for him. The captain, though I worshipped him, could also be a real asshole when provoked or under a lot of pressure.

I spoke to the XO about the chief's complaint, but he cautioned me away from it. "You're a mustang, Don. Anything you say will be cast in that light . . . drop it," he wisely counseled.

Hopefully, he'd talk to Hethington about it, but I doubted it. Leadership wasn't always the navy's strong suit. It was a shame; we could be so much better. But, I rationalized, this had been true all through history. *It'll be different when I'm the XO or captain. Yeah! Sure.*

"The captain wants to talk to you, Bosun," the talker said, passing his sound-powered phone to the chief.

"Looks bad, Cap'n. Someone's got to go down there and unshackle the anchor from the chain so we can work the chain free."

The chief stood there silently looking up at the bridge. He was not about to commit himself. I felt the north wind on my face and sensed a lessening of the barometric pressure tingle my neck hairs. Three minutes passed. "You there, Cap'n?" the chief asked. More waiting. The captain won when the chief finally asked, "You want me and a couple of my boys to do it, Cap'n?"

I guess the answer was no because he passed the phones back to the talker and gazed at the city on Victoria Island only a thousand yards away. His left hand grasped the top lifeline as his right ran over his short black hair, back around his neck, and down his body to his flat stomach. He looked at his first-class petty officer and shook his head. "Officers," he mouthed.

Mr. Bluing stood on the bow as a Jacob's ladder splashed into the water. His eyes darted around under the face mask of the engineering department's shallow-water diving apparatus. His bloodless white face tried to look confident, but his shaking hands, continuously adjusting the mask, refuted any semblance of self-assurance.

The captain, standing next to us, his face flushed red, berated the hapless, small-framed man test-walking the rubber fins he wore. "We got half the crew waiting to go ashore because you fucked up dropping that second anchor, Mr. Bluing. You've always bragged how good you were as a navy diver, now show me how good you used to be earning all that extra dive money."

I turned my head in shame from the captain's badgering. I wondered what happened on the bridge. Bluing was a good ship handler, but I knew that neither the captain nor the XO liked him very much.

Two seamen pumped furiously on the hand pump supplying air for the diving rig as Mr. Bluing disappeared into the grimy water carrying big wrenches and the end of a steel cable to shackle to the loosened anchor. Air bubbles plopped to the surface, breaking through the trash-laden, oily film of the bay.

In five minutes he shot to the surface, ripping off the breathing mask, screeching as he frantically tore at a huge jellyfish squirming around his body, stinging him with its poisonous tentacles.

The boatswain's mate yanked off his shoes and dove in, yanking, pulling the jellyfish away from the screaming lieutenant. A line came down, the chief made it fast around himself, and the sailors hauled him up. Mr. Bluing, quieted now to a whimper, let a seaman and me half carry him to sick bay.

Pharmacist Mate Jennings, in his best set of tailor-made blues, stood at the entrance to sick bay as we approached. He looked ready to lock up and go ashore, and was probably inspecting his holy domain to ensure it was 4.0 before he left. If those asshole officers could ever get us anchored, he was probably thinking.

He quickly turned professional. "Not poisonous, just stings, sir. Hurts like hell, but you'll be okay after you shower and get the shit off you from the harbor. This salve'll take out the sting, and in a day or so you won't even have any red marks. It'll be okay," Jennings said in his finest bedside manner to an unconvinced, trembling naval officer. "Go take a long, hot shower, sir, and I'll be up to your stateroom in fifteen minutes."

Mr. Bluing hobbled off forward, holding his head and dripping slime as he went. "What was he doing in the water, sir? He shouldn't be doing that," Jennings said, shaking his head.

"Why not, for Christ's sake?" I asked.

"Because, sir," Jennings leaned over, conspiratorially whispering, "he had dysbarism once—you know, the bends—when he was a diver, and getting the least bit of pressure can hurt him badly. Only the captain and XO know. Don't say anything or it's my ass, okay, sir?"

"The rubbing—why does he rub his nose so much?"

"He suffers heavily from migraine headaches; rubbing his nose gives him relief I guess. He takes a tremendous amount of aspirin—I don't prescribe them. He's never asked me . . . we don't talk about it.

"I doubt if an hour goes by that he isn't in some kind of pain. The bends, I think, cause it. I don't know for sure, but when the nitrogen from the diving gas mixture of oxygen and nitrogen dissolves in your blood and you change pressure too fast, the nitrogen bubbles up and collects in the joints. It can cripple a man or give him pain for years, or forever, and we don't know what other effects it has either. Ever watch his temples pound?"

I had, and made fun of him. I made fun of his nose rubbing.

In pain all the time? I'm sorry, Mr. Bluing. I'm sorry. Why did the captain order him into the water? Was he that pissed about fouling the anchor? Is the captain that uptight? Did he forget about the bends, or was he just tired of Mr. Bluing being sick all the time?

In an hour the chief boatswain's mate and two of his men had unfouled the anchor. In another fifteen minutes liberty call sounded. Hong Kong—the land of inexpensive tailor-made suits, shoes, and Oriental bric-a-brac and good food and cheap liquor and beautiful, friendly girls—awaited our sailors.

The barometer held at 30.24 inches, rising once to 30.26 late Saturday afternoon. A score of bumboats—sampans and small junks—scurried around our waterline, bumping into one another, screaming and pushing, vying for the choice spots next to the ship. Women in filthy pajamas held nursing babies at their breasts, and young children hunkered down, watching the strange "big noses."

The raspy, singsong voices of the elders hawked their wares of "priceless" Chinese artifacts, where teak was made from packing crates, jade from Coke bottles, and silks from rayon. "Velly cheapee price, no, never mind. You buy, Sailor Boy . . . you want big boom boom, Sailor Boy, never mind . . ."

After liberty call at 0800 the next morning, Sunday, half the crew went ashore. Mr. Hethington wanted to go, so I took the CDO duty for him. I was in no hurry and just wanted to sleep. We'd received 452 movies from the destroyer we'd relieved, and assigned the duty IC man to issue out the ones we didn't want to save for ourselves. The captain and XO spent the greater part of breakfast making the decisions. We saved 22 for ourselves—a bit irregular, but who was I to question my leaders when they could pick such good movies.

Our IC man exchanged movies with the other IC men who arrived by boat to do their business. They brought mail sacks along and picked up any we had for them. These older hands had been here for a couple of days more than we were and recited all the adventures our duty section wasn't having yet, cataloging all the "good" places for them to go tomorrow.

The captain and XO made their obligatory social call to the embassy at 0830. The captain returned with the news that Mr. Graffey had the Shore Patrol duties well in hand. The bosun made the perennial deal with Mary Soo—the woman who painted ships for garbage—to paint our sides for exclusive rights to our garbage. Thirty minutes later five large sampans tended by very young, very beautiful Chinese girls arrived and bent to their task.

The duty section, one-third of the crew—except for the engineers who were on port and starboard liberty because we had to steam the plant while at anchor—gladly attended to anything extra the girls might need. Mary Soo, the captain told us, was doing the same business when his father was an ensign. There must be a lot of Mary Soos, he allowed.

"Did you put out the two anchors because of the north wind, Captain?" I asked as we strolled forward, casually inspecting the ship as we went.

"Yes. It's very strange. The glass is holding steady but the wind is wrong. I don't like it." Neither of us wanted to mention what it might mean.

"I've got number one boiler on the line for electrical power and steam, and every two hours I relight number three just to keep her hot. Maclin's idea."

The captain looked at me and then to the north. "You thinking what I'm thinking, Don?"

"If you're thinking typhoon . . . yes, sir, I've got a bad feeling."

"So do I, but there's nothing I can do about it. I'm certainly not going to curtail liberty for my men just because I'm feeling vaguely uncomfortable about the weather when the weather messages give no indications of a blow. It could be nothing. Maybe we're just getting old, Don," he said, squeezing my shoulder as he stepped into his in-port cabin.

The Star ferryboats making their way between Kowloon and Victoria Island passed our bow every ten minutes, one going one way, one the other. Merchantmen at anchor discharged their cargo into huge lighters, and junks and the water taxis plied their way to and from the ships. I counted eighteen naval vessels at anchor: mostly destroyers and auxiliaries such as oilers, AOs, and stores ships, AFs. The ammo ships, AEs, had to anchor way out at the "explosive" anchorage. Their boat ride to the beach must have taken forty-five minutes or so. The subs nested by themselves at the far end of the harbor. I couldn't tell how many were there.

A slight rain wet the ship. Mary Soo, looking around, sniffed the wind, shaking her head. I watched her, a comely woman of indeterminable age, standing there proudly directing her girls on the mastery of painting a ship. A small gust of wind caught her loose pajama clothes, pasting them to her body. She jerked her head to the north as her expression changed from rippling smiles to squinted-up foreboding.

Seeing me standing there, she pointed to the north, shaking her head even more. "Big wind come soon, all same officer man . . . big wind never mind . . . big wind. *Tai-fung* . . . *tai-fung* come soon never mind, must go must go all same, all same . . . must go . . ."

Tai-fung? Sounds like typhoon. Shit!

She turned from me to shout to her girls in Chinese. They swiftly passed up our paint rollers and partially used cans of red lead paint. The sky darkened. The rain increased as they frantically sculled away to the junk fleet and tied up to any pier or landing they could find.

"Mr. Sheppard, OPS IMMEDIATE from Weather Central says we're in for a big one," the duty radioman shouted, running up to me on the fantail.

"Shit," I yelled, walking fast up to the captain's in-port cabin. Officers never ran; it lacked dignity and frightened the men. "Raise the recall flag, give the whistle several short blasts every five minutes. Get the duty signalman to the bridge," I shouted to the in-port OOD on the quarterdeck.

The recall flag supposedly told all hands to return to the ship—a signal from the sailing ship days when all the sailors ashore sat in one or two taverns along the beach and could see their ships. Useless for a big city such as Hong Kong, but it was something. At least it would be seen by the XO and Mr. Graffey at the Shore Patrol headquarters, Queen's Pier, just off our beam at five hundred yards.

The whistle blasted. Recall flags fluttered up on the ships around us as I knocked on the in-port cabin door. It opened instantly and the half-dressed captain stepped out. I handed him the message. "Shit!" The captain jumped as our whistle blasted again.

"SOPA, sir?"

"I'll call him; you get hold of the XO and let him know what's happening. Cancel liberty," he said, moving out toward the radio room.

"Gaines, you. . . . Good!" I said, stepping onto the signal bridge. The wind seemed more brisk up here. "How come you're not ashore?"

"I took the duty for ma boys. I cain't go into a city of sin like that there Hong Kong, suh. Just ain't right."

I wasn't in the mood for his twangy moralizations. "Yeah, Gaines, try to raise the beach on your light."

"Already done that, suh. The XO's waiting for ya."

"Send: 'Typhoon on way. Expected arrival ten to twelve hours. Track erratic. Secure liberty. CO talking SOPA now. Sheppard sends.'" An aldis lamp blinked back a roger.

The captain, half-dressed without a shirt, spoke over the navy's harbor common for Hong Kong. "Roger, SOPA, understand you'll recommend all vessels under way when ready. I have canceled liberty at Queen's Pier. My XO on the scene. We'll do our best.

"Interrogative, do you know my orders require I remain on station? Over," the captain asked, then glanced at me as he awaited the reply.

"Affirmative, Station, we expect to get under way in about two hours. Take care of any of my boys I leave behind. Good luck, Station."

SOPA, senior officer afloat, was nominally in charge of all navy units within his sphere—in this case, Hong Kong harbor. Now, it was a four-striper skipper of an oiler moored several thousand yards astern of us. His *recommendation* would be for all ships to get under way, if feasible, and sortie the harbor. It was usually easier to fight a large storm at sea rather than in a harbor, that is, if you're seaworthy. The choice lay with the individual captain and with him alone. Commanding officers were inexorably and completely in charge of their ships and their movements and safety, a legacy of World War Two storm losses.

We stood there as SOPA himself passed the message recommending all vessels get under way as soon as possible. All reported affirmative, giving their estimated underway times. I wondered how many skippers and XOs were on the beach, and how many CDOs chomped at the bit to "take 'er out" themselves.

"Wind's picked up to twenty knots, Captain, still from the north. Glass is at 29.9 and falling."

"I know, I know, Don. You don't have to tell me, okay?"

"Sorry, sir."

Junks and other small craft scurried to shore, and puffs of black smoke showed the fleet lighting off. Boats from the moored vessels headed for Queen's Pier, the city landing used for water taxis and for the liberty boats of the fleet, trying to get their men aboard. The weather here wasn't very bad yet. My mind jumped back to the North Atlantic, and the iced carrier deck, and Shaky Lyons and Rammin' Randall . . . and I was scared.

Mary

Mary, suh, that there's the name, Typhoon Mary. Been up-graded from a troppeecal depression. Heard it on the local radio station, suh," Gaines rambled in his insufferable southern accent. The captain thanked him for the information. Seconds later a radioman confirmed it with a message from Weather Central. The Star ferries quit running.

"Pass the word, Quartermaster—all officers and chiefs to the bridge." Whenever anchored we maintained a watch on the bridge to take bearings to detect any dragging of the anchor. I thanked the captain's foresight in putting out two anchors when it was easy.

Four chiefs and five officers showed up. Mr. Bluing, his eyes sunken, stood in the corner bracing his pale body against the nav table. The captain briefed the men. I was glad to see Chief Maclin. He rarely strayed far when *his* plant was lit off. Chief Burton, in charge of damage control, was also here, which calmed me a little; at least any damage would be seen to fast enough. Doc Jennings, having stayed aboard to keep an eye on Mr. Bluing, also came to the bridge even though he wasn't a chief. He was special.

Roger Wachifsky stood next to me wondering what was going on, complaining he was detained onboard to exchange U.S. dollars for Hong Kong dollars—7.6 to 1 he had told me when he was passing them out earlier. I wished the bosun was here. "Get the duty 1st Division petty officer to the bridge," I whispered to the quartermaster.

The wind increased to thirty knots as the captain spoke. "We can't leave; we have to fight out this one at anchor, which won't be easy to do. Before the storm's over we'll be steaming into the anchor chains; with any luck they'll hold. It's a pretty good bottom."

Our motor whaleboat came alongside with ten more of the crew. Mr. Banning stepped on deck and headed for the bridge with the bosun at his side. The crowded city landing thinned out as fewer liberty boats arrived. The wind increased to thirty-five knots as the AO with the ex-SOPA onboard steamed by. On harbor common he passed SOPA to us.

Three submarines, their black hulls shining from the increasing rain, slinked by us with their decks awash. A terse message from *Cat Fish* flashed over to us. "Good luck." Four merchantmen slowly hauled in their anchors. The chop in the harbor increased to three feet. A water taxi on our port side swamped. The captain diverted our motor whaleboat but called it back when no one came to the surface. Four merchies, black smoke pouring out of their stacks, steamed by, their hulls down to the Plimsoll marks.

The quartermaster tapped the glass to ensure that the barometer still worked. "It's dropping, sir, 29.75."

"Signal the XO to wrap it up and get back here right away," the captain yelled to Gaines over the wind on the signal bridge as it held steady from the north.

I could see the water level rise at Queen's Pier from the typhoon-generated swells and the low barometric pressure. *Henshaw* strained at her anchors, not dangerously but enough to let us know the wind hadn't forgotten us. "Set the steaming watch, Mr. Sheppard," the captain ordered, his voice almost a squeak. "Boatswain's Mate, pass the word for the bosun to get lifelines rigged, especially to the fo'c'sle. We're going to have to put a man up there to sound the chains."

How dicey was this going to get?

"Make a message to COMSEVENTHFLT, info the commodore," the captain called down to the radio shack on the 21MC. "All naval vessels except *Henshaw* under way clearing Hong Kong harbor. Will remain on station, station ship Hong Kong, until in extremis. Situation presently tenable but eye of storm might pass over Hong Kong. All naval boating secured. Will keep you advised."

A very wet XO reported stoically to the captain that all was secure at Shore Patrol headquarters. "I brought back twenty-one men from other ships. What's our manpower situation?" He looked at Mr. Bluing supporting himself against the nav table. He narrowed his eyes, then whipped his head to me. "Mr. Sheppard?"

"I make it we got about half the crew, maybe sixty percent of the engineers. We—" I started to answer as the 21MC sounded from main control.

"Request permission to test main engines," Maclin asked.

"I have the watch, Captain," I sang out, knowing that someone had to have it. He nodded. "Engines, sir?" I asked. He nodded again. I turned to the quartermaster. "Test main engines!" I ordered, wishing my voice had come out an octave lower.

His shaking hand rang ahead one-third on the port engine, waited a second, then pulled back the telegraph handles to stop. He repeated it on the starboard. Ten seconds passed. "Engines test satisfactorily. Main control ready to answer all bells; number one and three boilers on the line. Be advised cannot maintain full vacuum in main condenser, and distilling capacity down to fifty percent due to silting from the disturbed bottom. Also, we'll have to turn the engines every three minutes to equalize the heat on the shafts."

"Spin as required," I answered, ashamed of having forgotten to give this simple, required order. *God, Maclin is a professional.* I took a deep breath and held it. *Settle down, Sheppard.*

"Quartermaster, shift the OOD watch to the bridge," the XO ordered. We watched the bosun and Mr. Graffey with their men rigging extra lifelines forward.

Good for you, Graffey, being out there with your men.

An hour passed with no change in the wind or barometer. It was only 1100, but the skies darkened as if it were late twilight. A water taxi came along our starboard quarter and the boatswain's mates made it fast to a cleat. Four figures clambered aboard and ran for the shelter of the superstructure.

A howling scream of wind battered the ship as an eighty-knot gust smashed us head-on, slamming us tight against our quivering anchor chains. We stumbled, grabbing for any handhold. The water taxi strained her lines, bucked a few times, then rolled over and sank. Mr. Chadwick, with blood dripping from a cut on his forehead, stepped into the pilothouse, breathlessly reporting his return aboard.

The captain jerked his head toward him, caustically yelling, "You came out in that water taxi, you goddamn fool! There's got to be three-foot waves in the harbor."

"Yes, sir, sorry, sir, figured you might need me," Chadwick answered with his head held high.

"You're right, Chess, you're right . . . well done," the captain said, getting out of his chair and putting an arm around him. "You're right, Chess. Well done. Thank you."

The wind-speed indicator, receiving its input from the spinning anemometer atop the mainmast 107 feet above the waterline, read fifty knots.

Corrugated tin sheets from the shanty huts built on top of the tall buildings sliced into the skies, carried on the wind like kites. The British flags flying from the flagpoles on HMS *Tamar,* the British forces headquarters, stood out straight, shredding themselves in this killer wind smashing in from the north and reinforcing itself from the funneling effect of the low mountains beyond Kowloon.

"Barometer 29.5 and dropping," the quartermaster reported. Rain drove down at us, creeping into every small hole in the pilothouse.

The XO stood next to the captain's chair staring forebodingly into the darkened skies. He seemed mesmerized by the clack, clack of the two-foot wiper blades arcing uselessly across the windshields. The captain grunted once, cleared his throat, and looked at his second in command. "We're probably in the path, XO; we might get it bad. As long as the wind keeps to the north, it means the storm is to the east but not very far."

He reached for his pipe, rubbed it against his nose as if polishing it, and said into the wind whistling through the pilothouse, "The eye could hit us soon. I don't know how long that could be, but then we'll get the back half with the wind veering to the south. All we can do is wait. And pray. You think, XO, we should have gotten under way?" the captain asked in a slow lament.

The XO thought for a moment. If he said yes, he would be criticizing the captain's decision. If he said no, it could be interpreted as toadyism. "Our orders are pretty specific, sir, on remaining here no matter what."

"I know, XO, but I have contradictory orders on maintaining the safety of my ship . . . no matter what."

"We don't know what it's like out there," the XO wisely answered.

Atop a tall building, one side of the huge Mercedes Benz sign, a Hong Kong landmark for years, twisted off its pedestal. I watched through my binoculars as it whipped back and forth, then lifted off, twisting, circling, slicing into the roof of another building, into the poor Chinese huddled there for safety.

Sixty knots. Pressure 29.2. The surface search radar antenna, perched high on our mainmast, groaned, trying to rotate into the wind, screeching as if begging for help. I could just imagine the havoc its gears were taking. "Secure the surface search radar," I ordered, receiving the captain's nod in approval.

I could barely see the man huddled on the bow, unprotected except for a lifeline tied around him and the huge, orange kapok life preserver and goggles he wore. He had a hammer tied to his hand. "Bridge . . . Bow," I barely heard over the amplified sound-powered phone speaker. The shriek of the wind distorted his words. "Steady strain on the chains; I can feel them shake a little, Captain. Tension's growing; they're starting to sound."

"Thanks, Bosun. Lemme know when."

"Captain, I assume he's hitting the anchor chains with a hammer to determine the change in pitch as they come under strain," I said.

"Yes, we're going to start steaming into them mighty soon. I've never done it before . . . we'll have to play it by ear," he said, then burst out laughing as he realized the pun. I returned a weak smile. "Bluing's out of it, I'm afraid," the captain said. "Poor bastard, I shouldn't have let him go over the side. I shouldn't have let him," the captain said, turning away.

Let him, Captain, let him?

"You take the watch, Mr. Sheppard."

"I have the watch, Captain!" I said again as I glanced at the XO. He raised an eyebrow for an instant, then turned away, both of us knowing the old man must be pretty uptight not to remember I'd taken the watch more than a half hour ago.

I keyed the 21MC. "Chief Maclin, Sheppard here, we're going to start steaming into the chains pretty soon. I've never done this, Chief, you?"

"Yes, sir, back when I was a third class. It's tough; you gotta feel it. We'll give you just the turns you ring up. Keep my ass off the beach, *Mustang.*"

Seventy-knot winds hurtled into our huge forward superstructure, smashing against it like ten thousand pro-football guards. I rang up the first bell, ten turns. Nothing. Fifteen turns. "It's easing," came the bosun's garbled report. "Gimme a little more." I added three more turns. "OKAY! OKAY!" he yelled.

The junks around the ferry piers and down as far as I could see were now a jumble of pounded wood and canvas. The people once living on them were tossed into the white water or heaved bodily onto the streets, where they rolled and scampered for some nebulous safety. Scores of bodies whirled around us, most of them dead, the others flailing hopelessly in the confused throes of the three-foot waves.

These junk people numbered in the thousands. They lived their whole lives on these junks, never going ashore, never seeing anything except from the perspective of their sun-burnished, floating homes.

The captain tried not to notice. I tried not to notice. I wanted to talk. I went over to the man bearing the responsibility for staying here in harm's way. His bloodshot eyes locked onto my face, squinting, as if trying to remember who I was. "It's a typhoon . . . ah, Don?" he said, putting his grandfather's binoculars to his huge eyes as if he could see anything through the impenetrable, rain-blocking gray wall.

"Yes, sir," I answered, unable to comprehend the awesome responsibility this man must be feeling for not getting under way when he had had the opportunity. What torment: the conflicting responsibilities of staying here to possibly evacuate the embassy if the CHICOMS attacked—as if they could in this storm—or getting under way and fighting the storm at sea. He would never be censured for getting under way, but he would be if he lost his ship by staying here.

"Crew fed?" the captain asked.

"Yes, sir," I answered. "Drop two turns."

A garbled voice whooshed over the bosun's speaker. "There's a body tangled around the port chain. Whadaya want me to do?"

"Nothing, Bosun," the captain answered. "Just sound the chain . . . how we doing?"

"The tension is less but it's still jerking a bit." The swish of the wind in his mouthpiece made his words almost undiscernible.

"Captain, 29.0."

"Never seen it that low," the XO commented.

The driving rain gave definition and dimension to the savage wind. It no longer fell; rather it drove itself horizontally, smashing into everything in its path, sounding like a thousand .22 shells banging into and echoing around the enclosed steel pilothouse.

"Add two turns." I tried to feel the chain, sense its tension, and answer to relieve it. "Drop one turn." My body shivered from the cold even though the outside temperature was sixty degrees.

"The engine spaces are hell, Captain," the XO said, returning from one of his constant inspection tours of the ship. "Most ventilation has been shut down. The rain's coming too hard against the vents, drowning out the fans, soaking the spaces. Water's coming down the stacks and into the boiler air intakes."

Roofs of small buildings flew into the air, slicing their knifelike edges into trees and people still scurrying about. Where were the Chinese to go? The doors of the big commerce buildings were locked early on and barricaded, the XO had reported. "Drop one turn," I ordered.

Where were our eighty or so sailors hanging out?

"Wind seventy-five knots gusting to eighty, sir."

"Tension on the chain . . . tension on the chain. It's getting mighty bad up here, Captain," came the bansheed voice of the bosun.

"Can we relieve you?" the captain asked very slowly and distinctly over his phone, knowing his words would be hashed. Then turning to the messenger, he said, "Get Mr. Graffey up here."

"Add two . . . no, three turns." My body rebelled at the misery my mind was putting to it. I had to pee; I needed to sit down for a moment. The ship jerked once, twice, moaning its agony to me. "Add four turns." We rolled ever so slightly. I was overriding the chain; we were yawing. "Drop ten turns," I yelled. If I got ahead of the chains we would override them; when we compensated, the ship might yank backward with such force that the anchor might pull out. "Add five turns. It's the gusts, Captain; can't predict them."

"No one can, Don. You need a spell on the deck?" The dark skies and rain made our binoculars useless but we tried anyway to see through them. I mostly kept mine on the fo'c'sle to see the bosun. The XO and quartermasters tried to take fixes to determine if we were dragging the anchors or not. Their fixes just weren't that good in this low visibility.

A bewildered Ensign Graffey reported to the captain. "Mr. Graffey, did you make provisions to relieve the bow?" the captain asked, his tone too harsh for the occasion.

"Yes, yes . . . sir, we've got extra lifelines attached and we can physically drag him back. A pulley system is rigged to pull another man up," the blanched-faced first lieutenant answered. His sweat-soaked shirt gave evidence of the shut-down ventilation system. I could only imagine the torture of the main spaces, where the temperature must be around 120 degrees.

The steady strain on the ship returned and I dropped two more turns as I leaned against the midships pelorus. The pressure of this imprecise control drained my body of all thoughts except maintaining some nebulous control of the tension on the anchor chains. Chess Chadwick appeared beside me. I hadn't heard anyone call him to the bridge. "Ready to take the conn, sir," he yelled against the wind. I looked at the captain, appreciating his nod.

Chess watched me for several minutes. "Taking on any water? What's the condition of the ship?" I asked while devoting 95 percent of my efforts to the chain tension.

"Except for the ventilating, not bad at all. The depth charge racks are twisted and useless and the motor whaleboat was flooding badly until a boatswain's mate crawled up in it to remove the drain plug. Mighty stupid to forget that when we hoisted it in. It's just scary, that's all . . . the noise, and the god-awful humidity and heat in the spaces."

"Add two turns."

"I think I got it, Don," said Mr. Chadwick. "Is the chief doing any good up there on the bow?"

"I don't think so. I'm not hearing much of what he says and I think I have a better feel from up here."

He winked. "I relieve you, sir. This is Mr. Chadwick, I've got the conn," he bellowed. My body went limp as I sank back against the after bulkhead of the pilothouse.

"This is Mr. Sheppard, I've got the deck," I mumbled the obligatory response to ensure the bridge team knew of my continuing responsibilities. "Captain, I gotta pee."

"Use my sea cabin and then come and talk to me, Don. I'll take the deck. . . . This is the captain, I've got the deck," he shouted.

I stood in the tiny head relieving myself into the captain's own urinal. God, it felt good. I looked enviously around his eight- by ten-foot spartan sea cabin, reveling in the thought that this would all be mine someday. Not this one, of course, but one bigger and better to complement the daring destroyer captain keeping the sea-lanes open for the greater glory of the Western concept of democracy. But in the meantime, it was great just to stand here and empty my bladder.

"Mr. Sheppard, bring back the bosun," the captain said as I walked over to him, my body relieved of its hard-stomached burden.

The bosun buffeted his way back forward along the main deck, pulled by unseen crewmen out in the now hundred-knot winds. He slewed from side to side, jerking as the winds tried hard to lift him like a sail, to toss him into the shrieking maelstrom. As he passed out of sight under the pilothouse, the captain released his death grip on his armrest. Even in this darkness I could see the blood returning to his hands.

"Add two turns," said Chadwick.

"Pressure 28.4, winds one hundred three knots, sir," Morton, the quartermaster, shouted as if his reports made a damn.

"Add three turns!"

A huge freighter bore down on us stern first, yawing back and forth from the now four-foot confused waves. It looked as though we were going to collide. We were both powerless to alter the event. "Sound the collision alarm, Boatswain's Mate," the captain yelled, bolting from his chair and running to the port side.

"Add two turns."

She was big, riding high in the water because of her empty holds, her huge propellor, one-fourth out of the water, churning the air uselessly, splashing torrents of water as it tried to bite into the sea to gain headway. Her stick masts lay bent over and broken, and the crane wires flung themselves around, whipping, destroying everything in their deadly path. Her lifeboats hung uselessly along her sides, ripped out by the wind.

"She'll miss us, Captain," reported Mr. Chadwick, seemingly unfazed. "She's drifting left . . . close, but she'll miss us." Chadwick had the best position to determine this from his station at the midships pelorus. He had been watching her bearing drift slowly to port. "Add one turn."

Her hull showed a German name I couldn't make out as she bore down on us. She passed no more than sixty feet down our port side, two of her large hatch covers missing and her starboard twenty-degree list becoming more painfully obvious. She'd taken on a lot of water in her empty cargo holds, and it could only be getting worse. Her two anchors dragged uselessly taut as they plowed through the bottom of Hong Kong harbor. How many underwater cables had she parted on her way to destruction?

A man assisted by two others forced open her pilothouse door. A man started to step out. The wind picked him up, raising him like a feather, and smashed him into their superstructure, swept him down to the main deck, where a slashing crane wire sliced him in two, and dumped him into the harbor. His primordial scream penetrated the wind and steel around us and ricocheted frightfully through my mind.

A light flashed from their pilothouse. "International signal, suh, 'REQUEST IMMEDIATE ASSISTANCE,'" Gaines shouted, standing there with the portable aldis lamp in his hands, aiming it at the freighter.

The captain paused for a moment deep in thought, then walked over to Gaines on the port side. He smiled. "Cagey bastard," he said, then shouted, "Send, 'Regret, due to heavy weather, unable to maneuver or put boat in the water. Cannot assist. Suggest prayer.' Quartermaster, enter that in the log . . . secure from collision quarters."

The captain looked at my quizzical stare. "He's sharp, Don. He's thinking of the claims and lawsuits later. He can say a contributing factor to his grounding was the failure of a U.S. Navy ship to come to his aid after being requested to."

"He's not too sharp, Captain. He got caught in a typhoon in port with empty holds."

"Better for an empty merchy to stay in port than try to fight it out at sea. It takes time to load a ship. I doubt if he could have lasted more than an hour out there. But, shit, I don't know. I do know, Don"—and he pulled me over so his mouth was no more than six inches from my ear— "I do know that I made the wrong decision by not getting under way when we had the chance. It's just too late now. I couldn't even get a crew up there to dump the anchors. I fucked up, Don, big time. Don't you ever do it!"

The captain was back. He'd come to grips with his decision. "Don't fuck with a fait accompli," he'd once told me, and I guess he remembered. I felt safer now.

"All ahead two-thirds; add two turns," came Chadwick's unruffled orders. He was doing better than I had done. No jerking of the chain, no drops in turns, just a steady increase as the wind howled louder and louder. The two-thirds bell meant we were steaming at least eight knots ahead into the anchors. I didn't care to check.

"Winds constant now at one hundred thirty-eight knots, barometer steady at 28.31 inches for the last fifteen minutes," Morton reported as if he was giving the time of day. The captain and the just-returning XO walked over to see for themselves. They glanced at each other in some senior officer communications I wasn't privy to. "Get 'em up here, XO."

"Drop two turns."

The officers and chiefs came on the bridge again. "Soon we'll be in the eye of this mother and we've got to replant the anchors. Once the vortex is here we'll have maybe an hour of no winds—choppy sea but no winds—and that's when we'll do it. If we don't, we'll twist around to the south and cross our anchors and then who knows their holding power. After the eye, the way out is just as hairy as the way in. My plan is to raise the anchors, twist around, and replant 'em heading south in the other direction. Any questions?" the captain finished.

Mr. Graffey and the bosun shook their heads no. Chief Maclin said nothing. The bosun looked at his first class: "You see any problems? I won't be able to give you much help," he said almost too softly for the noise in the dank pilothouse as he held up his bandaged hands. The stinging wind and rain had cut them badly as if a meat grinder had been used. His bandaged face had fared no better except where his goggles had been. He had not once complained nor commented on the problem when he had been lashed to the fo'c'sle.

"No problems, Chief," the first class said, "My boys are ready for anything to get some fresh air."

"Wind dropping to one hundred twenty-eight knots. Pressure 28.2."

"Drop two turns."

"Mr. Chadwick," the captain said, walking over to the midships pelorus with Chief Maclin and me in tow. "When the wind starts to drop, it'll go down fast—god-awful fast—and when it happens get your turns off immediately or you'll override the anchors, maybe fouling them and taking our sonar dome in the bargain."

Chadwick looked at Chief Maclin and said with a maturity I'd never seen before, "Chief, I've got turns on for nine and a half knots now. When the wind drops, I'll ring back one-third while you close the ahead throttles and at the same time open the astern throttle. It'll take two men to do it. Any problems with that?"

"Why, no, sir, that's a good idea and I think we can do it," Chief Maclin answered, trying to keep the sarcasm out of his voice and the smile off his face. He winked at me as he turned to leave, saying in a whisper, "The kid's learning."

The wind held steady as the glass dropped, but now I could swear the wind blew more and more upward than horizontal. Our pounding against the waves grew less as I tried to comprehend.

Strange. How long have I been up here? How long have I been on my feet? What time is it? 1703.

I'd been on my feet for nine hours, hadn't eaten since 0615. I sent the messenger down to combat to bring up a stool. The captain watched it arrive.

"Drop two turns."

I sat down on it, looking at him sheepishly as I waited for the blast. Sitting down on watch was a crime, equal to but ranking just behind, defecting to the Russians. I didn't care. The relief surged through my body like an orgasm. The captain winked at me with that approving smile that said, not too shabby. The sonovabitch had been testing me again. He called down to the wardroom for sandwiches.

"SIR! barometer dropping fast; it's 27.6. I can actually see it fall . . . goddamn, sir!" the quartermaster blurted.

"Stand by, Mr. Chadwick, the wind'll be next," the captain commented needlessly.

"Drop one turn. Tell main control to stand by for a backing bell . . . anytime, it's getting close."

The rain was aiming up. Damn, even in this wind the rain was going almost straight up. Intellectually I knew that the spinning typhoon pulled the wind up as it spun its deadly circle. But emotionally its strangeness scared the hell out of me.

We all felt it, but Mr. Chadwick acted first. "All engines back one-third." There was no wind; it was quiet, spooky. We surged forward, but the fine hands of the engineers caught the bell in time and we slid almost to a stop. "All STOP . . . ALL BACK ONE-THIRD . . . all stop." And we bobbed in the water with our chains hanging loose.

The bosun's pipe shrilled the ship to attention over the 1MC, followed by, "Now hear this . . . Now hear this! Set the anchor detail. I say again, set the anchor detail. On the double, ON THE DOUBLE."

First Division poured out of the forward watertight doors and ran across the slippery deck. "Take in the port anchor," the bridge messenger passed to the fo'c'sle. The phone talker on the bow repeated the message, screaming it so loudly we heard it on the wings of the bridge.

"Wind confused at three knots, sir; barometric pressure—sir, the glass reads only 27.25. Goddamn, Captain, it's down to 27.25. I ain't never heard of a glass that low," the quartermaster reported unprofessionally.

"Port anchor aweigh."

"Take in the starboard anchor," Mr. Chadwick ordered.

The wind was nothing but a gentle downdraft. I stared out; we were surrounded by a circling mass of black clouds so ominously dark that I felt I was in a deep well looking up. The seas ran every which way sometimes joining to form higher waves, sometimes waves canceling each other out.

The ship moved sloppily in this water. I bloated from the low pressure. My clammy skin demanded I scratch, but if I did, I knew I'd cut myself and burst.

Our minds were numbed by the past fury of the wind and the rain. The quiet was even more frightening, knowing we'd be in the storm again in a few minutes. *How long? The oppressive heat—where did it come from?* The sun broke through, beaming down the tunnel, mocking our temporary haven at the hub of this killer wind.

Through my binoculars I spotted the German freighter, half over on its side, stranded hard upon the rocks down by the Happy Valley racetrack. Overturned junks and floating bodies filled the water around us. Three merchies were stranded in various degrees of tilt. That was all—we were the only ship afloat. A look toward Victoria Island showed macabre scenes of bodies jammed against one another in grotesque piles on the windward side of buildings. I tried hard not to vomit.

"Port anchor in sight. Starboard anchor aweigh."

"Under way."

Sweat poured down my face, filling my eyes, nearly blinding me, as I heard, "Starboard anchor in sight . . . both anchors out of the water."

Mr. Chadwick opposed his engines, twisting the bow due south. Ventilation fans whined at full power to cleanse the air in the ship. Their sound, the only sound, sang eerily in the noiseless harbor. "Let go port anchor," Mr. Chadwick ordered. The chain rattled out. The anchor struck bottom; he backed to dig it in.

"Moored."

Playing out the port chain, Chadwick twisted again, slowly moving forward away from the first anchor, then dropped the starboard hook and backed down gently to seat them both together. "Beautiful job, Chess," the captain said, patting him on the back.

The XO took a round of bearings and marked our position.

A sprinkle of rain. Cooling. A slowly approaching rumble assaulted my ears. A distant train in the night crowded into my consciousness. I lay tied to the tracks. Harder rain. The southern side of the black well charged like the Four Horsemen of the Apocalypse. Wind vertical. Louder rumble. Fear.

"Barometer rising, 27.6, wind confused."

Mr. Chadwick, with the captain behind him, gently twisted the engines, holding our heading south and off the anchor chains, the captain's

encouragement adding to his confidence and skill at the job. I had nothing to do. "Ship's buttoned up, Captain," the XO reported, adding,
"SHIT!" as he stared at the approaching black wall.

We'd lost all our whip and long wire antennas, making it impossible
to communicate even if the storm would have let us. All canvas works
were gone. The huge air search radar antenna was gone and the smaller
surface search antenna was twisted horribly. But we weren't on the beach
as those poor merchies, nor were we lying piled up dead against the
windward side of the buildings.

I looked at the captain; his face betrayed no emotion, gave no instructions. I made a move toward Mr. Chadwick to take the conn. The
captain's arm shot out, stopping me. *How'd he know that?* He smiled and
shook his head no. I nodded.

"Stand by for a two-thirds-ahead bell, Chief," Mr. Chadwick called
down to main control. "Give it to me fast; we're going to need it when
this hummer smashes into us. Fuck, Chief. Anytime, Chief. Anytime . . .
goddamn, Chief, anytime. It's coming," Chadwick's voice quivered his
message to main control over the 21MC.

Visibility disappeared. Darkness.

It hit us like a body blow from a sumo wrestler.

But, as if he'd done this every day, Mr. Chadwick had rung up ahead
two-thirds three seconds before the cliff of water engulfed us. It sounded
like the crash of a speeding Mack truck into a steel wall. The anchors
jammed taut, vibrating as if in excited anticipation of running free.

Slowly the chain tension eased as the screws took the load. Mr.
Chadwick asked for a cigarette, placed it in his mouth, and coughed as
the messenger lit it for him. It was the first he had in his life, and he
puffed it the way a hurtin' junkie inserts a needle.

As the wind passed eighty knots on its way up, the windows of an
entire twenty-story building, the one that held the Mercedes Benz sign so
long ago, blew inward in a shattering flash. What panic it must have
caused to the frightened "round eyes" thinking they were safe, huddled
in their concrete hideout. Very few Chinese had been allowed in, certainly not the lower-class kind.

"Winds ninety knots; glass at 28.4."

In an hour, a pale Mr. Bluing relieved me of the deck; Mr. Graffey
took the conn. I stayed on the bridge until I pompously felt they knew
what they were doing. In twenty minutes I realized they did; shivering

from the cold, I requested permission to go below. My endurance had not escaped the captain's attention . . . nothing did. "Thank you, Don, well done."

It was 2005.

An apologetic voice brought me to. "You've got the 0400 watch, sir; it's 0315—time to get up."

The ventilating fans were on. "How's the storm, Baxter?" I asked the seaman.

"Winds forty knots and the bare . . . o . . . meter—"

"Barometer, Baxter."

"The barometer reads 29.4 and rising. Quartermaster Morton said you'd wanna know that," he cheerfully added.

"Where's the captain?"

"Asleep in his chair, sir."

"Thank You, Sir"

Our old steaming buddy, *Haney,* waited outside Hong Kong harbor ready to escort us to Subic. With no operating motor whaleboat and no radar or radio antennas except for one we jury-rigged, we needed help. We had been relieved of station ship duties by another destroyer who had missed the worst of Typhoon Mary. We heard that our carrier was nearly trashed and the ships that had sortied from Hong Kong suffered damages, some heavy, and were already on their way to Subic.

We were alongside *Haney*'s starboard side on course 170, transferring the chaplain back to our ship and receiving our mail. The beautifully clear, crisp morning gave me a sense of deliverance from the horrors of the typhoon. I had the conn. Nothing could daunt the intrepid seaman of *Henshaw.* The captain, in a rare instance, wasn't on the conning platform supervising; he stood in the pilothouse reading a message from COMSEVENTHFLT that the XO had just brought up. It congratulated *Henshaw* on a job well done for toughing it out in accordance with our orders.

"All lines free," came the report. I checked for sure, then gave the command, "Come left to course 174." Nothing happened as I expected to ease out to starboard.

"SIR, say again, sir," came the hesitant questioning voice from Morton on the helm.

"Come left to course 174!" I ordered again.

Again Morton's voice came back more loudly, almost angrily, "SAY AGAIN, SIR!" he yelled.

I bent down from the conning platform and shouted out the order again in a harsh, angry tone, but halfway through I felt a lightning bolt jam up my ass. I screamed, "BELAY THAT . . . BELAY THAT, RIGHT, RIGHT TO COURSE 174."

"Right to course 174, AYE! sir," he yelled, spinning his helm to the right away from the destroyer we would have hit if he had blindly obeyed my errant "come left" rudder command.

We slowly eased away. When nearly perpendicular I gave the conn to Mr. Banning, who immediately ordered right standard rudder to take us to station a thousand yards astern of *Haney*. I couldn't have handled it. As he slid handsomely into position, my body slumped and my heartbeat eased to normal.

My sweat-soaked khakis squished as I stepped into the pilothouse and walked over to the helm. My hand clasped Morton's well-muscled arm as I looked into his eyes. His smiling black face looked back, his shirt as sweat soaked as mine. "I owe you big time, Quartermaster. Thank you."

"It's nothing, sir."

"It's one naval career to me, Morton. Thank you," I said, squeezing his arm again. "One naval career, Quartermaster . . . I owe you."

Our three-second drama seemed to have gone unnoticed, thank God, and I nervously tried to be a noncocky OOD for the rest of the watch as my eyes kept glancing back to the stupid little sign pasted on the forward bulwark by the midships pelorus: "A collision at sea can ruin your whole day."

We were tied up at the Repair Facility, Subic, and a high-pitched voice droned in our ears. "I've heard good things about *Henshaw*," the soon-to-be new captain addressed his soon-to-be department heads at an informal meeting over coffee in the wardroom. Mr. Bluing looked better.

"I will, of course, meet with you separately to get a feel for your departments. The incumbent—*stupid word to use for my captain*—says you're all good officers. I hope he's right, and I hope you serve me as well as you've served him. But, of course, I know you will." And his too small mouth eked out a smirk.

What a crock of bullshit. Do they teach that in some how-to-be-a-senior-officer school?

"I haven't been to sea for quite a few years and I *may* be a little rusty," he said with a pathetic grin, "and I *may* need your help . . . a *little*." I hated myself for chuckling with the others at his inane remark.

Four days later I looked good in my dress whites with the high, stiff collar. My sword belt and sword lay on my rack; I had worn it only once, at graduation from OCS. I couldn't help but draw it and play a little. I was careful. Many officers had wounded themselves and others by playing with these things, but I couldn't help it.

I was Errol Flynn in *Captain Blood,* I was Nelson at Trafalgar, and I was a chief petty officer petrified with fear as an officer stood on the pier on the Isle of Rhodes in the Aegean Sea with his sword point sticking ever so slightly into my neck.

The three-year-old memory haunted me again. I thought it was over. We'd steamed out of the North Atlantic en route to the Mediterranean and joined COMSIXTHFLT to finish off our cruise, the memories of the heavy weather in the North Sea all too fresh in our minds. We visited Greece. We visited the Isle of Rhodes. At Rhodes the officers had a formal party; I never knew what for, nor did I care. Most of our younger pilots acted like spoiled brats anyway when they weren't flying.

I was the Shore Patrol chief at the boat landing as the drunken aviators staggered onto the pier to wait for a launch back to the carrier. This was the officers' landing, somewhat protected from the wind and the light rain starting to fall. The officers rode in covered launches while the enlisted men rode in open liberty boats. I couldn't understand why it was okay for enlisted men to be huddled up wet in an open boat while the officers rode back in dry comfort. Perhaps, I thought, I'd find out one day. Surely it must be right or the navy wouldn't do it. It was my fault that I didn't understand.

"You're Sheppard, aren't you?" a feisty, short officer, who looked perhaps eighteen, scowled at me, his putrid, liquored breath offending my body.

"Yes, sir, can I help you?"

"You smart-ass bastard—you've helped me enough, you sonovabitch," he bellowed, drawing his too-long-for-him sword from its scabbard.

"I don't understand, sir," I pleaded as he flicked his sword and in a deft movement pinned me against a light pole with the point of the sword pressing into my neck over my shirt collar.

"Fencing team, Princeton . . . yeah!" he shouted, positioning his feet like a trained swordsman. "You sonovabitch asshole. You helped me out all right, detecting that fuckin' Russian submarine and keeping us at sea for another week."

The sword flashed at my neck. A drop of blood trickled amongst my sweat down from my Adam's apple. "I missed it, you asshole, and it's your fault. And that suck-ass Martin grabbed all the glory. It was your fault I missed the birth of my first child and I'm going to kill you for it," he slurred.

The guy was crazy drunk; I knew he wasn't going to do it. I knew it, but I wasn't all that convinced. A slight movement of the sword's tip painfully widened the hole. I kept my eyes directly into his, trying to face him down. I tried to reply as he ranted on, but my fear-constricted throat would not let the words come out.

A gathering of young officers crowded around, yelling for him to knock off the horseplay. A glance showed Lt. (jg) Rammin' Randall moving up behind him.

"Look at me, you tall motherfucker; your height isn't going to help you now. WE ALL HATE YOU," the short officer shouted with a flourish of his left hand that encompassed all the commissioned onlookers.

In a flash Randall's left arm went around his neck, yanking him backward, while his right hand pulled the sword away. He held the banty officer by the neck, as he wrestled the sword out of his hand. He threw it into the bay as he applied an armlock on him.

The officers' launch arrived in another second, and Rammin' Randall threw him from the dock into the forward compartment. *Thanks again, Rammin' Randall.*

The woeful humidity of the Philippines brought me back as I sheathed my sword, shuddering at the memory, and walked to the fantail for the change of command ceremony.

To the parade of lined-up officers and men of *Henshaw,* Chaplain Layman spoke of the responsibilities of freedom and the power for good that *Henshaw* possessed. Captain Baker thanked the men for serving the ship so faithfully, and Commander Jackson said how proud he was to take command of such a fine ship. Then each of the two three-stripers read their orders. Captain Baker became Commander Baker and Commander Jackson became Captain Jackson and we officers went to a reception at the O club.

Commander Jackson's wife and two daughters had flown in from San Francisco to revel in the new power of *their* man. They acted like the beautiful queen and the fairy princesses. It became quite obvious that his wife would "wear his stripes" and wallow in the authority and prestige of her husband. Many officers' wives did; I hated it. I drank.

As the party wound down, Captain Jackson toasted the navy and nodded to Commander Baker for a speech. Commander Baker stood and raised his glass. "My speech, gentlemen, and ladies, is contained in the record of *Henshaw*, but I toast you naval officers, the last proud vestige of the American aristocracy." Faces paled at the audacity of the remark. Not a whisper followed, not a clink of a glass. I was proud to have served him and I clapped.

As the invited guests from the other ships and the naval station departed, Commander Baker made the rounds of his ex-wardroom. I didn't relish my turn. I harbored the childish notion that he was deserting me.

I stood in a corner pretending I was having a good time. I was the last one. He took my hand, not shaking it but holding it as we were about to shake. Neither of us spoke for what seemed a long time. "Thank you, sir," I managed to get out through the *imaginary* lump in my throat while my eyes constricted and a drop of *imaginary* moisture oozed uncontrollably out of my right eye.

He still didn't speak. He was doing it to me again. "I'll miss you, sir."

"Thank you, Don. I'll . . . No! Just thank you, Don," he said, then turned and walked away. In a second he stopped, twisted his head back to me, and said, "And, Mr. Sheppard,"—his eyes twinkled—"may I suggest in the future you not give the helmsman an order to turn into the ship you happen to be alongside of." He smiled and walked through the door. I'd not see him again for thirteen years.

The sonovabitch knew, goddamn him, he knew.

The queen and the two fairy princesses stood waving on the pier as Captain Jackson made one of the sloppiest underways I'd ever seen. At sea he was neither good nor bad, just a commanding entity who lived on the bridge. I served him well due only to my ingrained fidelity, but I offered only an unimaginative attention to duty. His condescending demeanor and biting sarcasm elicited no more. He played it by the book with huge margins for error.

It wasn't fun anymore.

*   *   *

FRAM was a year of frustration and education, but in the end the Vallejo Naval Shipyard did a great job. They had overhauled all the machinery, and the superstructure was completely new. We had ASROC and MK 44 torpedoes and had lost a five-inch gun mount in the trade. They weren't very effective anyway. A new XO had taken over before we got there, and Captain Jackson had his CO tour cut short. The navy didn't need a three-striper for this job.

The new XO, designated now as only an officer in charge (OinC), left most of the overhaul to Mr. Chadwick and me. We were the only officers attached the entire time. Of course we kept Chief Maclin and the bosun; it would have been unthinkable to lose them. The OinC wasn't an engineer and didn't want to sully his hands by association. He played golf a lot, which was okay with Chess and me. My promotion to full lieutenant, an O-3, came through early.

Thank you, Commander Baker.

The new crew started showing up along with a new captain as we came to the end of the year-long conversion. With his organizational expertise shining through, the OinC organized the crew and set the ship right for sea. The day of the sea trial—four boilers on the line pumped out 30.9 knots—she ran magnificently. Maclin had his boys as smoothly trained as a drill team.

"Stand by for emergency backing bell," came the word from the bridge.

This was part of the sea trial, and the most demanding evolution the engineers could run. It was fraught with danger, and every man had to do the right thing at the right time. No errors. I was in main control; Chess was in the after engine room. He'd come a long way and had found his niche. He was to relieve me as chief engineer. He knew his stuff and he and Chief Maclin admired and trusted each other.

The engine order telegraph flew back from ahead flank to back full— once, then twice indicating an emergency situation. Wild, choreographed activity opened huge valves and little valves and closed huge valves and little valves. We sweated and cursed, and the noise deafened us. We ground to a stop in one and a half ship lengths, shuddered, dug our stern deep into the water, and lurched astern at fifteen knots. *Bloody great!*

"All ahead standard, make turns for fifteen knots." It was over—my swan song. That night Chess, Chief Maclin, the bosun, and I got drunk, maudlinly drunk, and in the morning I left for my new duty station.

*   *   *

"Commander First Fleet arriving," came the call over the heavy cruiser's 1MC. As was naval custom, whenever the commander of a unit came aboard, the quarterdeck called out his command, not his name. We did the same on *Henshaw*, ringing four bells and calling out "*Henshaw* arriving" whenever the captain came aboard or ringing four bells and calling out "*Henshaw* departing" whenever he left.

It was my boss coming aboard. I was his fleet scheduling officer, five strata below him. A choice billet, supposedly: a fitness report signed by a vice admiral.

My sole job consisted of taking the "proposed" schedule of each ship from the list that the type commander's staffies sent us and collating them into the First Fleet Master Schedule, thereby anointing them with the three stars my boss wore.

Also, when a change had to me made, I wrote the message as dictated to me from the type commander's staffies and entered it in my book. Boring. I could accomplish my job in about a half hour per day except for the end of the quarter, when it demanded my attention for a full hour.

My idle hands created a devil's workshop. To pass the time I started making a list of watertight doors in bad condition and sending the list down to the cruiser's DCA. He didn't like a staffie pointing out his responsibilities.

On the extremely rare occasion when we were under way, I asked to stand bridge watches. No! of course not; you're on the staff. What about CIC? No! of course not; you're on the staff. Main control? No staffies allowed.

COMFIRSTFLT had the task of fighting a sea engagement if the attackers hit the West Coast. We really didn't have a job since all ships in EASTPAC belonged both administratively and operationally to their type commanders. Not like the Seventh Fleet in WESTPAC or the Sixth Fleet in the Med. Our counterpart in the Atlantic, Second Fleet, didn't have a job either and everyone knew it but me. I thought I just didn't understand.

I met the admiral for the first time at a reception for someone I hadn't heard of, but I went because my immediate boss, a full captain, pay grade O-6, said I should. The admiral and an O-6 sitting next to him both wore a blue ribbon with tiny white stars, the Congressional Medal of Honor.

The admiral got his in World War Two for submerging his submarine down to the conning tower in the middle of a Japanese convoy and fighting them all alone up there, giving firing orders to the crew below. I never found out why he had to do that, but he reputedly sank at least ten merchies and two destroyers. I guess the shallow depth of his boat was undetectable by sonar, and the Japanese didn't have good radars.

The O-6 sitting next to the admiral, I found out later, won his award when he was a seaman in World War Two. As the helmsman of an LST, he took command when the bridge was destroyed by a Japanese shell, killing everyone on it but him. He took command of the ship without anyone below knowing it and brought the ship to safety.

I often mused which one deserved it most. The admiral made a conscious choice to expose himself and fight the convoy on his own while exposed on the conning tower. The O-6 was a victim; he had no choice, and for self-survival he did what he had to do. Commendable? Certainly.

I thought of the Medal of Honor winners who got their medals posthumously for throwing themselves on live grenades. Commendable? Certainly. And what about the man who charges a live machine-gun nest? He too is often a recipient of the medal. Knowing the workings of severe adrenaline release, I would question the sanity of a man who throws himself on a grenade or who charges machine-gun nests. A tremendous jolt of adrenaline could render them insane.

One effect of adrenaline is to pull blood from the brain and feed it to the muscles and the skin, leaving the brain to act mostly on instinct and reflex actions. Could sufficient blood have been diverted from their brains so the machine-gun charger or the grenade diver were no longer in conscious control of their actions? Could they merely sense an overwhelming threat such as the sight of tusked woolly mammoth charging them and attack instinctively? I didn't know. I did know, however, that I wanted medals of my own but didn't have a war to feed them to me.

It was 1962. The Cuban Missile Crisis came up. Big talk around the staff said we were going to take a fleet and neutralize the Commie bastards. Excitement permeated the staff. And as good naval officers are wont to do, we ached for a fight. Cuba. My mind drifted back to Havana and my one trip there.

The ASW S2F squadron I was attached to had transferred to Key West, Florida, for joint operations with the squadrons out of Norfolk, Virginia. Every Friday an old R4D, the naval version of the venerable Douglas DC-3, made a courier run to Havana.

The squadron CO awarded four of us enlisted men the trip because of the fine job we had done keeping the squadron's electronics gear up. As we deplaned, I saw men on stretchers being lifted off another R4D—actually a C-47, the army version—and carried off in their blood-soaked bandages into an ambulance. They were parked right next to us. After the stretchers left, a group of ten or so men with their hands tied behind their back were thrown out of the plane's huge cargo door.

Three of them made a break for it, running the best they could with their hands tied behind them. Two submachine guns opened up. One man lurched forward from a hit but continued running until another blast found him. He tumbled four times before dropping. The other two stopped when they heard the submachine guns and turned toward the guards. The guards fired again and both men went down.

A man in an officer-looking uniform walked up to the closest one, drawing his pistol as he stood over him. He fired twice into the man's head, then walked over to the next one and fired a bullet upward under his chin. He leaned over the third man—lifting him up by his long hair—then, as in disgust, shoved him away. As the man tried haltingly to crawl, the officer-dressed man placed his pistol into the back of the man's neck and fired.

Machine-gun fire came from the edge of the airfield as we walked out of the terminal. I was twenty-seven years old; the others were in their low twenties. It took a lot of cheap Cuban rum and many fair ladies to help us forget our arrival.

First Fleet didn't go to Cuba, and we had little else to do.

To my immediate First Fleet boss, who also hated being a staffie, I expressed my desire to go to the Naval Post Graduate School to get a baccalaureate degree. The procedure was simple: apply and have two years of college credits; if your fitness reports were good enough, you'd get an appointment when one opened up. My boss, with little enough to do himself, took on this task. He searched what navy schools I'd gone to and got credit authorization for those that counted. Even OCS gave me four credit hours. It ended up that I had to take four more courses: math to calculus, English, physics, and psychology. It would have been more, but during FRAM I attended night school at a local college three nights a week.

He made me order all four correspondence courses at the same time. I studied at home at night. I studied during the weekends. I studied during my lunch hours. When business was slow, I studied in my stateroom on the cruiser. My boss was a math major and he helped me, he mentored me, he drove me to excellence. He never let up. And in a year I completed the courses and, with the fitness report he wrote, for the admiral's signature, I was accepted. Watch out, Chess Chadwick. Watch out, Rog Wachifsky: Phi Beta fucking Kappa.

The Naval Post Graduate School sat in a beautiful location in Monterey, California, with rigorous professors and a grueling curriculum. But it was a piece of cake for most of us already used to the demands of duty and the long hours required. We only had to maintain a B average. Going to school was our only duty; our fitness reports reflected simply our grades, unless, of course, we did something really stupid.

The air force started it all. They thought it prestigious to have most of their officers holding advanced degrees. The navy, not to be outdone, purchased the old Fremont Hotel to establish their school. The army followed with a school of their own. The navy took care of the marines and coast guard.

By a quirk of World War Two, an undergraduate program existed for naval aviators who entered flight school with only two years of college. They'd been promised their last two years would be free whenever the chance came up. Twenty years after the war, the program still existed, and I took advantage of it.

I had my two years' worth of credits, didn't I?

No tension, no pressure, no storms, no night catapult shots, no duties, cheap liquor and good food at the O club; the good life prevailed. The cotton was high and the livin' was easy. We could drink and party all we wanted—as long as we maintained that magical B average.

I was in the general course heading for an undesignated degree in engineering. If I took extra courses I could get a designated degree in whatever subject I chose. I graduated with a second BS in International Relations at the age of thirty-six.

College had a mild storm or two. One was an elective called American Traditions and Ideals. It was a no-brainer and considered an easy A. It taught how marvelous the United States was, how we had never done anything wrong and how, in fact, could not do anything wrong.

The professor's lectures were perhaps better suited for the fertile minds of grade-school children. The idealistic professor firmly and unequivocally believed in what he taught. I, like most of my classmates, listened with only half an ear, saving our minds for headier things such as differential calculus and organic chemistry.

The simplistic drone of the professor bored us two hours a week for ten weeks. I measured his words against what I knew of the United States from my courses in political history. We weren't lily-white, and one of my history professors made a strong case that we caused the Japanese to attack us at Pearl Harbor. President Roosevelt didn't like the Japanese expansion in Southeast Asia in the late thirties and early forties. Every time the Japanese tried to secure their supply of raw materials, the United States moved in and countered them with dollars. Their backs were against the wall and they attacked.

Our gunboat diplomacy and excursions in Latin America could be looked at as raw-toothed imperialism. And what about Mexico and the American Indians?

The only exam was a final: two hours of filling up a small blue essay book on some subject dealing with an American tradition or ideal. I wasn't prepared for this; I thought he'd ask us questions. After frittering away twenty minutes, an inspiring topic came to me. I'd make a case that the United States was the second coming of Christ. *How clever you are, Lieutenant Sheppard!*

Two days later the professor threw the essay book on my desk. "BLASPHEMY" in thick red ink was slashed across the blue cover, with a larger D for a grade placed an inch below it. He looked at me, his face a scowl as he passed out the other essay books to my fellow students, all smiling over their A grades.

He wouldn't talk to me in the classroom. I followed him into his office. He dismissed me. I stayed. "What do you mean, blasphemy?" I demanded, pissed now at the bigotry of this skinny civilian as I tossed the essay book on his desk. "This wasn't a religious class," I argued. "Did I develop my case?"

"Yes," he admitted, his hands shaking a bit as I loomed over him.

"Did I present my premise adequately? Did I develop the hypothesis? Did I draw the right conclusions from what I presented? Couldn't the breaking away of the colonies be likened to the birth of Christ, like the birth of a savior for the world?" I paused. I felt I was on a soapbox. I even began to believe my paper.

"Couldn't the bountiful nature of the land be the same as Jesus turning water into wine and feeding the masses from a basket of fish? Magic? Where does it say Jesus would return as a man?"

He stared at me while running a handkerchief over his thick glasses. He looked down at the offending blue book on his desk where it had landed, his eyes squinting to see it. It was upside down to him. He turned it around with a pencil, as if leprosy would rot off his hand if he touched it. He paused, then scooted it closer to himself.

With a pencil in his left hand, he held down a corner of it, and with a red pencil in his right, he marked through the D and wrote an F. Then with both pencils he flipped it to the floor in front of me. "BLASPHEMY!" he shouted. I picked it up and marched out.

I went to see my class adviser. He concealed his laughter as he gave me permission to see the dean.

The four-striper captain read the blue book, looked up at me, and smiled. "Not too shabby. I don't agree, but it's scholastically correct. Imaginative."

"The grade, Captain, it's not fair. Can you make him change it?" I half pleaded, my ego on the line.

He picked up my record. "Grades aren't bad," he murmured while doing some math on a yellow legal pad. "You could get Fs from now until graduation and still have a B average. We can't legally influence a professor's grades. What difference does it make? Maybe if it would cause you not to graduate we could use some subtle muscle, but that's not your case. Forget it! Though I can perhaps get your D back for you."

"But Captain," I pleaded. "It's the principle."

He shook his head as if dealing with a child, lit his pipe, and said, "Principle, Mr. Sheppard, is what the weak fall back on when logic has failed. Good day, sir." *Shit!*

The war in Vietnam was going into high gear. I volunteered and received my orders. Command, the brown water navy, the riverboats. Glory danced through my heart. Adventure. The skirl of a bagpipe. The tap of a drum. The call of a bugle . . . and I was afraid.

Epilogue

T he wind freshened, driving the damp sea air across San Francisco Bay deep into my bones. I raised my collar higher as the biting cold chilled me. I shook my head to clear out the thoughts of my junior officer days. They were over. I watched despondently, heavyhearted, as the lights of the destroyer *Cambridge* grew dimmer in the waning light.

Like a jabbing pain, the realization of my loss dug into me. I was no longer in command of her—no longer her captain.

Again she whispered farewell. I kissed my fingertips and waved to her. I thought of the killing days in Vietnam and my time as XO of the destroyer *Kramer,* and the long road ahead to command.